JOY

from

FEAR

Copyright © 2019 by Carla Marie Manly
All rights reserved.

Published by Familius LLC, www.familius.com

Familius books are available at special discounts for bulk purchases, whether for sales pro-
motions or for family or corporate use. For more information, contact Familius Sales at
559-876-2170 or email orders@familius.com.

Library of Congress Cataloging-in-Publication Data
2018961640

Print ISBN 9781641701211
Ebook ISBN 9781641701709

Printed in the United States of America

Edited by Katharine Hale and Sarah Echard
Cover design by David Miles
Book design by Brooke Jorden

10 9 8 7 6 5 4 3 2 1

First Edition

JOY
from
FEAR

Create the Life of
Your Dreams by Making
Fear Your Friend

CARLA MARIE MANLY, PHD

This book is dedicated to all of those who courageously embrace the journey with transformational fear. May the loving self-awareness you cultivate bring true freedom and joy to your soul and your world.

I offer my deep, humble gratitude to Love. You have been faithfully at my side and in my soul; you have never failed.

Contents

PREFACE

I am ever grateful to the extraordinary researchers, authors, and clinicians who have informed my work. From the works of Carl Jung to Thomas Moore, I have been enlightened and guided by those who have gone before me. *Joy from Fear* but scratches the surface of many areas that deserve in-depth, focused attention.

As with any important life journey, it is recommended that you consult with your primary caregiver and engage the active support of a trained psychotherapist when needed. It is my prayer that this book offers you a guided introduction to greater joy, well-being, and transformation.

It is important to note that the case studies in this book are representative amalgamations. Though their names and stories have been changed to maintain privacy, the journeys and realizations depicted in them are real. They are not intended to, nor do they, depict any one actual person or situation.

Why Fear Makes a Much Better Friend Than Enemy

I want you to throw away your preconceived notions of fear, along with any particular opinions of anxiety and its causes. In doing so, in opening your mind and your spirit to what might be an entirely new way of thinking and of being, you will embark upon the most challenging, illuminating, and richly satisfying journey of your life.

If you feel as though you are sometimes drowning in a lonely sea of unhappiness, in meaningless chronic anxiety, depression, or hopelessness, this book—this journey—is for you.

Whether you are struggling to discover or maintain nourishing relationships, a fulfilling career, financial ease, or greater harmony within your family life, this book will offer you welcome assistance. If you are searching for a deeper understanding of who you are as an individual— from your sense of spirituality to a greater depth of inner awareness—you will encounter fulfilling guidance. If you are searching for a life that is free from the weight of anxiety and stress-induced illnesses and for a healthy sense of delight within your physical being, you will find well-honed tools in the pages ahead.

You might be wondering how one small book can offer so much. The answer is both simple and complex. It is one familiar aspect of fear that strangles us, holds us back, and keeps us living lives filled with stress, unhappiness, and emptiness. It is another hidden aspect of this same fear that—when listened to and understood—affords us the opportunity to engage in the lives of our dreams.

This book will welcome you into the world of transformational fear, where you will find that fear has two faces, not just one. The first face, destructive fear, keeps us tangled and immobilized. The second face, constructive fear, is a hidden ally we can come to recognize and know. Through this journey, you will come to notice and appreciate this trustworthy ally; you will come to make transformational fear your friend.

From Living a Lie to Living Free

In a few simple sentences, I will tell you about a woman I know very well. On the outside, she seemed to have it all. She had the right education, the right house, the right kids, the right clothes, the right husband, and even the right car. She was a successful high-performer, working dutifully from dawn to well after dusk. She did everything that was expected of her and far more. She wanted everyone to be happy and pleased; perfection was her goal.

No one knew that she was dying on the inside. The woes of her difficult history had been repressed but not forgotten. The perfect marriage was a farce. The job that paid the bills was not the one of her dreams—far from it. It was a job of duty and subjugation; it was entirely devoid of joy. Yet she continued to smile, to carry on. She might have walked off the earth's edge had it not been for the bright light of her two sons; she wanted to survive and thrive for them.

At what seemed to be a most inconvenient time, a momentous epiphany hit her smack in the face. *She realized that she was modeling for her children how to accept a barely-lived life.* Hers was a life of gray, endless days of toil, a loveless marriage, and a job that fed upon her soul. She'd come to feel that she was a pitiful shell of a woman who accepted far less than she wanted and far less than she deserved. This woman was unwittingly trapped in the grip of a nearly inextricable, invisible web of fear that kept her constrained and internally dead. This devastated woman, as you may have guessed, was me.

Unwittingly, largely unconsciously, I began my journey away from fear in the early months of 2005. I woke one morning and whispered to myself, *I would rather live under a bridge than live this life.* I truly meant those words. I had no idea where I was going, how I would get there, or if I would survive the rigors. I knew one thing only: that my life was not worth living if I did not try. Despite complete uncertainty about what the future—my "new world"—would hold, I had decided that I would rather die than live the smothered, suffocating, and meaningless life I had come to accept.

Had you told me at the time that my life thus far had been ruled by fear, I would have stared at you uncomprehendingly, staunchly and whole-heartedly disagreeing. I would have averred that I was an independent, strong, tenacious, and determined woman. Had you pushed me further, I might have recounted my varied external successes, my accomplishments, my sound capacity to tend to whatever business was at hand, and the highlights of my education and career. I would have tossed my head back, looked at you with fierce eyes, and steadfastly ignored that I was dying—actually suffocating—inside.

And yet, with an objective backward glance, I now clearly recognize that I had lived the vast majority of my life in the silent, overpowering grasp of fear. Much of what I am now able to acknowledge, now that my inner gaze and sense of self is much clearer, was impossible for me to see when I lived in fear. Fear had served to mask my vision, to slowly infiltrate my world until I did not recognize it for the jailer it had become.

I see in my not-so-happy childhood that much of the way I was raised—indoctrinated—was based in fear. As the ninth child in a large Catholic family, I was raised to fear my father, my eldest brother, and God (in that order). I was taught to fear leaving the "safety" of the family. I learned to fear the world in general, for strangers might discover the secrets, woes, and frail stability within the family. Without my realizing it, pervasive fear had become the glue that held our family together. It was this glue of fear, this internal message, that unconsciously permeated my life.

As I grew older, I learned to mistrust myself. On those rare occasions that I took a step on my own—a move toward natural autonomy and self-trust—I was admonished and warned that I was wrong, that I would fail, or that I wasn't being "smart." In essence, I was trained to fear walking my own path and becoming independent. I came to doubt my strengths and my abilities. I did not learn to value and become who I innately was as an individual but who I was *expected* to be.

Even so, my inner voice occasionally balked, but I was hushed and taught to follow the "right" path. Head down, eyes lowered, I listened and, fearful of the consequences, did as I was told. In fearing and doubting my own capacities, I put my faith in others rather than in myself. I attributed to others the power and wisdom that were inherently mine alone. I was taught to distrust others, yet instead I grew to doubt and mistrust myself far more than I doubted those around me. In abandoning my true self, I grew into someone I did not recognize. Without having words to express it, I lived with a chronic sense that some critical element within me was amiss.

Most interesting to me is how little I actually realized that I was driven by fear. In retrospect, I now see that the bulk of my decisions about vital, life-shaping topics, such as education, relationships, marriage, and career, were motivated by fear: fear of being unloved, fear of not receiving approval, fear of being disowned by my family, fear of God, fear of physical retribution, fear of a failed marriage, fear of financial instability, or fear of not being able to manage on my own. I was immobilized and desperately unhappy, yet I did not have the understanding or the tools to extricate myself. Although my spirit felt that something was gravely amiss, my daily struggles and closed mind precluded my realizing that such angst could be used to transform my fears into freedom.

I did not possess the ability to recognize the Medusa-like aspects of fear that serve to both terrify and sustain. Fear has the ability to bring us to our knees in self-doubt. It also has the capacity to bring us to the greatest heights of who we are.

In working through my own fears, I came to appreciate fear's unique and intricate role in the journey of life. Although at first unaware of the nature of my process, I now realize that I wrestled with what I came to call "transformational fear" on an intimate level for many years. Blind fear had me in its grip. Once I realized this fact, I was stunned. Once I accepted its truth, the real work of transformation—and my true life—began.

It has not been an easy path, for the work of self-confrontation and inner awareness often appears endless, yet the reward of finding myself has been invaluable and incredible. Once I have faced and conquered one aspect, another rises to greet me with a knowing, half-familiar grin. Progress comes in being able to more readily recognize the force of transformational fear, and to use it—not fight it—in my continuing journey.

I now know fear for what it is—both an immobilizing force and an unparalleled teacher. I have personally experienced the "dark night of the soul" and witnessed its potential for bringing profound illumination along with exquisite, intense pain. I have learned that a life lived in immobilized, destructive fear is a life scarcely lived, and I can now never return to such a barren existence. There is immense power in the realization that transformational fear has the capacity to lead to the unearthing of my own buried treasures. I have realized that there is no need to live within this fear. In fact, if transformational fear were to speak with us directly, I believe it would command, "Do not succumb to my darker, negative side. Notice that another side exists—an enlightening, positive side. Look at me, learn from me, and use me—*your fears*—to transform your life into what it was meant to be."

Here I am, this many years later since the tentative commencement of my journey, a vibrant testimony to the incredible, life-changing powers of fear. I finally pursued my lifelong dreams of becoming a clinical psychologist and helping others through their own life journeys. I have learned to notice and confront the demons that told me I should act in ways that were not right for me. My days are not spent in the confines of offices geared toward financial gain; instead, my days are spent loving, guiding, and soothing others. The changes I made were hard-won, yet my soul now knows a vast and true freedom. The source of this energy stems from inner love and a sense of divine connection that is wise to the ways of destructive fear. I am no longer stifled, confined, and accepting of that which is not good for me—that which suffocates or undermines me. Instead, I strive to know my essence, stand in my truth, and reach toward ever more wondrous heights by helping others as I have helped myself. Through the power of transformational fear, I have been given the journey of my life—an extraordinary labor of pain, love, and incomparable rewards. I made a vow that I would use my learnings to help others successfully accomplish the same journey. I want you, too, to know the power of transformational fear.

The Devil We Know: Destructive Fear

Let's take an even closer look at the destructive face of fear—the one we are so familiar with in life. Although the following pages may feel disheartening at first glance, trust that the goal is to cast light upon the shadowy aspects of this devilish fear. By delving into the silent and often unnoticed depths of destructive fear, we have the opportunity to become more aware. In being more consciously attentive to both the causes and indicators of fear, we increase our capacity for liberation from the ravages of fear. With steady eyes and a curious mind, let's look at some of the all-too-familiar aspects of the beastly side of fear.

We have all met challenges that bring us face to face with our fears. Fear hounds us perniciously; we worry that there won't be enough money to cover food, shelter, and medical care. We fear that we cannot properly care for our families—our children, ourselves, and our aging parents. From college tuition to astronomical health insurance and hospital fees, we fear that we do not have the time, the strength, and the financial resources to juggle such formidable realities. We are afraid that we are getting older, that the ravages of age will take over. Comparing ourselves with airbrushed facsimiles of humanity, we fear that we will be replaced with younger, "better" models. A nip here, a tuck there, a stimulant pill or caffeine drink downed, we are promised that all will be well if we only look better, do better, or accomplish more. Many of us live with a silent voice that chides, *You are not enough. You are not good enough. You never will be.* We are mercilessly hounded. We live with the fear that a debilitating disease will come knocking. Millions search the web, seeking affirmation that they have not succumbed to some form of cancer or other virulent disease. We self-diagnose a host of ailments—many of them imaginary—as we read fearfully through the list of symptoms that seem to decide our fate. We bolt our doors, lock our windows, and set our alarms. In essence, we fear that we simply are not safe.

The sensitive inner spirit lives within this maelstrom of fear. Whether you are rich or poor, whether you live in a tiny city apartment or a beachfront mansion, there is often an underlying sense that life is a precariously balanced house of cards, and that one slight wind or move in the wrong direction might bring the walls crashing down. Notice the deep, enveloping fear that silently underlies all of these worries. Yet it does not end there. This unremitting sense of insecurity is merely the first layer of destructive fear's stealthy influence.

Day in and day out, we wake blearily to tend to our families and ourselves. A cup of coffee for fuel, we trudge to a job that is not the one of our dreams. Texting here, emailing there, a cell phone as a ubiquitous accessory, we have no space for serenity. If a moment of quiet does seep through, we are often anxious—too accustomed to nonstop techno-chatter to feel comfortable with the silence. Many of us feel that things are amiss—even that we are nonexistent—if the cell phone does not ring. There is a fragile sense of holding tight, of being on alert throughout the day. As the day fades into night, we make the bleak trip home again and into the realm of quickly devoured dinners, blaring televisions, and the simulated relief provided by the blue computer monitor or television screen. Stretched thin, we live with tight necks, unsettled stomachs, tension headaches, and jagged tempers; our bodies feel the strain. As the stress and anxiety rise, a host of physical ailments set in. The body and the psyche know the truth of our fear, of our deep unhappiness. We mindlessly overeat to assuage the gnawing emptiness. Beer, wine, and drugs dull the pain, the anxiety, and the feelings of depression—but only temporarily. Minds numbed, bodies worn, spirits frayed, we fall asleep with the unsettling realization that we'll wake to do it all over again.

Even the respite of sleep is hard-won, for the fears and anxieties that lurked about unseen during the day percolate and surface in the blackness of night to remind us that, though pushed away, they are not forgotten. The use of sleep medications continues to rise, yet sleep remains fragmented and riddled with fear. There is no natural falling to sleep with the setting of the sun and waking with the light of dawn. Instead, there is the haunting evening news, the incessant chatter of the techno-world, and vast array of sleep aids that carry us into uneasy dreams. The anxious, frayed remnants of our beings toss and turn through the night; we know, deep down, that this sort of life is not right.

Fear takes advantage; it feeds on those who feel cut off from themselves and from society. Our fears make us lonely, depressed, and anxious. Where people once gathered to sew, read, and play in nature and community, many now regress to the isolative confines of bedrooms, where television shows and computer games replace real life. Many find quick relief by turning to the illusory television world, where joy and pain are created by a Hollywood producer. Others release stress by striving to win the fight against computerized demons and soldiers. Better to escape to a world where evil is created by a computer graphic artist and can be controlled with feverish taps of buttons or a joystick than to feel stressed and powerless in a life that seems so very out of our control. Better to waste away the hours between dusk and sleep with the engaging pseudo-relationship of the computer screen than to feel isolated, empty, and alone. Although the underlying emptiness, anxiety, stress, and depression persist after the "off" button is hit, it is easier to escape to these realms than to reach out, talk with each other, and truly connect. It may seem better to pretend and remain unaware than to acknowledge that something has to change, yet the undercurrent remains: *This is not right; this does not feel good.*

There comes a time when we must each look in the mirror and ask, "Is it better for me to hide from my fears than to look at them? If I am unhappy, then am I ready to face fear on my terms? Is this the life I accept—the life I want to live?" It is your call; you get to decide. Do you want to stay in a place of fear, convincing yourself that all is well, that you will accept what life has brought you? Or do you want to listen to your body and that inner voice that is desperately unhappy, anxious, and living in fear?

This is where the sweetness of your own power can be awakened to make a difference in your life. It is here that faith and hope may rise, knowing that with steadfast effort and dedication, you can change your life. You needn't be shackled in a life of fear. You can choose to learn more about how we have become susceptible to the wily forces of fear. To that end, with a brief investigation of fear's propensity for taking advantage of our culture's separation of the body, mind, and spirit, let's shift our attention to fear's intriguing tendency to divide and conquer.

The Unified Self: Body, Mind, and Spirit

In the twenty-first century, we have been racing ever faster toward a separation from our fuller selves. Looking back in time, we can follow the various theories that led to the idea that the mind and body are two separate entities. In the 1600s, René Descartes argued that the mind and body are essentially separate. He believed that the two intersected at the pineal gland, where the mind connected to the brain.[1] Emanating from the early work of Descartes, the school of Cartesian thought propelled the concept that the body operates much like a machine, largely divorced from the psychological and spiritual aspects of the individual. Historically, many cultures believed otherwise: that the human body, mind, and spirit were interrelated and, in fact, largely indivisible from each other. In viewing the person holistically, as an interconnected and multifaceted form, there was a natural appreciation for the inseparability of human thought and emotions from physical form. Before the separation of the physical body from its other components that came with Cartesian thought, there existed a more organic trust and fundamental belief in the interplay of "the one" (the individual) and "the three" (the body, mind, and spirit).

When we subscribe to the belief that there is no split between the body and the mind, we acknowledge, quite literally, that we are one. What the body experiences is felt throughout the mind, the spirit, and the soul. Likewise, that which is experienced by the spirit, soul, and mind is also perceived by the body. The fear that riddles us in the external world takes root in our psyches and in our bodies. The soul, too, is cut off and suffocated; its messages are lost in the cacophony of anxiety and fear. The individual often suffers silently. Depression and anxiety set in. Shopping malls are filled with consumers ready to plop down an almost-maxed-out credit card to get the feel-good fix of the latest designer handbag, pricey athletic shoes, or bit of technology. Closets fill, waistlines broaden, credit card bills surge, and stress increases. The temporary fixes we purchase online, in stores, and at the doctor's office only serve to deepen our anxiety and broaden our fears. Medicine cabinets fill with sleep aids, antidepressants, and anti-anxiety pharmaceuticals. The underlying causes are not always addressed; in the interest of saving money and finding a "quick fix," the symptoms are simply medicated. The real issues—the root problems—are ignored.

The individual is, of course, not alone in this predicament. We all swim in the same fish tank of humanity. In sharing the same "water of life"—a collective consciousness—that which affects one individual ultimately affects us all. The destructive, fear-based messages that pour forth through the news riddle every person's psyche. When its formidable powers are disregarded, fear amasses its strength, growing wildly under the nose of our ignorance. As individuals turn inward in anxious isolation, fear turns ever outward, stretching its arms and running rampant throughout society.

The Messenger We Want to Know: Constructive Fear

If this sounds all doom and gloom, fear not. As Henry David Thoreau wrote, "Nothing is so much to be feared as fear."[2] His words remain solid and true, for although destructive fear often has us in its grip, that needn't be the case. Fear gains power over us because we are too blind or ignorant to understand that *each and every one of us* has the ultimate power over the destructive aspect of fear. We regain our power by becoming aware of and utilizing the second aspect of fear: constructive fear. Constructive fear allows us to dismantle destructive fear, rendering us more knowledgeable and aware of the inner self. Through embracing this hidden, wondrous side of fear, we ignite our inner power—the power of transformational fear.

A simple metaphor may enliven this unfamiliar concept. Imagine a tough, fierce bully in the middle of a busy sidewalk, a spot that he has claimed and owned for years. This bully is so strong and demanding that no one dares to approach him. He shouts, screams, and terrorizes—often in unintelligible ways. This bully controls travelers with his arbitrary, destructive ways that leave people angry, stressed, immobilized, or scurrying in fear. Yet what would happen if we paused and shifted the customary scene? What if we had the courage to walk up to this bully and inspect its hidden backside—the side we usually rush by in our fear? What if there was another face on this hidden side that was wise and friendly, with a soft voice telling us there is much to be learned from looking at both sides of fear? What if we were to embrace both aspects, turn the bully around, and transform that busy sidewalk into an avenue of freedom and joy? This sidewalk is your life. It is *our* life. Fear is not merely a tyrannical bully. Fear also has the capability to be one of our greatest teachers; this is the constructive aspect of fear. Unite both—learn from both—turn the awareness into action, and you have ignited the full, tremendous power of transformational fear.

Transformational fear is the force that arises when we move forward to notice and embrace the illuminating, *constructive* messages hidden within the bullying, *destructive* aspect of fear. Transformational fear wants us to notice and tame the untended, bullish side of destructive fear. It does not want fear relegated to the dark corners of the night and the bleak recesses of the mind. Transformational fear wants us to notice both of its sides; it wants you to be free of the controlling fear that surfaces through clenched jaws, tormented sleep, and angry outbursts. Transformational fear wants to introduce you to the constructive face of fear. It wants you to recognize, hold close, and use constructive fear as a tool for greater self-discovery. This constructive, friendly aspect of fear is far too often hidden, unseen, or unheard. This powerful, friendly side of fear calls out to say, "If you will look at me and discover the messages within me, I can lead you to the life of your dreams. Do not run from me, but listen to me. Your very fears have the power to lead you into a fuller knowing of yourself and, thus, into a life that is free of the false chains of fear." When set in motion and utilized, this constructive element of fear becomes transformational fear at work.

Still, you might be resisting this idea of fear as an ultimate driving force in your life. You may feel more or less content in your daily regimen—comfortable with the status quo. You might be afraid to shake things up. You might, on some level, *want* things to stay the same. This may bring you to ask, "How does this affect *me*?" I then reply, "In every possible way."

It's often easier to go through life with our heads stuck in the sand. We often think, *Hey, what I don't know can't hurt me.* However, that is not the case here. What you don't know—and what you don't *want* to know—may be affecting you more perniciously because of your lack of awareness. What you ignore does affect you, and it affects every aspect of your being, inside and out. Are there parts of your life that could benefit from a bit of illumination and freedom, even if it makes you uncomfortable? If so, this adventure with transformational fear is for you.

Yes, the journey is arduous and never-ending, yet the resulting inner light of awareness and unity is a joy beyond compare. To live a life infused with anxiety and deadened by the strictures of fear requires a resigned settling, an unspoken agreement to merely exist through a series of days upon end. To live within the embrace of transformational fear is to open the windows of the soul to the greater world.

By engaging with both aspects of fear and developing a relationship that is appreciative, informative, and non-adversarial, transformational fear becomes the energy that actually creates greater freedom and self-awareness. Even as you ponder my words, you might resist this novel concept. You may counter, "Well, what can *I* do about it?" I offer, "You can do everything to change fear's impact in your life, and by changing your relationship to fear, you will affect every person you come into contact with throughout your life."

It is vital that you set aside everything you ever learned about fear. Put it in a box. Set it on the windowsill and leave it there for just a bit—long enough for some new thoughts and ideas to enter. Truly entertain the idea that we are all *afraid* of fear. It is our fear of fear that does us in. Fear is not innately "good" or "bad;" fear just *is*. It is what we *do* with our fear that makes all the difference. Our perceptions of fear make all the difference in our lives, our inner spirits, and our world. We are taught that fear is a strongly negative force, that it keeps us down, and that we should conquer it, overcome it, or even be entirely fearless. I shout, "No! Pay attention to your fears! Notice that there is more than one side to fear. Let fear serve you, not hold you back! Use fear! Learn from fear! Explore who you are— and who you want to become—through the extraordinary, dual-sided nature of fear. Dare to let your life be *transformed* by fear."

In the chapters ahead, you will read case examples based on my clients who have successfully faced and risen above their own fears. These illustrations are offered to provide you with encouragement and inspiration as you move forward on your own journey. I prescribe concrete exercises that offer you the opportunity to face your own fears at a pace that is comfortable for you. These exercises will allow you to begin to notice your fears, move to explore them, and then engage in the life-changing thoughts and behaviors that will make your life your own. As you dismantle your destructive fears, you will steadily notice significant shifts in your attitude, thought processes, behaviors, and physical body. You will begin to truly know how it feels to live a life free of the harmful constraints of fear.

Once you have progressed on your journey, you will look back and wonder what took you so long to "get to it." You will laugh at what once held you back. You will marvel that you once accepted a life that felt poorly lived. You will bask in the joy of knowing that you no longer compromise or accept that which feels wrong for you, beneath you, or unacceptable to you. You will smile, knowing that you have gained your integrity and that you stand in the truth as you know it to be. You will shine with an inner light that comes from loving yourself, from radiating the beauty that was once held in the dark cave of fear. The claws of pernicious anxiety and depression will be remote memories, for you will come to know them for what they are. You will call out to others to join you by your very being, for you will be the fullest version of your true self.

Old or young, male or female, rich or poor, the journey into transformational fear is an essential journey of love and freedom. In opening up to the exploration of your deepest fears, you begin to truly know yourself. As you become more aware of your personal fears, you learn to face them and even open your arms to them. As you move more deeply into the journey, you begin to leave self-judgment behind. In committing to the process, your self-appreciation increases. In undergoing the process, you gain a deep love and appreciation for yourself. You accept—and fall in love with—the person in the mirror at a level you may have never dreamed possible.

In learning how to recognize and make use of your own fear, you are taking your first steps toward a life lived in true freedom. Do not be afraid of fear; draw it ever closer. I entreat you: *allow yourself to be afraid*—simply put one foot in the front of the other and take one moment at a time. Have faith that you are meant to be happy, free, and filled with love. Know that only good can ultimately come from removing your shackles and learning more fully about yourself. You are not meant to be less; you are destined to become more. Come along for the journey; you won't regret it. In fact, by reading these first few pages, I welcome you, for your journey has already begun.

CHAPTER I

Fear as a Fire-Breathing Entity

Fear Is More Powerful Than You Think

As I drove home from work one chilly winter evening, the sky unleashed a furious downpour. The car in front of me suddenly swerved, skidding sideways in the pouring rain. I reacted instinctively, my mind keenly aware as I turned the wheel and slid wildly onto the gravel shoulder. My hands, through the instinctive senses of my mind and body, had reacted with a smooth dexterity I didn't know I possessed. Stunned and shaking, I sat in the sudden stillness. I noticed that my hands, once calm, trembled uncontrollably as I searched for my cell phone. Reacting to my inner fear and profound sense of fragility, I wanted to call a friend to share my terror, to somehow connect after feeling that I'd just nearly missed meeting my own death. My breath was shallow and shaky, and I reminded myself to breathe slowly. As the long minutes passed, I began to relax. My state of panic subsided as the rain lessened in intensity. My thoughts became clearer, and my hands stopped their frantic search in the darkness. Focusing on the steady rhythm of the windshield wipers, I turned off my car as the strain of ambulance sirens filled my ears. Relief soaked my being. Despite my rational fear for my life, I had used my instinctive abilities—skills I didn't even know I possessed—to move through an intensely challenging situation.

We have all experienced an intensely fearful reaction like what I just described—*rational* fear based on *actual* or *perceived* danger. Whether threatened by a snarling dog, a stranger on a dimly lit street, or a jolting awareness that a loved one is in danger, we are neurobiologically hardwired to face threats with a "fight or flight" response. Although the physiological effects of fear will be detailed later, a brief overview of the body's fear-based responses may be helpful at this point. In short, the sympathetic nervous system quickly kicks into action when a potential threat in the environment arises. As the body goes on alert, various physiological responses occur, such as increases in heart and respiration rates. As the environment is scanned, the heart pounds, breathing changes, the pupils dilate, and perspiration increases. Within seconds of perceiving a danger, the situation has been evaluated and a decision has been made to fight, flee, or freeze. This built-in survival mechanism, the body's "fight or flight response" (sometimes termed the "fight, flight, or freeze response"), works well to allow us to respond quickly to potentially dangerous, fear-inducing situations.

In this sense, fear is viewed as a normal and beneficial reaction that allows us to take unconscious, evaluative notice of a threat. When an actual threat exists, this rapid response system normally works in our service, saving us from all manner of dangers—whether they are relatively minor or truly life-threatening. The body's capacity to react and adapt so magnificently has, in fact, ensured the survival of our species. In this realm, fear is highly beneficial to us. Its purpose is to keep us safe from harm. When we think of fear and fear-based responses, it is this physiological type of fear—and our unconscious, instinctual responses to it—that first comes to mind. In fact, fear is commonly and primarily defined as a feeling of agitation and anxiety caused by present or imminent danger. We are so accustomed to this particular definition of fear and our one-dimensional perception of it that we are nearly blind to the other faces of fear.

The Destructive and Constructive Faces of Transformational Fear

I ask you to consider that an altogether different form of fear exists, a form of *irrational* fear that is *not* based upon the perception of a realistic threat. This type of fear is less obvious to us because it is so pervasive in our daily lives. Very different from reality-based fear, this brand of fear has life-changing powers. For this reason, I have termed this type of fear "transformational fear." As you may recall, transformational fear is the process of embracing constructive fear to become free of the bullying force of destructive fear. Once an individual is empowered by awareness and understanding, the active work of transformation can take place.

First, let's take a deeper look at destructive fear. Much like the ubiquitous weeds that slowly infiltrate and choke a once-promising garden if left unchecked, the adversarial side of fear moves stealthily and steadily to gain ever-greater ground. Precisely because destructive fear blends in with our world, because it is so ever-present and subtly shaded, it takes hold and its roots grow deeper every day. In failing to notice this fear, it becomes an enemy to us. Rather than making use of its messages, we often either ignore it or react to it. Instead of moving toward the fear to allow further inspection and understanding, we run away in avoidance or fight it as an adversary. We have become accustomed to treating this fear as an actual threat, and we often unconsciously adopt a "fight or flight" stance. By responding in this way, we become a victim to fear; we become enslaved by the nature of our own behaviors. This fear is not based upon an actual, realistic threat; it is not a fear that is warning us to evade danger. Instead, it is a pernicious, imagination-based fear that serves no purpose but to bind us in upon ourselves. This brand of fear, insidious and depleting, heightens our pervasive sense of anxiety. As a result, we unconsciously and chronically see the world through fear-tinted glasses. This type of fear—destructive fear—sneaks in through the back door of the mind to plant seeds of insecurity.

Through the story of a dear friend I shall call "Cindy," let's take a brief look at this powerful and destructive element of fear. For well over five harrowing years, Cindy lived in a fear so deep and entrenched that she came to second-guess everything from her job performance to whether or not to leave a tyrannical and abusive marriage. A dedicated, highly intelligent, and competent woman, Cindy consistently strove for success in all areas of life. As is her habit, this accomplished, intense woman had refined a work project to the point of absolute perfection; as usual, she'd left no piece uncovered, no diagram anything but clearly and brilliantly detailed. The evening before the presentation—an event for which she was overly prepared—fears began to overtake her. Cindy telephoned me to share her doubts and unload, but my words of support were of little comfort. In the throes of a divorce, she had uncharacteristically imbued the task ahead of her with such intense emotions that she made herself quite literally sick to her stomach. I made the short drive to her home to offer my support in person.

"If I don't get this right, they will fire me," she cried. "I'll lose my job, and I won't ever see the light of day again. I won't be able to pay my bills. I won't get custody of my daughter—it will all be gone. I can feel it. I'm ruined. I should've just stayed in the horrible, stupid marriage. I've lost it all. How could anyone be so completely . . . stupid?"

From personal experience, I knew all too well the depths of her self-doubt, her fears. I knew, too, that any words I could offer in the midst of her angst would be unheard. No matter how unrealistic and unfounded I knew her fears to be, I realized any objective feedback would, at this point, be futile. Shaken and overwhelmed, she slowly sipped the tea I had made. I listened as she spoke, attending to both her verbal language and her body's messages. By homing in on the cognitions and feelings that were working against her, we slowly unraveled the tentacles of fear that had invaded her spirit. Her agitation diminished, and the clarity of her perceptions increased as the evening wore on. As her overwhelming emotions subsided, she once again believed—not just in her head, but in her spirit—that the daughter she had raised would never be removed from her care. From her supposed stupidity to the incomprehensible idea that she'd be fired by a company that openly considered her its greatest asset, each corrosive fear was given attention. As though every careful illumination of a fearful thought caused it to spark and then burn out to nothingness, the strong, self-assured woman I'd known for so many years came back to life before my eyes. No longer catastrophizing the situation, she was able to look at her fears for what they were—unrealistic seeds of self-doubt that had flourished deep inside her spirit. Without her conscious awareness, the fears had moved in and taken hold; as they did so, the true nature of her inner self had been pushed aside and diminished.

The above scenario reflects how fear conspires against us to gain control. Once we are immobilized—whether in an untenable marriage, an unfulfilling job, or a web of negative self-talk—it is far too easy to lose sight of our strengths. When we are stuck or feeling powerless, a loss of confidence in the self may follow readily. As fear gains greater hold and becomes more entrenched, a nebulous sense of despondency descends. Often, we feel that something is not right. Subtle warnings (the well-known "gut instinct") may arise, but these caution signs are often quashed or ignored. When we ignore these signals, fear takes the opportunity to set in more firmly. Confusion, desperation, and feelings of depression soon follow; it is not long before a sense of overwhelming helplessness arises. The last stronghold—faith—begins to disintegrate; belief in the self, life, and the future diminishes. We are often wholly unconscious of this process. In what seems to be the blink of an eye, the face in the mirror is asking, *How did I get here? What happened to me?* In general, this is how destructive fear works on an individual level.

Fear, ever cunning and practiced, does not stop with the individual. Its methods are equally clever when working on a mass scale. As we saw with the attack on the Twin Towers on September 11, 2001, when the United States—and the world—reeled from the impact of the terrorist attacks, fear has the capacity to wreak havoc upon entire nations. On that terrible autumn day, we stood in disbelief as individuals and as a nation. Glued to radios, television screens, and computer monitors, we were unable to comprehend the magnitude of what we had witnessed. As the initial shock and numbness subsided, fear quickly took hold. Airport security was elevated to unparalleled levels, turbaned foreigners became the embodiment of terrorism, and feelings of hostile suspicion were directed toward *any* potential or perceived threat. Americans stood before the world, angry and strong—all the while trembling in fear. The media fueled the fear, and we sat within our homes and offices, captivated by replayed scenes of the horrors of "9/11." We were filled with anger, confusion, and alarm, but most of all, we were filled with terror—an unshakable and intense fear. Fear had us in its unruly, masterful grip.

Revulsion, rage, horror, and a blanket of grief moved in to cover the powerful, deep fear that had crept into our marrow. We stood in ever-increasing airport security lines, submitting to invasive, often bizarre, and always time-consuming searches. We eyed those next to us with suspicion as lights flashed, alarms beeped, and faceless recordings warned us to leave no bag unattended. The rise and fall of the Homeland Security color-coded "terror alert level" furthered citizens' anxiety; the possibility of a "red alert" loomed large in the collective American psyche. Often retreating to the safety of our homes, we became captives in a world that seemed riddled with danger at every turn. We had become a nation immersed in fear. However, we had also joined ranks to become a country unified by our visceral terror and anger. We shared the specter of catastrophe; we were united by fear's throttling grip. Although 9/11 is now a more distant memory, our psyches have shifted in an almost permanent manner. Fear has made its home in our very core.

Whether operating on an individual scale or a more global level, this type of fear shares similar roots in all its manifestations. More obviously, this facet of fear is crippling, isolating, and limiting. This form of fear creates barriers to trust and peace. With practice, we can sit back and objectively list additional destructive elements of transformational fear. What is more difficult—only because we are unaccustomed to such a study—is to notice and delineate the *constructive* aspects of transformational fear. You may ask, "Constructive? How can fear of this sort possibly be constructive?"

Just as an instinctive reaction to a physical threat can be used to identify and react in a life-saving manner, this type of fear, too, can be used to salvage and foster one's inner life. It can be deconstructed to reveal the psychological and spiritual lessons hidden within its layers. Our souls and our bodies can become free and enlivened. With care and attention, fear can be explored to discover incredible, curative lessons that offer invaluable inner guidance. By using its constructive powers, fear can guide us toward greater self-discovery, increased awareness, and the liberation that comes with inner wisdom. For example, imagine that you have a destructive internal voice that says you are stuck forever in an unfulfilling, dead-end career. Consider what might happen if you were able to listen to a wise inner voice that could actively guide you to pursue a different career and the life of your dreams. If you listen, this wise guide will strive to help you get unstuck; it may suggest going back to school, joining a support group, or investigating other jobs. This inner wisdom is constructive fear at work. It sets the stage for transformation in your life. Due to its ability to propel transformation—to morph a mercurial, destructive force into a constructive force via intentional action—the term "transformational fear" seemed a natural choice for this incredibly powerful aspect of the human psyche.

In accepting the novel idea that fear contains both constructive *and* destructive components, it is important to remember that fear also has many layers and degrees in between the two counterparts. We often slip into the habit of forcing our thoughts and feelings into opposite poles; it seems easier to perfunctorily compartmentalize issues into "good or bad," "love or hate," or "black or white." To notice and distinguish the shades of gray, the nuanced spectrum, takes time and energy. To differentiate and discriminate challenges us and exposes us; it makes us think about and feel what we normally block off.

It is much the same with transformational fear. Transformational fear contains a vast and incredible treasure trove beneath its shadowy and unfamiliar surface. Many of us stop at the point when we sense that we are afraid. We prepare to fight or shy away. In either case, nothing is resolved, and we continue anxiously on our way. In doing so, we think we have "escaped our fears," but we haven't. They only wait in hiding. Sometimes they wait quietly and patiently to be noticed; at other times our fears fester and proliferate, turning into a psychic infection of sorts. We may think we have hidden our fears very well, but they often mount and arise in symptoms that range from persistent anxiety to panic attacks. Yet we continue to pretend that all is well. We convince ourselves that we have things under control.

Although we often think we have outsmarted our fears through aggression, avoidance, or repression, we have actually missed an incredible opportunity to become more self-aware. Out of blindness, we have ignored the waiting arms of transformational fear. When we don't stop to notice and tease apart the elements of fear that beg us to look closer, we have only shortchanged ourselves. The aspects of fear that we ignore or run from are often the very aspects that contain the subtle messages we need the most. These profound messages have the potential to become powerfully constructive tools for the careful, fear-aware user. These messages hold the keys to self-knowledge and personal transformation.

The Relationship between Fear and Anxiety

It is important to have a fuller understanding of fear and its various aspects before moving further into a journey with transformational fear. To notice fear, to work with fear, and to move *through* fear, a deeper study of fear and its various expressions is essential. Just as you might want to be able to

identify various snakes before embarking on a journey in unfamiliar territory, it is helpful to understand more about the shades of fear that are often
part of our daily journey through life. For those of you who crave facts
and figures, the following pages will be especially intriguing for you. Even
if you normally eschew statistics, the information I offer might encourage
you to see fear in a new light.

Anxiety, by far the most commonly acknowledged manifestation of
fear, pervades our culture. In the world of Freudian psychology, fear "has
an object," yet anxiety is considered to be fear "without an object." In
more understandable terms, this means that when we see something that
is potentially threatening, such as a strange figure in a dark alley, we react
in fear to that alarming "object" or situation. In contrast, anxiety is more
amorphous and cloudy; there is often no specific target ("object") to which
sensations of unrest and worry are attached. Instead, anxiety lingers and
lurks nervously in the mind's shadows as a manifestation of fear. Often
sitting just below the surface of consciousness, anxiety stealthily perme-
ates the psyche. We cannot escape the sense that things *just aren't right*.
Anxiety leaves us with the inexplicable feeling that *something*—the stress,
the pressure, the tension, the pace—is just too much. Without the overt
symptoms of full-fledged panic attacks, this pernicious form of anxiety
often escapes our radar. It just "lives" inside of us day to day, and we cope
with it as best we can.

If you question the ubiquitous presence of fear in our daily lives,
researchers offer very sobering information. According to the Anxiety
Disorders Association of America (ADAA), "Anxiety disorders are the
most common mental illness in the US, affecting 40 million adults in the
United States age 18 and older, or 18% of the US population." Anxiety
manifests itself in many forms, including panic disorder, agoraphobia,
social phobia, obsessive-compulsive disorder, post-traumatic stress disorder, acute stress disorder, and generalized anxiety disorder. According
to the ADAA, 6.8 million adults in the United States—3.1 percent of the
population—suffer from generalized anxiety disorder. Women are twice
as likely to be affected by this psychological disorder as men.[1] These figures for adults are assuredly daunting, yet keep in mind that such statistics
normally capture only those individuals who have sought treatment and
been diagnosed. Given the millions of Americans with no health care or
inadequate health care, the actual number of those suffering from anxiety-related disorders is sure to be much higher. On a positive note, some of

the increase in published statistics may be attributable to sufferers' growing comfort and willingness to reach out for necessary support.

Anxiety disorders often develop over time, and symptoms may arise slowly and perniciously. Many psychological conditions, including anxiety-based disorders, are rooted in a host of complex risk factors. Each person's unique combination of neurobiology, genetic makeup, environmental factors, and life history affect how and if psychological disorders are manifested. In the case of anxiety disorders, what is consciously or unconsciously feared can surface through a litany of anxiety-based symptoms such as sleeplessness, hyperactivity, and physical ailments. Particularly when repressed and avoided, fear and the resulting symptoms of anxiety will flourish.

According to statistics offered by the National Institute for Mental Health (NIMH), 19.1 percent of the US adult population was affected by an anxiety disorder in the past year; the level of impairment ranged from "mild" (43.5 percent) to "severe" (22.8 percent). This is troubling news, and it only gets worse. According to the NIMH, the far-too-young age of eleven is the average age of onset for an anxiety disorder. This means that, for many children, the actual age of onset can be much earlier.[2]

Due to the potentially serious effects on growth and brain development, researchers have questioned the efficacy and appropriateness of several common psychotropic medications being administered to children as young as preschool age.[3] Why are an increasing number of preschoolers—who can be as young as three—on medications for psychological disorders?

Sit back for a moment and reflect on what you have just read. Where are we headed when our elementary school children are suffering from anxiety? What can we do when learning that researchers question the long-term effects of the psychotropic medications administered to *preschoolers*? What has gone wrong when approximately one-fifth of our adult population has been formally diagnosed with an anxiety-related disorder? To what extent is fear controlling our world—our very psyches? If fear and its various manifestations are really this powerful, what can be done about it? Notice your thoughts and notice how you feel when you allow the full weight of this information to settle over you. Are you shocked, saddened, or surprised? Or have you been numbed?

Can you picture in your mind's eye how you felt at the young ages of seven, eleven, and fifteen? What were you doing in your youth? Were you riding your bicycle, climbing trees, dancing, playing baseball, swimming, studying, or taking music lessons? Or were you sitting in a doctor's office, texting, gaming, and surfing the web on a cell phone while awaiting a medical evaluation for anxiety, attention-deficit hyperactivity disorder (ADHD), or depression? Are our children living in environments so infused with fear that they, too, are suffering the consequences of fear-based, fast-paced, anxiety-riddled living?

Are you, as an adult, living the life of your dreams? Or does fear have you by the tail? Does stress, anxiety, or depression rule your realm? As you move at a breakneck pace throughout your day, does your left hand forget what the right one has done? Does your head pound with tension? With the roller-coaster effects of days on end still within your body and mind, does sleep elude you at night? When sleep does come, is it interrupted and restless? Does one pill put you to sleep and another help you awaken? Is there one medication in your drawer for depression and another in your pocket or purse for anxiety? If this doesn't describe you or someone you love, count yourself among the very fortunate. If this does describe you—even in some small way—have faith that you are not destined to continue on such a rocky path.

The High Cost (and Sometimes Low Value) of Medication

Before moving on toward various solutions to fear-based living, it is important to have a more focused grasp of some of the underlying problems. Clearly, our country's overreliance on pharmaceuticals as the "quick fix" is misguided and potentially harmful. After reviewing published literature on the efficacy rates of psychotherapy versus antidepressants, England's National Health Service selected cognitive behavioral therapy (CBT) as a first-line treatment for mild and moderate depression. Their decision was based upon research showing a "poor" risk-benefit ratio for antidepressants.[4] From anti-anxiety medications (anxiolytics) to antidepressants, the United States holds the dubious title of the world's top consumer of psychotropic medications.

The use of anti-anxiety medications to combat a host of psychological conditions continues to increase dramatically. Primary care physicians are often put in the position of prescribing medications for mental health concerns such as depression and anxiety, yet in-depth mental health care is often beyond the scope of their practices. These physicians often face many bureaucratic constraints, including appointment time limitations and pressure from healthcare companies to take the quick-fix, "pill popping" route. As a result, the client seeking pharmacological mental health treatment is often not given appropriate attention, critical follow-up care, and necessary psychotherapy. This common pharmacological approach to treating mental health issues can be likened to throwing prescription darts and hoping to hit near the bullseye; this is unacceptable. A model that provides mindful, individualized care is necessary, as each person's unique genetic makeup can make it difficult to predict the nature of a response to a medication. Without tools such as in-depth genetic testing, the prescriber does not know how or if an individual will respond to a certain medication or what negative side effects may result. When a medication is ineffective or problematic, many individuals feel ashamed, as if they are somehow to blame. This additional stress can lead an already anxious or depressed client to feeling even worse. These individuals are rarely—if ever—told that it is the approach, not the individual, that falls short of what is needed. What are the answers? Given the current state of psychopharmacology, care should, at a minimum, offer a thorough clinical evaluation and in-person follow-up care at least every three months. Each individual deserves thorough and mindful attention based on teamwork and informed decisions, not a random approach that often benefits the insurance and pharmaceutical industries. The field of pharmacogenomics is focusing on developing and providing safe, effective medications and medication dosages customized for each client's genetic makeup. Such individualized approaches offer a much-needed move away from the standard "one size fits all" approach to psychopharmacology. The options are increasing for those suffering from mental health issues, but concerted patient advocacy is necessary to create change.[5]

This section is not intended to demonize or disparage individuals who find relief by pharmaceuticals, nor is it intended to demonize specific pharmaceuticals. Certainly, there are many individuals who would face needless suffering or even danger without the benefit of their medications. Some are able to "get on their feet" and address underlying issues only as a result of the beneficial effects of their medications. Many courageous individuals will find that medication improves their lives, enabling them to engage in life and even embrace transformational fear. Yet after medications are dispensed, far too few receive sufficient psychological support to address the issues beneath the often-debilitating symptoms.

The problem lies not with individuals but with insurance and drug companies that profit from pushing medications in place of effective—but costlier—holistic treatment. The statistics in this section are not meant to shame those taking medications for diagnosed mental health disorders, but rather to offer support in requesting and advocating proper treatment. Sadly, insurance companies continue to place limitations on mental health services. Although individual therapy is often vital, it can be prohibitively expensive. However, no-cost or low-fee options are often available through venues such as community clinics, college campus services, and religious organizations. Some mental health practitioners offer sliding scale rates or low-cost group therapy services. Remember, too, that the self-work you are undertaking in this book can be a tremendous complement to professional psychotherapy.

According to an American Psychological Association (APA) publication, the percentage of the general US population making use of psychotherapy services during a nine-year period remained relatively unchanged. However, medication-only visits rose during that timeframe. The use of psychotherapy-only services dropped from 16 percent to 10.5 percent. Alarming but true is the fact that more than 57 percent of patients now receive medication without psychotherapy; this is a 13 percent increase from the former medication-only rate of 44 percent.[6] As our population increasingly suffers from the debilitating effects of pernicious anxiety and other disorders, insurance companies save money and pharmaceutical firms witness ever-higher profits. All the while, the root causes of the mental health issues are usually left unattended and unexplored. The long-term costs can be devastating.

Psychotherapy, although potentially costlier upfront, can address the root causes of many disorders and their symptoms. However, a significant research study found that the amount spent on healthcare funding for psychotherapy actually decreased over the ten-year period studied. During this same time period, the amount spent on psychotropic medications increased threefold.[7] The skyrocketing economic burden of healthcare costs is not increasing the level of care for the public. The vast arrays of medications, many of which have considerable and often highly undesirable side effects, do little to address the underlying causes of the symptoms. Additionally, new research is contesting the efficacy of pharmaceuticals as compared to placebos, finding that placebos are often as effective as their costly pharmaceutical counterparts.[8]

A study commissioned by the ADAA determined that anxiety disorders alone account for nearly one-third of the nation's total annual mental health bill. The study found the annual cost of treating anxiety disorders was over 42 billion dollars per year. The costs are not going down; they continue to rise at alarming rates.[9]

As noted in an APA journal article, American consumers spent over eleven billion dollars on antidepressants in the reported year alone. This same publication noted that adult Americans increased their overall use of psychotropic medications by 22 percent over the course of nine years.[10] The Centers for Disease Control and Prevention (CDC) recently reported that the use of antidepressants increased 65 percent in the last fifteen-year period studied.[11] According to the pharmaceutical industry's data, one in five adults currently uses at least one medication intended to treat a psychological disorder such as anxiety, depression, or ADHD.[12] This figure does not, of course, account for the medications frequently "borrowed" from the medicine cabinets of spouses, friends, and parents.

Data emanating from various disciplines that include medicine and psychology warn of the dangers of improperly prescribed—and improperly used—medications.[13] Of course, it is not that the medications themselves are inherently "bad." It is our misuse and overuse of them that wreaks havoc. When used with discretion and care, psychotropic medications can be extraordinarily valuable tools in the treatment of psychological disorders. Unfortunately, prescriptions are often offered as a unilateral quick fix, and the underlying issues—the real sources of the problems—remain largely untreated. We know enough to improve this situation.

A New Vantage Point

If pharmaceuticals were the answer for many of our mental health issues, we might expect a decline in the incidence rates of the disorders being treated with these medications. Instead, there is a consistent increase in the diagnosis rates of many psychological disorders. Given the steady increases in diagnoses and the large number of unsuccessful treatment efforts, there is no time like the present to find a few different answers. What can be done to approach anxiety and other fear-based disorders from a new vantage point? It makes sense for us to take a step back and learn from what has not been working. Rather than continuing to pour resources into *covering* symptoms, we would be far better served by addressing the underlying *causes* of depression, anxiety, panic disorders, sleeplessness, and a host of other treatable mental health issues. Those who continue to suffer live with the internal agony of conditions that never seem to be truly resolved by pharmaceuticals. Many feel that they have made some ill-fated mistake that now dooms them to a life of psychological misery. Operating in the age of science and the rational mind, we want to believe that a quick-fix pill will cure all, but the results tell us otherwise. The psyche knows differently; what is ailing within demands thoughtful and diligent attention.

The psyche is often undervalued and marginalized in today's externally focused world. The human psyche may be thought of as the totality of the mind's conscious and unconscious aspects. The word psyche is derived from the Latin *psyche*, or "animating spirit," and the Greek *psyche*, or "soul, mind, spirit; breath; life." Interestingly, the Greek term also refers to "the invisible animating principle or entity which occupies and directs the physical body."[14] Clearly, humans have long believed that the psyche has a direct impact on the body itself. When the psyche is thriving, the physical body feels lighter and free. When the psyche is not doing well, the body will suffer.

Although a later chapter will focus on destructive fear's negative effects on your overall health, it's important to draw a few key points to your attention early on. As you read, open your mind to the idea that your psychological health and physical health are deeply interrelated. A simple illustration underscores this connection: When you know that you have a deadline at work, does it affect your body? Does the mental deadline make your body feel the pressure? Do your shoulders tense up? Do you feel a headache coming on? Does the coming deadline affect your ability to sleep? These are but a few of the ways that a mental concept, one as common as a work or school deadline, can affect your physical body.

As another example, have you ever felt "punched in the gut" when someone called you a horrible name or said something terribly unkind? Did a mere word or sentence result in feelings of hurt, sadness, or anger inside your body? Did your heart pound? Did your belly feel queasy? Maybe your throat constricted. Did your stressed physical reaction then make your mental state all the worse? These common reactions show how readily the body can be affected by the mind and how the mind can be affected by the body.

Looking at one last illustration, can you recall a time when you were really afraid about doing something new or unfamiliar? Did the mental idea of giving a speech, meeting new people, or traveling to a different place make you feel anxious or uncomfortable? Did you get butterflies in your stomach? Did you have an urge to flee the situation? Did your chest constrict or your breath become shallow? Perhaps your heart beat so frantically that you thought it would explode. All of these reactions are the body's way of saying, "Hey, anxious mind, I am registering and feeling what's going on with you. I know you are scared. I feel it. I am connected to you. I respond to your thoughts. I *get* that you are afraid."

For better or for worse, the mind has great power to affect the physical body, and the physical body has great power to affect the mind. The above examples focus on how the body responds quickly to stressful circumstances. Yet the body also has the power to slow down, soothe, and heal. Can you recall a time when your stress or anxiety were lessened by the sound of familiar music or a loved one's kind words? Maybe you can remember how your body and mind felt when you received a warm, gentle hug. Indeed, you might readily recollect a time when deep, belly-aching laughter felt immensely relieving. That mood-elevating laughter made your body and psyche feel lighter; it was better than any medicine you could have ordered. This is how the body-psyche connection works. Often unnoticed, it works behind the scenes every minute of every day. It is through this connection that we see the world and live our lives.

It's likely that you face some sort of stress every day of your life. If you're lucky, maybe you feel stressed only every now and again. However, in our hectic, busy world, most people live with far too much stress in their lives. Perhaps you live in a world that leaves you stressed from morning until night. Maybe anxiety never leaves you, whether you are awake or asleep. It might be that you've gotten so "good" at managing your stress that you don't notice it anymore. It might have become so chronic that life might feel strange, maybe even too calm without it. Like an undetected termite infestation, ongoing stress has the power to do a great deal of damage without you even knowing it. Stress, all too often rooted in destructive fear, is more harmful than you may realize.

Of course, it is important to note that psychological and physical difficulties can be rooted in factors other than fear. For example, certain mental health disorders stemming from genetic factors, serious medical conditions, and intractable physiological issues are outside the parameters of general fear-based disorders. However, many problematic issues do have a strong basis in issues related to our fears. In determining those conditions and situations that will respond to fear-based treatment techniques, a mindful approach is the key. By consciously considering your unique situation and needs—as well as your healthcare professional's advice—you will find the path that is right for you.

Additionally, when anxiety and depression are discussed in this book, I am most often discussing *feelings* of depression and anxiety rather than a mental health disorder. Remember that while feelings of depression and anxiety are to be expected in our hectic, stressful world, there is a difference between these feelings and a mental health disorder such as major depressive disorder or generalized anxiety disorder. Although it can be tempting to self-diagnose, professional guidance is often helpful and necessary. When in doubt, reach out to your mental healthcare professional or physician to have your concerns fully addressed.

Getting to Know Your Fears—Exercises and Moving Forward

Now we can move on to the especially intriguing place where the enlightening work with transformational fear begins. The exercises presented in this book are an important, supportive aspect of your journey. In general, they will improve your overall self-awareness and offer helpful structure. Some exercises are focused on generating personal insights that may be transformative in themselves. Others are designed to help you learn and establish positive patterns; the more you practice your new skills, the more familiar and natural they will be to you. The exercises build on each other, allowing you to move forward with greater awareness and confidence.

Whether working with the initial gentle exercises or the more complex exercises that will arise later, a few basic instructions are necessary:

1. Always take care that your surroundings are peaceful; ensure that you are psychologically and physically in a place of spaciousness and sufficient wellness for this work.
2. Have a pen, pencil, and notebook with you. This notebook will become a very important chronicle of your journey with fear. Indeed, you may come to embrace this personal journal as a dear friend.

3. If any exercise or aspect of an exercise does not feel appropriate or safe, simply move past it; honor your unique responses. If at any point an exercise does not feel right to you, take a break and breathe. You may choose to return to the exercise later if you like, but never feel compelled to complete an exercise. Every time you notice, honor, and accept your own internal messages, you are increasing your self-awareness. For example, if an exercise makes you feel panicked, set it aside and breathe. If you choose to return to it later, complete it only if your emotional responses feel appropriate and manageable.

4. Feel free to take breaks before, during, and after any exercises; do what feels best for you.

5. Finally, you will be reminded to breathe at the conclusion of the exercises in this book. These breaths, which I often refer to as "cleansing breaths," will allow you to release energy and thoughts that are not helpful. As you gently breathe in through your nose to the count of four, allow your chest to expand fully and allow your belly to float outward. As you exhale through your mouth, release your breath slowly and fully, drawing your navel back toward your spine. These full, slow breaths will allow you to naturally return to a state of calmness and clarity. Of course, if any breathing exercise feels harmful, do not continue. Various breathing techniques, sometimes known as "breath-work," will be discussed in greater detail later, yet this brief introduction to cleansing breaths may serve you well in many situations. For those who are used to breathwork through yoga, meditation, or other pursuits, this exercise may be easy. For others, the breathing exercises may seem odd and unfamiliar; in such cases, patience is key.

As your opening exercise, simply practice breathing as described above. Take a deep inhalation through your nose as you count to four. Then exhale slowly through your mouth. Repeat this four times. When you are finished, notice how you feel. Did focusing on your breath help your mind become still? Did you feel more present and aware? Perhaps you found the breaths soothing? Were you less distracted? Without judgment, simply notice how the breathing exercise made you feel, even if you felt nothing different at all. Then make a few notations about your experience. You are now ready to move forward to the next step. Excellent!

What Is Fear to You?

Let's continue to expand our understanding of fear through your first personal exercise with fear. Ensure that you are in a space that feels relaxed and safe to you. As with all future exercises, have your pen and notebook at your side. When you are physically and psychologically ready to proceed, pause to breathe. Prepare to investigate fear through your own unique lens.

Fear is often defined as a "state of apprehension, agitation, or uneasiness." For an interesting and very apt historical interpretation, a quote attributed to Aristotle offers, "Fear is pain arising from the anticipation of evil." Do you feel the difference between those two definitions? It is Aristotle's centuries-old version that resonates within the psyche; it feels as though the psyche knows the truth of fear's power. Refer once again to Aristotle's simple phrase. You might find that another word fits more appropriately for you in the place of the word "evil." Maybe it is the word "uncertainty," "failure," "death," "rejection," or "nothingness." There is no right response here; there is one word that will feel most true. Although other peripheral words might arise, for now, simply home in on the *one* word that lingers foremost in your being. Close your eyes. Hold onto this key word; make note of it.

Whether you use Aristotle's phrase unchanged or insert a different word that most resonates for you, repeat the phrase out loud and cement it in your mind. Close your eyes as you repeat it again. Notice—simply notice—what happens in your body as you say, "Fear is pain arising from the anticipation of _____." Pause to write down your complete phrase in the notebook you are devoting to your journey. Make any other notes that feel important to you. Complete the exercise by breathing in deeply and fully, allowing your chest to expand with fresh breath and then allowing a deep release on your exhale. Repeat the breathing exercise a few more times. This was your first discussion with fear. Well done; it is time to move on.

Let's have another look at anxiety. Particularly in the field of psychology, anxiety is often viewed as the "state of agitation or apprehension that arises from anticipating an event or situation that is perceived as threatening." Interestingly, the relationship of anxiety to fear is often ignored. In his book entitled *Original Self*, author, clinician, and lecturer Thomas Moore offers a more interesting definition of anxiety. Moore notes, "Anxiety is nothing but fear inspired by an imagined future collapse. It is the failure of trust."[15] This simple definition of anxiety, one that clearly reflects anxiety's relationship to fear, also offers an important clue to anxiety's connection to a loss of trust. To take this concept one step further, anxiety and its parent, fear, are both rooted in a lack of faith. Devoid of a centered, internal trust—a core belief in the power of faith—fear lurks at the corners of the psyche, gaining leverage as it eats away at whatever vestiges of positive conviction remain. In later chapters, we will look more closely at the fear-faith connection; for now, simply contemplate that such a connection exists.

Recall that fear is generally deemed to be the body's response to an actual or perceived threat, whereas anxiety is often viewed as the body's response to a more amorphous danger. Recollect that Freud conceptualized anxiety as a response to an "object-less" threat. The traditional view of fear comes alive in an illustrative example of a person's terror-stricken reaction to a robbery attempt; the ski-masked robber would be the object of the fearful response. In the case of anxiety, no particular item, person, or situation may be identifiable; instead, a lurking sense of panic or apprehension floats within, often creating a constant sense of impending doom. Chronic anxiety does not benefit the individual; instead of moving the individual toward either "fight" or "flight," it infiltrates the body and the psyche as a wayward instinct that has moved into overdrive. The exhausted sufferer feels constantly on alert, often overcome by a vague sense of worry and agitation that seems to have no particularly identifiable source. This type of anxiety, often simmering just below the surface of conscious awareness, can have wide-ranging deleterious effects. Clients have described this chronic anxiety in many ways, from a "headless monster that lives in me" to a sense of "constantly walking on eggshells."

Unfortunately, we often attend only to the symptoms of anxiety as they surface. Rather than attending to the underlying causes of the anxiety, the root fears are often minimized or ignored. Most commonly, we look externally for solutions to alleviate the anxiety; by popping pills, shopping too much, overeating, or downing a few drinks, the disquieting feelings are temporarily vanquished. The benefits of alternative methods of addressing anxiety, such as yoga, walking, breathing techniques, relaxation exercises, meditations, and psychotherapy are often overlooked in favor of readily available quick-fix "cures."

Anxiety at Work in You

Before moving on, take a moment for another brief exercise, an introductory exploration of anxiety. Without judgment or a need to censure, allow the idea of your own anxiety to come into focus. Think only on the one thing that makes you *most* anxious today. Do you have health concerns lurking? Are you haunted by a heavy burden of responsibility? Do you have a strange sense of being un-fulfilled? Are you feeling friendless or isolated? Do you have some financial worries? Or is "it"—the anxiety—something else that you cannot quite put your finger on?

Close your eyes and gently—very lightly—notice that sense of anxiety. Do not respond to it. Just watch it float into your mind and into your being. Simply notice how it makes you feel and let it pass out again. Where in your body did you tighten, contract, or shiver? Take a moment to breathe in and out deeply, to restore your sense of quiet. Make notes on what you noticed. You touched your anxiety; you noticed it. Breathe fully in and out again. Well done. Notice, in the gentlest way possible, if you sense any changes in your body. Has any tightness, constriction, or other uncom-fortable sensation eased? Perhaps you noticed a slight increase in discomfort, or maybe you experienced no change at all. Notice any sensations and, if it feels appropriate, take some additional cleans-ing breaths. Make a few notes of your experiences. Excellent work.

Fear has many manifestations, and it is often helpful to have tangi-ble examples to increase our understanding. So let me introduce you to Clarissa, a woman in her mid-forties who contacted me to "work on self-confidence issues." Attractive and dressed stylishly, Clarissa arrived on time for her first appointment. When I greeted her, she offered a quick, nervous smile. Yet despite her lovely exterior, Clarissa seemed strangely haunted and fragile. Once inside my office, Clarissa's façade melted away as she broke into sobs.

"I never cry like this," she mumbled through her growing wad of tear-soaked tissues. "I don't know what's wrong with me. I usually do such a good job of holding up."

"Well," I told her, "it sounds as if you needed a space to let go. This is a good, safe space to let yourself feel, to let yourself cry." As she shared her story, I learned that Clarissa was suffering deeply despite the lovely appearance—the empty shell—she offered to the world. She had married well and given up her career early on to care for her two children. With all the benefits money and status could provide, one might imagine that Clarissa had everything a woman could hope for, yet this was part of her misery. As Clarissa said, "I *should* be happy. I know women would *die* to be me and have what I have. I feel so guilty that I'm not happy—the guilt makes it even worse. I've been taking the medications my doctor pre-scribed, but I feel more anxious and depressed than ever. What's wrong with me?" Clarissa's eyes begged for an answer, a simple quick fix, but I knew that the keys were within her and that we would find them only through careful exploration. Although I couldn't answer Clarissa's ques-tions *for* her, I did tell her that she had the power to create change—to free herself of the negative thoughts and patterns that were holding her back in life. With a somber but genuine smile, Clarissa responded, "Well, let's get to it then. I still have half of my life ahead of me, and I want to really live it. No more faking it for me." With these simple, honest sentences, Clarissa's journey toward healing had begun.

Our first session didn't allow Clarissa enough time to unpack the mounting load she had quietly carried for years. Over the course of many hours, I came to know her secret, sad world. During one session, Clarissa allowed her innermost thoughts to spill into the room. "You know," she said, "I always thought I was doing the right thing. I've always had a lot of energy and passion, so it was natural for me to put all of my time and effort into my family. I volunteered at my children's schools. I took them to their sports and stayed to watch the games. I make dinner every night. I keep the house tidy. I try to take good care of myself without going over-board—I do my spin and Pilates classes a few times a week to stay in shape. I'm a good, dedicated wife, but I barely see my husband. I didn't realize it, but somewhere along the line he turned into the kind of guy who gave me gifts instead of affection and love. I never wanted to make a fuss or seem ungrateful, so I never said anything. It's embarrassing to say, but we rarely have sex—that connection went by the wayside after the kids. Now, when I actually look at my life, I feel so stupid. I've spent my last twenty years focusing on my husband and kids, just trying to make everyone happy, but I'll have an empty nest in a year. What will I do then? I'm not the kind of person who is going to be content with shopping, manicures, and exercise classes. I want to matter. I want to have a purpose. I've been out of the workforce for decades—who would want to hire me at this point? Maybe that wouldn't be so bad if my husband and I weren't so distant. I don't know who he is. And, to tell the truth, I don't know who *I* am or what I want. I'm afraid I'll have nothing—that I'll *be* nothing—when my youngest son leaves for college. I don't regret my kids or marriage, but half of my life is gone, and I have no clue who I am. There are times I am so anxious that I actually feel frozen in fear—like the anxiety is taking me over. My physician increased one of my meds a few months back. It's supposed to be getting better, but it's getting worse. I really need help." I knew that Clarissa had what it took to create the transformation she so dearly wanted. Clarissa was her own greatest asset—she was willing and ready to change.

Faced with the specter of a large, empty home and a husband she barely knew, Clarissa dove into therapy with the passion she had devoted to other areas of her life. In time, she came to realize—with great resistance—that she had unconsciously modeled her life after her parents, who had both passed away. Her mother had been a "saint," loved by her family and community, but Clarissa felt she never really knew the woman behind the crisp, elegant façade. Her father had been a dynamic businessman, a highly critical perfectionist who ruled his home and office with an iron hand. As Clarissa said, "We were raised to believe that children should be rarely seen and never, ever heard. Now that I think of it, I think this applied to my mother as well. I don't think she was allowed to be seen or heard. I wish I knew—I wish I could ask her. Yet I'm not sure she'd tell me in any event. I never saw her cry—not once. She put up a good front. I would never have known anything was amiss if I hadn't found a bottle of antidepressants by accident in her medicine cabinet when I was home from college one time. I'll never forget that. I was looking for sore throat medicine, and that bottle with her name on it was staring back at me. I picked up the bottle and held it. I wanted to talk to her. Instead, I put the bottle back on the shelf and never said a word."

At first, Clarissa fought the idea that her "model" childhood home environment had affected her own life in any long-lasting way. She didn't want to "blame" her parents. She always assumed she was well-loved, for she had everything she needed as a child—good food, nice clothing, a lovely house, and a good education. Yet, after quite a few sessions, Clarissa sat with tears in her eyes and said, "I'm getting it. This isn't about blaming my parents or anyone else. It's about seeing what worked for me in my childhood and what didn't work so well. It's about seeing the patterns— positive and negative—and noticing how they affected me." Clarissa was a quick study. She realized that destructive fear had moved into her during her childhood. It told her young brain that she must be a "good, quiet girl," that she must never make waves, that she must do as she was told, and that she must—*must*—please others. Of course, Clarissa didn't understand this consciously; she simply put down her head and followed the behaviors that were modeled for her. Long before she was an adult, Clarissa had unconsciously accepted her expected role in life: she would grow up to be a good, quiet woman who never made waves, who did as she was told, and who strove to please others. As she continued her journey, Clarissa was able to uncover and dismantle the unconscious memories, patterns, and thoughts that held her back. Through this process, she was able to fill her internal void with new life and joy.

Over the next year, Clarissa came to life before my eyes. With every session, Clarissa left with a slightly increased sense of self-awareness. She learned to use breathing techniques to ease her anxiety. Daily meditation became an easy, no-frills routine that gave her substantial and lasting relief from her spiraling, negative thoughts. As she learned more about the causes of her symptoms, she understood that her medication was a necessary, supportive tool for her well-being and that she need not be afraid or ashamed of it. With conscious awareness, positive self-talk became the rule rather than the exception. Clarissa practiced new communication skills with me and then took them home to practice with her son and husband. Clarissa began to take greater interest in her own self-care, from attending to her sleep schedule to enrolling in college courses to refresh her skills. She formed several friendships through her classes, relationships that she felt were "genuine and real." Clarissa's self-doubt eased, replaced by strong sense that she was, for the first time in her life, beginning to create and follow a path that was right for *her*. As Clarissa tuned in to her own needs—to what she really desired for herself and for her own life—the voice of destructive fear lessened its hold.

Clarissa's journey was not easy; it took great courage and perseverance for her to create the transformation she desired. The long-term anxiety and depression had wrapped its debilitating tentacles about and within her. She had ignored it as best she could, immersing herself in caring for others. Yet over time, Clarissa had lost her sense of self even more. She had moved forward—going through the motions of living—but her inner self had withered. Feeling alone and hollow, Clarissa's self-doubt had grown stronger year by year. Fed by the voice of destructive fear, Clarissa felt doomed and alone—stuck in her seemingly empty, purposeless world. She could have stayed there, but she didn't. The whisper of constructive fear—the idea that something beautiful waited inside and in front of her— prompted her to seek change. With courage, patience, and dedication, Clarissa began to shift her fearful self-doubt into joy.

Self-doubt often takes hold slowly and tenaciously, leaving the victim with the sense that inner life is steadily ebbing away. Without a belief in the self, inner confidence dissipates, and what remains is often silently felt as a giant void, a gaping and cavernous hole within. Even a highly confident person can be negatively affected by the destructive aspects of anxiety. For example, a toxic long-term relationship (whether it be a romantic part- nership or an employment relationship) can leave a formerly self-assured individual mired in anxious self-doubt. However, those reared in environ- ments of constant criticism and disapproval (or environments where the child is not "seen" and is essentially ignored by their caretakers) often are the most vulnerable. Those who are raised to believe that they somehow fall short and that they simply are not "good enough" are highly suscep- tible to the corrosive effects of self-doubt. Fear infiltrates those weakened areas of the psyche. When we are insecure, fear moves in stealthily to gain a foothold in the crevices that are most vulnerable. Chronic anxiety, one of fear's most persistent manifestations, whittles away at the psyche until the world is viewed with worry and dread. Yet when a person chooses to "look within" rather than seeking the singular "cure" of a prescription, self-med- ication, or overt denial of problems, the psychological and physiological rewards are often immense.

Having met Clarissa, you may now sense that aspects of yourself are riddled with anxiety. You might now more easily recognize the effects of anxiety in your own life. The symptoms of anxiety, though often sharing a common foundation, materialize differently within each individual's psyche. Additionally, your physical body and your mind will sense your anxiety in an entirely different manner than any other person. Now that you have a better understanding of what fear and anxiety look like and mean to you, we are ready to move a bit deeper.

Fear as an Archetype

At nearly every turn, I see and feel the tremendous, connective power of archetypes. They are within us and without us; they have existed since the dawn of thought. Regardless of factors such as nationality, race, language, or sex, archetypes exist throughout humanity, bearing remarkable similarity from human to human, culture to culture, and epoch to epoch. You might be asking, "But what is an archetype?"

An archetype might be best viewed as those psychological and spiritual images—often with mythological foundations—that are historically common to all mankind. For example, when speaking to a group of people, I might offer the word "hero" as an archetype. Each person in the room will conjure up a personal image of the word, yet certain underlying themes (such as strength, independence, courage, and bravery) will be shared by all. Whether the "hero" image that arises is of one's parent, a superhero, or mythological figure, an undeniable commonality exists as to the foundational significance of the term. Moreover, each member of the group will often have a deeply internal sense of the image. Unlike more static images (e.g., sock or spoon), the archetypal images speak to us—often stridently— on an intrinsically personal *and* communal level. Many oft-spoken nouns quietly carry an immense weight of our shared history. Common words such as child, mother, father, orphan, victim, goddess, angel, tyrant, lover, king, and queen are but a few of the fundamental archetypes. We often use such words without realizing that these seemingly simple terms hold vital, ancient messages that pervade the individual unconscious and the collective unconscious. Simply put, the collective unconscious can be viewed as a "universal field" composed of the archetypes—the primordial images and mythological themes that permeate humanity across all space and time. This concept is important, for fear lives within the collective unconscious. As we pay more attention to the archetypes and the feelings and thoughts they evoke within us, the power of archetypes becomes clearer and more wondrous. Throughout cultures, throughout the ages, such words arise with the power to evoke similar thoughts and reactions; they bring individuals and multitudes to unify in common, even unspoken, understanding. Such is the command of the archetype.

Fear itself is an archetype. In fact, I maintain that fear is one of the most influential and omnipotent of all the archetypes. If we depart from the traditional understanding of fear as being merely a physiological response to an external threat, we are able to move into a more encompassing understanding of fear as an energetic, far-reaching power that often has little to do with realistic dangers. In redefining fear, we learn to appreciate the reverberations of fear's archetypal nature. By attending to fear in this manner, we begin to notice that fear invasively affects us internally and externally on both individual and collective levels.

In refocusing on fear as an archetypal force, we are able to take a step into objectivity. In this movement away from the constraints of our inner subjectivity, we are able to notice fear as an *entity*. Fear, as an entity, has constructive (light) and destructive (dark) aspects with which we can learn to wisely engage. This stance affords us greater clarity as we journey into learning about fear. It also allows us to form a relationship with fear from a place of curiosity and personal power.

Visualizing Fear

When you are ready, slowly read the following paragraph that describes the "Visualizing Fear" exercise. If it makes you feel more comfortable, you can choose to read this entire section before proceeding. Through this profoundly important exercise, you will have the opportunity to gradually engage with fear on a personal level. You may be able to access the archetypal power and energy of your own fear. In a gentle way, you will begin to actually explore who—or what—within you is afraid. This exercise has the power to positively shift your relationship with fear; it can help you open up to a new, transformative relationship with your fear. Once you understand what the exercise will involve, take a few moments before proceeding further. Pause to soak in the depth and wonderful possibilities of your work in this next step. Remember to engage in cleansing breaths when you conclude your exercise. If you find that you feel tense or anxious during the process, gentle breathing exercises are often helpful in restoring a sense of calm and relaxation.

For this exercise, you will need your notebook and a pencil. You will want to be in a quiet spot where you can relax in comfort and security. When you are psychologically and physically ready to proceed, close your eyes and bring to mind an image of fear. Allow it to unfold as it will. It may take a form within your mind's eye, and it may even choose to speak. Simply remain quiet and notice the effects upon your physical and emotional body. When the process is complete, open your eyes and draw your experience of fear upon your paper. If words come to mind, simply write them without self-editing. If a face, an image, or a presence arises, allow it to take form. What lies before you may reflect your archetypal image of fear. Without judgment, notice it—how it speaks to you, how it makes you feel. Notice how and in what places your body responds to the image—a cramping in your stomach, a tightness in your chest, a marked tension in your neck. All of this, your visualization of fear, is your personal response to the archetype of fear that your own psyche has offered to you. Take note that there is no right or wrong outcome. There is nothing to be fearful of in this exercise, for all that arises is from your inner self, that which is already an inherent part of you.

After this portion of the exercise, you may feel the need for a rest or perhaps a desire to stroll outside or take a freeing hike. It is important not to judge your experience or to dissect it with your thoughts. In fact, it is often best not to return to this exercise for a day or two in order to allow the images and any attached meanings to unfold naturally and without critical judgments. The psyche often seems to do its most precious work when we attend to it, open it gently, and then allow it to settle and sift through the process in its own subtle way. We are accustomed to analyzing the products of our efforts, so this technique may be unfamiliar to you. This type of exercise will plant important seeds; trust that your unconscious mind, the depths of your psyche, will unfold its truths for you in time.

After a small space of time, return to conclude this exercise and contemplate the fruits of your efforts. Again, make certain you set aside a time and environment that is gentle and spacious. Behold your creation—and any thoughts and feelings that arise—with the eyes and heart of a child. Set your analytical, rational mind aside. To accomplish this, you may find it helpful to close your eyes and breathe softly for several moments. Imagine that you are four or five years old—a time when your mind was playful, creative, and nonjudgmental. Notice the spaciousness created by this uncritical attitude. When you are ready, open your eyes and look at your drawing with childlike curiosity. Simply soak in whatever is before you with a curious and interested attitude. Ponder in amazement the untold gifts that lie within you. Notice any thoughts or feelings that arise as you behold the results of your efforts. Again, take care to avoid any judgmental evaluation of your work; let it speak to you as it is. When met with openness and acceptance, your psyche, your deepest inner spirit, will become more alive to you in these processes.

Let me offer you an example of my early work with fear. Although this profound experience occurred several years ago, it is emblazoned in my memory as if it took place just moments ago. Even now, I recall the deep, internal shifting as I began to stop struggling in the mire of fear. The more I noticed my fears, the less I felt plagued by them. The more I attended to my fears, the more I felt free of them. As this dance unfolded, I felt compelled to give fear a new face—a new identity that melded with the unfamiliar powers I was discovering within fear. Fear kept coming to me, calling to me, asking me to notice it more. I was at a nascent stage in my journey with fear. I had, reluctantly, begun to release the illusion that I was tough, strong, and "not afraid of anything." This was the period that a growing respect for the dual-natured power of fear began to take root within me. A mentor suggested that I engage more deeply with fear through an imaginative exercise. I pondered the idea and later engaged in my own version of the "Visualizing Fear" exercise outlined above.

With pad and pencil in hand, I found a quiet space underneath the giant limbs of an oak tree. It was there, in the soft glow of an early summer morning, that I undertook my first dialogue with fear. I closed my eyes and gradually relaxed, and what followed was truly stunning. I can readily visualize the large, looming figure that slowly approached me that day. As he neared, I stood strong, if not hesitant and mesmerized. He was massive and godlike, with pure white robes that flowed behind him as he strode toward me. His long beard, silver-gray strewn heavily with white, matched his thick pelt of silvery white hair. His face was terrifyingly intense, aged and lined yet beautiful in its antiquity. The fierce eyes were dark orbs that stared piercingly into mine.

Feeling both infinitesimal and strangely powerful, I stood firm, resolute in my wary, righteous inspection of the intimidating force before me. I asked him a question—I wanted to know this creature—and he threw his head back in wicked delight at my impertinence. He deigned to respond, his commanding eyes matched by the deep intensity of his voice. As I continued to probe, he adopted an unperturbed, seemingly amused attitude. It seemed he was strangely pleased, but hardly intimidated, by my demanding examination of his being. As I fired question after question, he remained imperturbably tolerant. A cool calmness filled the air, and I was suddenly struck by his wisdom and his grace. My inquisition complete, he motioned to me in a gentle, if imperious, manner. My curious eyes followed the waving flow of his right hand, and as the curtain of his robe settled, I saw two white beds resting side by side. "Here," he said in an unexpectedly tender tone, "come lie beside me."

Struck by the intensity of my interlude with fear, I opened my eyes to find soothing shades of summer foliage about me. Slowly, not wanting to lose a single thought or phrase from my encounter, I reached for my pad. I scrawled page after page, relentless in my outpouring of each nuanced word. My fingers flew as I drew Fear as he had appeared to me, formidable, intense, and somehow lovingly courageous. I did not edit my thoughts or feelings but allowed the pages to become saturated with the varied shades of my experience. I wrote and etched until my psyche's messages had run their course and my fingers slowed to stillness. I noticed that I had unconsciously darkened and capitalized the figure's name; it was not "fear" to me but **FEAR.**

It was not until the cool of the evening, so many hours later, that I was able to reflect upon what I had written, to open the doors of my mind to what my spirit had witnessed. Still later, the image of the two beds waiting side by side remained a lingering question. A part of me recoiled from the image, for I was afraid that Fear had asked me to die, to rest alongside him rather than continue my incessant exploration. I felt haunted, for an inner aspect of me knew that I'd drawn the wrong conclusion. It took a conversation with my mentor to illuminate the obvious. "Ah," she said without skipping a beat, "isn't it lovely—spectacular—that Fear wishes you to be his friend." With that simple explanatory sentence, the full weight of the image came to me. I understood. Fear had asked me to carefully draw him close, to get to know his immense forces intimately, to treat him not as an adversary but as an ally. I know enough about Fear to refrain from any misapprehension that this mercurial force is purely my *friend*. Fear is cunning, ruthless, and tyrannical. Fear is also wise, instructive, and clever. Fear is often patient with the mindfully curious yet merciless with thoughtless drones. The dual nature of Fear—its formidable ability to both paralyze and aid each one of us—is to be honored, respected, and understood. Fear asks to be questioned and revered. Fear does not appreciate our blind, foolish willingness to succumb to tyranny. Fear, both foe and ally, is a Janus-faced entity.

On that unforgettable summer morning, I found that Fear—my archetype of fear—had profound and compelling lessons to teach me. The wide-reaching effects of my first tête-à-tête with Fear continued to astound me for months afterward. At every turn, I would encounter something— poetry, music, or an intriguing situation—that would foster my journey. It was as though something much greater than me was at work to focus my attention on the concept of fear. The more I investigated the signals, listened, and learned, the more I found that I had barely scratched Fear's surface.

I became accustomed to heeding the inner voice that frequently called me to attend to yet another nuance of Fear. I came to accept that Fear seemed to have deemed me its messenger, and it was, apparently, a task from which I could not be readily freed. I realized that the journey would be one of intense devotion, for I had come to love, respect, and appreciate Fear. I took up the challenge with all the grace and strength I could muster. *Me, an emissary for Fear?* I came to consider this idea a duty, a challenge, and a privilege.

Your Personal Relationship with Fear

In your own unique conversation with fear, you have the same opportunity to explore your past and future relationship with this extraordinary archetype. As you develop an understanding of the role of fear in your life—particularly with a foundation of an archetypal perspective that brings fear to you in a highly personal, elemental fashion—fear becomes accessible as a valuable guide. In this light, greater psychic movement is possible, and aspects of the self that have been immobilized are set free. Such shifts are generally not instantaneous; they occur over time as self-awareness increases.

Following your "Visualizing Fear" exploration, you may find that your experience continues to work within you in the days ahead. In fact, that particular conversation may be one that you remember for a lifetime. You may also note that something within you wishes to return to further conversations with fear. As a silent part of you is now awakening, you may notice subtle changes in the way you begin to sense, think, and feel. It is strange, indeed, to come to know a part of the self—a part of the psyche— that has been hidden for so long.

At this point, you may be questioning the purpose of the challenges I am setting forth. You may also feel a quickening, a glimmer of interest at the prospect of no longer living under the silent, ubiquitous control of fear. I ask you to stay the course, to continue reading, to further your understanding through brief exercises and inner explorations. This may feel like foreign ground, yet it may also feel strangely familiar—as though an ancient part of you is stirring. That stirring, I suggest, is both fear and your own inner self beginning to acknowledge fear's intense, pervasive presence. Do not be afraid, for I truly believe that fear does want to walk *with* you. Just as a bully feels internally isolated and inherently weak in its polarizing force, I sense that fear, too, wishes to be known for more than its obvious capacities. Do not be surprised if you hear a tiny inner voice suggesting that you might be best to close this book, to settle with life as it is. This, too, is fear talking. This is the aspect of fear that desires control and strives for homeostasis. Indeed, this is the dark face of fear we all know too well. Within the pages of this book, this negative aspect of fear will be described in various terms—*destructive fear, enemy fear, dark fear, cruel fear, immobilizing fear,* and the like. One term does not suffice to describe the artifice and power of this negative side of fear. With courage, you can ask this destructive force to release its grip to allow you to welcome the beneficial face of fear into your life. This friendly aspect of fear holds vital transformational power. This constructive aspect of transformational fear—which will be referred to as *friendly fear, constructive fear, beneficial fear,* and *helpful fear*—can become a most cherished force in your life. Simply put, constructive fear wants to help you notice how destructive fear has kept you from becoming your highest self. With this awareness, the active force of transformational fear will support you in becoming the finest version of the individual you want to be.

In taking a step toward fear, you are moving in the direction of becoming less afraid. You are moving toward greater self-awareness and a fuller expression of your own being. As you notice and welcome the constructive aspects of transformational fear, you will benefit from its valuable messages. Your inner strength and sense of freedom will grow as you befriend this helpful fear. As constructive fear takes root in your life, the power of your destructive, dark fear will lessen. Remember that both sides of fear are within you. The more you become conscious of them, the more they are within your control. Your life will change as you embrace constructive fear, all the while releasing yourself from the grip of destructive fear. By acknowledging transformational fear's incredible constructive and destructive powers, you will become empowered. You will have the awareness and courage to translate this awareness into essential action. As you move forward with wise, intentional actions—the full power of transformational fear—your life becomes your own.

I want you to know that I used to cringe when I reflected on my past. I now see how easy it was to flee from fear in the short run, to remain on a well-known and familiar path. I paid a steep price for not freeing myself from the chains of immobilizing fear early in life. Yet I simply did not know any better. I did not know the insidious power of destructive fear, and I had never encountered the life-changing power of transformational fear. I learned that there was no need to blame others or myself. I learned to become conscious of my own thoughts, emotions, and actions. Most of all, I learned that no one could save me or free me from my fears except *myself*. I have no regrets, just a deep gratitude for all that I have learned. I know that were it not for my intensely difficult journey, I would not be writing to you now. Transformational fear is my companion—my dear friend.

If the above rings true for you, do not sink into a place of blame or regret. Many of us—possibly *most* of us—are raised and taught to live within the confines of destructive fear. We cannot live freely if we are not exposed to people and situations that support and model inner freedom. We cannot shift our lives if we do not know or understand how to shift. Maybe for the first time in your life, you are ready to step into a journey that gives you the joy and freedom you crave. Maybe you are ready for transformational fear to become your friend.

CHAPTER 2

Cold Sweat: How Your Body Reacts to Fear

To Fight, Flee, or Freeze?

H uman beings are highly complex, yet we are also very primitive in many ways. When exposed to a fear-inducing stimulus, the body responds in a predictable, instantaneous manner. The immediate, unspoken question is, "How can I survive this situation?" Whether the circumstances involve an encounter with a wildcat in a forest, a menacing figure in a dark alley, or a highly volatile spouse, a fear-induced response arises immediately. The brain doesn't slow down to differentiate between a wildcat attack and an angry partner when it is in survival mode; it simply knows a threat has been perceived. In an instant, your brain strives to determine if you are best off running, fighting, or freezing. This vital, natural reaction is exceedingly beneficial when situations are life-threatening. Unfortunately, this response can be triggered and become an unconscious pattern even under nonthreatening situations.

As previously mentioned, we are neurobiologically hardwired to respond to perceived threats in a lightning-fast manner. Humans have survived through the ages as a result of finely honed instinctual reactions. When you feel threatened by a stimulus, your body kicks into action to protect you. On a wholly unconscious level, a step-by-step process occurs almost instantaneously within your body. First, the brain's amygdalae—two small, almond-shaped groups of nuclei that are part of your limbic system—send signals to activate your autonomic nervous system. Biochemical changes occur in your sympathetic nervous system and the HPA (hypothalamic-pituitary-adrenal) axis. In this stressed state, a range of adrenaline-charged responses stake claim in the body and mind. As your body prepares to fight, run, freeze, or appease, you might experience sensations such as racing heart, sweating, tightened muscles, and other physical responses. On a primitive level, your body knows that it must conserve resources in order to flee. To improve survival chances, your cardiovascular and muscle tone increase while other systems such as digestion slow down. At the same time, your physical and psychological states are greatly affected as biochemicals such as cortisol and adrenaline surge in your system to help you prepare for action. Whether these instinctual responses are triggered by an actual threat such as a home robbery or a perceived threat such as a stressful conflict at work, your body's systems respond in much the same way.

These responses are life-saving when you are faced with an actual threat. However, when your body learns to respond to non-life-threatening circumstances in the same way as it does to situations that are life-threatening, the results can be damaging over time. Research continues to show that chronically elevated levels of cortisol and adrenaline can lead to health issues that include chronic inflammation, a weakened immune system, and an increased risk of heart attack and stroke.[1] Given the wide-ranging importance of the health concerns involved, we'll take a look at this topic in more detail later. For now, it will be helpful enough to remember that chronic fear, in whatever forms it might arise, might be physically and psychologically harming you.

How Does It Feel to Be Threatened?

If it feels safe and appropriate, recall a minor, mildly challenging situation when you felt threatened. For example, you may remember a time when you didn't finish a project and feared that your boss might be angry. You may recall a time you confronted a friend who broke your trust. Perhaps you remember a situation with your partner when you felt worried or mildly threatened. Whatever the situation, pause to notice how you responded. Was your instinctive response to fight, run, freeze, or appease? Did your responses indicate fight, flight, immobilization, or appeasement? Can you recall how your body felt? Did your heart race? Was your stomach queasy? Was your breath rapid? Did other sensations arise? Can you recall how you felt at that time? Were you frightened? Angry? Sad? Worried? Anxious? Whatever feelings arose, can you feel them inside you now? If so, just notice what they are and where in your body you feel them. Use your cleansing breathe to consciously release these feelings. Pause to breathe. Well done!

Simple exercises such as the one above, when done in a safe and relaxed space, can help you learn how fear works within your own being. Although you share a great deal with other human beings, you are not the same as any other person. Your individual personal experiences make you even more unique and complex. As such, it's important that you learn about *you*. Certainly, you will share certain traits and general life experiences with others, but no one will actually experience them, feel them, interpret them, and hold them in exactly the same way that you do. Your very uniqueness is one of the key reasons it can be so wonderful and yet so very difficult to learn how to work with your own fears. Yet the more you persevere, the more you will learn how to notice both destructive fear and constructive fear. As you become more in tune with your own being, you are forming the foundation for your journey with transformational fear.

How the Body Stores History: A Case Study

Let's look at a case that spotlights this issue. A client, let's call him Harry, came to my office for his initial appointment. A generally successful man in his mid-thirties, Harry is tall and heavyset. Surly and sarcastic, Harry wanted me to know that he was in control. Yet before our third session was done, Harry "lost it." As he sat in an oversized chair, tears ran down his cheeks. "What did you do to me?" he stuttered. "I don't think I've ever cried in my entire life. Third session with you, and I'm sniveling like a stupid girl."

My actions did not create the shift in Harry. Surely I listened and asked questions—and then I listened some more. As Harry talked, I also watched him carefully. I paid attention to Harry's fears. So what did cause Harry's shift to occur? Was it that I gave Harry the close attention he needed? Or was it simply that Harry was ready for change? Perhaps it was a combination of many tangible factors. Whatever the causes, it was *Harry* who made all the difference. Harry let me in. Harry let me into an old, dark world where fear had ruled him. For the first time he could recall, Harry let down his defenses. He was open and ready to explore. This was just the beginning.

During that session, Harry and I discovered that he was still hurting from childhood psychological wounds. As a thin, awkward boy, he was bullied by his older brother at home. At school, he was assaulted by bullies in the classroom and on the schoolyard. He was afraid to go home, and he was afraid to go to school. His busy, single mom seemed unaware of his pain. With every passing year, he became more isolated and defensive. Three things gave Harry comfort: eating, video games, and listening to music. Whenever possible, Harry retreated into the safe haven that these familiar, soothing behaviors offered. As soon as he was able, he obtained a part-time job to earn extra money—and to avoid going home. Although he grew tall and sturdy in late high school, the fear never left him. Even though he was no longer bullied by his peers, Harry felt shunned. At home, Harry never felt at ease, even when his brother eventually moved out. When Harry graduated from high school, he began a full-time job repairing electronics, a job that required little human interaction. A deep fear lived inside Harry even though he was no longer bullied; this fear affected his ability to relate to other individuals. Afraid to let people into his tormented world, Harry developed a sarcastic, gruff attitude that effectively kept people at a distance. Harry's fear had also affected his ability to attend college. Year after year, he signed up for college courses, but fear had a hold on him. As he drove to the campus, his anxiety would rise. Once inside the classroom, his heart raced, his cheeks burned, and perspiration soaked his clothes. The only solution he knew was to bolt in a cold sweat. Feeling embarrassed and defeated, he never returned for a second class. Realizing that he couldn't secure the new job he wanted without a degree, he had enrolled for courses again—and, once again, he had run. This is what had led Harry to me.

At the end of our third session, Harry stared at me and said, "I should be way past this stuff. No one has bullied me for nearly twenty years. I can't believe it still affects me. It doesn't make sense."

I smiled and looked into his eyes. "Fear doesn't know chronological time. It doesn't know if you're nine, thirty, or fifty. It just knows that you're hurting and afraid." Even though twenty years had passed since Harry experienced bullying at the hands of others, fear had become his personal bully. Physically and psychologically, he had unconsciously held on to the terrifying experience of being bullied.

In later sessions, Harry was able to describe in detail how he felt on the schoolyard. He learned to identify the self-protective pattern he had developed in order to attend school. Over time, Harry was able to recall how fear would set in the moment he woke up each weekday morning. He was able to remember how the fear grew as he dressed, nibbled at a cold cereal breakfast, and took the short walk to school. In time, Harry was able to recollect the nuances of his school years and how the fear usually remained throughout the school day. As we unraveled the memories, Harry was also able to recall a few bright spots where he had found safety. He had forgotten how the school library had sometimes been a safe haven. He now remembered the smell of the books and the kind face of the redhaired elementary school librarian. He would smile now and again as he remembered a science teacher who had inspired him in middle school. These few positive fragments had been lost amidst the heavy grasp of fear.

As Harry felt safe, he shared deeper hurts from his school experiences. There were many poignant, shame-based memories that had been etched into his mind. Although he recalled a few terrible punches and bruises, it was the emotional pain that had lived on in Harry's memory. Long after the black-and-blue marks had faded, the emotional damage—the living fear—had remained. At times, Harry would recount an experience as vividly as if it had just occurred. During one session, Harry looked through me with pained, fearful eyes and said, "I was wearing a yellow shirt. I didn't have many shirts; it was the only one I even liked. The one kid, Colin, kicked me in the shins and said I was ugly and stupid. He pushed me to the ground, and the shirt got torn and dirty. It was after school. The other kids laughed. Someone started yelling 'Loser! Sissy!' and the others chimed in. I'll never forget that day." A few moments passed, and he looked at me. "I have a thousand memories like that. They're there when I sleep. They're there when I am awake. They haunt me. They make me afraid to live. It chokes the life out of me."

This is how fear works in the mind and the body. In his past, Harry felt chronically unsafe and unprotected. He couldn't fight the school bullies; he was too small and didn't know how to fight. Harry didn't bother running; he had tried that once and suffered a terrible beating. Harry froze and did his best to cope with whatever came his way. Underneath it all, his body was coursing with fear. Harry's sympathetic nervous system was desperately striving to help him stay safe, but safety wasn't possible. There was no one present to protect Harry, and he had no skills to help him bring his parasympathetic nervous system online. This occurred over and over again with no reprieve. Harry lived in a place where fear and immobilization were hardwired into his very being.

When pieces of a school bullying memory came forth, Harry slowly shared what felt safe to him. From our earlier work, he had built greater self-awareness and was learning what felt safe and right to him. Using a 0-to-10 scale, Harry could home in on his emotional state. He would smile and say, "I'm feeling a little scared right now—it's at 1 right now—so I can share more." If he felt too fearful and unsafe, he would say, "My fear level is getting up toward a 5—or maybe a 6—I want to take a break." Harry also learned that he could use a vast array of words to describe how his body felt. When feeling highly anxious, Harry might say, "I feel angry. I'm afraid, too. My stomach feels really queasy. My cheeks are getting red hot. I'm sweaty." These skills allowed Harry to increase his sense of personal power. Harry learned that he could turn toward his fears and not run away from them. Harry learned more and more that his fears held vital information that would allow him to heal. He no longer had to keep his fears in a closet where they had the power to haunt him. He could open the closet—as he felt safe—and learn from his fears. In this way, he could set himself free.

As our work deepened, Harry offered occasional glimpses into his home life. The routine mistreatment by his older brother—along with his mother's lack of interest—were far more painful to Harry than the school bullying. Understandably, Harry was terrified of fully recalling and sharing the memories. In one later session he noted, "The memories are there— dark and muddy. They more or less live behind a locked door. If I open the door to that hell, I am afraid I'll never recover. If I go there, I might start crying and never stop. Or maybe I'm afraid that it will be such a dark abyss that I'll fall into it forever." Indeed, it seemed that Harry's childhood home life was filled with experiences that triggered his fight or flight response. Yet he could do nothing. He was too small to fight his older brother. His mother was not present or available to shield him or fight on his behalf. He could not flee, for he had nowhere else to go. Instead, he was immobilized and forced to live in a chronic state of fear. Even as he grew older, the fear remained inside him.

As Harry felt comfortable, we edged deeper into his experiences with his brother and his mother. Using the same skills that he learned in our earlier work, Harry was often able to identify his level of fear. He found that he could determine when our sessions felt right for deeper work and when his body and mind needed a lighter session. Harry began to listen to himself, to listen to the wise whisper of fear. Sometimes, if he'd had a particularly hard day at work, Harry would say something like, "I'm tired. I'm not afraid of working on things today, it's just that my body feels really heavy. My stomach feels sick and my neck is really tight. I'd just like to talk about what's going on at work." Often, a few deeper things would "pop out" as we worked, but Harry learned when—and if—he wanted to explore them more fully in that session. On other days, Harry would rush in, sharing his newfound excitement in life. "Hey," he might say, "a troubling memory came back to me. I really want to work on it. I had a dream that seems to go along with it. I want to tell you about it!" He'd meet my gaze, offering a glimpse into the hazel eyes that were less haunted and far more alive. During these sessions, Harry shared and explored with greater ease as he used his new skills. Sometimes he'd take two steps forward and sometimes a half step back. Most importantly, Harry never ran. Harry learned to talk to his fears, to detangle them, and to love the lessons they taught him. In this courageous way, he looked his fears in the eye. He found that he didn't need to run any longer. He was learning the power that had been hidden all along within his fears.

Easing the Body

Your life experiences may be vastly different from Harry's. However, they may share some common themes. Many people have experienced bullying behavior at home, school, work, or other social settings. In fact, it's likely that every human being has experienced some form of harassment or mistreatment at some point in life. Depending upon your unique physiology and personal history, the way in which you experience and respond to a situation will be entirely your own. Additionally, life experiences will affect you to a greater or lesser degree depending upon the duration, frequency, and overall impact of a situation. I emphasize these factors frequently because many people tend to evaluate or judge their experience based upon comparisons to others. Unfortunately, such comparisons do nothing but let destructive fear walk in the back door of your mind. When you notice a comparison or judgment arising, this is an opportunity to see the constructive face of fear; this is an opportunity to turn fear into your friend. For example, when reading Harry's story, you might have found yourself thinking, "Well, I didn't have it *that* bad. My experiences are nothing compared to Harry's." If such voices come into your mind, notice that this is the judgmental voice of fear at work. Notice that this voice is trying to distract you from your healing efforts. Try to detach from any comparisons that arise. The comparative mind can be quieted by repeatedly and patiently returning to your own experience. If judgment surfaces in one form or another, simply remind yourself, "I want to notice and honor my *own* experience. I will focus on my unique perceptions and responses." In this way, you will be able to appreciate and honor your own fear-based life experiences and their effects on you. As you practice doing this, your self-awareness and self-compassion will increase as the constructive side of fear steps in. Over time, the destructive grasp of fear will lessen its hold on your body and your mind.

Exploring Fear in the Body

This next exercise will allow you an opportunity to practice what I described above. As always, remember to honor your responses. If at any point the exercise does not feel right to you, take a break and breathe. You may choose to return to the exercise later if you like. When you are ready to begin, return to the beginning of Harry's story. As you read the paragraphs, notice any sections that grip you. Notice any thoughts, emotions, and bodily sensations that arise. Without judging your responses, simply make notes about your experiences. For example, you might have felt angry as you read the words *The one kid, Colin, kicked me in the shins and said I was ugly and stupid. He pushed me to the ground, and the shirt got torn and dirty. It was after school. The other kids laughed. Someone started yelling "Loser! Sissy!" and the others chimed in. I'll never forget that day.* Perhaps the bullying Harry suffered evoked memories of hurts you experienced as a child or adult. As you read, simply notice if any thoughts arise. Also take note of your feelings. Do certain portions of the story bring up frustration, rage, irritation, sorrow, or other feelings? Notice, too, how your body responds as you do this exercise. Does your breathing change? Do your shoulders tighten? Does your stomach feel queasy? Maybe you notice that your head aches or that you feel agitated. Whatever your experiences might be, make note of them without judgment. Through this exercise, you may be able to "feel" your fear. You may find the places where fear tends to live in your own body. You might notice how certain words or phrases trigger feelings or bodily responses. This important exercise allows you to explore your fear through your responses to another human being's story. When you complete the exercise, use your cleansing breaths. Well done!

Anxiety in the Body: A Case Study

Let me introduce you to Amanda. If you saw this spirited and outgoing young woman, you'd likely never guess that Amanda lives with chronic anxiety and suffers from severe panic attacks. In fact, it was Amanda's third panic-related emergency room visit that resulted in her deciding to seek psychotherapy. Raised in a very health-oriented family, one of Amanda's chief concerns was her desire to discover and attend to the root causes of her anxiety issues. She hoped that psychotherapy would allow her to eventually discontinue her anti-anxiety medication, a very common, highly addictive pharmaceutical in a class of psychoactive drugs known as benzo-diazepines. Although regular use of her prescribed medication effectively eased much of her chronic anxiety, an increase in her breakthrough panic attacks signaled that her situation was worsening. Additionally, Amanda confessed that her use of the medication made her feel ashamed. As she noted in her first session, "My parents would be upset to know that I'm using meds. They'd want to help me get to the bottom of things so that I don't become addicted to the stuff. Besides that, I don't want my friends or coworkers—and certainly not my boss—to know that I don't have my life under control. Only my boyfriend knows how much I struggle with this. After that last ER visit when I was practically paralyzed, he made me promise to get help." As panic attack symptoms often mimic those of life-threatening conditions such as heart attacks, panic disorder sufferers like Amanda often end up in emergency rooms. With a host of symptoms that include heart palpitations, chest pain, shortness of breath, shaking, dizziness, sweating, and a fear of dying, panic attacks—which can last ten minutes or more—are absolutely terrifying for the sufferer. As she told me more, it became clear that fear—arising through general anxiety and wors-ening panic attacks—was ruling nearly every aspect of her life.

In her second session, Amanda described the anxious world she lived in every day. Each weekday morning, she would wake to the beep of her phone's alarm. As Amanda's anxiety worsened, she found it increasingly difficult to leave the safe, dark cocoon of her blankets. To give herself more time to get going, she set her alarm an hour early. She'd hide under the covers, agonizing over the day ahead. Eventually, she'd reach for her morning medication and wait for it to kick in. After her shower, Amanda would weigh herself and log the weight. Invariably, she would be filled with self-loathing when she noted the numbers displayed on the digital scale. The self-loathing would turn into anger and agitation as she dressed for work. Her anxiety would rise if her slacks, shirt, or dress felt too tight. With nothing but coffee in her system and a bagel in her hand, she'd set off, fuming at herself for never losing weight. Amanda's morning diet of caffeine and carbs didn't help her; the caffeine increased her agitation and the bagel's high glycemic index created blood sugar–level fluctuations that left her feeling edgy. As she walked to work, Amanda felt anxious, certain that others were judging her for being "too fat" or "odd in some way." Once in the office, her anxiety continued to percolate. If a coworker stopped by her desk, she could feel her anxiety rise. If an email from her boss popped up on the screen, she was terrified. Although Amanda was a valued employee, she was "always prepared" for bad news. Just before lunch, she would take another anti-anxiety pill; it helped her ease her fear of going outside the building. The pill also helped ease the fears that arose if she decided to eat her lunch inside. Throughout the day, Amanda was acutely aware that anxiety was always with her in some form or another. Once she returned to her apartment, particularly if her boyfriend was coming over, Amanda would finally find some ease. Yet both her home life and boyfriend could become sources of anxiety. Certain television shows and commercials could trigger comparisons, self-loathing, and fear. Her boyfriend, whom she described as being "super sweet, smart, and accepting," might inadvertently say or do something that would result in her feeling "fat and unlovable." During one session, Amanda described how easily she could be set off. "Just last week," she explained, "he brought over soup and salad for dinner. I immediately thought that it was a not-so-subtle message that he wanted me to lose weight. When he saw my reaction—I was actually shaking and crying—he asked what was wrong. When I told him, he just smiled and hugged me. He told me he loves me as I am and that he brought soup and salad as a change of pace. He thought I'd be tired of our Wednesday night pizza. But that's how it works for me. My anxiety keeps me looking for something—anything—that might signal I'm not acceptable or good enough."

As her description clearly outlines, Amanda lived in constant fear—fear of being rejected, unworthy, and unloved. Destructive fear had her firmly in its powerful grasp. Her fears were with her day and night, taunting her incessantly and causing her to live in an anxious world of self-doubt. As Amanda explained, "Barely a moment passes that I'm not afraid of what someone else is thinking of me. I'm terrified that I am not doing 'it' right—whatever 'it' is at the moment. It could be my work product. It could be my hair, my clothes, or even my shoes. It is *always* my body issues. I'm so afraid that I'm too overweight to be really liked. I am not even sure what my boyfriend sees in me. I'm a nice person and all that, but he could do so much better." Fear had stolen Amanda's self-confidence. From the inside out, fear was eating her alive.

Amanda's story may sound familiar to you, for many aspects of it are common in our fast-paced, externally oriented world. It is the norm rather than the exception to focus on fitting in, looking good, and doing things "right." In a world that is highly geared toward material success and external appearances, the "soul" of our humanity suffers. This suffering emanates from a place of fear. If you are continually worried that you are imperfect, not good enough, or not getting things right in some way, you are living in constant fear. This fear lives in the mind, a constant source of scorn and unrest. As the mind is connected to the body, it makes perfect sense that this manifests in constant, merciless anxiety. This anxiety—rooted in fear—plagues millions.

In Amanda's case, fear initially latched onto her in early childhood through body image concerns. One of her first memories is that of her father chiding her for eating cookies. Amanda explained, "I was probably only five or so. I wasn't a fat kid by any means, but I was never a stick. My dad came in while I was eating chocolate chip cookies in the kitchen. I still remember the cookies and even the plate. He took the plate, threw the cookies in the trash, and said, 'You're getting fat. You don't want to be fat like your mother. Men don't like fat women. Get exercise and watch what you eat, or no boy will ever like you.'" From that day forward, Amanda remembers having a love-hate relationship with her father and food—chocolate chip cookies in particular. As if fear saw an opportunity to torture her, it moved into Amanda's psyche. As Amanda became increasingly fearful of eating, she ate more. She lost a natural relationship to food as a source of nourishment; food became an enemy, another manifestation of her fear. Additionally, Amanda lost a friendly, appreciative relationship with her body. Her rounded belly became a constant source of angst. Before her nighttime baths, she would inspect her naked juvenile body with growing disgust. Amanda began seeing the image in the mirror as a cluster of imperfections, not as a beautiful, youthful form. Fear had found its entry point; it wanted to make her body its home.

In this way, destructive fear began to live inside Amanda on a nearly full-time basis. She quickly learned to fear her father. If he approved of her, she felt loved. If she didn't meet his approval, she felt unloved and very unsafe. As she grew, she learned to fear connection with others. She imagined disapproval in the eyes of friends and schoolmates. Criticism, real and imagined, terrified her. Perfection at school was her goal; any grade less than an "A" sent her into panic and a downward spiral of self-loathing. She learned to fear her clothing, for it represented far more to her than fashion. If an item fit well, she was "good." If it didn't fit well, she was "bad." With every passing year, Amanda became increasingly intimate friends with many aspects of destructive fear. Constructive fear was invisible to her.

With concerted effort, Amanda slowly learned how to observe the destructive, fearful voice of self-doubt. She noticed that the negative messages often filtered in as though her father was talking to her. A stern voice often said, "You will always be a mess. You will always be a disappointment. Who are you trying to fool?" Constructive fear helped Amanda learn to slow down and notice the negative voice. She learned to pause, breathe, and detach from the voice. With practice, Amanda began to respond with self-love and strength born of constructive fear's wisdom. She learned to tell the destructive voice, "Go away. Leave me in peace. I am a good and wonderful person." The more she noticed the negative voice and stopped it in its tracks, the more the hold of destructive fear lessened. Amanda also learned to notice how self-doubt felt in her body. When self-doubt kicked in, she could often pinpoint a feeling of anxious dread building in the center of her stomach. As she became more adept at noticing her body's responses to triggering thoughts or events, Amanda was able to use her tools before her destructive fear took control, one of which was the soothing power of imagery. Constructive fear guided her to envision a calm, blue ocean when she was triggered. When anxiety began to take hold, Amanda learned to pause to imagine herself sitting on warm sand with the ocean before her. No longer controlled by the voice of destructive fear, Amanda found that constructive fear had the power to guide her toward healthy thoughts and actions. To support her progress, Amanda covered her bathroom mirror in self-affirming sticky notes. The sticky notes offered her positive thoughts of loving kindness to replace the negative words she was accustomed to hearing in her head. What I term a "food-mood journal" became Amanda's new best friend. When she felt hungry, Amanda paused to pull out her journal. She would then write a sentence or two about her emotional state. Next, she would write down if her stomach actually felt hungry. She would also note if she felt thirsty. Then, Amanda would write down what she was choosing to eat or drink. Without judgment, Amanda would simply notice what *she* wanted—not what a destructive voice had customarily told her to do. Amanda embraced the structure and safety of this process; it allowed her to slow down, listen to her needs, and make healthier choices guided by constructive fear. Although destructive voices plagued her now and again, Amanda learned how to notice them and choose to listen to the gentle, kind voice that guided her into the arms of positive action—the powerful wisdom of transformational fear.

A Memory of Fear

As your last exercise for this chapter, take a moment to recall an event in your life that might have allowed destructive fear to step into your world. In Amanda's case, the chocolate chip cookie incident was this type of event. If it feels safe, let that memory unfold before you as if you are watching a movie. Allow yourself to notice the people involved, the setting, and your own presence. Then notice just yourself. Notice how your body felt. Notice if any words or phrases come into your mind. Notice any feelings that arise. Then notice your body again. From the top of your head down to your toes, scan your body as if you can see your very muscles and bones; notice any areas that feel tight or constricted. Notice if your heart is calm or racing. Simply notice whatever arises. When you are finished, make notations in your notebook about your experience. Without judgment, let the experience give you a little more information about how the enemy side of fear has lived in your body. Let this exercise be a guide into noticing when or how destructive fear might have first moved into certain areas of your life. Remember to use your breathing exercises. If additional experiences or memories come forward to inform you, treat them as messengers and helpers. As you feel ready to accept them, allow yourself to notice—without judgment—the ways that destructive fear might have controlled your life. For example, you might notice that you are haunted by the critical voice of a parent, sibling, or other influential person. Pause to notice any phrases or images that plague you. Notice any bodily sensations that arise when you think of these phrases or images. Recognize these bodily sensations as an indicator of impending negativity and practice detaching from the phrases and images rather than getting hooked by them. For example, if you hear a parent's critical voice saying, "You will never get it right. You are such an idiot!" imagine the words encapsulated in a gray balloon. Imagine that you've been holding tightly to this balloon—and others like it—all your life. Imagine letting go of the balloon; let it drift away. You may need to practice this type of "letting go" over and over again. This is normal, for the memories have been in place a long time and will want to hang on. As you consciously disengage from the negative words or images, the powerful grip of destructive fear will lessen. Next, practice inserting words of loving kindness or soothing, peaceful images to replace the negative. For this step, imagine an empty, translucent balloon. Fill up this balloon with words that are supportive and kind. For example, the words in this balloon may say, *You have strength and courage. You are bright and capable.* Imagine this affirming balloon—and others like it—floating above and around you. It will take time for your mind to get used to replacing the negative gray balloon with the positive translucent balloon, and practice is key. The more you patiently repeat these simple steps, the more positive energy you will have. As you practice this process, you are allowing yourself to listen to the wisdom of constructive fear and take action into the powerful world of transformational fear. Well done!

This chapter serves as an introduction into some of the ways that destructive fear can present itself in the body and mind. The destructive side of transformational fear tends to be rather devious, often shifting its face and form to avoid detection. Yet, just like any intruder, the detection of harmful fear is half the battle. You may now know how this fear first began to hold you in its grip. You might be more aware of how destructive fear manifests in your mind. You may be able to identify verbal or visual triggers (words, thoughts, people, objects, etc.) that initiate anxiety and other fear-related sensations. In understanding yourself and your fear a little bit better, you are on your way to greater freedom. As you practice noticing your destructive fear without judgment, you will become increasingly detached from it. When fear-related sensations begin to move in, you will be less controlled by them; you will be an observer. As Amanda said, "I am slowly learning to feel more in control. Fear and anxiety aren't my masters any longer—my awareness is. When my negative self-talk begins, I can feel my throat tighten and my belly constrict. I remind myself that it's just my old fears talking and that I don't need to listen to them—that I don't need to get pulled into fear's game. I feel so much more powerful when I work with my fear this way. I'm learning that fear has messages for me. I never knew that fear could actually be helpful—that it could be my friend."

It's important to be patient with yourself during this journey. As you practice your new skills, you are rewiring your brain and giving loving attention to your entire being. You are becoming more aware of how the destructive side of fear has held you back. This gives you the freedom to choose the helpful, constructive side of fear. As you become more familiar with the dual components of transformational fear, you will naturally begin to tease them apart to create inner freedom. You have the ability—and the power—to notice the helpful voice of constructive fear. As you acknowledge both the negative and constructive elements of transformational fear, your self-awareness and sense of personal power will increase. You will be able to translate your awareness and power into action—the full force of transformational fear. You have the power to make transformational fear your ally—and even one of your dearest friends.

CHAPTER 3

Trauma: Wounded Souls and Coping Mechanisms

What Is Trauma?

During an initial session with a client, I am often asked, "Do you think I have PTSD?" My first response is, "Do *you* think you have PTSD?" The reason for this particular response is simple. Many people feel traumatized even when they do not exhibit the range of symptoms required for a clinical diagnosis of PTSD. What I find most important in the assessment of trauma is not my opinion or someone's comparison to another person, but whether a client feels that he or she has been traumatized. Trauma surfaces in many forms, only one of which is PTSD.

Trauma is so pervasive in our world that you may see yourself or loved ones within the pages of this chapter. Indeed, I believe that many people suffer from undiagnosed PTSD and other forms of trauma. This idea is not novel, for we live in a world filled with disturbances and terrifying events. No matter where you go, media outlets provide an endless stream of traumatic situations that assault the body, mind, and spirit. As we move through our daily lives, we are constantly assaulted with images, words, and sounds that affect and wound the psyche, giving fear a place to live. Interestingly, the word *trauma* arises from the Greek language and refers to physical wounds, hurts, or defeat. Over time, trauma came to include the psychological wounding that can be defined as a deeply distressing or disturbing experience. It is through this inclusive lens that we can best understand and appreciate that trauma affects many people. Trauma does not discriminate; it affects people regardless of age, socioeconomic status, race, sex, or religion. In some way or another, trauma affects every one of us.

Understanding Post-Traumatic Stress Disorder

PTSD, the acronym for post-traumatic stress disorder, is well known in our tumultuous world. PTSD is commonly defined as a psychiatric disorder that develops after witnessing or experiencing extremely traumatic events, such as combat, crime, an accident, a natural disaster, or a physical, emotional, or sexual assault. An important aspect of this definition is the phrase "extremely traumatic events," for the *impact* of an event is a tremendously individual issue. A situation that is "extremely traumatic" to one person may affect another person on a very low level.

When evaluating a client for PTSD, the vital first step is to determine if the individual feels that the situation experienced was "extremely traumatic." In exploring this issue, a critical aspect is whether or not the traumatic experience created anxiety or other issues that cause distress or significantly interfere with daily life (e.g., social life, home life, or employment). As a result of the traumatic event, stress-related symptoms that were not present before the event become a source of significant disruption or despair.

Because of the prevalence of PTSD, it's important to better understand this diagnosis and its symptoms. The *DSM-5* (*Diagnostic and Statistical Manual of Mental Disorders*) outlines the specific criteria necessary in order to meet a clinical diagnosis of PTSD. For example, a diagnosis of PTSD requires that an individual be exposed to actual or threatened serious injury, threatened death, actual exposure to death, or actual or threatened sexual violence in at least one of the following ways: witnessing the trauma, direct exposure to the event, indirect exposure to trauma details (e.g., in the course of first responder duties), or finding that a friend or close relative was exposed to the trauma. Among other criteria, the symptoms must be present for at least one month before a formal diagnosis can be made.[1]

In general, an individual suffering from PTSD may experience symptoms including but not limited to:

- reliving the experience through flashbacks, intrusive thoughts, chronically disturbing memories, and nightmares.
- the avoidance of situations, people, and things that trigger reminders of the trauma.
- a sense of detachment, emotional "numbing," and self-isolation that may arise as an unconscious means of avoiding reminders of the traumatic experience.
- heightened emotional arousal that may include hypervigilance (feeling constantly "on guard"), sleeplessness, difficulty concentrating, irritability, high startle reflex, and angry outbursts.
- negative feelings or thoughts that began or worsened after the traumatic experience, often reflected by a loss of interest in regular activities, negative attitude, or exaggerated sense of blame related to the trauma (magnified blaming of self or others).[2]

It is important to note that symptoms of PTSD may arise immediately after a traumatic event, or they may develop over a period of time. In PTSD, the individual's stress-related responses do not resolve on their own and may increase in intensity as time passes. Some individuals with PTSD struggle with ongoing issues such as chronic anxiety, depression, and substance abuse. On an unconscious level, an individual suffering from PTSD often moves through daily life with a constant search for anything that might be a threat. It is in this space of constant, anxious vigilance that fear deepens and grows.

As we delve more deeply into trauma and transformational fear, it's important to resist the reactive temptation to label yourself or others in your world. There is no need to place yourself in any specific "box." However, if having a name or diagnosis for what distresses you is helpful in your healing process, then allow yourself that benefit. The theories and models presented are modifiable principles; they are not singular, rigid doctrines. Feel free to work loosely with the concepts presented, accepting what fits and moving away from what does not. If the term "trauma" feels too strong (or not strong enough) for your situation, then find your own descriptors that better match how *you* feel.

Traumatic events—and the psychological traumas that can result—are ever present in our current world. Indeed, the National Institute of Mental Health estimates that 50 percent of adults in the United States will experience at least one traumatic event during their lives.[3] The Nebraska Department of Veteran's Affairs provides even higher figures. This government agency states that 60.7 percent of American men and 51.2 percent of American women reported at least one traumatic event during their lives.[4] Note that these figures only include those who reported their experiences; many people do not report traumatic experiences. Whether they do not make a report as a result of shame, embarrassment, lack of awareness, guilt, or other issues, underreporting is all too common. As such, the percentages provided—as alarmingly high as they are—may be far lower than the actual statistics. Although it is noted that most people do not develop PTSD after experiencing a trauma, many do. It is this segment of the population—those who develop PTSD and other related disorders—who often live in constant agony. When a person lives in agony as a result of unaddressed trauma, the root of the suffering is *fear*—fear that a horrible experience will occur again.

Of course, PTSD is just one of the many disorders related to trauma. This chapter focuses on PTSD simply to provide a platform or avenue to encourage a greater understanding of the impact of traumatic events. Whether or not a traumatic event results in a PTSD diagnosis, it is the *impact* of the trauma that is most relevant. As you will see, traumatic events have a different impact on every person. Although certain trauma response patterns are common and somewhat predictable, every individual will respond to trauma in a different way. Indeed, an individual's *response* to a traumatic or threatening event is often more significant and influential than the traumatic event itself. The individual's unique physiology, history, felt experiences, and perceptions of the situation have a profound impact on how that person responds to a traumatic event.

Let me explain this concept with a dramatic metaphor. Imagine that I am in a horrific airplane crash. Imagine that I, along with five other passengers, survive the traumatic event. During the crash, I was wide awake, feeling and seeing almost every aspect of the sudden, terrifying tragedy. The other passengers had a different experience. One sixty-year-old man had taken a sleeping pill and was sound asleep during the crash. Another man in his forties was anesthetized by several rounds of alcoholic beverages. A thirty-year-old mother and her six-year-old child were the third and fourth survivors; wearing headsets, the pair had been focused on an animated movie. The fifth survivor was a young teenage girl who had been immersed in a game on her laptop during the crash. Her parents did not survive. Every single survivor experienced the same crash, yet every survivor's *perception* of the event will be very different. How the airplane crash ultimately affects each person—the nature and degree of the trauma experienced—will rely on many factors. Some of these variables include genetic makeup, personal history, perceptions of the event, and the individual's *felt* responses during and after the event. This is how trauma works; it affects every person differently. Trauma has one constant: its ability to infect the survivor with a virus of fear.

According to the statistics provided by The Nebraska Department of Veterans' Affairs, it is estimated that 7.8 percent of Americans will develop PTSD during the course of their lives. Women, at 10.4 percent, are over twice as likely to experience PTSD as men (5 percent) at some point in their lives. About 3.6 percent of US adults aged 18 to 54 have PTSD during the course of a given year. The traumatic events most often associated with PTSD for men are rape, combat exposure, childhood neglect, and childhood physical abuse. The most traumatic events for women are rape, sexual molestation, physical attack, being threatened with a weapon, and childhood physical abuse.[5]

In my capacity as a clinical psychologist, I work with trauma cases day in and day out. Some of the individuals suffer from PTSD or complex PTSD. Others suffer from chronic anxiety, depression, and other disorders that are often rooted in trauma. Whether working with my private clients, offering pro bono assistance to our veterans, or volunteering in the world of drug and alcohol rehabilitation, I see unresolved trauma and its devastating effects at every turn. In these unresolved trauma cases, deep, unresolved fears are resting—festering—within the sufferer. The symptoms of trauma are easy to detect in some individuals, while others mask their struggles well. These individuals appear to move through life as if they are "fine," but they are suffering within the secret cage of destructive fear. Whether their symptoms are obvious or hidden, trauma sufferers often feel alone and isolated, sometimes believing that they are broken, damaged beyond repair, and hopeless. When hopelessness sets in, destructive fear intensifies, becoming ever darker and heavier.

A powerful antidote to hopelessness is constructive fear. With its informative, illuminating powers, constructive fear has the power to remove the chains of these festering fears. This powerful, beneficial face of fear has the power to ease the suffering that is so often rooted in trauma. The light of hope and truth is cast upon the dark, secretive powers of destructive fear. Constructive fear offers the wisdom that allows doubt and hopelessness to fade as positive, new ways of being are discovered, explored, and adopted. Additionally, by adding meaning to the trauma—through creating understanding and compassionate awareness that gives attention to the cognitive, emotional, and body-based elements of trauma—transformation can slowly occur.

Trauma in the Body: From Childhood Forward

Maybe you think that you or a loved one left childhood traumas behind simply because you grew older. This is wishful thinking. When trauma is not addressed and properly resolved, it persists. It might be hidden from public view, but it persists in the psyche and the body. Simply put, a child *raised* in fear and trauma *lives* in fear and trauma. As that child grows, the fear and trauma remain—and sometimes grow stronger—until the time that the trauma is properly addressed and resolved. The seeds of destructive fear often sprout and grow roots during childhood. Like weeds, they can proliferate and grow stronger year after year. The more trauma that is added, the more the dark fear grows. In childhood and adulthood, certain coping strategies may make things look fine on the surface, much like pulling off the leaves and fluffy head of a dandelion; the visible element may be gone, but the stem and roots remain intact. For those who don't look very closely, the grass may seem perfect and pretty, but the weeds are there, even if well-camouflaged in the grass. This is how the effects of fear and fear-riddled trauma live, breed, and hide.

I emphasize this point throughout this book for one key reason: an inordinate amount of suffering in adult life stems from unresolved childhood trauma. In fact, research has found that 80 percent of chronic mental disorders begin in childhood. Sadly, approximately 70 percent of children experience three or more adverse childhood events (e.g., traumatic incidents of domestic violence) by the time they reach a mere six years of age.[6] Many people are unaware of—or prefer to avoid—these simple, sad truths and their profound, lifelong implications. Sadly, unaddressed trauma—with its roots deep in destructive fear—affects many aspects of later adult life. The unconscious, fear-based patterns are continued in intimate personal relationships. They infect and destroy marriages, ruin friendships, and harm social relationships. They contaminate work environments. They result in addictive patterns that manifest in drug and alcohol abuse, excessive spending, unhealthy sexual behaviors, overeating, and other significant difficulties. And, very sadly, they are inflicted on the next generation through unconscious, unhealthy parenting. In this way, the destructive element of fear uses trauma to perpetuate itself.

Let me offer you another way to think of this vital concept. If you are faced with a physical health concern, whether it is as straightforward as a broken arm or as challenging as breast cancer, the issue does not resolve itself. The body needs help to heal properly, so you would seek medical attention. For example, in the case of breast cancer, treatment often involves intense, ongoing care that may require surgery, radiation treatment, chemotherapy, and implants. Without focused care and attention, healing and recovery would not occur. The psyche works exactly the same way. It needs proper attention and care to resolve the wounds that have left it suffering in destructive fear. Left unattended, the psychic wounds will only worsen and cause needless anguish.

Clearly, psychological wounds do not magically disappear over time. Chronic childhood stress often results in extended periods of emotional dysregulation; such prolonged dysregulation is believed to cause damage to the brain while also increasing the child's use of primitive, instinctive coping mechanisms. Indeed, an individual with a history of childhood trauma may be more susceptible to the effects of stress and trauma in adulthood. We cannot escape the truth that our childhood environments affect us deeply—psychologically, cognitively, and physiologically. When unhealthy behaviors are learned in childhood, they persist into adulthood unless time and effort are put into conscious, positive change. When old, unbeneficial behaviors are changed, the physical body and psyche can reap substantial benefits.

The above section may help you understand yourself better. If you were affected by trauma at an early age, it is quite probable that the fears related to the trauma still live inside you. Clients often say, "I'm older now. So many years have passed since I was a kid. It's not possible that I'm still affected by what happened way back then." Remember, trauma has no sense of chronological time. It just lives inside of you, telling you to be afraid. Whether you were the victim of your father's alcoholic tyranny, your mother's uncaring detachment, your stepparent's sexual abuse, or some other form of trauma, the old, unresolved fears live inside of you.

Due to the highly sensitive nature of the brain in early development, experiences during infancy and childhood have a particularly significant impact on overall behavioral, cognitive, social, and psychological functioning. The individual's experiences and neurobiological makeup from infancy forward directly affect the individual's ability to cope with stress and trauma in a healthy and adaptive manner. Early trauma can instill fear-based patterns that affect the way the child views the world. Rather than seeing home, parents, and life as "safe," fear sets in to issue constant reminders that more trauma is waiting just around the corner. Although such fear is designed to protect the child—helping him or her stay alert to danger—the chronic, ongoing state of arousal is terribly destructive. Children thrive on safety, security, and love; healthy development is hampered in environments rife with neglect and fear.[7]

Research suggests that traumatic relationships in early childhood affect right brain development and thus lead to an inability to cope well with stress.[8] It may come as no surprise that individuals who experience trauma in childhood often do not respond well to stressful situations. When faced with stress—which increases the individual's state of arousal—the traumatized person may respond as if faced with earlier traumatic experiences. Certain situations, words, smells, objects, sounds, and other stimuli can provoke heightened, irregular responses. As a result, the individual may feel as if the trauma "held" in the body is being literally relived. In this state of stress, the sufferer simply does not have the capacity to differentiate between the original trauma and a current event that may bear little or no resemblance to the original traumatic experience. Indeed, these primitive, fear-based responses home in on one thing: survival. No matter how many years have passed since the original trauma, and no matter how different the current trigger may be from the original trauma, the sufferer unconsciously "returns to the scene" of the original trauma. Once again, it is fear—fear of harm of some sort—that lives in the body like a toxic, festering beast.

Sadly, those who are deeply affected by trauma often revert to harmful patterns when faced with stress. Even after substantial psychological healing has occurred, a trauma survivor may regress into familiar, destructive patterns of behavior during stressful times. For example, you may recall situations where you or a loved one reacted instinctively to a fairly low-level stressor in a highly exaggerated way. One client, whom we'll call Marcus, exemplifies this dynamic very well. Here is how he summarizes his discovery and subsequent improvement: "I am now more aware of my old patterns and my fears. I understand that my angry outbursts come from my childhood—my stepfather's emotional and physical abuse. He seemed to thrive on being unpredictable. He was brutal—mean and critical. As a kid, I was always on guard, terrified of doing anything wrong that might prompt an attack. I felt so helpless—angry and scared, but helpless. I was always hyper-alert for danger. When I first started working with you, I didn't believe that all that old crap was still inside of me, that it could set me off. I get it now; I was unconsciously confusing the real trauma of my past with anything that remotely looked or felt like it in the present. More and more, I can slow myself down and step back to observe what's *really* going on inside of me. The old fears don't rule me like they used to; I listen to the constructive fear that wants to help me. I don't have to—I don't want to—react like a tortured kid on the defensive. In the past, I'd blow up at my wife over anything that even hinted of disagreement—anything that made me feel criticized. In one instant, I'd go from being the normal, nice guy to being a monster. Things have gotten better slowly but surely. I have an awareness that gives me real power—the power to choose how I want to respond. It feels great not being ruled by those old fears, those crazy inner monsters from my childhood. My wife is slowly getting more relaxed. She says she feels safer now that she's not living in constant fear of me or what I might do next."

Situations like Marcus's are exceedingly common, for unresolved childhood trauma has great power to affect adult behavior. As a form of destructive fear, the unresolved trauma can actually dictate an individual's reactions. Indeed, when stressed or threatened, the traumatized individual reacts to the emotionally stored traumatic memories, *not* the current situation that may bear little or no relation to the original trauma. In a sense, it appears that unresolved trauma—the vessel for fear—lives in the psyche in a semi-dormant state. Stressors can provoke the trauma and the fears it holds, causing it to rupture into active mode. The behaviors that arise are often illogical to others until it is understood that they are the familiar, protective responses that the trauma survivor learned long ago.

These hard-wired patterns, so rooted in primitive fear responses, can only be healed with ongoing attention and perseverance.

As we prepare for another exercise, it's important to note that unresolved trauma requires special attention. Such trauma normally can't be resolved without proper psychotherapy. This book is intended only to acquaint you with the fears that might be living inside of you. As you explore and understand more about your inner life, you may discover that you have unresolved trauma that deserves professional attention. As always, feel free to skip this or any exercise that does not seem appropriate. As this exercise deepens your work with fear, remember that you can pause or completely discontinue the exercise at any time. An important aspect of this exercise is for you to cultivate a growing awareness of what is best for *you*. As you learn to listen to your needs, the constructive elements of fear will respond and grow ever stronger. As always, pause to breathe or rest whenever you would like.

Exploring the Grip of Threat

If you desire to move to this next exercise, be sure that you are in a physically and emotionally safe space. With your notebook and pen at your side, pause to breathe. Proceed when you are ready. Recall a situation from your childhood or adulthood when you felt threatened. As always, select an experience that feels *very* manageable to you. You may choose a relatively low-level situation, such as a minor disagreement with a friend. If it feels appropriate and safe, you might choose a more stressful situation, such as being the victim of bullying or heavy criticism. Can you recall how you responded? Did you run? Were you immobilized? Did you fight? Notice if memories of the event (words, faces, or other details) live on vividly inside of you—almost as if the event just occurred. Then notice if you can you recall your bodily sensations. Did your heart pound? Was your throat constricted? Did a chill or a wave of heat run through you? Notice if you can recall your emotions. Were you angry, scared, confused, furious, or numb? Notice if anything else arises in your body or mind. Consciously release any negative emotions and energy; imagine it all floating away in a balloon. Breathe.

Take this opportunity to make notes that feel important to you. Feel free to include thoughts, feelings, and bodily sensations. Breathe. Pause to appreciate the exploratory work that you have done. If it feels appropriate, take a nap or a gentle walk. Well done!

Before reading further, let at least a few minutes pass. Then pause to look at your notes from the above exercise. Notice how much—in what ways and to what degree—the old fear rose up inside you as if you were back in the threatening event itself. Notice you may feel some of the old fear rising up in your mind and body. Depending upon various factors—such as the surrounding circumstances, your unique physiology, your personal history, and how safe you felt during and after the situation—fears related to that previous experience may still be living inside of you. Indeed, even if you successfully fled from a bully or managed to hide to avoid a threat, your body and psyche might very well remember and hold onto the fear that you experienced. In noticing whatever arose for you during the exercise, you may now more deeply appreciate how you have been affected by certain difficult events in your life. There is no way to go back in time to "fix" or "reverse" the harm that was done, but you can *heal* the wounds. As you explore the big and little traumas of life that are stored inside of you, you are facing your fears. As you face your fears rather than hide or run from them, fear becomes your friend.

The Impact of Childhood Trauma in Adulthood: A Case Study

Let me introduce you to spirited, hopeful Ellie. If you met this outgoing woman, you might not realize that Ellie secretly lives within a cage of fear. I first met Ellie while she was in recovery for substance abuse. As she learned early in life that a cloak of cheery detachment was her best defense, Ellie kept up a strong front. Yet when Ellie recounted her horrific childhood, fresh pain moved in. Unused to letting her feelings come through, she quickly brushed away the tears that burst through; crying was a foreign, still-uncomfortable experience. In telling her story, Ellie recounted being sexually abused by three of her mother's "boyfriends" by the age of five. By the time she was in third grade, she no longer kept count of the various men's offenses against her. Ellie learned early on in life that marijuana—provided by her mother—helped her dull her emotional pain. By age eleven, she sought relief from alcohol. Before too long, illicit drugs entered the mix. Then, barely an adult, she found herself pregnant—and addicted to meth. In the rehabilitation facility, Ellie no longer had alcohol or drugs to dull her pain. She stood face to face with her fear—the horror of her history, the unknowns in her future, and all the painful, unfamiliar feelings that lived inside of her.

Ellie's courage and honesty made it easy for me to appreciate her as a human being. Straightforward and spunky, she sat with her hands rubbing the giant mound of her pregnant belly. The trauma that she lived through made her a picture of perseverance and resilience. "You know," she told me with clear, intense gaze, "I'll give this baby a better life than I ever had. That's my mission. I won't let anyone hurt her. I'll get my life on track. Up until now, I've always been addicted to something—it numbed me. This is the first time in my life that I'm actually feeling my feelings. I didn't even know what feelings were before rehab. Well, I guess I had *a* feeling before—it was rage. Now I feel the hurt, the sadness, and the anger, too. Sometimes I feel a little joy, especially about the baby. But, mainly, I feel the hurt and the pain—and I *really* feel the fear. I think that's the worst. I'm terrified that I'll screw up, that I'll end up being like my crackhead mother. I'm scared that I'll be back on the street—living that way for the rest of my life. I'm afraid that all of these huge feelings will overtake me. You know, I'm even afraid that if I start crying—really crying—that my tears will never stop. I'll tell you another thing. I'm afraid that I'm so messed up that I've already ruined my life forever, that no one will give me a real chance. I am so scared that I am broken beyond repair. I have this thing in my head that tells me I'm damaged, too damaged for anyone 'good' to really want me. Like, 'Who do you think you are that anyone nice or good could really love you after all the crap you've been through, all the bad stuff you've done, and all the bad stuff that's been done to you?'" Ellie paused, wiping at the silent tears that had escaped her notice. I smiled warmly, and she continued. "You know, this 'feeling stuff' takes a lot more work than just walling off. When I'm calm, I can see why I need to make sense of my life, my own story. The more I work at it, the more I feel myself breathing a little. I'm actually feeling less anxious and even sleeping better. Sometimes I want to shut it all away and stuff everything back inside—to wall off again—but that's when my cravings start coming back. I know that I'm just at the beginning of my sobriety journey, but I'm going to make it through. For my little baby—and for me, too."

Ellie had lived her young life in a walled-off cell of fear. As long as she pretended that horrible things were not a part of her everyday life, she could cope well enough. This strategy helped her survive through her very early years. As she learned to use marijuana to dull her pain, she felt more detached. Her chronic fear of her abusers made Ellie feel constantly on edge. She never knew which predator would come into her room, and she never knew when. With a mother who failed to protect her, who simply did not seem to care, Ellie was terrified and alone. Ellie lived in a place of powerlessness, of chronic fear. The soothing effects of alcohol brought welcome, temporary relief. As long as she was buzzed, her inner terror— her fear—was quiet. A "friend" introduced Ellie to meth, and she loved the high it gave her. It also blunted her emotions, and she felt anesthetized to her inner pain. Meth helped her ignore the bad memories that were stored inside her mind and her body. Meth helped her pretend that she was not afraid; it kept her from noticing her fear.

Ellie's past is extremely horrific, yet the themes are terribly common. Trauma, in whatever depth and form it arises, has the power to affect every person's body and mind—and when the trauma is chronic, its roots are often far deeper. When the trauma occurs early on, it has inordinate power to affect the individual on many levels. In a case such as Ellie's, the trauma began early, and it persisted throughout her childhood. As such, the fear created by the trauma was entrenched inside Ellie's body and mind. Ellie numbed her painful fears in a variety of ways; none of them really worked. As she moved into adulthood, the fears continued to live on inside of Ellie despite her best efforts to numb them and push them away. This is how the cruel fears that arise from trauma live on in the body. They cannot be tricked into leaving. They cannot be ignored, numbed, or escaped. The only way out of their grip is to face these fears. The only way to freedom is by finding the healing messages within fear and moving forward with fear as your friend.

Trauma: Transforming Fear with Humor, Truth, and Love

We are used to letting fear act as the enemy. Running or hiding from fear can be the familiar way out. Facing fear is often very uncomfortable and unfamiliar. It takes time, dedication, and energy to find the constructive messages within fear. Indeed, dismantling general fears can be a demanding process. When it comes to deconstructing fear instilled by trauma, the task can be far more complicated and difficult.

It is an arduous task to pull apart one's history to gain understanding, yet I know of no other way to find healing. Clearly, pills don't do the trick; they offer only symptomatic relief. Alcohol and drugs numb the pain, but when the "anesthesia" wears off, the pain remains. Add the shame and guilt that often arise afterward, and it's clear that alcohol and drug use does far more harm than good. Not one of these commonly used "crutches" addresses the underlying fear that is the source of the angst. Fear waits, hoping that its transformative power will be noticed. Fear waits, hoping to become your ally and your friend.

How can we dig deeper to better understand the transformative and friendly side of fear? Using Ellie's situation as an example, it's helpful to remember her comments about fear. As Ellie so honestly stated, "I'm *terrified* that I'll screw up, that I'll end up being like my crackhead mother. I'm *scared* that I'll be back on the street—living that way for the rest of my life. I'm *afraid* that all of these huge feelings will overtake me. You know, I'm even *afraid* that if I start crying—really crying—that my tears will never stop. I'm *afraid* that I'm so messed up that I've already ruined my life forever, that no one will give me a real chance. I am so *scared* that I am broken beyond repair. I have this thing in my head that tells me I'm damaged, too damaged for anyone 'good' to really want me."

Stop here. Read Ellie's sentences again. Even if your own fears are quite different from Ellie's, you might understand the essence of Ellie's fears. You might notice in her words the unfriendly, cruel side of your own fear.

Using Ellie's fears as examples, we'll do a low-level, basic dismantling of each theme. As each theme is explored, we'll investigate the cruel, threatening side of fear. We'll then move to transforming the fear into a message that is helpful—we will encourage a relationship with the friendly side of fear. This section will give you a template for dismantling and transforming your inner fears. The work may seem simple at times, yet transformation occurs with these simple "adjustments" that change the way the mind and body perceive the world. By noticing and shifting the unconscious thoughts and beliefs that stem from the cruel face of fear, the psyche and body begin to enjoy a sense of relief. Life viewed through a lens of cruel fear is far different than life viewed through a lens of friendly, helpful fear. With the former, there is no upside; with the latter—friendly fear—the possibilities for transformation are endless.

Starting with Ellie's first two sentences (*I'm terrified that I'll screw up, that I'll end up being like my crackhead mother. I'm scared that I'll be back on the street—living that way for the rest of my life*), the message is clear. Ellie is afraid of making mistakes that will doom her for the rest of her life. Fear-based internal messages like this have vast, negative power. There is no upside to living with a mindset that is terrified of failure. That mindset will only drain Ellie's positive energy, keeping her in a constant loop of self-doubt. The truth is that Ellie may never relapse. The truth is also that Ellie *may* relapse. But even if that were to occur, Ellie would not be doomed. As a result of her recovery program, she has far more helpful tools than she ever knew possible. She has a support system and a safe place to put her head at night. Ellie also has a growing sense of respect for herself that will help her move forward. Ellie now understands that she is courageous and resilient. Additionally, Ellie has a reason to change: she wants to be sober to provide her baby—and herself—a life that is happy and safe. Now that we understand the fear and how to find the possibilities within the fearful message, we can see that Ellie is *not* doomed. Ellie has the power to keep moving forward, and if she relapses, she will be able to stand up and try again. Friendly fear wants Ellie to listen to its voice: "You are strong. You are resilient. You are courageous. You can—and will—create the life that you want and deserve. If you stumble, do not worry; you will get up and use the situation to become even stronger and more aware. You have support. You are not alone."

Next, Ellie admits, "I'm afraid that all of these huge feelings will overtake me. You know, I'm even afraid that if I start crying—really crying—that my tears will never stop." Although her words might seem dramatic, they are extremely common for those who have learned to cope by bottling up their emotions. People detach from their emotions for many reasons. Often, parents or caregivers don't permit emotional displays. Sometimes teasing or mockery teaches a child that "emotions are for sissies." Some families believe that logic is more important than "irrational" emotions.

In Ellie's case, she found that her emotions made her feel more vulnerable and scared, so she cut off her emotions without realizing that they were still there, festering inside of her. Now, when Ellie is faced with the deep well of her unfamiliar emotional world, she is terrified. She is afraid that her feelings will consume her. She fears that her tears will be endless and that she will cry forever. However, when we look at this objectively, we realize that cruel fear is simply trying to keep her emotions walled up inside of her. Cruel fear wants Ellie's emotions to remain bottled up; that fearful voice wants what is *familiar*—even if it is harmful to Ellie. The cruel face of fear does not like change; it is very, very afraid of change. So how can we transform this fear? In this particular case, a bit of humor, a dose of truth, and a lot of compassion are the most helpful tools. We might say to the cruel fear, "Is it really possible for emotions to take me over? If I become sad, will I always and forever be sad—so sad that I never leave my bed? If I feel my anger, will I turn into a beast? If I let my tears come, will I turn into a puddle of water? Will I become so lost in my emotions that I won't ever think right again?" Then we might laugh a little at the images that have shaken off the fear just a bit. We might then look at the truth of the fears with a healthy dose of compassion. Yes, it is possible that Ellie may feel lost in her emotions. When the walls that have kept her emotions stored away come slowly tumbling down, she may feel intensely sad. Ellie may feel terribly scared. She may feel very angry. But she will need to be reminded that those feelings will not last forever. Despite how much she may *feel* that they will consume her, she will learn to trust that her feelings will not harm her. As she grows stronger, she will find that she can sit with the discomfort that may come with unfamiliar feelings. She will learn that her feelings have a great deal to teach her. These are just some of the transformative messages that awaited Ellie's discovery. Within such messages lies the friendly, helpful side of fear at work. If friendly fear could speak out loud to Ellie, it would tell her: "You are safe. You are learning that feelings are good and helpful; they give you important information. Don't worry; you won't lose yourself in your feelings—you will learn from them. You will understand yourself better by acknowledging your feelings. You will use your feelings to grow more self-aware. You will learn to let your feelings work for you, not against you. You will learn to use the feelings that arise—all of them—in healthy ways."

Finally, let's move to the last of Ellie's fearful confessions. She said, "I'm afraid that I'm so messed up that I've already ruined my life forever, that no one will give me a real chance. I am so scared that I am broken beyond repair. I have this thing in my head that tells me I'm damaged, too damaged for anyone 'good' to really want me." Ellie's fears are not at all uncommon. Many women and men have revealed very similar fears to me. The theme of this cruel fear tells the individual, "You are not lovable. You are unworthy." This menacing fear rests on an insidious assumption of perfection—that one must have lived some sort of perfect life or be some sort of perfect person in order to be loved. Yet the essence of love has nothing to do with perfection. This assumption of perfection gives enemy fear a terribly strong upper hand.

Love, in its purest form, accepts unconditionally. Love may ask that future behaviors be different from past behaviors so as not to cause harm, but pure love does not rely on perfection. Cruel fear does not want this truth to be absorbed. When friendly fear moves in to offer loving acceptance, the body and mind are often quick to constrict. As in Ellie's case, she will instantaneously and unconsciously react through the lens of her past. She will recoil, remembering that the "love" offered by those in the past was not kind or accepting. Indeed, the "love" Ellie experienced as a child was certainly not pure, unconditional love; it was the opposite of love. Friendly fear nudges Ellie to absorb the idea that a pure form of love does exist, and that she is truly worthy of such love. Friendly fear wants Ellie to push away the insistent, cruel voice that tells her she is not good enough to be loved. This helpful, kind face of fear wants Ellie to know that she is worthy and lovable as she is. Friendly fear wants her to know the truth: "You are a precious soul. You are loved. All humans are imperfect. You are not defined by your past, but by the courage of your journey. You are lovable. You are strong. You are resilient. You are courageous. You can—and will—create the life that you want. You may stumble, but you will get up. You have good support. You are not alone."

Reframing Destructive Fears with the Wisdom of Constructive Fear

If you feel ready for another exercise, you now have an opportunity to practice reframing your destructive fears. As we did with Ellie above, you can now work with a destructive fear—or set of destructive fears—that you would like to transform. When you are relaxed and in a safe space, take out your notebook. Write out a destructive fear that is holding you back. Don't think about it too much; just write out whatever comes to mind. For example, you might write, "I can't get the job I want. I'm stuck forever where I work now." Then ponder what the destructive fear is saying to you. Imagine what you could do if you were able to set yourself free from that destructive fear. Constructive, friendly fear might say: "You are a solid, excellent employee. You are smart and committed. When you get home tonight, set aside an hour to work on updating your resume. Then, tomorrow night, send out that resume to three different companies. You can do this. Repeat and repeat until you find the job you want. You are never stuck. You are free." Continue this exercise for as long as it feels valuable. When you are finished, pause to breathe. Review your notes and make a commitment to yourself. Your constructive fear is already partnering with you to transform your life. You are amazing.

Beyond Cognitions: Healing Stored Fears

The word "healing" has many meanings. When working with the concept of transformational fear, this term will be used to draw your attention to the idea of "reducing suffering." Whether a person is suffering from mental distress, emotional distress, or the physical distress that often arises from various forms of psychological distress, the intention of healing work is to reduce suffering. What feels like suffering to one person may not feel like suffering to another; the nature and degree of suffering is a subjective experience. What matters most is whether *you* feel that you are suffering. If you are, the kind and helpful face of transformational fear—when noticed, embraced, and put into action—has incredible power to help you heal.

Trauma cannot be healed by shifts in cognition alone. If it were that simple, logical attention to an issue would "fix" psychic wounds. Additionally, the insights that might arise from rational contemplation would allow a person to "move forward" after a traumatic event. The psyche often responds best to healing through a holistic approach. Such an approach involves a process of discovery that allows cognitive understanding and meaning as it supports emotional and physiological awareness and release. Remember, the enemy side of fear can dwell in pockets inside the body and the psyche. If these pockets are not "cleaned out," the fears sit and fester.

New clients often say something to this effect: "I've talked about my trauma in the past. I understand my issues. Now that time has passed, it doesn't make sense that I don't feel better. I don't understand why I still get bothered." We expect the psyche to heal with the passage of time, but the psyche does not work that way. The psyche heals when—and only when—we give it the attention it deserves. Someone who has "resolved" a traumatic experience by "thinking through it" has only put the issue in a compartment. That's why it still arises in various forms including nightmares, emotional outbursts, depression, and anxiety.

Trauma sufferers often believe that they can put the issue behind them by simple analysis of the trauma. This type of intellectualization is actually a defense mechanism that can do great harm in the long run. The enemy side of fear thrives on intellectualization. Although it temporarily dispels internal conflict, it does not address the root problems. Intellectualization is not a tool for healing; it is a tool used to avoid the underlying emotions. Healing asks that we move into the spaces where enemy fear lurks and hides. This takes patience, courage, and perseverance.

Many people want to find an easy route to healing, but that easy route does not exist. If trauma could be healed by "thinking through it," the person suffering would be able to say, "Well, I was abused. I was betrayed. I am angry and hurt. I understand all of that. Now, I feel better. I don't need to use food, drugs, alcohol, sex, or shopping to avoid the real pain. Now that I can logically outline what happened, I am completely healed." Clearly, it's not this simple. Far more is needed to heal the wounds that life brings. The psyche and body must be supported in making meaning out of the entire experience and its effects. This includes attending to the underlying thoughts, the emotional world, and the body that has stored memories of tension, anger, and sadness. There is no quick fix, and this is a scary, unwanted concept for a world that has come to rely on quick fixes. The enemy aspect of fear wants you to believe that a quick fix will do the trick. It wants you to reach for a pill, a credit card, or a quart of ice cream. Friendly fear asks you to stop. It wants you to take good care of yourself. It wants you to take the time to meander through your body, mind, and emotions to find what's going on inside.

Alexander the Gentle Veteran: A Case Study

The effects of trauma run deep and rampant in many of our veterans. In an effort to make a positive impact, I donate my services to veterans through an organization based in a major city. One of the men I worked with through this program—let's call him Alexander—suffered from childhood trauma, adult trauma, and wartime trauma. Alexander appeared in my office as a tough, intense civilian. His haircut, gait, and posture made his military background obvious. As with most of my veterans, he chose to sit with his back to the wall and his eyes toward the door. He scanned me, and then my office, assessing the situation. He was alert for possible danger. Alexander smiled with an appreciative, "Yes, please, Doctor," when I offered him tea. As he chose from my tea selection, I chatted. I watched Alexander relax slightly during this simple interlude. His jaw softened, and the set of his strong shoulders eased. Within the first fifteen minutes of our initial session, Alexander's veneer cracked. As he described one of the reasons he finally sought help, tears poured down his cheeks. Seemingly oblivious to the tears, he ignored the box of tissues on the side table and continued to speak. Besides the tears, the only hint of his inner pain was the occasional crack in his measured speech. Like most of the veterans I have worked with, there is far more to the story than meets the eye.

Over time, Alexander let me into his world. It was a slow, slow process, for he needed to be able to trust me. He'd been betrayed so many times in his life that he was fearful I would be yet another in his long line of betrayers. I understood this. I had to be patient, straightforward, and true. Alexander had to see and feel that I would be genuine with him. Alexander tested me in many ways, from offering payment for my pro bono services to vigilantly watching for any signs that I might judge or criticize him. He found over time that I could be trusted. The more he trusted me, the more his stories poured forth. As I heard more of Alexander's story, I learned that his combat trauma was significant, as was the trauma he experienced outside the military—from childhood forward.

In exploring this case, you might notice how combat trauma and adult trauma "built upon" childhood trauma. Through this lens we are able to appreciate the long-term effects of trauma and destructive fear. The fears instilled in Alexander as a child made his later trials all the more difficult to bear.

When Alexander was a small child, his father termed him the "Stupid One." Even when Alexander's performance in school belied this moniker, his father would laugh and say, "Stupid One, you will never succeed in life. Everything you do will turn to crap. I'll bet money on it." As Alexander said, "I came to believe that I really was stupid. Anytime I did well at school, I believed that the teacher was being nice, that the class was for dummies, or that someone made a mistake on my grade. I felt like a fraud—I was always waiting for someone to discover just how stupid I was. My father's criticisms stuck in my head no matter where I went—even in the military. No matter where I went or what I did, I could hear his voice mocking me—'Hey, Stupid One!' That voice made me believe I would always fail. I didn't let anyone know it, but I had zero self-confidence." Alexander recalls bringing home a report card displaying straight As. His father tore it to pieces, accusing him of foul play. Alexander remembers his mother scuttling away as she always did; she didn't want the father's cruelty turned her way. Such encounters were normal in Alexander's youth. When his father passed away from a heart attack, Alexander secretly hoped things would change. They did, but for the worse. An "uncle" moved in and made Alexander his target. The physical, emotional, and sexual abuse that resulted was horrific. Alexander told his mother; she accused him of being a liar. She told the "uncle," and the beating Alexander received forced him into silence. As Alexander put it, "I walked on eggshells all the time. I didn't know what was going to happen next. The only thing I could trust was that my mother would let anything happen to me to make her life easier. That was the one thing I could count on."

Alexander recounted a childhood filled with chronic stress and anxiety. He pushed his emotions aside, numbing himself to prepare for the next attack. Both before and after his father died, Alexander lived in terror. Alexander was never protected by his caregivers; they were his abusers. Day after day, Alexander lived in this world of unsafety. He was afraid of living. Even his tiny bedroom, where he often hid under the covers, was not a safe place. He startled easily, jumping at unusual or unexpected noises. His nearly constant state of anxiety kept him hostage. If he sensed any possible threat, his anxiety would switch to full-blown, silent terror. As Alexander describes it, "I was always on the alert. Something bad was always going to happen—I just didn't know how or when. When I was a kid, my dad would come in my room when I was sleeping. Sometimes he'd just give me a cold, nasty look and say, 'Hey, Stupid One.' Other times he'd dump out my drawers. It was the same kind of thing with that 'uncle.' It was unpredictable. If I was lucky, he'd just scream and call me names. Sometimes he'd haul off and hit me. Other times, it was a lot worse. I never knew what would come next. I just had to be on the alert, to survive as best I could. I didn't do it consciously, but now I see that I got really good at noticing details. That's the upside, I guess. I could read gestures, looks, and even a change in footsteps. The more accurate I got at noticing and tracking the little signals, the better I could prepare."

As is sadly common in such environments, Alexander's state of fear became part of his way of being. In essence, the fearful state had taken up residence inside him. It had become trait-like, affecting every aspect of how he perceived and experienced the world he lived in. Alexander's chronically stressful environment affected his ability to adapt to stress on a daily basis, and it also affected his long-term ability to cope with stress. Situations and experiences that others might handle with ease often felt intensely frightening for Alexander. As is common for those who live in chronic fear, Alexander often responded to everyday stressors with exaggerated reactivity. Alexander felt abnormal; he couldn't help but compare himself to others. He did his best to keep his terror secret. He played strong. He stayed tough.

Children learn by observing. Their young brains become trained by watching what their parents and caregivers do day in and day out. Whatever they observe, be it positive or negative, becomes the template for future action. Children do not have the mental ability to logically think through situations. When a child feels an emotion, a reaction "pops out." If parents model behaviors that are explosive or harmful in other ways, the child will adopt these same patterns. If unskillful or harmful behaviors are modeled, unskillful or harmful behaviors result. If poor coping strategies are modeled, poor coping strategies will be learned.

Given his unsafe, stress-filled environment, Alexander unconsciously found himself caught in a chronic pattern of trauma response. The coping strategies and patterns he had needed to survive became a part of his life. He moved through life as though everything was a threat. Living in a constant state of protective hyperarousal, Alexander did not stop to differentiate between what was safe and unsafe. He grouped everyone and everything into one category: unsafe. The defenses he unconsciously erected to keep himself safe became a wall of fear. It was a wall that kept others from hurting him, but the wall also kept him within the world of fear. To others, he looked like a "normal, fun guy," yet Alexander felt deeply fearful and alone. Alexander knew two things: *I cannot trust others. I cannot trust myself.*

Although he moved away from his mother and "uncle" as soon as he could, Alexander's later years brought no relief. Now deeply hardwired to fear relationships, Alexander moved from woman to woman. He sought comfort through sex, but the comfort was temporary at best. He began to lie to cover his tracks, secretly promising one woman his fidelity while seeking escape in the bed of another. The more complicated things got, the more he found himself lying to cover his tracks. He sought comfort through alcohol, but that comfort, too, was fleeting. Although one part of him felt proud of the array of women he had collected over time, another part felt deeply ashamed of his behavior. He became angrier and angrier, sometimes exploding into a rage over small issues. Alexander became interested in the sport of boxing. He liked the adrenaline surge and power he found through the sport, but the feel-good state never lasted long enough. As Alexander put it, "I wanted to put my past behind me. I didn't want to think about it—I wanted to pretend it never happened. So, my world became about three or four things: making money, boxing, sex, and women. I don't think the women or sex actually mattered. I never let myself get close enough to anyone to actually care. It was just a power and ego thing for me. Well, no matter how much I tried to pretend that having sex with a lot of women somehow made me more desirable—somehow lovable—deep inside I guess I knew that the opposite was true. I used women, sex, and whatever came my way to avoid dealing with the horror of my past. I have lived my whole life in a constant state of stress. In my past, I had no way to control my stress except through women, alcohol, and boxing. I had no idea back then that my actions were controlled by fear. I thought I was a 'tough guy'; I didn't know that the toughness was just another mask—a way to get by."

Fast-forward to Alexander's military career. Alexander liked the routine and predictability of his life in the military; the structure made him feel somewhat safe. The training, the combat, and the accompanying adrenaline rushes further entrenched Alexander's fear-based responses. Alexander enjoyed the power and ego-driven aspects of the military, yet part of him suffered deeply. He became more detached from personal relationships, numb to the effect that he had on others—particularly women. His military training honed his sense of detachment. His temper flared now and again, but it wasn't out of the ordinary in the military environment; he had learned when and where he could explode. In the military, Alexander carried on with life as usual, seeking comfort and release through sex, alcohol, and sports. This behavior was common in the military world; Alexander liked that he did not stand out. Military life seemed to suit him perfectly.

Alexander's life changed the day an IED (improvised explosive device) took the life of his best friend. This friendship was the only really close relationship Alexander had ever allowed himself to form. His friend had died before his eyes. Numb to everything else in life, this experience "broke" Alexander. Survivor's guilt ate at him. Further complicated by the traumatic brain injury and wounds he personally suffered as a result of the incident, Alexander could no longer cope as he had in the past. Thoughts of suicide began to torture him. He didn't have a plan or a means of killing himself, but the idea of ending his life was tempting. As he told me, "I don't think I really wanted to kill myself. I guess I think I'm too tough for that. But I just didn't have any other ideas for how to stop the constant demons." The trauma Alexander had experienced in his past was now compounded. The primitive coping strategies he had learned to use were no longer effective. His life was falling apart.

In desperation, Alexander sought relief where he could find it. Several months after his honorable discharge, he married a woman he had known for two months. The stress of a new marriage—and the baby that soon resulted from the union—only made matters worse. Routine became even more important to Alexander; repetitive patterns gave him a sense of safety and security. He became increasingly intolerant of any disruptions in his schedule. He also avoided new situations. As Alexander noted, "I hated unpredictability more than ever. If I made a change—if it was something I decided to do—I'd be okay. But if someone else tried to mess with my routine, I'd fly off the handle, especially if it was my wife. My wife started accusing me of being a control freak, but I couldn't see it. I'd just go off on her. I never hit her, but I came close. The things I've said to her—I've really made her suffer. I wish I could take them back." Destructive fear haunted Alexander. It tormented him, and he, in turn, tormented those close to him. He could not control his terrifying internal world, and his external world was out of control.

Nothing external could solve Alexander's internal trauma. No temporary salve, be it in the form of marriage, sex, alcohol, or the adrenaline-rush sports he no longer enjoyed, could heal his trauma. Healing was possible but only if Alexander was ready to face his destructive fears and work with them to embrace the constructive, friendly face of fear. It was in my office, in the safe, friendly arms of fear, that Alexander began to find the relief he had been seeking for a lifetime.

You might want to believe that Alexander's story is uncommon, but it's not. The rates of childhood physical, sexual, and emotional abuse are alarmingly high for both men and women, and much of it goes unreported due to fear. A child who is raised in a state of fear stores and retrieves information differently than one who is raised in a stable, relaxed environment. A child who lives in a constant state of stress, anxiety, or "numbing" often suffers from significant impairment in emotional and social functioning. As portrayed by Alexander's story, a traumatized child often has highly developed defensive skills that result from consistent exposure to the chronically stressful environment. When a child is raised in an unsafe, unpredictable environment, the child's physiology is actually changed by the ongoing stress. The negative impact, which affects everything from interpersonal relationships to stress management and general learning abilities, can be profound and long lasting. These effects, as you can readily see in Alexander's poignant case study, do not disappear after childhood; they grow and strengthen into adulthood until they are faced and given proper care and attention.

Trauma, Stress, and the Brain

Let's pause for a moment to understand a little more about the physiological effects of trauma. This is a perfect opportunity to touch on the topic of stress, for the effects of chronic stress and trauma can be similar in many ways. Bear with me for two important paragraphs that will help you understand and appreciate the long-term effects of chronic stress and trauma-induced stress. It is helpful to remember that our life experiences and how we process them have a serious impact on the body as well as the psyche.

An important part of the brain's limbic system, the hippocampus works in concert with the cerebral cortex (the outer layer of the brain often referred to as "gray matter") to encode and store certain memories. Among the other functions, the hippocampus is involved in reality testing and inhibition of the amygdala (a key part of the brain responsible for processing emotions such as fear). The hippocampus plays a key role in an individual's response to stress and trauma. Here's where it gets interesting. When you are extremely stressed, your body releases certain chemicals such as cortisol and adrenaline. These neurochemicals can temporarily affect the hippocampus; normal memory storage does not occur when severe or ongoing stress affects the ordinary functions of the hippocampus. Simply put, when faced with a traumatic experience or chronic stress, the brain's ability to properly consolidate and store certain memories can be seriously impaired.

Glucocorticoids, a class of steroid hormones produced by the body's adrenal glands, are essential for human life. Cortisol, sometimes called the "stress hormone," is a commonly known glucocorticoid. Glucocorticoids have many functions, one of which is to prepare the body for "fight or flight" as a response to a threat or stressor. When the "fight or flight" response triggered by the stressful event resolves, the level of glucocorticoids is reduced. However, in chronically stressful or traumatic environments, the body is constantly flooded with a high level of glucocorticoids. The body is meant to return to its unstressed state and normal level of functioning; chronic stress and trauma prohibit a return to this healthy state. Ongoing stress can actually cause hippocampal damage due to the prolonged, abnormally high levels of glucocorticoid hormones in the body. Among other problems, glucocorticoids play a significant role in disrupting immune and inflammatory responses as well as cell growth and reproduction. Remember that your body—from your heart to your skin and everything in between—is made of cells. Clearly, ongoing stress— whether created by a traumatic experience or a life filled with chronic stress—does substantial harm to the body that is your home.

This type of long-term damage can be avoided by getting to the root of the issues. By reducing the cause of the chronic stress, whether it is related to trauma or some other source, your physical body and psyche will benefit. If you continue to ignore any sources of chronic stress in your life, the long-term impact can be significant. Destructive fear works to continue the often-unconscious thought patterns and behavior cycles that perpetuate chronic stress. It is possible to have a life that is largely free of ongoing stress and toxic, trauma-related residue. When you reach out to embrace constructive fear, you will find that relief is in store.

Healing Trauma from the Inside Out

Human beings instinctively want to recover from trauma. We thrive when our bodies and psyches are in good form. Pain, whether it exists in the body or the psyche, wears on our ability to flourish in life. Transformational fear has the power to seek out where fear has taken hold in the body, mind, and emotional world. It has the power to expose the distressed areas, release them, and promote healing. You are not meant to live mired in sadness, anger, hatred, or shame—you are not meant to live in fear.

It's important to note that healing from trauma is not a simple journey and often requires extensive psychotherapy. The healing of long-term, chronic trauma such as what Ellie and Alexander experienced requires substantial time and effort. The healing process may take years, often leaving the individual with trauma residue that arises now and again, particularly during times of stress. Singular, less influential forms of trauma may resolve rather readily. Many forms of trauma require a level of care and attention that lies somewhere between these two poles.

Are you ready and willing to heal and set yourself free? A nine-step outline will help you answer this important question.

1. You must have the *desire* to heal.
2. You must have a sincere *readiness* to undertake the journey.
3. You will need to have a *commitment* to the process—to stick with it even and especially when it is difficult.
4. You must have a *willingness to reach out* for additional support when necessary.
5. You will need to *care* enough about yourself to make your healing a priority. Destructive fear may want to sidetrack you with distractions (television, binge eating, video games, etc.); it may also tell you that you're too busy.
6. You will need an *open mind*, as some concepts may seem odd or unfamiliar.
7. You will need to be *patient* with yourself and your journey; your destructive fears did not arise overnight, and they will not disappear overnight.
8. You will need to be *kind and tender* to yourself, appreciating your hard work every step of the way; you deserve as much TLC as you can get.

9. You must have a *nonjudgmental attitude.* This necessary space of nonjudgment allows you to focus on the present, never blaming yourself or others for the past. (Blame gives destructive fear a foothold in your life. For this reason, your healing process *needs* to be free of blame.)

The nine prerequisites for healing may seem simple, yet they are sometimes difficult to achieve. But I know that you can do this. You have the power to embrace transformational fear, to use it to heal and set yourself free.

Emotions and Feelings: A Little Background on a Big Issue

Although your emotional world might seem overly complex, certain key points can help make it understandable. From a physiological model, an emotion is an instinctive bodily response to a stimulus. The limbic system, historically referred to as the brain's emotional processing center, processes stimuli rapidly and prepares you for a speedy response. This important system allows you to form a quick impression of a situation and then utilizes your history to determine how to best respond in the current moment; this system provides necessary information to let you know if you are physically and emotionally safe. Among its other functions, the limbic system controls your emotions to help ensure your survival. When you involuntarily react to a stimulus in fear, it is your limbic system telling you to act this way. Through learning to manage your emotions, you can slow this process down to help ensure that you react to stimuli in a healthy, beneficial way.

As you delve into your emotional world more fully, it's important to have a basic understanding of how your feelings and emotions work. We often use the words *emotions* and *feelings* interchangeably, but they are quite different from each other. Emotions are the body's response to an environmental stimulus, and feelings are the brain's response to the felt emotion. For example, if you see a person (the stimulus) who hurt you, your body might instinctively respond with the *emotions* of anger and fear. A *feeling* would arise as your brain interprets your body's emotional response to this person; you might feel anxious, worried, terrified, or furious. In short, emotions arise in your body as a response to an event. Your thoughts then kick in and combine with your initial emotional response to create your feelings. One or more of the basic emotions underlies every one of your feelings.

How many emotions and feelings do you have? Many theorists have offered their opinions on the number and type of human emotions. Some say that there are only four core emotions—fear, sadness, anger, and joy.[9] Others add emotions such as disgust, shame, and surprise to the list, and some theorize that humans have many more emotions, with one researcher offering a list of twenty-seven.[10] Robert Plutchik's psychoevolutionary theory offers a basic, yet inclusive, outline of human emotions: joy, sadness, trust, disgust, fear, anger, anticipation, and surprise.[11] There is no hard-and-fast rule; you can adjust this list to make it feel right for you.[12]

Interestingly, although there are relatively few primary emotions, the English language has thousands of words to describe the vast array of feelings that stem from this basic set of emotions. Our language gives us the freedom to choose from a myriad of words to describe how we feel. With this freedom comes an interesting responsibility. Indeed, it's not always easy to slow down to access the appropriate words to describe how you really feel. Our culture does not necessarily support feeling-based communication. Sometimes, we are so shut down that we don't know what we are feeling. When someone asks, "How are you feeling?" common responses might be, "I'm fine," "I'm good," or "I feel OK." None of these sentences actually describe feelings. Examples of feeling-based responses include, "I feel frustrated right now," "I feel very excited," and "I feel gloomy." Many people simply never learned about feelings and therefore might not have a good vocabulary of feeling words. If feelings confound you or scare you, don't worry; you can learn how to express your feelings—all of them—in positive, healthy ways.

Emotions are extremely important and worth investigating more fully. The emotional world can seem overwhelming and even frightening, yet emotions give flavor and depth to life. Without them, we would move through the world with all the personality and flair of a computer. As you learn to understand your emotions, you will find them a wonderful source of healthy expression and inner freedom. Actual physiological changes arise in your body when you experience an emotion. When you feel afraid, you may tense up and your heart might race. When filled with joy, you may have more vibrant energy and a sense of buoyancy. If feeling sad, you may be tearful, sluggish and weary. When feeling angry, you may be highly irritable and very edgy. Your emotions, whether you notice them or not, are experienced in your physical body, the "home" of your emotional world.

You might have noticed that joy is the only "positive" emotion in the core, four-item list of emotions (anger, sadness, joy, and fear). Anger, sadness, and fear are commonly termed "negative" emotions, yet the emotions are not inherently negative; it is how an emotion is used (or misused) that can have negative results. That said, why would humans be hardwired to feel more negative emotions than positive ones? In short, our emotions are designed to protect us; they are part of our basic survival system. Our emotions are designed to warn us away from dangerous experiences. For this reason, we are predisposed to negative emotions because they are intended to keep us safe. Each emotion carries with it an impulse to take action. Joy carries with it the urge to connect and engage with others, to reach outward in a positive way. Conversely, sadness makes us want to deactivate and turn inward, to contract, hide away, and self-soothe. Fear can make us want to run, fight, freeze, or appease; the strongest urge is often immediate flight. Anger is activating; it turns on the powerful urge to fight, to destroy the enemy. The primitive, basic purpose of human emotions is to propel the individual to some sort of protective or helpful action.

These concepts are extremely important; they are the foundation for how you experience yourself and how you experience your life. If you grew up in an environment where emotions and feelings were disregarded or not allowed, this work will be particularly helpful for you. Be patient with yourself, for the process of increasing emotional awareness is both rewarding and challenging. Remember, your journey with transformational fear relies on your awareness and understanding of the fundamental concepts you are learning. You might want to think of them as pieces of your basic toolkit in the life-changing work ahead. The more familiar you are with each tool—each aspect of what makes you who you are—the more capable you will feel as you venture forward. When you feel informed and capable, you will embrace and utilize your vast inner power to change.

The Basics of Healing Trauma

Emotions do not affect every person in the same way. Human beings are not all the same physiologically, and this includes the realms of emotional sensitivity and emotional intensity. Research has revealed that some people are physiologically more sensitive to emotions.[13] It is important to note that these physiological predispositions can be affected by other factors, such as active addictions and trauma history. Indeed, research reflects that those with a history of trauma are more vulnerable to the "negative" emotions of fear, sadness, and anger.[14]

Emotional regulation is not only an important aspect of healing from trauma, it is also a vital component of overall psychological well-being. Emotional regulation is often described as the mental and behavioral processes used to influence emotional states. Those who do not have sufficient skills in this arena may tend to feel overwhelmed or controlled by their emotions. If you can recall a time in your life when you felt completely overcome by your emotions—wild anger, debilitating sadness, or immobilizing fear—you know how terrible this sense of overwhelming emotion can feel. Unmanageable emotions can make us feel as though we have been hijacked by something that is, all at once, inside us and yet completely beyond our control.

One of the most damaging effects of trauma is its ability to erode the sufferer's sense of self-efficacy. Self-efficacy, sometimes referred to as confidence, is often defined as the belief in one's ability to succeed in a certain situation or accomplish a set task. When you recall both Ellie's and Alexander's case studies, it may be clear to you that the trauma they suffered affected each person's sense of self-efficacy. Although both Ellie and Alexander could function in certain areas of life, neither person had an inner sense of being able to cope with life in healthy ways. Both felt out of control—afraid of being irreparably damaged, afraid of being unlovable, afraid of emotions, afraid of relationships, afraid of failure, and afraid of life. A foundational sense of self-efficacy is necessary for psychological healing and well-being. For this reason, it has long been recognized that effective treatments focus on increasing self-efficacy, because they support the individual's coping abilities. A beneficial treatment axiom might sound something like this: "You have the ability within yourself to move in a positive direction. Others can be of *assistance* in your journey, but you have the ability to access helpful tools and coping strategies. You have this power within yourself." Treatment strategies based on the concept of increasing self-efficacy validate the individual. You might notice that self-efficacy is built and strengthened by working with transformational fear.

Those who suffer from trauma and chronic stress may lack the flow of ease and flexibility that might be commonplace for others. When the psyche is stressed, the world often seems chaotic. As a response, the trauma sufferer may shut down and become more rigid. At the opposite end, the sufferer may feel extremely agitated, responding in a dysregulated fashion. Whether the emotional cycle is one of immobilization, heightened emotional response, or both, the sufferer can become terrified of the cycle itself. In this way, the cycle of fear—fear of being overtaken or immobilized by emotional experiences—is perpetuated. Experiences that support emotional regulation increase the sufferer's sense of self-efficacy. Healing occurs when the individual learns how to slow down, self-regulate, and cope in healthy ways. When an individual learns to modulate fear-induced emotional responses, new neural pathways are created. These pathways allow the formation of improved patterns of emotional responses, patterns that reinforce self-efficacy. Indeed, having power over one's emotions can be immensely relieving and confidence-building.

Trauma can best be healed by addressing the sufferer's emotional, cognitive, and body-based experiences. Research shows that the most effective healing treatments focus more on the individual's *internal* experience of the trauma rather than the traumatic event itself.[15] For example, if you were the victim of an assault, it would be important to explore and understand the impact of the actual assault. However, the majority of the focus—the actual healing work—would be accomplished by focusing on the unresolved, often unrealized, impact of trauma through your internal experience. This internal experience involves your emotional responses and the way your body felt during the event. Your internal experience also includes the way your body held and stored the trauma. Remember, your body is a warehouse for all the emotions you have been unable to process and feel.

Suppressed emotions live a secret (or not-so-secret) life inside the individual; the individual suffers, fearful that this energy will explode. In Alexander's case, his anger would actually detonate in rushes of raw, unfiltered fury. Alexander had, in a sense, become addicted to his anger cycle. Emotions certainly can have an addictive quality to them. Over time, emotional responses can become hard-wired behavior patterns. When the emotion takes charge of the situation, the individual is no longer in control. An emotion in itself is not bad or negative; it is the way the emotion surfaces in a dysregulated state that can be damaging. Unregulated emotions can feel overwhelming and incapacitating; they can make us feel powerless. Overly strong emotions can narrow our ability to notice other options; they limit our capacity to see and consider choices that are beneficial. Additionally, emotions often have a timeless sense about them, as if they will last forever and never allow a respite from their hold. For these reasons, it is natural for us to fear primitive, uncontrollable releases of emotion—it can be deeply terrifying for both the person experiencing the emotion and any person nearby. Although his anger gave Alexander a sense of power, it also terrified him. Alexander's anger had become his master; he was captive to its destructive force.

Through his journey, Alexander found that a host of emotions and feelings were hiding beneath his anger: sadness, frustration, hurt, fury, sorrow, and shame were just a few that he found simmering underneath. Men are often raised to believe that anger is the singular acceptable emotion. Sadness and fear are often thought to be for "sissies" only. By contrast, women are often raised to avoid or shut down anger; as such, many have no idea how to work effectively with angry emotions. In this way, destructive fear steps in through the emotion of anger.

When any emotion is shut off, whether as a result of personal history (e.g., parental modeling), societal expectations, or other forces, something else moves in to take place of the unfelt emotion. Here, again, destructive fear gets a dose of power. No matter which emotion is shut down, avoided, or cut off, it will arise in another form. Passive-aggressive behavior is a potent example of anger gone awry. Individuals who feel angry but who do not know how to appropriately express their anger may resort to passive-aggressive behavior to get their needs met. These unhealthy, fear-based patterns manifest in many ways.

For example, imagine a wife saying to her husband, "Oh, there are weeds in the garden." The husband feels angry—he's actually hurt—but he doesn't say anything. He sulks and stuffs down his feelings. Later, these feelings come out in an angry outburst: "I get no appreciation around here. You think you're perfect, but you are impossible to live with. No matter how hard I work, you are never satisfied." Sadly, the wife may not know the cause of the outburst. She may just be left with the hurt from the sarcastic, negative comments. Rather than using passive-aggressive behavior, the husband could reach out in a way that would lead to understanding. He might say, "Honey, I felt hurt when you made that comment about the garden. It felt like you were criticizing me for not doing the weeding. Is that what you were doing?" The wife might then say, "Honey, I apologize. I didn't mean to hurt your feelings. I was thinking out loud—I meant to do the weeding last week. I just didn't get to it. Maybe we can have fun gardening together this weekend." These minute modifications in emotional awareness are incredibly empowering. Although they often seem minor in the moment, these small shifts can help prevent—and heal—intrapersonal and interpersonal disruptions, many of which arise from patterns learned in childhood. In this way, destructive fear loses the power to insert itself. Constructive fear steps in to create emotional intimacy, transforming the misunderstanding into a connective experience.

As another example, a woman may want to purchase something that she knows her husband won't support. Afraid of discussion and confrontation, the woman goes behind her husband's back and makes an especially costly purchase out of resentment. In taking this approach, she avoids having to face the emotional discomfort of speaking her mind and discussing the issue. Her relationship with destructive fear grows stronger every time she resorts to passive-aggressive behaviors. In this case, the wife would be far better served by being assertive and openly stating her need or desire to her spouse. The resulting discussion, even if it proved difficult, could be used by the couple to build healthy, connective patterns. Although the shift in behavior might bring up anxiety and fear due to entrenched, unhealthy patterns of behavior (behaviors that, once again, most likely began in childhood), the old patterns—once replaced by healthy patterns—will begin to relinquish control. The helpful face of constructive fear would move in to guide the couple in discussions that promote emotional awareness, transparency, and fluidity in the relationship.

Later chapters will touch on communication and emotions in more depth. Yet the above examples may give you a basic understanding of how simple shifts in emotional awareness can be used to create substantial transformations. These little changes are accessible to you. With practice, you can hone them and make them part of your routine. As you continue to increase your awareness, you will notice that small, seemingly insignificant fear-based patterns created big clogs in your life. You will become generally more aware of what is healthy for you and what is not. You will find yourself choosing constructive behaviors more and more often. Every positive change that you make, every piece of awareness that you gain, will create a shift in your life. Although the shifts may seem small and barely perceptible at times, the fear-based patterns that have been holding you back will start to release their hold.

Noticing Stuck Emotions

This next exercise will help you build your emotional awareness. It also creates an opportunity for gentle self-healing. First, make certain that you are in a safe, relaxed environment. Check in with yourself to be sure that you are well-rested and psychologically ready to continue this part of your journey. Remember that an absence of self-judgment is very important. Simply allow yourself to observe what arises. Do not judge it; just observe.

With your journal and pen at your side, imagine stepping back from yourself. Imagine a time that you felt *stuck* within a certain emotion. Imagine the situation in detail. For example, you might recall a time you felt so angry that you wanted to throw a plate against the wall. You might recall even acting out by throwing the plate. You might recall feeling so sad, so heartbroken, that you cried in bed for two days. Perhaps you have a memory of being so frightened that you literally could not move; you were frozen in your tracks. Whatever the situation, notice it in detail as if you are hovering above yourself. Notice the emotion. Notice how it felt in your body. Notice, if you can, how the emotion felt in your body when it first "arrived." Notice if it grew stronger. Notice what, if anything, made the emotion intensify in your body. Notice how long the emotion seemed to last. Notice, if you can, how long the emotion *actually* lasted. This is important, for emotions often feel like they last much longer than they actually do. Notice what made the emotion dissolve—was it a person, a thought, a behavior (e.g., exercise), the passage of time, or something else? When you are finished, make notes. Breathe. Sit with yourself and notice if other thoughts or bodily sensations arise. Make notes that are important to you. Utilize your cleansing breathes to relax. Well done!

You are now ready to go a little deeper. By exploring Alexander's patterns of emotional dysregulation, your understanding of emotional regulation will grow. Alexander's history is highly complex, yet it is easy to relate to many aspects of his overall situation. How could Alexander begin the healing process? First, Alexander needed to feel *safe*. Essential to healing is the ability to work in a safe, supportive environment. Alexander had to feel connected and safe with me (his "guide") and the surroundings (my office). Then, Alexander was ready to *learn* about emotions. He felt more confident when he had the ability to label what he was feeling inside. Next, Alexander learned how to *identify* what emotions he was feeling, He learned to notice when an emotion was "coming on" or forming in his body; this awareness gave him relief. Alexander became adept at identifying how his body felt when various feeling states arose. He got used to the "tingles" of anxiety. He became familiar with the "edginess" of frustration. He became aware of the encroaching "heat" of early anger. As Alexander came to *acknowledge* these aspects of his emotional world, he felt more aware and more in control of his intrapersonal world. With a great deal of patience and effort, Alexander learned that he had the power to self-regulate, to slow himself down. He found within himself the capacity to feel his emotions and then choose the responses that would work for him, not against him. In this way, Alexander found freedom. What Alexander developed was a deep, solid sense of knowing he could trust himself to respond in generally healthy ways. Alexander no longer lived in fear of his emotions; he did not worry that they would consume him. Alexander used his constructive fear to tease apart his emotions; over time, he made friends with every emotion in his repertoire.

The work that Alexander undertook was not easy. At first, he would "relapse" into old, hardwired patterns. With patience and conscious awareness, he continued to work on improving his emotional regulation abilities through each day. He found early success with low-level triggers, such as frustration when his doctor's office rescheduled a medical appointment. By utilizing the healthy emotional regulation strategies he was learning, Alexander began to take charge of his emotions. He discovered the power of simple strategies such as slowing down to breathe, counting to ten, and identifying how he was feeling. Relationship issues were more difficult for him, but he didn't give up. His wife was supportive, and he persevered. As is common, Alexander had learned that his old, fear-based habits tended to reemerge under times of stress. Whenever Alexander felt hungry, angry, lonely, or tired (HALT), he knew he might be more susceptible to outbursts and other harmful patterns. The acronym HALT reminded him to be especially mindful if he was in any of these states. Alexander also came to notice that being hungry or tired made him more likely to engage in old, problematic patterns. Interestingly, this became a bonding opportunity for Alexander and his wife. She became more aware of Alexander's eating habits and needs; she supported him by offering frequent, nutritional snacks. As Alexander said, "I like the food she gives me, but I really like the attention and the TLC." Alexander became more aware of his sleep hygiene, and he began to realize that he was much less irritable and on-guard when he was well-rested. Laughing at himself, he told me, "A well-rested and well-fed Alexander is a much happier Alexander."

Alexander found it helpful to make a very specific outline that supported his emotional regulation efforts. He kept one copy of his personalized strategy on his refrigerator and another one on the bathroom mirror. The visual reminder gave Alexander additional safety and security; he liked knowing that his customized protocol was readily accessible. He also felt comforted knowing that his wife was supportive and aware of every step of his process. At the top of his outline, he had written, "I have the power to make good choices. I don't need or want to act on every urge I have." Below the heading, he wrote:

1. Notice my emotion.
2. Breathe.
3. Feel it coming in my body.
4. Breathe and count to ten.
5. Acknowledge the emotion—give it a name.
6. Communicate the emotion ("I feel———!").
7. Don't act on the emotion.
8. Take a break (walk) if I need or want more time.
9. Consider and choose healthy responses.
10. Do something that feels rewarding (hot tub or shower).
11. Give myself positive feedback.

In general, emotional regulation can be accomplished through patiently practicing several important steps over and over again, just as Alexander did. Patience and perseverance are key, for old habits are very strongly hardwired in the brain. As you become more adept at managing your emotional world, your new responses will become natural. The old habits that have harmed you will fade away. Although old patterns may want to resurface during times of stress, your tools will help you navigate even the most stressful situations. The steps below are highly detailed; they

can be modified to suit your personality and individual needs. I call this
outline "Simple Steps for Healthy Emotional Regulation."

1. Notice when an emotion is starting to negatively affect you
   (when you feel "hooked" by it).
2. Notice the sensations in your body (racing heart, constricted
   chest, shallow breathing).
3. Slow down. Breathe. Count to ten. Remain focused on your
   breath.
4. Identify and name the emotion or feeling (irritation, sadness,
   shame, rage, etc.).
5. Slow down. Breathe. Count to ten again. Remain focused on
   your breath.
6. Notice, once again, the sensations in your body (racing heart,
   constricted chest, rapid breathing).
7. Notice where the emotion is stuck or held; allow it to move.
8. Notice if aspects of the emotional energy are shifting; notice if
   you can release or "let go" of that energy.
9. Express the emotion or feeling by saying "I feel angry," "I feel
   hurt," "I feel sad," "I feel criticized," etc.
10. Refrain from acting on the emotion.
11. Distract yourself with a visual, situational, or mental shift.
12. Avoid additional known triggers that might worsen the emotion.
13. Move your body in a way that feels beneficial (take a walk, step
    outside, stretch, or do jumping jacks); refrain from aggressive
    actions such as hitting a punching bag.
14. Check in with yourself; notice how you feel (tired, weary, spent,
    energized, etc.).
15. Engage in a self-soothing behavior (taking a warm shower, medi-
    tating, drinking a cup of tea, etc.).
16. Anchor or ground yourself by sitting on the floor, lying down on
    a firm surface, or placing your flat hands on a wall. Breathe.
17. Reward yourself with a kind statement or other reinforcing
    behavior.

By taking the above steps, you slow down your emotional response
system. You build a healthy awareness of your learned, hardwired patterns, and you learn how to create new ones that work *for* you, not against
you. Remember, emotional responses are addictive in nature and are

fundamentally reinforcing, even when they cause you significant distress and pain. Your emotional behavior patterns, be they constructive or destructive, become self-reinforcing. As you practice, your constructive patterns will get stronger and your destructive patterns will weaken. You will learn how to "sit" with your emotions—how to not be controlled or ruled by them. With practice, you will learn not to react but to respond; you will learn how to choose your behavior. You will learn how to expand your ability to pause, breathe, and slow down your system; you will learn to self-regulate. During this journey, you will learn how to transform your world through the slow, steady wisdom of transformational fear.

Increasing Your Emotional Awareness and Emotional Regulation

In this chapter's last exercise, you will have the opportunity to increase your emotional awareness and work with emotional regulation. First, make certain that your environment is safe and relaxed. Check in with yourself; it's important to be well-rested and psychologically ready for your exercise. As always, allow yourself to observe whatever arises for you; do not judge your thoughts or emotions. Have your journal and pen with you.

Step into the role of an observer, as though you can see yourself in a movie. Now, imagine a time that you felt overwhelmed or controlled by a certain emotion or emotions. Recall the nature of the emotion and give it a name (e.g., raging anger, blue sadness, gripping fear). Recall the way the emotion felt in your body. Remember to remain as detached as possible. Imagine the situation in detail, even your surroundings. Now imagine the situation that triggered the emotional angst. Then focus on your own being. Look at yourself with an attitude of acceptance and compassion.

Imagine that you can see *into* your body, as though you are wearing special glasses through which you can see energy, colors, and shapes. Look into your body to see where the emotion took hold. Notice the color, shape, and movement. Was it red, black, yellow, or some other color? Did it grow bigger? Did it stay in one place? Notice the details as you observe yourself.

Next, imagine breathing *with* your imagined body. Notice if the breathing helps the emotional energy shift. Continue slow and steady breathing with the imagined self. Notice what happens. Are you able to go back into the situation to calm yourself by breathing slowly? Are you able to calm yourself by focusing on counting to ten? Perhaps it works to imagine feeling the emotion and then "letting go" of it. Then imagine taking yourself into another room. Does that feel better? Perhaps the angry, hurt, or scared self feels soothed with a distraction (knitting, writing, listening to music, or watering plants). Notice what does and does not work to lessen the hold of the overwhelming energy. Now see your imagined self doing something "grounding." Perhaps it feels good to lie down on the floor, sit on a chair, or place both hands on a cool, solid wall. Maybe you choose to go on a walk, meditate, or take a bath. Notice what feels good to your body. Notice how much power you have to choose behaviors that make you feel more at peace. Notice what made the emotion dissolve more fully in this exercise. Were you able to better regulate the emotion by distracting yourself, releasing the emotion, moving, and grounding yourself? What were you able to do—what did you create and choose—that made the situation better? When you are finished, make notes. Breathe.

Sit with yourself and notice if other thoughts or bodily sensations arise. Make notes that are important to you. Then notice that you have created a template for your own self-regulation needs. Breathe again. You now have made a new pathway in your brain for helpful, constructive patterns. Congratulate yourself on a job *very* well done.

As you may have noticed, this work is not easy. There are times in your journey that you may want to reach out for additional guidance and support; this is normal and beneficial. What is most vital in this section is this message: Healing, whether it is focused on small issues or larger ones, is absolutely within your reach. With the power of transformational fear at your side, you have the ability to access the tools you are creating and putting into action.

It takes time and energy to let transformational fear move into your life. As you explore your personal history, your triggers, and your emotional world, some of your old wounds will surface. Your old, destructive fear may rise up and tell you to run, that it's too much work. It might tell you that you'll always be broken, that you'll "never get better." Remember, this is just the enemy face of fear talking. The constructive, friendly face of fear wants to help you. It wants your psyche and body to release the pain they have been holding. This is how constructive, beneficial fear works. It allows the old psychic wounds to call out; they want your attention. By working with whatever arises in a "holistic" way (taking care of your body and psyche), you will find greater relief. You will see, experience, and practice new possibilities. You will not give up. You will embrace the full power of transformational fear, and it will set you free.

CHAPTER 4

Fear-Based Patterns and Health: Moving into Wellness

What Is Wellness?

This chapter is all about *you* and your overall well-being. So get ready as we delve into the world of wellness—a place where destructive fear often sneaks in to make a home, creating patterns that work against your physical and psychological well-being. To move toward greater wellness, it's helpful to have a working definition of what wellness means to you, for wellness can be defined in many ways. Some describe wellness as being free from illness. Others define wellness as eating and sleeping "well enough." Some see wellness through the lens of a scale, feeling well only when their weight is within a certain range. Still others need to be able to exercise, laugh, and play to feel well. Some who have suffered through cancer treatments or life-threatening surgeries describe wellness in terms of "knowing I have survived." Others see wellness as the absence of health issues. When we think of wellness, we often confine our description to the familiar, physical plane of life.

Over time, my personal description of wellness has become very inclusive. My current definition of wellness is this: an active, conscious, and evolving process of making ever-wiser choices that benefit the body and psyche to create a dynamic, positive life filled with joy, love, and serenity. Personal definitions are important, for each one of us really needs to know what is required to feel well. What one person may find essential may be unimportant to another. Your definition of wellness may morph over time. Indeed, a significant life change can initiate a revamping of wellness and related priorities. Yet all too often, we move through life without attending to or being aware of these vital aspects of our lives. This chapter will allow you to slow down and explore more of your inner world. It will give you the opportunity to tune into yourself and what you *really* want and need.

Creating Your Initial Description of Wellness

This exercise provides the opportunity for you to reflect on your personal definition of wellness. There is no right or wrong definition of wellness nor any need to define it in fancy terms. Your personal reflection—the generation of your own, unique definition—is most important. So prepare for this chapter's first exercise. Create a safe place, and pull out your journal and pen.

Draw an image of wellness. Then write out the whatever wellness-oriented words come to you. Let your imagination flow. Then write out your own definition of wellness—a sentence or two is plenty. Ponder the definition you have created. Feel the emotions that arise. Imagine this aspect of wellness forming, growing, and manifesting in your life. If destructive fear comes in to tell you that wellness is beyond your reach or power, simply notice its presence. Do not feed it with judgment or commentary. Just go back to your image of wellness. Instead, feed the constructive face of transformational fear that beckons you to imagine a life filled with wellness. Make any notes that feel important to you. When you have finished, breathe deeply. Well done. You have taken another important step forward.

You are not alone if creating wellness hasn't been at the forefront of your to-do list. We take much in life for granted, often ignoring the simple beauty and fluidity of life—until something goes awry. It's often only during a time of physical or psychological challenge that you might pause to notice your own well-being. When you are so stressed that you forget to pay your bills or you are plagued by a cough you can no longer ignore, you might pause to say "Something is off!" or "I don't feel well." Sadly, we often give focused attention to ourselves and our lives only when difficulties arise. Much of the time, we merely struggle to get by, often ignoring the tune-ups and careful attention that will keep us truly *well*. When you are run down, you are far more susceptible to the invasive tendencies of destructive fear. Remember, destructive fear will want to keep you stuck in patterns that keep it going. Constructive fear will want to guide you away from these harmful patterns and toward behaviors that give you serenity and joy. Transformational fear will allow you to create wellness no matter what the day brings your way.

In our hectic world, the struggle for daily physical survival can seem overwhelming. Emotional well-being can seem unimportant for those who are struggling to stay afloat. Many people tend to downplay the importance of mental health, favoring areas that are easier or more familiar to them. For example, some people readily call the doctor's office at the sign of a cold or stomach ache, and some are far more inclined to check their bank balance than the status of their internal, emotional world.

Psychological well-being often takes a backseat. Whether as a result of societal stigmas, lack of awareness, or simple indifference, psychological issues are all too often ignored. For those who undervalue the importance of a healthy psyche, I ask them one question: If you were faced with the choice of having only one healthy part of your being, your body or your psyche, which would you choose? This is an important, telling dilemma; it helps puts the personal definition of well-being into sharper focus. If you had a perfectly healthy body but your mind was unsound, would you be happy? If you had a perfectly happy mind but your body was unsound, would you be happy? I ask myself this very question now and again. Although I'd prefer never to be faced with having to choose between a healthy body and a healthy psyche, I would choose the healthy psyche, for I know a perfectly fit and healthy body would do me no good if my psyche were lost in a place of fear, darkness, and despair.

Now it's your turn. Pause to reflect before you arrive at your response to the above dilemma. Does your response align with the definition of wellness you created in the exercise above? As always, there is no correct or incorrect response. This is simply an opportunity for you to explore and understand yourself a little more fully. With transformational fear as your guide, you will enliven and expand this vital area of your world.

Moving into a Deeper Relationship with Wellness

When we look at wellness holistically, we can better appreciate how all dimensions of personal wellness are interconnected. Although personal wellness includes many factors (physical, psychological, spiritual, intellectual, social, financial, occupational, and environmental), this chapter will focus on certain physical and psychological components of your relationship with wellness. The other aspects of wellness will be included peripherally within areas of this chapter, whereas others—such as spiritual wellness—will be explored in later chapters.

As you delve into the realms of your physical, psychological, and spiritual wellness, you will naturally notice how you are faring in each one of these dimensions. This awareness will help you become more connected to your sense of overall wellness. You might sense that certain areas of your personal wellness are balanced and vibrant, whereas others are dormant or constrained by fears. This tuning-in process will allow you to consider those areas that might benefit from more attention. This type of reflection provides the opportunity to shift your priorities as needed in order to gain balance and wellness in your life as a whole. As you read, notice if destructive fear wants to step in and foster judgments, criticism, or blame. If you notice this happening, allow constructive fear to enter with its wise, compassionate voice that will say, "Breathe. This journey of life and transformation is a process. Let's leave judgment and negativity outside the door."

The following pages will guide you into an exploration of physical and psychological wellness in a gentle, step-by-step manner. As you read, you may notice that each dimension is intertwined with other aspects. Wellness is much like a living organism; the whole is affected by the various parts. You may find that personal wellness is a much bigger and more important arena than you thought. Notice if certain areas seem to be more interesting to you and if some sections seem to "call out" for attention. Notice if destructive fear wants to chime in and judge you as you read. Notice if it wants you to close the book or ignore certain sections. If this happens, let the voice of constructive fear remind you of your courageous journey into wellness. Let constructive fear whisper to you: *You are worthy and valuable. You deserve wellness. You deserve to let go of all the things that hold you back. You deserve to embrace the things that bring you true health and joy.* As you read, notice how an in-depth look at wellness brings your own being—your entire world—into sharper focus.

You and Your Physical Wellness

Let's first look at your overall physical wellness. Although some of this may seem rather basic, our busy lives make it easy to miss some of the essential components of good self-care. Physical health includes proper medical care, a healthy diet, regular exercise, sufficient sleep, and generally maintaining your physical body (showering, brushing your teeth, etc.). Some of these aspects of physical wellness are in your own hands—decided, administered, and nurtured by you. Others rely on the support of professionals, such as routine medical checkups, taking medicine as prescribed, and seeking proper medical care when needed. In our busy world, it can be easy to overlook these essentials.

When it comes to medical care, it's vital that you create a partnership with your medical team. It's easy to become fearful or to rely heavily on medical staff to make decisions for you, but those in the field of medicine are only human. Before visiting your doctor, it is helpful to prepare a list of questions to help you obtain answers that are clear and understandable. If you don't feel up to being your own advocate for any reason, a friend or family member can take the lead. If you are on medication or dealing with a chronic health issue, consider keeping a log to track any changes in mood, weight, behavior, or other important factors. Self-advocacy is an important component of physical wellness. In general, life's challenges and stressors will be much easier to handle when you give proper attention to your physical health. As you consider making changes to improve your physical well-being, note that it's vital to consult your physician before altering your diet, health care, or exercise routines.

Destructive fear wants you to believe that you can "get by" without paying too much attention to your physical health, yet cumulative damage to the physical body accrues over time. Although an occasional glass of wine or bar of chocolate may do your spirit good, continuing patterns of excess are unhealthy. A balanced lifestyle allows for treats now and again. Take the time to notice if your habits are *generally* healthful or *generally* unwholesome. Is a dinner of french fries and burgers or pizza the routine or the exception? Has fad dieting become a way of life, or have you embraced a healthy diet as part of your lifestyle? Notice as you read if destructive fear wants to step in to support and rationalize any behaviors that might not be very healthy.

Alcohol

Alcoholic beverage consumption is an area where daily use is often minimized. It has generally been recommended that women of all ages and men over age sixty-five have no more than one glass of alcohol (12 fluid ounces of beer, 5 fluid ounces of wine, or 1.5 fluid ounces of distilled 80-proof spirits) per day. For men sixty-five and under, the general recommendation has been no more than two alcoholic drinks per day. However, new research recommends no more than one drink per day for all adults.[1] When working with clients, I've noted that problematic behaviors such as excessive alcohol consumption are often underestimated. For example, I listened as a wife "came clean" on behalf of her highly stressed husband. As he sat shaking his head, she declared, "He says he has only two drinks every evening, but you should see the size of his glass. For each drink, he puts in over half a cup of vodka, ice, and a can of tonic in a giant-sized tumbler. That has to be the equivalent of at least six or seven drinks a night." Another client mentioned that she had "a little bit of wine" every evening to deal with her chronic anxiety. Her husband offered an important clarifying adjustment: "When she says a 'little bit,' she really means that she drinks one full bottle and a 'little bit' of the second one." Another client felt that her alcohol consumption was troublesome. This single woman noted, "I drink more during the week; it helps me not feel so alone. On the weekends, I use alcohol as a social lubricant. But I don't track how much I really drink." I suggested that she buy a small notebook to log her alcohol consumption. After two weeks of tracking her usage, she brought in her log. "I can't believe it!" she exclaimed as she pointed at her notes. "I'm averaging two glasses of wine every night, and three or more on the weekend evenings. I wasn't paying attention before—or maybe I just didn't want to know."

Stories like these are not uncommon, for destructive fear tends to work its way in stealthily; once present, its grip can be very strong and unyielding. Yet its power begins to lessen the moment you begin to become aware of its presence in a nonjudgmental, curious way. If you or a loved one tends to minimize excessive alcohol consumption or some other unhealthy habit, begin to notice how destructive fear might be at work. Pause to notice *why* you are drinking. Is it because you enjoy the taste? Does it help you connect socially? Or is because you feel as if you *need* to drink to cope? If you are drinking in order self-anesthetize or cope, which of life's stressors (e.g., work, relationships, or financial issues) are you hoping to avoid by numbing yourself with substances? Let constructive fear come in with a gentle prod toward noticing what is going on within you. Imagine creating more healthful, balanced behavior patterns that are based in transformation rather than fear-based avoidance. Allow constructive fear to offer alternatives, such as reaching out for support, taking a walk, or meditating. Notice when your old patterns want to keep you stuck in behaviors that ultimately harm you. Remember, destructive fear likes to downplay harmful habits; it does not want you to make positive changes. It's important to note that excessive alcohol consumption and other addictive behaviors can be highly resistant to change; substantial time, focus, commitment, and support are often required to reap lasting relief. Constructive fear will be your patient, informative guide as you utilize the power of transformational fear to create and institute lasting changes.

Diet

A consistent, healthy diet is an important factor in your overall wellness, for when we don't eat well, we tend not to feel our best. This section will touch upon the general key elements of a healthy diet, offering you a few basic, guiding principles. As with other areas of wellness, the principle of balance is critical. In our fast-paced world, it is easy and tempting to get into the habit of eating fast food, prepackaged convenience meals, and frozen dinners. When we resort to processed foods now and again, no real harm is done. However, chronically unwholesome patterns can sneak in and become a way of life. Constructive fear wants to help you eat and live healthfully.

In a nutshell, research continues to show that diets low in processed foods and sugars along with plant-based diets consisting mainly of dark green leafy plants, fruits, beans, whole grains, and fish are the healthiest.[2] According to the American Heart Association, a largely plant-based diet is "associated with a 42 percent reduced risk of developing heart failure among people without diagnosed heart disease or heart failure."[3] If this sounds wholly unpleasant, take heart; as you learn to care for your body, many of the unhealthy foods you formerly found tempting will lose their appeal.

If creating a wholesome diet is a weak spot for you, notice if destructive fear is holding you back. Notice if your eating habits are based on thought patterns that lead you down the wrong path. Destructive fear often sneaks in by saying that making healthy food is too time consuming. It might tell you that healthful food is too expensive or unavailable.[4] Its insistent voice might say that three cups of coffee or an energy drink is just what you need to get through the day. This negative fear might try to trick you by telling you that you "deserve" to eat a pint of ice cream or a half box of chocolates as a "reward" of some kind. Begin to notice how destructive messages sneak in. Let the healthy, constructive voice make itself known. Allow it to tell you that you are worthy of wholesome food. Let it remind you that healthy, fresh food need not be out of reach. Try these easy tips:

- Choose your least busy day to do weekly meal prepping. You can cook one huge meal and save the leftovers for meals throughout the week. If you make more than you need, freeze the extras for later.
- Inexpensive slow cookers are an increasingly popular tool in creating low-cost, healthy dinners for those low on time.
- Create a shopping list in advance. You can minimize costly impulse purchases by sticking to the list.
- If a discount grocery store is an option, items can cost substantially less than those found in traditional stores. Look for low-cost store brand options that are of equal quality to expensive brand name products. Check store fliers for weekly sale items.
- Buy in bulk. For example, a ten-pound bag of potatoes often costs only slightly more than a five-pound bag.

As you explore your new relationship with food shopping, preparation, and consumption, your awareness in these areas will expand. As you open up to new options, constructive fear will make food your friend.

One of destructive fear's favorite tactics is to divide food into strict categories of "good" and "bad." When the "bad" stuff becomes off limits, it can become more tempting. Indeed, this is a very devious face of fear, for this sly message leads to and perpetuates many unhealthy behaviors. Allow constructive fear to tell you the truth; let it remind you that balance is key. Let this friendly aspect of fear allow you to create healthy treats that are *true* rewards to your body. For example, I once had a penchant for mint truffles; they became an often-forbidden reward. As I learned how to bring greater wellness into my life, my relationship with food also changed. When food became my friend—not my enemy—I discovered that my tastes shifted naturally. As I learned to listen to my body, I lost my fear of food—the fear of eating too much or too little. Although an occasional chocolate can taste lovely, I am not pulled by the "power of the forbidden." When nothing is completely "off limits," balance can be learned and nurtured.

As you learn to listen to your body, you will know when it is hungry and when it is not. You will notice when your stomach starts to become full, and you will naturally want to stop eating when your stomach says "Enough." When destructive fear steps in to tell you to continue eating, let the friendly face of fear remind you that you're full. The friendly face of fear will tell you to take the rest of your food to go or to wrap it up for tomorrow's dinner. Destructive fear might plead, "Oh, just eat it all now; it tastes so good." It might take the voice of your parents and say, "You'd better finish every last bite—there are starving children in Africa!" As you listen to yourself more and more, you will notice how devious these old thought patterns can be. You will learn to step back and listen with a non-judgmental attitude. The voice of constructive fear will become stronger as you learn to pause and listen. To help this process, you may consider starting a food-mood journal like Amanda's as described in chapter 2. As you take the time to truly consider what you eat, this beneficial fear will help you notice when you are satiated. It will help you notice what foods taste healthy and nourishing. It will help you steer away from foods that leave you feeling heavy and sluggish. Constructive fear will help you see food as a source of healthy energy—not a source of chronic angst. It will allow you to see food as a friend—not an enemy.

As you become accustomed to this new relationship, food will no longer have a symbolic power over you. You will learn to listen to your wise inner self as you journey forward with transformational fear.

Sleep

Consistent, good sleep is a vital, often discounted aspect of physical wellness. The Centers for Disease Control and Prevention found that over one-third of American adults are not getting sufficient sleep, defined as less than seven hours per night.[5] Surveys have found that up to seventy-five percent of people experience sleep difficulties at least a few nights every week. These statistics are troubling, for the risk of developing a serious, chronic disease is associated with insufficient sleep. For example, diabetes, depression, obesity, stroke, heart disease, and high blood pressure have all been linked to sleeping less than seven hours per day. Research shows that interrupted or restless sleep can be even more harmful than insufficient sleep.[6]

Sleep is the vital time when your body rests and restores itself after a long day. As the following examples will highlight, the human body requires sufficient sleep to repair itself and function efficiently. In general, cellular repair and memory consolidation occur during sleep. Sleep gives your heart, blood vessels, and other vital body systems time to rest and heal. Without proper sleep, the all-important immune system suffers and does not respond as effectively to infections. Diabetes has been linked to sleep quality, for the body's response to insulin is affected by insufficient sleep. Sufficient sleep is necessary for proper brain function; deficient sleep contributes to poor decision-making, emotional dysregulation, inattentiveness, problem-solving difficulties, and lack of focus. Because poor sleep hampers the brain's ability to process emotions, the symptoms of anxiety and depression often increase when the sufferer is sleep-deprived. Those who are affected by issues such as anxiety often have a lower tolerance for interrupted or deficient sleep. Sadly, those who suffer from disturbed or insufficient sleep are often unaware of both the short-term and long-term effects. Some become so accustomed to insufficient sleep that they move through life in a dangerously sleep-deprived state. This is not only self-destructive; it also increases the risk of accidents that result from sleep-associated human error. Many of these problems can be prevented with proper sleep hygiene. When good sleep habits are maintained, the body's systems function at their optimum level—brain cells fire properly, the body's organ systems are rejuvenated, and muscles are rested and ready for the day ahead.[7]

As you might imagine, destructive fear has its hand in sleep deprivation. With its penchant for causing problems, destructive fear thrives on instigating seemingly little actions that snowball into big issues. Many people stay up late to watch "just one more" television episode, finish that last video game, or polish off another school or work project. Late-night texting, computer use, and cell phone use regularly interrupt or delay sleep for countless sleep-deprived individuals. Research continues to show that school and work productivity diminish as a result of poor sleep.[8] When sleep hygiene suffers, so do the personal relationships that are affected by the ensuing frazzled emotions, poor judgment, and reactive minds. Sadly, it's hard to hear the helpful messages of constructive fear when exhaustion has set in. Even as constructive fear pleas for sleep and relaxation, destructive fear's voice often overpowers it. A report from The National Institute of Health states, "After several nights of losing sleep—even a loss of just 1–2 hours per night—your ability to function suffers as if you haven't slept at all for a day or two."[9] Reflect on this statement again, for it is profoundly important. *A sleep loss of only one to two hours per night can affect you as if you had no sleep for one or two days.* Destructive fear thrives in situations where sleep deprivation is chronic.

When you don't give proper attention to your body's sleep needs, your overall wellness suffers more than you may have appreciated. You now have a greater awareness about the importance of sleep. You now can see how poor sleep is often propelled and worsened by destructive fear. Constructive fear wants you to take steps to help create healthier sleep hygiene:

- Have a set bedtime each evening that allows you to obtain at least seven hours of uninterrupted sleep.
- Shut off electronic devices at least two to three hours before bedtime.
- Follow a simple bedtime routine (flossing, brushing, meditating, etc.) that allows you to unwind.
- Keep your bedroom free of electronic devices including cell phones, computers, and televisions.
- Avoid stimulants after lunchtime; this includes coffee, caffeinated tea, and energy drinks. If you need an evening snack, complex carbs are better choices than sugary foods or junk foods.
- Keep a notepad next to your bed to "write off" any thoughts or to-do items that arise to interfere with sleep.
- Use your breathing exercises to help your mind turn off; a calm mental state can lead to great sleep.

- Ask your doctor for a sleep apnea study to ensure that medical issues are not contributing to poor sleep.

Constructive fear thrives when you are well-rested and refreshed; it is strongest when you are aware and tuned in. Consistent, good sleep will support your transformation; it will support your wellness.

Exercise

Let's take a walk in another direction—it's time to home in on the importance of exercise. Our physical well-being relies on staying active. As a species, we are meant to move and play. In the not-so-distant past, our ancestors spent most of their days farming, walking, hunting, crafting, and searching for life's necessities—they moved throughout each day. They were active and busy, waking with the sunrise and falling into exhausted sleep not long after sunset. Within the last few hundred years, daily life has changed dramatically. In today's world, many of us either sit down or stand in one place for the bulk of each day. Our routines generally lack the variable activity that our ancestors relied on for good health. All too often, we wake only to sit down for a quick breakfast. Then we sit down in a car or bus to go to work or school. Depending upon our job, we then sit down at a desk or stand on our feet until lunchtime. Then we sit down at a table (or desk) to eat lunch. Not too long after, we find ourselves back at our desks or standing on our feet until we sit, once again, in the car or bus for the ride home. At home, we sit down once again—this time for dinner. After all of that busyness and "exercise," we often feel too exhausted for the aerobic and weight-bearing exercise our bodies sorely need. Instead, we sit to watch television or focus on a computer screen. Exhausted, we then fall into bed where—if we are blessed with good sleep habits—one-third of each day is spent recharging our bodies so we can do it all over again. This is unfortunate, for the human body is meant for so much more movement and variation—our very physiology is designed for plentiful and varied activities.[10]

It's easy to fall into bad habits, for they sneak into our lives slowly—often under the guise of being harmless. As one single mother confessed, "My son is getting chubby. He eats terribly; I find energy drink cans, empty potato chip bags, and candy wrappers all over. I want him to get off the couch and exercise, but he fights it. He's either on the computer or watching TV. I wish I'd never got him a cell phone. I thought it was a good idea to stay connected and in case of an emergency, but it's a problem. He takes it to bed, and I know he uses it during the night. I shouldn't complain. I need to make changes in my life, too. I need to eat better and get some exercise, but I'm just so exhausted." As this parent later discovered, she could make small, healthy changes that improved her son's life and her own. One of her first steps was to walk ten minutes a day—rain or shine—after work with her son. Before long, they were preparing healthy meals together and living electronics-free after 8 p.m.

Life, indeed, can become very busy, with days filled from dawn to dusk with tasks. Yet the recommended amount of exercise per week—150 minutes[11]—is not that much time; it boils down to just over twenty minutes per day. Think about it! By investing just twenty minutes daily into a physical activity at a moderate or vigorous level, you would be on your way toward greater well-being. If it's difficult to fit in or complete longer periods of exercise, research shows that you can still benefit by separating the physical activity into smaller ten-minute chunks.[12] What matters most is that you consistently engage in a brisk, aerobic physical activity that supports your well-being.

Whether you enjoy exercising solo or find extra fun and connection through exercising with others, consistent physical activity offers profound benefits. Aerobic exercise increases blood circulation and brings more oxygen into your entire body—including your vibrant, wonderful brain. Exercise can result in greater mental clarity and overall improved brain function.[13] Additionally, research shows that the feel-good neurochemicals released during exercise are highly beneficial.[14] Physical activity is known to stimulate the release of endorphins, dopamine, norepinephrine, and serotonin; when you exercise, the resulting flood of these neurochemicals has a positive impact on your overall mood. Even a brisk, ten-minute walk has the power to reduce symptoms of depression and anxiety, decrease your stress level, and fight fatigue. If that's not enough to get you off the couch, remember that regular aerobic exercise improves your overall cardiovascular health. You'll feel better about the amazing body that is your home, for exercise also increases your metabolism, reduces fat, and helps you burn calories. You deserve to exercise, and you deserve the wide-ranging, healthful benefits that exercise brings.

Five Messages to Increase Physical Wellness

This exercise is designed to allow you to reflect on your physical wellness a little more deeply. Remember, the key components of physical health include proper medical attention as needed, a healthy diet, sufficient sleep, exercise, and body maintenance (showering, brushing your teeth, taking prescribed medication, etc.). When you are ready to begin, find yourself in a relaxed, safe space. Have your notebook and pen at your side. Then simply allow yourself to consider five ways that destructive fear may be controlling your physical wellness. It can be helpful to close your eyes for a moment, noticing how this enemy may have stealthily infiltrated your mind. Whatever thoughts come, simply notice them without any judgment attached. For example, destructive fear may be telling you, "You are just too tired to exercise—besides, you have no time for it." It might say, "A regular bedtime is not for you. You have too much to do. Besides, you *like* staying up late." When it comes to diet, destructive fear might say, "You deserve to eat whatever you want and plenty of it. Besides, you're too busy to cook healthy meals. Fast food is good enough." Destructive fear might take another tactic. It might say, "Food is your only comfort; it's the only thing that makes you feel good." Whatever negative, controlling thoughts come, notice them. Use your notebook to write down five of these destructive thoughts. Notice how you feel as you read these messages. Make notes if you wish. Pause to breathe.

Next, carefully shift each message in your mind; let the voice of constructive fear guide you. Using the above examples, constructive fear might prompt you to write, "You can make time to exercise every day at lunch. A brisk, twenty-minute walk is doable and would feel great." For the next item, you might note, "Being well-rested is important; going to bed consistently by 10:30 p.m. will make me feel so much better." As to diet, constructive fear may say, "You deserve to eat healthy food that makes you feel good and also keeps your body healthy. You can make time every Sunday night to cook healthy food that will last you through the week." The last example might be constructively shifted in this way: "You can notice and create other sources of comfort. You can learn to enjoy food as nourishment, not as a replacement for companionship or as a way to drown your fears and feelings of depression." Notice how you feel as you look at the positive messages in your notebook. Make any notations that feel right to you. When you are finished, pause to breathe. Well done! You are moving forward! By inviting transformational fear into your world of wellness, your life will truly change.

You and Psychological Wellness

As you might suspect, your psychological (emotional and mental) wellness is a most critical aspect of your general well-being. Yet what may be a high priority for your own psychological well-being may not be a top priority for someone else. This is where focus and personalized attention will help you notice what is vital for your own emotional and mental health. Although there are many definitions and aspects of psychological wellness, we'll focus on several key factors: self-esteem, self-efficacy, and self-care. Much of this book focuses on utilizing transformational fear to create greater wellness in your overall life. In this section, we will home in on these three specific areas of psychological well-being that deserve a bit more attention and emphasis. As you read, you will notice that these three vital arenas overlap each other. Indeed, optimal psychological well-being generally relies upon the healthy growth, positive interplay, and overall balance of all facets of wellness.

From understanding and accessing your emotional world to creating beneficial coping strategies, the world of psychological wellness may seem endlessly vast and deep. Yet as you learn to harness transformational fear, you will find that you have incredible abilities and resources at your disposal. You will come to utilize and benefit from consistent use of the simple, powerful tools you are learning and personalizing. As you move through this section, you will have the opportunity to notice the areas of your psychological well-being that are riddled with destructive fear. You will continue to work with constructive fear to become aware of your abilities, new possibilities, and transformative changes. Through this work, you may notice actual shifts in your psychological well-being; this is your personal power—your transformational fear—at work.

Self-Esteem

Let's take a close look at self-esteem. Like many words, self-esteem can have different meanings to different people. In the world of psychology, self-esteem is often seen as an enduring personality trait that reflects the individual's overall sense of self-worth or personal regard. (If you suffer from low self-esteem and the word "enduring" brought a jolt of fear, do not worry; self-esteem, like other characteristics, can be transformed over time with dedicated care and attention.) Going a little deeper, your sense of self-esteem is indicative of how you perceive your personal value—how much you value yourself and how much you believe you are valued by those in your world. Our perspective on self-esteem will be broad and encompassing; it will include how you *feel* about yourself and how you *think* about yourself—both positively and negatively. In general, those with a strong sense of self-esteem deeply and genuinely value, like, and appreciate who they are as individuals.

High self-esteem is vital, for it provides supportive roots and the structure necessary for a lifetime of growth. Good self-esteem provides the inner strength and self-belief that foster self-awareness and personal success. The word *esteem* has its origins in the Latin word *aestimare*, the meaning of which is "to estimate or appraise."[15] Self-esteem becomes the lens through which the individual evaluates two important questions: *What am I worth to myself? What am I worth to my loved ones—to the outer world?* Given the fundamental nature of self-esteem, it affects how we think, how we feel, and how we act in public and in private. Our sense of self-esteem affects how we relate to ourselves, our loved ones, our friends, our coworkers, and the world at large.

It's important to pause to distinguish between self-esteem and its rather distant cousin, self-confidence. Self-confidence is often associated with how strong or successful an individual appears to the external world—regardless of the person's actual level of self-value and self-respect. Those who are truly self-confident have trust in their abilities, whether in general or in specific areas, such as math, business, or cooking. Self-confidence is often built after successful life experiences that might include sports, school achievements, or work accomplishments. Self-confidence can also *lead* to successful experiences in life, for it can afford the inner conviction that is needed to undertake certain tasks. Given its limited scope, a person can be self-confident in one area of life yet highly insecure in other areas. Indeed, a person who appears to be self-confident may have very low self-esteem. True self-esteem does not rest on external achievements or successes but comes from a place of internal self-value that reveals itself to the world through genuineness. For instance, a person may appear self-confident to the outside world—wearing the trendiest clothes, driving the most expensive car, or buying the latest gadgets—while feeling like an impostor inside. Some go out into the world with their hair styled, makeup on, and smile fixed—not letting anyone, even those closest to them, know about the wreck inside. An *attitude* of self-confidence can be projected even when the actual quality is lacking; self-confidence can be worn as a mask to cover an inner world filled with feelings of unworthiness and shame. When it comes to illusory self-confidence, you might be fooled by what meets your eyes or ears.

Ultimately, healthy self-esteem can be seen through a person's actions. Those with high self-esteem value themselves and others. Unlike those with poor self-esteem, they have no need to fill a void inside with an array of possessions, relationships, substances, or sexual escapades. Qualities such as respect, honesty, integrity, humility, and kindness are primary when self-esteem is strong. As a result, external pursuits (such as status and wealth) become secondary. Overall, a person with high self-esteem is nonjudgmental, treats the self well, and treats others well; such an outlook promotes self-acceptance and acceptance of others.

One of the beauties of strong self-esteem is the absence of the need or desire to "wear a mask"; no vital internal energy is wasted to create an artificial front. A person with solid self-esteem can be counted upon to be honest and filled with integrity at home, at work, and in society. Key handymen of destructive fear such as artifice and deception are noticeably absent in those with solid self-esteem. Instead, an individual with strong self-esteem is trustworthy to the self and to others.

"Whew!" you might exclaim, "That's a tall order!" It may be, but constructive fear will tell you, "The nature of strong self-esteem may seem demanding, yet it is tempered with wisdom and tolerance." It is conscious, accepting, and compassionate. It doesn't expect perfection—it simply asks for conscious effort and good intention. Strong self-esteem knows that mistakes are a truly inevitable, necessary part of life. Solid self-esteem sees mistakes as a vital opportunity to build greater awareness and strength. It doesn't make excuses or create defenses; it simply wants to learn and grow. Positive self-esteem uses life's mistakes and challenges to foster resilience and inner capacity. When these friendly, uplifting messages from constructive fear are noticed and welcomed, *self-acceptance*—an integral component of self-esteem—moves in to replace the negative voice of destructive fear. The negative, judgmental voice of destructive fear will begin to fade as you leave self-judgment and blame behind. In these ways, positive self-esteem is a close friend to constructive fear. A solid and true sense of self-esteem is an essential component on the journey of transformational fear. Your self-esteem will naturally grow as you learn to listen to the voice of constructive fear. This voice will lead you to notice and envision the positive changes that will make you feel good about yourself and your life. As you take action to make the changes you desire—as you embrace transformational fear—your self-esteem will steadily increase. This is one of the greatest powers of transformational fear. Your self-esteem will grow as you read this book, learn to listen to constructive fear, and take action with the power of transformational fear at your side.

Transforming low self-esteem doesn't happen overnight. It takes desire, time, and ongoing dedication. Strong self-esteem is foundational for overall well-being; it is not optional for those interested in creating lasting joy and transformation. Your sense of self-esteem is a vital element in the matrix of your world. Without good self-esteem, destructive fear will rule you from the inside out. If you are ready and willing, constructive fear will take you by the hand and lead you forward into the wonders of positive self-esteem. As you take action, your life will transform.

Self-Efficacy and Communication

As we move into the next arena of psychological wellness, self-efficacy, you might remember that we touched on this topic in chapter 3. You may recall that self-efficacy is the belief in one's ability to succeed in a certain situation or competently accomplish a specific task. A strong sense of self-efficacy provides the important inner sense that one has the skills and coping strategies necessary to make it through life's daily challenges. For example, when you feel capable of positively handling a difficult emotional situation with your partner, your sense of self-efficacy would be high. As another example, when you readily handle a situation at work that was formerly challenging, your sense of self-efficacy would improve as a result of your achievement. In short, when we feel good about our abilities and capacities, our sense of self-efficacy grows. When self-efficacy is low, feelings such as frustration, anger, shame, and worthlessness can set in and take charge. Indeed, the enemy face of destructive fear promotes negative thoughts and behaviors that eat away at a sense of self-efficacy. Destructive fear wants you to live in a place of self-doubt and insecurity. Destructive fear wants you to be stuck in uncertainty; it knows that doubt will fuel the anxiety that keeps you stuck in its negative grasp. Constructive fear lets you notice these negative issues and helps set you free to embrace the positive, supportive power of self-efficacy.

Trust that your work with self-efficacy will help you slowly and steadily develop your inner resources. As you journey forward, your emotional world will be more understandable and user-friendly. Your communication skills will improve. Your personal boundaries will be clearer and stronger. You will better understand your own needs and foster the skills to help you obtain what you need. As your inner resources become stronger, you will feel and see shifts in your life. You will find yourself learning and growing from your life experiences instead of getting stuck in thoughts of what you did wrong in the past or what you might mess up in the future. As you feel more competent and capable of handling your internal world, your external world will begin to open up and blossom.

Solid communication is an important aspect of self-efficacy and general well-being. Indeed, our daily lives are built on our ability to communicate. When we are able to successfully communicate with others, we feel empowered and capable. However, we often simply never learned how to communicate effectively. Many parents and caregivers do not possess good communication skills themselves and, therefore, are not ideal models in this regard. As a result, this basic, essential skill is often an obviously underdeveloped ability in childhood and adult life. Poor communication can create increased stressed and unnecessary, avoidable interpersonal difficulties.

In our busy world, words are often used haphazardly and without regard for true meaning and impact. Sadly, it can be all too easy to build up an arsenal of resentments that result from unfiltered or thoughtless communication. For example, if a friend were to call you "goofy," your feelings might be hurt if this term holds a negative connotation for you. However, the friend might consider this word an endearment and remain entirely unaware of how it affected you. If you weren't comfortable letting your friend know in a positive way that the word "goofy" holds a negative charge for you, the hurt might turn into a resentment. If your communication skills were well developed, you might say, "My dad teased me a lot when I was younger; some of that still sticks with me. I want you to know that I felt hurt when you call me 'goofy.' I'm OK with 'silly,' but 'goofy' strikes me the wrong way even after all these years." This simple, minor example sheds a strong light on how even small words can affect relationships in often subtle—yet important and lasting—ways.

Destructive fear flourishes when communication is poor, for it uses this arena as a place to draw in anger, hurt, disrespect, and uncertainty. Poor communication is often at the root of many interpersonal difficulties and misunderstandings. Many people simply never learned to state their needs in a kind, clear, and straightforward manner. This common problem can lead to negative patterns, including passive-aggressive, passive, and aggressive communication. Effective communication relies on assertive communication that is open, direct, and respectful. Yet destructive fear keeps people stuck in cycles of poor communication. Notice if any of these common examples—all of which are problematic and give destructive fear power—sound familiar to you:

"I was only joking; you are too sensitive."

"It's your fault, not mine."

"You're so irrational. Just be logical for once."

"You're such a jerk. I can't stand you."

"Oh, yeah, as if *you* are the sharpest tool in the shed."

"Stop your whining. I don't care about your feelings or opinions. Just shut up."

Every one of these examples shuts down positive communication, allowing destructive fear to move in and perpetuate negativity and friction. Unhealthy tactics such as blame, sarcasm, intellectualization, ridicule, black-and-white thinking, and deflection are common in everyday communication. These unhealthy methods reduce trust and intimacy; they also promote unrest, disrespect, and negativity. Destructive fear thrives in harsh, disrespectful environments where communication is used as a weapon, not a connective tool. If negative communication is at work in your world, trust that you have the power to create positive change.

Constructive fear knows the importance of good communication in your life journey. The shift toward healthy communication takes time, dedication, and focus. It may take quite a bit of time and effort to notice long-lasting change, particularly when old, negative patterns have long been in place. Yet as you learn to listen to the friendly, instructive voice of constructive fear, your communication patterns will become increasingly positive—benefiting you and those in your life. Constructive fear asks you to take note of seven simple steps that will lead to better communication. Although the steps are simple, they are often difficult to use in the real world where communication is affected by many factors, including mental state, emotions, situations, and personal history. Destructive fear will want you to revert to unhelpful communication patterns, yet you can create lasting, positive changes with patience, practice, and perseverance. It can be helpful to post a copy of the steps outlined below in a visible place for easy reference. Your communication skills will steadily improve with practice.

1. Pause to reflect before you speak. Know what you want to say, taking the time to formulate your thoughts into words before you speak. Many problems can be avoided when you mean what you say and say what you mean.

2. Do your best to communicate with clarity, kindness, and respect.

3. Know the power of "I" messages when talking about your own feelings or needs. For example, "I feel hurt when you don't call me to tell me you'll be late."

4. If you're unclear on a topic or feeling unheard, learn to "mirror" (repeat back) what you believe the other person said; this allows opportunity for clarification.

5. Take responsibility when you say something that is problematic, hurtful, or damaging.

6. Take responsibility when you notice that you shut down, close off, or withhold words of connection, help, or support.

7. Remember that many people have not developed appropriate communication skills. When communicating with someone who perpetuates negative communication, do not take it personally. Take a time out. Trust that your power lies in your own growing ability to speak kindly, honestly, and respectfully. Others may not yet have this capacity, yet they can choose to grow.

Practice and refine your new skills in front of the mirror, with your partner, and with supportive friends. It will take time and effort to learn to use these skills consistently. Be patient with yourself as you learn to notice—without judgment—when you are using your new tools and when you revert back to less effective behaviors. When you hear the negative power of destructive fear begin to creep into your communication, pause. Let the voice of constructive fear guide you into healthy, positive communication. By practicing and applying these skills yourself, you also guide others into changing their ways. Transformational fear has incredible power to lead you forward into life-changing, positive communication patterns.

Self-Care

It might feel wonderful to take a deep breath of gratitude as you move into this next section, for it focuses on self-care. If self-care is a foreign concept, these next few pages are especially important for you. True self-care involves giving intentional, careful attention to all aspects of your being—this includes physical, emotional, mental, and spiritual realms. Daily life can deplete our energy stores on many levels; self-care allows for purposeful recharging. In this way, good self-care gets us back to a place of feeling revitalized and balanced. Indeed, conscious self-care is not optional; it is critical to having a good relationship with oneself and with others.

We often think of self-care as being limited to getting a bit of rest and relaxation. Although sleep and time for leisure are very important, the essential elements of true self-care stretch deeper and wider. Self-care involves taking purposeful, deliberate actions that allow you to move through life feeling recharged, balanced, and at your best. Self-care can involve consciously limiting your social engagements and outside responsibilities to avoid becoming drained and overextended. Of course, giving conscious attention to your sleep, diet, exercise, and medical needs are also signs of good self-care. Taking daily time to unwind, whether through meditation, walking, stress-reducing hobbies, or other soothing practices, is a vital self-care element. Good self-care also involves loving, connective time with significant others. Too often, the importance of this vital element is minimized or overlooked; daily connective time with loved ones can be vital for bonding and healing intimacy.

When it comes to creating self-care, scheduling is a must. Although scheduling might seem counterintuitive or off-putting, we often tend to put some of our most important needs on the back burner. Whether it's setting aside time for exercise or being intimate with one's partner, life's "more important" pursuits often take center stage. It's easy for life's to-do lists to get in the way of what's really important. When self-care activities become scheduled into life as priorities, the benefits can be astounding. A critical element of self-care is purposeful scheduling that allows the psyche to fully acknowledge, appreciate, and benefit from the opportunity. By making active, conscious choices to engage in scheduled self-care activities, the level of commitment to well-being is also increased. Without a schedule, self-care often goes by the wayside; this leaves the psyche feeling all the more unimportant, untended, and forgotten. Self-care time is different from fun, spontaneous life activities; it is focused, intentional time that is set aside and prioritized. Mindfulness and other centering strategies maximize self-care time.

If you're already thinking *I'm too busy for self-care!* or *Self-care is selfish!* these next paragraphs are perfect for you. Whether you are male or female, single or married, childless or not, it's likely that your schedule is filled to the brim with necessary duties and tasks. If it's not, it's possible that certain activities have crept into your life that suck at your time and energy—making you *feel* as if you're too busy for self-care or even unworthy of self-care. Without good self-care, you are not as effective in your daily tasks. So, as busy as you might be, proper self-care will not only make you more focused and effective in your tasks, it will actually allow you to have greater appreciation for what you accomplish. As a result, good self-care will not only make you more productive in the long run—it will also leave you feeling more fulfilled.

How Destructive Fear Enters through an Overfilled Life: A Case Study

To illustrate this point, let me tell you a story about David. A master of to-do lists, David started each workday with a specific outline of what he needed to accomplish. To complete each item on his detailed lists, he often went to work early and stayed very late. David believed he had perfected the art of multitasking. He didn't like "wasting" time. Yet as detail-oriented as he could be, David found that paperwork would often "vanish" as he rushed from one task to another. Now and again, he spent precious time searching files or the trash can for misplaced documents. To maximize his daily output, he didn't take breaks or stop for lunch. Fueled by coffee and adrenaline, he rushed through meetings and phone calls, ever focused on the next item on his calendar. David found himself frustrated that clients and fellow employees didn't seem to listen to him—misunderstandings and confusion constantly arose. At home, the routine was much the same. David raced through his weekends with to-do lists at hand. Before he knew it, the weekend had evaporated. Unrested and cranky, he made his to-do list for the upcoming week, preparing himself for the nonstop week ahead. With his wife threatening divorce, David came to see me for direction. He said, "I thought I was doing everything right. I thought I was making everyone happy." David didn't realize that he had created home and work environments that allowed him to accomplish a great many tasks yet were devoid of connection, joy, and vital self-care.

You might see parts of yourself in David, for it's easy to get caught up in external goals and pursuits. In fact, our daily tasks and duties are an important, dynamic aspect of life; they add to our sense of meaning and purpose. However, when these elements are not balanced by good self-care, something or someone will ultimately suffer. As David learned, he could actually accomplish more—and feel a great deal better overall—by adopting good self-care strategies. By making conscious shifts in his daily schedule, his days became more fulfilling. Although the changes he made were unsettling at first, David was determined to do what was necessary to save his marriage. David set specific work starting and ending times, regardless of what was left over on his agenda. He began eating lunch daily, and he invited his wife to join him once a week. He took a silent ten-minute walk every weekday afternoon. David found himself being more attentive to others at work, and misunderstandings became less commonplace. No longer ruled by agendas and endless to-do tasks, David found that self-care allowed him to see that life was more than a series of accomplishments. He became more aware of what he was doing, how he was doing it, and how he *felt* during the course of his tasks. He also became more aware of the overall results of his accomplishments—the quality, not just the quantity, of his experiences. As David learned to slow down, he found that he began to actually enjoy life. As he put it, "I began to see— really see—my wife *and* my life. I fell in love with both all over again."

From this example, you can see that destructive fear had worked itself into David's being. It had given him the strong, clear message that he was a better man and a better provider when he accomplished more. David's psyche had become so riddled with this concept that he feared stopping. He had unconsciously concluded that he was unworthy if he stopped accomplishing. Destructive fear had taught him to focus on how much he could accomplish during his waking hours. Indeed, destructive fear had often kept him going with plans and lists as he faded off to sleep, during the night, and as he woke. Destructive fear had confused David into believing that he *was* his accomplishments. When David made friends with constructive fear, his life began to transform. More and more, he learned to listen to constructive fear's kind voice. It often told him, "David, take a time-out. It's okay and necessary to slow down. Breathe. Relax. Focus on your top to-do priorities today; what is undone can be completed tomorrow or the next day. Take care of yourself. It is good to relax and connect with yourself and your loved ones. Remember, *you* are a priority. Your well-being is important. You are a splendid man inside and out—you are far more than what you accomplish in any given day."

Many people believe that self-care is selfish and even narcissistic. If you tend to believe this is true, these next paragraphs may be enlightening and supportive. To begin with, let's turn the idea of "self-care being selfish" on its head. In truth, self-care is actually one of the most unselfish things you can do. "Well!" you might exclaim, "How can that be? It's selfish to take time out for personal care when others need me and there's so much to do. I should put others first!" You may now be able to notice that this is the voice of destructive fear. Constructive fear would say, "Slow down. If you don't take care of yourself, you'll ultimately be unable to properly care for anyone. If you're tired and stressed, you'll get run down. Taking care of yourself with rest and relaxation is vital so that you can move through life with balance, serenity, and overall good health."

Some confuse the concept of self-care with self-absorbed outings, shopping sprees, or expensive spa treatments. True self-care involves none of these. Indeed, self-care needn't cost a penny. Some of the most beautiful acts of self-care are very simple. Yet destructive fear wants you to believe that self-care is selfish, costly, or unavailable. It wants to keep you in the clutches of stress, anxiety, and overwork. Destructive fear does not want you to become intentional, conscious, and self-reflective—it wants you to stay away from these benefits of good self-care.

How Destructive Fear Works against Self-Care: A Case Study

Let me introduce you to Mandy, a diligent, spirited woman. Mandy sought my assistance hoping to reduce her "out-of-control" stress. As we talked,

Mandy told me that her nonstop schedule had worsened. From morning to night, she attended to the needs of her husband, children, boss, elderly parents, and friends. She explained, "I finally carved out time to make an appointment with you. It's been on my to-do list for ages. I am so stressed and irritable. My husband complains that I don't want sex anymore. He's right; I just don't have the drive or the energy. On top of that, I can't sleep. I pop nighttime sleeping aids, but they're not working anymore. The bags under my eyes are horrible. I'm making more errors at work. The stress is actually making work less rewarding. As if that's not enough, I got into a fender-bender last week as I rushed to yoga class—it was totally my fault. It's my one chance a week to de-stress, and I missed the class. Seriously, I don't even stop to pee when I need to! How crazy is that? I just can't keep up this pace much longer." Sadly, I've heard hundreds of versions of Mandy's story before. Destructive fear had her on its treadmill, and it didn't want her to get off.

As she talked, a few additional, important details of Mandy's life surfaced—they were places where destructive fear had seeped in to work against her self-care. When I asked Mandy how she spent her weekday lunches, she confessed, "I go to the mall. It helps me get away from work. It's how I take care of myself. It's my reward for working so hard—I deserve it. I love shopping for shoes and jewelry. Makeup is another favorite. Before I know it, my lunch hour is gone." Through our discussion, Mandy came to realize that her shopping "self-care" was doing her far more harm than good. Not only were her constant purchases a financial drain, but the items didn't add to her quality of life. Like many shopping habits, whether online or in stores, the purchases only temporarily filled the aches and voids she felt inside. In addition, the hour she spent in the confines of the shopping mall consumed precious minutes that might be devoted to a walk, journaling, or other soothing activity. Although that particular session didn't cure all of Mandy's woes, it did give her hope and ideas that sparked healthy change. "You know," she said with a laugh, "I didn't realize what a time and energy suck my little shopping excursions had become until now. The mall is an easy, mindless escape. I didn't realize that what I really want—what I really deserve—is to do something relaxing with that time. No wonder shopping never made me feel better; it wasn't actually de-stressing me at all. Isn't it strange that I somehow convinced myself that going for a walk or a yoga class was selfish, while going to the mall was somehow OK? If I use that same amount of time to consciously do something really good for myself, I know I'll feel better. There's a public garden just down the street from my office—I could go there to sit in peace or take a walk at the park. I'm committing to putting some much-needed daily quiet time on my schedule. Just thinking about it makes me feel lighter."

Mandy's story is a true reflection of how powerful the mere idea of self-care can be. As Mandy allowed the voice of constructive fear to enter, she was able to feel what she truly wanted and needed. What she really craved couldn't be purchased or found in a store, despite what destructive fear wanted her to believe. Mandy didn't need to buy more—she actually needed to "let go" and just allow herself to *be*. Mandy found that what she really desired and needed was quiet time to walk, sit, and relax. Indeed, she craved dedicated, solitary time for serenity and healing. As she later told me, "I am learning to create quiet spaces in my day where I can tune out the world and tune into myself. I call it my 'quiet time'—sometimes it is just ten minutes or so. More and more, I'm finding that my quiet times give me a sense of peace that lasts throughout the day. It's funny, too, that my kids have noticed. My son plopped down next to me the other day and said, 'Hey, Mom, can I do quiet time with you?' Within a few minutes, he fell asleep with his head on my lap. It was such a precious experience that I actually found myself crying. I didn't even know why I was crying—perhaps it was a mixture of joy and relief. Maybe it just felt wonderful to sit quietly with my son. Maybe I was just letting go."

Indeed, the healing power of crying is an often-missed element of self-care. Emotional tears are sometimes seen as inappropriate or a sign of weakness. Yet our tears are a most healing, powerful aspect of our humanity. Crying is a natural, vital means of self-soothing. Crying also provides an opportunity for others to reach out in comforting ways, whether with kind words or healing, physical touch. Tears have the extraordinary power to connect you to yourself and to others.

When it comes to emotional tears, interesting research shows that tears resulting from a stressful experience actually contain stress hormones.[16] Shedding emotional tears has also been found to increase levels of oxytocin and endorphins, the feel-good neurochemicals that give rise to a more positive mood. Indeed, when we give ourselves permission to cry, we often notice reduced feelings of stress, depression, or anxiety. Anyone who has felt the comfort of a much-needed cry knows that, although tears can leave us feeling spent and weary, they also allow us a substantial opportunity for relief. Additionally, the unremitting crying common to chronic depression has a constructive missive: "Your tears are a sign that it's time to seek outside help and support."

Yet destructive fears sneak in to stop the healing power of tears with harmful, negative messages from the self or others. It might exclaim "You are being too sensitive!" or "You're making a big deal out of nothing!" Destructive fear can also surface through the critical words of others who, many times, are uncomfortable with their own emotions and sense of powerlessness. A person who is not secure in their own emotional world might say "Stop crying!" or "Tears aren't going to do you any good." Indeed, harsh self-messages or negative commentary from others might get you to shut down your tears, yet the sadness and hurt will remain. Sadly, those unspent tears might lead you to reach for a bottle, a pill, a plateful of food, or a "buy now" button.

During a most challenging period a few years back, there were times when heavy tears came to me at the most inopportune moments. Whether I was out on a morning hike or walking to my car, the tears that came were a powerful force. These were no ordinary tears—they had a thick, viscous quality that seemed to hold a hundred years of pain. At first, I tried to push them away until I was in the privacy of my home, yet I realized that the tears wanted to be felt on their timeline, not mine. They did not want to be dishonored and pushed away until a more convenient moment; they had arisen for sacred reasons of their own. So I learned to honor my tears. I let them come as a healing element of my journey—as a gentle witness to the deep, eviscerating pain I felt inside. In this way, I learned to be more appreciative and in touch with my tears. Through listening to the voice of constructive fear, I learned that my tears are my angels, my messengers. I let them come when they may, and I remain grateful for them—never ashamed.

So if that old voice of destructive fear tries to get you to close down, trust that your tears have a healing message for you. Let constructive fear remind you of this truth: Those who are truly strong and conscious honor the healing, connective power of tears. Crying is a sign of inner strength and emotional intelligence—not weakness. If those around you haven't the emotional awareness to support your healthy tears, cry your tears in a serene place that is comforting to you. If desired, reach out to others who will honor your tears and enfold you with compassion. Listen for the voice of constructive fear as it guides you to feel and shed your tears. Your tears are a wonderful aspect of your being—welcome them as a natural part of your transformational journey. Allow your tears to become part of your constructive self-care.

The Vital Importance of Personal Boundaries

The next concept, *personal boundaries,* is often misunderstood. As a client once said, "How can I have boundaries if I don't know what they are? I never learned any. I never had any!" The good news is this: Even if your parents or caregivers didn't model appropriate boundaries—and even if your boundaries were unhealthy or violated in the past—you can develop healthy personal boundaries. Constructive fear will allow you to put any boundary issues of your past in your rearview mirror as you move forward to create and utilize boundaries that give you safety.

Simply put, an individual's personal boundaries are the rules and principles that identify what will and will not be acceptable to that individual. Each person has the right to create personal boundaries to ensure emotional, mental, and physical safety. Clear, responsible personal boundaries are vital, for they let others know what behaviors would be considered appropriate or inappropriate. Personal boundaries create necessary guidelines for interactions with others; they affect how a person relates to others as well as how a person expects others to relate to them. By increasing self-awareness and a sense of safety, properly set boundaries can actually decrease the stress associated with unclear or inappropriate boundaries. As such, healthy boundaries are a crucial component of self-care in all aspects of our lives—at home, at work, and in social settings. Additionally, clear boundaries provide for consistent, predictable responses when a personal boundary is violated. Three types of boundaries are generally recognized—rigid, porous, and healthy. Although you might expect a fourth category for those who appear to have "no boundaries at all," such individuals generally suffer from having overly porous boundaries.

Rigid boundaries can be prisonlike in nature. They keep others at a safe distance and act as a blockade against interpersonal interactions. In keeping others out, however, they also lock a person inside a tight, closed-off world. Those with rigid boundaries may seem "fine"—if sometimes detached—to outsiders. In close personal relationships, a person with rigid boundaries may seem distant and emotionally unavailable. A fear of rejection or unworthiness may be masked by the fixed, impermeable boundaries. Those with rigid boundaries are often highly protective in general. Additionally, those with rigid boundaries are not likely to reach out for the support or advice of others.

Porous boundaries are more fluid and open by nature. They can be appropriate in some situations yet not at all appropriate in others. In general, those with inappropriately porous boundaries tend to engage in behaviors that negatively affect their own well-being and, often, the welfare of others. Such behaviors range from the oversharing of private information to acceptance of unwanted sexual advances or other abusive behavior. Additionally, those with very porous boundaries may be highly dependent on the opinions or validation of others. Fearing rejection, they may engage in people-pleasing behavior, often finding it difficult to say "no" to others. Those with overly porous boundaries may accept abusive and disrespectful behavior in order to obtain "love" and "acceptance." In addition, individuals with overly porous boundaries may be overinvested and overinvolved in the lives of others.

Healthy boundaries are a vital aspect of good self-care. Healthy boundaries allow openness and emotional vulnerability in safe, intimate relationships. Healthy boundaries are flexible and balanced; they are not too rigid or too porous, and they adjust appropriately to the situation. A person with well-developed boundaries may use very strong boundaries in work and professional settings yet naturally ease into more permeable boundaries in intimate and romantic life. Those with healthy boundaries are able to say "no" in order to protect personal space and needs. It's important to note that "no" statements are not necessarily indicative of healthy boundaries; frequent "no" statements that are reactive or controlling can reflect a rigid type of boundary. Those with healthy boundaries respond to requests carefully, choosing a "yes" or "no" response that considers the healthy needs of the self and others. Those with healthy boundaries tend to be less reactive and more self-reflective.

In addition, a behavior that might be appropriate in one situation may prove to be a boundary violation in another. For example, a porous boundary within an intimate, bonded relationship would allow for the sharing of highly personal information—this would be safe and appropriate. Yet, the sharing of private, intimate information in a professional setting would indicate inappropriately porous boundaries. As another example, a rigid boundary may be extremely necessary and beneficial in a threatening environment. However, in a close, personal relationship, a rigid boundary would prevent bonding and intimacy. Finally, cultural background has an impact on boundaries; what may be normal and acceptable in one culture may be highly unacceptable in another. Some cultures have more fluid, porous boundaries; others may tend to be less relaxed and more rigid in style.

Your boundaries are important because they protect you. They give you the safety and security you need and deserve in life. They allow you to move through your days knowing that you have the ability to be "within your set space" (emotional, mental, and physical) without others impinging on that all-important private space. When it comes to boundaries, it's helpful to use a metaphor of a fence around a home. You might imagine that the fence is the type of boundary, the yard is your personal space, and the home is you—your sacred self.

Healthy boundaries might be envisioned as a well-crafted privacy fence with a gate. The fence has an open quality, yet it is strong and solid enough to keep intruders at bay. The gate can be opened for those who are safe and welcomed into the general, personal space. Overall, the home's fence (the boundary) offers safety and a sense of peaceful relief. The door to the actual home (one's most personal space) can be opened for those who are true and worthy friends. A key to the home may even be given to those sacred, intimate ones who have earned the deepest trust.

In looking at rigid boundaries, a compelling image is that of a home and yard surrounded by formidable stone walls. The walls are tall, and a drawbridge severely restricts entry. If someone manages to get inside, they are kicked out before long. Of course, no one ever gets a key to the door—sometimes not even the actual owner of the home. And sadly, the person inside the defensive stone walls does not get out to enjoy and grow from learning how to truly bond and connect with others. When the individual ventures outside the rigid stone walls, the emotional defensiveness remains, although outsiders may not notice it. And, of course, the formidable stone walls do not want to be moved, shifted, or changed in any way.

When it comes to inappropriately permeable boundaries, the image of a partially-constructed or dilapidated fence comes to mind. With this poor or insufficient boundary, all sorts of things—wanted and unwanted—might wander into or around the home. Indeed, the lack of any clear boundary might actually be seen as an invitation to others. The homeowner might feel anxious or stressed, ever on the alert for intruders. Additionally, the homeowner might feel obliged to open the door and welcome anyone who knocks. Seeking love and acceptance, a homeowner with very porous boundaries may give the key to the front door to almost anyone—oftentimes to those who never earned or deserved a speck of trust. The fence—the boundary—is sometimes moved or kicked down to please others. A fence that is indistinct, unsteady, or constantly changing does not feel safe in any way. Yet instability and uncertainty are the very nature of inappropriately permeable boundaries. In such an environment, anxiety and insecurity abound.

Such are the dangers of boundaries that are too rigid, too permeable, or too unclear. Of course, destructive fear prefers unhealthy boundaries. Whether boundaries are overly rigid or overly porous, destructive fear knows that unhealthy boundaries give it greater power and control. Destructive fear gains power when rigid boundaries prevent healthy intimacy, vulnerability, and connection. Destructive fear gives warnings that suit its agenda. At times it will scream, "People are out to get you. They don't really care about you—they'll only hurt you. Don't be vulnerable to anyone." On the other hand, destructive fear thrives on overly porous boundaries—it uses its power to create unhealthy vulnerability, exposing the individual to people and situations that are not healthy, appropriate, or safe. Its voice does great harm by chanting phrases such as "No one will like you if you don't do this. You must say 'yes' to be accepted. You must do this or that—it's expected." The voice of constructive fear is far different. Knowing and cherishing the importance of healthy boundaries, constructive fear whispers gently, "Slow down. Breathe. Be conscious and be aware. Listen to what is right for you in each situation. Learn to use flexible, healthy boundaries that are based on deep self-respect and respect for others. As you listen and learn, you will become vulnerable to those who respect you and have earned your trust. You will learn to reflect and pause, saying 'yes' and 'no' when it is healthy and appropriate for you. You will become aware of how to create safe boundaries. You will come to better notice and respect the boundaries of others. You will not let destructive fear hold you back. You will allow this work to transform you."

As you now may see, good self-care is far from selfish; it deeply acknowledges the vital importance of caring for oneself in a manner that will support optimal well-being. When we are immersed in self-care activities, we can often hear the transformative voice of constructive fear come through with profound, simple wisdom. In truth, when we optimize our well-being, we do ourselves and the greater world good. As constructive fear might say, "When we take the time and energy to engage in good self-care, we are our better selves. We are more aware of our basic needs, and we attend to them with wisdom. We are more aware of the needs of others, and we have the health, energy, and desire to help support them. We are more aware of the needs of our environment, tending to it with the same level of care we give to ourselves and our loved ones." This is how profoundly unselfish true self-care can be.

Five Messages toward Psychological Wellness

This next exercise is designed to allow you to reflect on your psychological wellness a little more deeply. This exercise focuses on the components of psychological health addressed in this section, the areas of self-esteem, self-efficacy, and self-care. When you are in a space that feels relaxed and comfortable, begin the exercise with your notebook and pen at your side.

First, allow yourself to consider five ways that destructive fear may be causing you stress and anxiety or generally controlling your psychological well-being. It can be helpful to close your eyes for a moment or two, noticing how the messages of destructive fear may have crept into your life. Whatever thoughts arise, simply allow yourself to notice them without any judgment attached. For example, when you approach the topic of self-esteem, destructive fear may be telling you, "Your behaviors and patterns are just fine. You've gotten along in life so far doing whatever you needed to do to get by. It's worked for you so far. Why change?" The negative voice of destructive fear might even say, "Self-esteem? You've never had any. Do you really think you're going to get some now?" When it comes to self-efficacy, destructive fear might quip, "You will never really succeed at this transformation thing. You are a failure." As to self-care, destructive fear might come on strong. It might tell you, "Hey, a glass of wine or a beer is great self-care. You feel more relaxed after you drink, so it's got to be good for you." Destructive fear might try other tactics and say, "Self-care is for wimps, selfish people, or those with too much time on their hands. People who are really strong just push on forward. You don't need or deserve self-care." Whatever negative, controlling thoughts come, simply notice them as they arise. Use your notebook to write down five of these destructive thoughts. Notice how you feel as you read the messages you chose to write down. Make additional notes if you wish. Pause to breathe.

Then consciously shift each message in your mind, allowing the voice of constructive fear to guide you. Using the above examples, constructive fear might prompt you to write, "Here is an opportunity to be honest with yourself. You are accustomed to making things look good on the outside, but you are just going through the motions. You absolutely have the power to be the person you want to be. You have the ability and wisdom to be proud of yourself from the inside out." Constructive fear might also guide you to state, "Healthy self-esteem is important to you. You have what it takes to create the thoughts and actions that align with what feels truly good and right for you." As to self-efficacy, constructive fear might say, "You can do this. You have the power and ability to transform your life. You can—and will—slowly but surely make the changes you need and want to make." Moving to self-care, constructive fear might also note, "Quality self-care isn't to be found in substances. Imagine what you really want—what you really crave. Is it a daily walk after work to release stress, time to meditate, or maybe a workout? This will do you good physically, mentally, and emotionally. This is not wasted time—it is necessary time." Constructive fear might also note, "There is wisdom in taking time for self-care. Far from being selfish or weak, carving out time for daily self-care takes dedication and focus. Good self-care is necessary to optimize your well-being and the well-being of those you love and care about."

When you have completed your notes, pause to notice how you feel as you look at each positive message in your notebook. Make any notations that feel right to you. When you are finished, pause to breathe. Congratulate yourself on a job well done! By slowing down to dismantle the voice of destructive fear, you are allowing constructive fear to work its quiet, subtle magic. With every step of your courageous journey, you are inviting the power of transformational fear to take you into a world of greater well-being.

Your Overall Wellness and Chronic Stress

Given the serious effects of chronic stress, it is important to emphasize some important points before moving forward. On both physiological and psychological levels, research continues to investigate the negative impacts of chronic stress.[17] Physiologically, chronic stress can contribute to high blood pressure, heart disease, diabetes, and obesity. Stress can have a seriously negative impact on the body's all-important immune system. Additionally, ongoing stress can cause chest pain, fatigue, decreased sex drive, headaches, stomach irritations, and muscle tension. In the psychological realm, research shows that chronic stress can lead to anxiety issues, depression, restlessness, irritability, decreased motivation, and difficulties with paying attention.[18] Chronic stress often results in self-isolation and a withdrawal from social activities; this is unfortunate, for humans thrive on supportive interconnection. The joint psychological and physiological impact of stress can be readily seen in many areas. For example, chronic stress can lead to eating issues, drug and alcohol abuse, tobacco use, and other addictive behaviors. Those who are stressed often exercise less; this alone has a significantly negative impact on physiological and psychological health. Last, but far from least, is the impact of stress on sleep. Most of us are awake and busily engaged for at least two-thirds of every day. Sleep gives the body the opportunity to restore and repair itself. The human body generally requires at least seven hours of sleep for much-needed cellular repair. Among other negative effects, sleep deprivation decreases mental clarity and emotional regulation capacities. Simply stated, your body and psyche need less stress and more sleep. As destructive fear is at the root of stress, you might think of it this way: I need and deserve less destructive fear and more friendly, constructive fear. My body and psyche crave a new way of being.[19]

Not All Stress Is Bad: The Benefits of Optimal Stress

Now that you've focused on a basic outline of the negative effects of chronic stress, it's time to tell you about an upside to stress. The concept of optimal stress—which is far different from chronic, traumatic stress—is an important one. Optimal stress is the ideal low or moderate level of stress that keeps you productive in life. Optimal stress is that personal, necessary level of stress that gets you out of bed in the morning and allows you to accomplish tasks in a clear, beneficial, and effective manner. If the level of stress is too low, you might stay in bed or on the couch day after day. If an opportunity or challenge came your way, you would likely not have the energy or motivation to pursue it. However, if the level is too high, you might rush around feeling anxious, out of gas, or as though you were running in circles. Unlike high-level stress, optimal stress has the quality of being energizing rather than toxic to the self or those proximate to you. If you have trouble differentiating between optimal stress and chronic stress, ask yourself these questions:

- Is the stress I feel temporary and manageable?
- Does it propel me to take an action that is ultimately helpful?
- Does the sense of being stressed diminish once I take action?

If your answer to these questions is "yes," it's likely that optimal stress is at work to help motivate you. If your answer to these questions is "no," it's likely that you are experiencing chronic stress.

Stressful incidents of all shapes and sizes occur throughout life; unexpected challenges and difficult situations are inevitable. We can't prevent these life stressors from occurring, but we can learn how to effectively respond to challenging incidents. Without effective tools, life's challenges can exact devastating physical and psychological tolls. Although we often have very little power to control the difficulties that appear on our doorstep, we do have great power to learn how to face and move through these stressors effectively, thereby minimizing or even avoiding unnecessary damage to our physical and psychological well-being.

Through the reading you have already done, it may be clear to you that the impact of a stressor is reduced when you are able to process and integrate the stressful experience. So whether the initial focus or impact of the stressor was your physical body or your psychological being, your greatest defense is your ability to *synthesize* the incident—to make a congruent whole out of the fragmented pieces of the stressor. The tools you have been accruing and practicing throughout these chapters are geared to help you process and integrate challenging life experiences more fully and effectively. As you apply them to your daily life experiences, you will find that chronic stress becomes a thing of the past. The skills you have been practicing will help make you more effective at facing life's stressors.

This is where the concept of optimal stress can become deeply meaningful in your daily life. Indeed, you might prefer to think of optimal stress in terms of motivational energy. As a metaphor, you might envision optimal stress as the salt in your soup. You want just enough, but not a speck more than is absolutely essential, to improve the taste; too much can be disastrous. As you become more attuned to your own well-being, you will find that an intentional level of optimal stress is helpful, for this level of stress helps you grow, learn, experiment, face challenges effectively, and ultimately evolve throughout life. Destructive fear will fight this; it will want you operating in familiar, chronic stress—stress that will harm you, hold you back, and keep you running in anxious, adrenaline-fueled circles. Constructive fear wants to be your guide and ally; it wants you to slow down. It wants you to take the time to notice your healthy and unhealthy patterns. Constructive fear wants you to nurture what works for you, and it wants you to let go of what does not—this is the essence and beauty of transformational fear.

Getting Comfortable with Being Uncomfortable

With all the background reading and hard work you've done up to this point, you might be ready for the next step. Indeed, this next stretch offers a provocative concept: *It's time to get comfortable with being uncomfortable.* "What?" you might exclaim. "I don't want to be uncomfortable. Isn't the whole point of this journey to find a way to be peaceful and stress-free all the time? Isn't being comfortable the whole point?" Yes and no.

As you read the preceding chapters and bravely engaged in the exercises, you have already been developing your ability to sit with discomfort. I didn't note early on that you were experimenting with the concept of "being comfortable with being uncomfortable." This was intentional, as this might have brought up unnecessary fear and actually made you too uncomfortable to progress. Indeed, this is another way that destructive fear can sneak in; it can make you so afraid of what might be coming that you don't allow yourself the full benefits of whatever the actual experience might be.

In actuality, it is possible to become so anxious that the fight-flight response is triggered just by the idea of potential discomfort. For example, imagine that you've prepared yourself well for an activity, such as giving a speech or performing on stage; you may be quite comfortable with your ability to do the task. In your mind, you know that you're capable, but the mere idea of the activity makes you so uncomfortable that your actual performance falters. This is destructive fear at work. It sidles into your body and mind to trigger self-doubt. As you walk into the room to give your well-prepared speech, destructive fear would want you to focus on what might go wrong. It would want you to get stuck in some sort of discomfort—whether the thought of a knot in your stomach or the possibility of forgetting an important topic. Destructive fear would try to convince you that your discomfort is too much to bear. It might make you want to vomit or run from the room. Destructive fear does not want you to be able to tolerate the idea of being uncomfortable. Destructive fear wants you to be *uncomfortable* with being uncomfortable. Interestingly, destructive fear also wants you to be uncomfortable with being comfortable. Imagine slowing down and pausing to breathe before giving your speech or performance—trying to calm yourself and become comfortable. Destructive fear might very well creep in to undo your efforts—it would want to make your anxiety and stress level rise. Destructive fear, in short, does not want you to be comfortable in any way at all.

As you are learning, the focus of constructive fear is far different. It wants to help you move out of these destructive cycles; its goal is to help you transform. Constructive fear knows that new behaviors are unfamiliar and uncomfortable by nature. It knows that change and growth are simply not possible without some degree of discomfort. Constructive fear knows this sad truth: so much potential is never fulfilled—in the self or in relationships—because people run from discomfort. Whether we do not tolerate the discomfort of a rough patch in a relationship, the difficult discomfort of letting go of an addiction, or the discomfort of a change in life, so much beautiful life potential is lost to the voice of destructive fear that demands complete comfort or unsettled discomfort.

Constructive fear wants you to notice the negative messages of destructive fear, and it wants you to learn from them. Using another example, imagine having a difficult heart-to-heart talk with a loved one. Perhaps deep conversations are not your forte, and that the mere idea of moving into the intimate, emotional realm is frightening. Maybe you're more accustomed to talking of work, sports, or more superficial matters.

Destructive fear might want to raise your anxiety. It would want you to view the talk as a threat. It would creep in to warn you, "Heartfelt talks are bad! They're unnecessary! They are no fun! You'd better fight or run. Get out of this unfamiliar territory in any way you can. Get out now!"

Constructive fear would help you see through this negative, destructive tactic. It would help you to compassionately slow down—to take a step back to notice your discomfort without judgment. It would help you become aware of your emotional state and how destructive fear is trying to take over. Constructive fear might say, "Heartfelt discussions are simply new and unfamiliar to you. You learned as a child and through adulthood to be frightened and to avoid these discussions. Yet you can learn to become more comfortable with them only by practicing. Just notice that you are a bit anxious and scared. Breathe. Pause to check in with how your body feels. Remember that intimate discussions are actually very healthy; they are a vital and essential element of truly bonded relationships. You have the courage and ability to talk about intimate matters—the most important elements of life. Take a step forward into this new behavior. It is natural to be a bit uncomfortable. Allow yourself to tolerate the discomfort; you have what it takes to be 'comfortably uncomfortable.' You will transform and grow as you strengthen this ability. You will build true confidence in your power to speak your truth—to safely and securely talk about anything with dignity, courage, compassion, and respect."

In many ways, we get too used to being "comfortable" in life. As humans, we generally want to be comfortable all of the time. Couple this with our culture's "quick fix" mentality and the idea of learning how to be comfortably uncomfortable goes by the wayside. When we have a headache, we reach for a pill. When we are lonely or sad, we reach for a pint of ice cream. When work is stressful, we reach for a box of cookies or a bag of potato chips. If we are unhappy, we reach for an antidepressant. If we are anxious, we reach for an anti-anxiety pill. And so it goes. We down pills, drink booze, have hookup sex, overeat, and overshop to avoid discomfort. None of these tactics work to tackle the underlying issues. By refusing to get to the bottom of what's causing the issue, we do not address the discomfort. We get caught in the vicious cycle of running from discomfort and running into it again.

There is a far different, more conscious and powerful way to move through life. With constructive fear at your side, a healthy threefold process becomes your ally in learning to utilize discomfort. These three steps are simple yet highly effective.

1. Let constructive fear help you investigate what causes the discomfort—the underlying messages of destructive fear.
2. Use the voice of constructive fear to guide you into noticing options that don't keep you stuck in old patterns that are deeply unhealthy and uncomfortable.
3. Practice being uncomfortable in a healthy way. Build your ability to tolerate the discomfort that arises as you approach your life experiences in a new way. You may even enjoy it as a sign of positive growth.

Remember, destructive fear wants you to be uncomfortable with the slightest discomfort. It wants you to run away. It wants you to stop conversations with yourself and others that might help you change negative pathways. Constructive fear will help you become aware that learning to be comfortably uncomfortable is a vital element of your transformative journey.

The Power of Letting Go: Forgiveness and Change

It is often difficult to get unstuck—change can be scary and tough. Yet when we do not let go of unhelpful emotions, feelings, thoughts, or behaviors, an opportunity for freedom is lost. When a thought or feeling is permitted to continue, it forms a stronger pattern in the mind. Just like a muscle in the body will grow stronger with routine exercise, the same pattern of growth occurs in the mind. This concept applies to all self-work. When we allow an old memory or fear to haunt us, it will come back more frequently. When we notice it and refuse to be "hooked" by it, the memory eventually fades; remember this powerful lesson as you continue to work on releasing yourself from destructive fear. Destructive fear wants you to be stuck in toxic habits and negative thoughts. As you work with constructive fear, you will see how these patterns have held you back; you will want—you will actually *crave*—the act of "letting go."

Once upon a time, I held a hurt deep in my heart that I could not release. Someone close to me had harmed me, and I could not find a way through to truly "letting go." I meditated, I prayed, and I wished the hurt away. I didn't realize that my inability or unwillingness to forgive was holding me back. The person I hadn't forgiven wasn't the vital piece of the puzzle; in fact, that individual was far away in body, carrying on with life as usual—most likely completely unaware of the deep, heavy pain in my heart. What was critical was not what that individual had done to me but my fear of releasing the pain and the hurt—my inability to set myself free. Destructive fear didn't want me to move forward. It didn't want me to be free, for it liked this dark control of me. Constructive fear came to me, suggesting that I confide my deep sadness to a wise, honorable friend. That very evening, I reached out to a trusted mentor to discuss the complex situation. Magic happened. He offered an unexpected suggestion that changed my world. The patient, wise mentor said, "First, feel compassion for your own being. You must forgive yourself for not standing up sooner. Forgive yourself for putting your head in the sand. Then, as if the person were in front of you, ask forgiveness for not standing up sooner for what was right, allowing this person to hurt others in the same way. Indeed, the intensely destructive power this person had may have been quashed or minimized by your strength—yet it *grew* as a result of your fear." As I listened to this odd twist in confused discomfort, my head spun. The room itself spun. Shivers coursed throughout my being. I could feel destructive fear wanting to well up in anger. It wanted to grow and move inside me. It told me that it was the other person who should be begging *my* forgiveness—not the other way around. Destructive fear did not want me to let go; it did not want me to do what was necessary to set myself free. Constructive fear embraced me with compassion and wisdom. As I shook off the dark, invasive voice of destructive fear, I could feel my power grow. I needed to—I *wanted* to—release the negative energy in order to move forward. In the silence of that room, I forgave myself. I then sent forgiveness to the individual who had caused such great harm and pain. In taking this wise, brave course, a tremendous miracle happened; I could feel that I was truly free. My heart—my very soul—was lighter and more expansive. When I forgave myself for not doing more, I was truly able to forgive the other; this released the person's invisible hold over me. I was connected to a light and power beyond myself—one that I had not been able to fully access through a lens of unforgiving fear. "Yes," the wise voice of constructive fear said to me with a soft kiss upon my forehead, "this 'letting go' is magical; it is your key to being free." Indeed, I have never been the same since that day. Although many years have passed since that moment, I can still recall the shimmering, connective energy that arose in that moment that will last a lifetime. The wisdom of constructive fear allowed me to experience and own the vastly freeing gift of truly letting go.

I share this deeply personal part of my story with you due to its incredible impact; it is one of the most powerful treasures I hold. It underscores the importance of compassion, perseverance, humility, and letting go. As you move forward in your journey, you will notice the importance of continuing to develop greater forgiveness, patience, and compassion for yourself. Destructive fear may try to hold you back by telling you not to forgive yourself or others for old behaviors. True forgiveness is necessary and beautiful—it is deeply freeing. Forgiveness of the self and others is necessary to move forward; it is essential for the art of letting go. As you move forward, notice the spaces that might need a touch of compassionate forgiveness. Allow yourself this gift. Let constructive fear be your guide in learning to embrace this essential element of transformation.

Remember that destructive fear has many tricks in its bag. It will not want you to let go of old ways of being. It may want you to get impatient and to fear that "change is too tough," that you're "not making progress," or that you'll simply "never feel better." Let constructive fear remind you that the opposite is true. Remember that change may be challenging, but it is not "too tough" for you. As to progress, you are absolutely moving forward—simply by reading and engaging with your thoughts and feelings. Constructive fear will tell you that "feeling better" is a process. As you notice the pockets of relief, calm, and joy that you are creating, you are emphasizing and nurturing these natural, "feel good" states. You have this power within you. Whether the positive changes you notice are small or large, focus on them. In this way, you are building patterns of positivity within your being. You are making them stronger bit by bit and day by day. As you let go of destructive fear's negativity, you will feel the freeing, light voice of constructive fear. By following that wise, friendly voice, you will transform—you will set yourself free.

Wellness and the Body-Psyche Link: Connecting the Dots to Move Forward

You have learned so much through these first four chapters. You have bravely engaged with a wide variety of concepts—some that may have been easy and familiar and others that might have proven unfamiliar and complex. All of this courageous work will continue to grow and manifest in ways that will support your ongoing transformation. As you "connect the dots," your life will slowly transform in the simplest, most beautiful ways.

During your journey, you may have noticed that you are "feeling" more of your emotions and that you are more connected to what is going on inside of you. As you notice and channel these emotions with wisdom, you will experience your life differently. You may realize that you had cut off a vital source of information—a source that is now coming to the surface after having been pushed aside or ignored for far too long. Indeed, the emotional body, which is often thought of as the "bridge" between the physical and mental aspects of the self, stores a lifetime of energy. When emotions are not adequately felt and processed, they are "held" within this part of the self. The emotional body can contain residue from various experiences that include psychological trauma, hurtful life experiences, and the emotional effects of physical trauma. Interestingly, the emotional body's reservoir of pain and fear is often held and "mirrored" in the physical body. For example, a person who felt emotionally strangled by her mother may have chronic neck and throat tension. Emotional energy is a powerful, often silent force in the body and the psyche. You are building your capacity to utilize this force with wisdom and conscious awareness.

The physical sensations that arise when you experience your feelings can be uncomfortable or unfamiliar. You are already building your capacity to tolerate—rather than ignore or run from—sensations that might bring up feelings of unease or discomfort. Remember, these sensations can be eased by noticing them, feeling them, and then releasing them. As you practice this, the physical sensations that are part of the emotional experience will diminish in intensity; they will have less power over you. By practicing this release of emotional energy, you will feel more comfortable with the vast array of feelings available to you. You will not be afraid of your feelings. Remind yourself that your feelings are your friends; they are not your enemy. Remember, the constructive face of fear is your guide in becoming consciously aware of your emotions and the amazing information they offer. Trust that you are becoming more adept at wisely noticing and utilizing your emotional energy. You are becoming more mindful and conscious. Allow yourself to appreciate and enjoy these changes.

Simple, Effective Tools for Balance, Mindfulness, and Letting Go

The following exercises are designed to help you on your transformational journey as well as your daily journey through life. Play and experiment with the exercises. Find those that work for you, personalizing them in whatever ways are beneficial. These simple, helpful skills will become part of your foundation for greater well-being. The more you practice and apply them, the more they will become a familiar and accessible part of your toolkit. In general, the exercises will be most beneficial to you when you are in a seated or reclined position. Feel free to use pillows or other props to make yourself more comfortable. There may be times that you want to close your eyes during your exercise; at other times, you may find more benefit and ease with your eyes open. Make whatever adjustments are necessary to optimize your experience. It will be helpful to practice in a quiet, relaxed environment at the beginning stages. As the concepts and tools become more familiar, you may find that you can use them effectively in a greater variety of settings (e.g., while you are sitting in an airport or waiting for a meeting).

As always, use your tools wisely and in accord with your individual personal and medical needs. If an exercise brings up undesirable feelings or sensations, stop the exercise and focus on a calming activity or thought, such as sitting on the ground or recalling a fond memory. Additionally, many of the tools invite deeper states of relaxation and require that you respect your body's and psyche's need for rest and inactivity afterward. Activities that involve driving, machinery, or fine motor skills are not appropriate after states of relaxation. In general, be careful and consciously attentive with your use of these important tools for centering and relaxing.

Breathing Exercises for You to Enjoy and Explore

During the course of each day, we often breathe mindlessly, using only a fraction of our lung capacity. Breathing is one of your most effective, portable tools, and you will find increasing power in using your breath consciously. As emotions arise, breathing patterns change. Indeed, when we feel frightened or tense, our breathing often converts very quickly from normal breath to panic breath. Panic breath—sometimes called survival breath—is fast and shallow. During your work in the preceding chapters, you may have become more aware of your own breathing patterns. You may have become more consciously connected to your ability to shift and control your breathing patterns by using calming strategies such as cleansing breaths. In doing this, you have utilized your own breath—a most beautiful and powerful element of your being—to relax mindfully.

This section builds on the basics of the cleansing breaths technique you have been using throughout this book. Strive to prioritize these exercises; use them as soon as you begin to feel stressed or anxious. By getting ahead of the anxiety or stressor, it will be much easier for you to control it—to get the negative energy to shift or dissipate. If you put off the exercise, the negative energy will often get stronger and more difficult to control.

There are many benefits to breathing exercises. One of the chief benefits is the sense of personal empowerment you will likely experience as you find that breathing techniques help you reduce your stress and anxiety. Breathing exercises take the busy mind into the present moment, allowing the psyche to calm and heal. As well, by decreasing stress and bringing vital oxygen into your system, simple breathing techniques can bring incredible healing benefits to the body. In general, it is recommended that you breathe in through your nose and exhale through your mouth. Experiment with the breathing techniques outlined below to find those that feel right for you.

Extended Cleansing Breaths:

Breathe in as deeply and fully as you think possible, then lengthen the inhalation for two more counts. Breathe out as deeply and fully as possible, then continue the exhalation for two more counts. After the exhalation, relax and pause for a moment. Repeat for five or fewer slow cycles of breath. In time, you may choose to increase this exercise until you reach ten slow, extended cycles of breath.

Three-Part Breathing:

In three-part breathing, you will actively engage three areas of your body—abdomen, diaphragm, and chest—as you breathe, giving conscious attention to each of these areas in turn. To begin, breathe in deeply. Imagine filling up with fresh oxygen—begin with your belly, then move to your lower ribcage, and finally to your upper chest (just above the sternum). Next, exhale slowly—beginning at the top of your chest, then moving to your lower ribcage, and finishing in the lower belly. Imagine releasing toxic energy with each full, slow exhalation. Continue for up to five cycles. As you learn this method, you may want to move your hands upward along each of the three areas as you inhale—feeling your breath expanding each area. As you exhale, you may enjoy moving your hands downward until you complete the final exhalation at your belly. Once you are familiar with this technique, you may wish to leave your hands at your sides. Ultimately, three-part breathing will become so familiar that you may feel a wave of energy moving up through your torso as you inhale and down through your torso as you exhale.

"Between the Brows" Breathing:

Focus on the area between your eyebrows. Imagine a small circle—no larger than a pencil eraser—in this area. On the inhalation, imagine that your breath increases the size of the circle between your brows. Pause for a moment. As you breathe out, imagine that the circle between your eyebrows diminishes to the original small size. Continue for five or fewer slow cycles of breath. Over time, you may find that you enjoy increasing the number of breath cycles—possibly to ten slow repetitions.

"Joy" Breathing:

Begin this exercise in a relaxed, safe space. First, imagine a very positive image—someone or something that brings you great joy. It could be something as simple as a child's face, your favorite flower, or a divine image. Whatever the image might be, hold it in your mind's eye. Then practice your simple cleansing breaths as you focus on the beautiful image of joy. If thoughts come to distract you, simply set them aside as you return to your joyful image. Continue for five or fewer cycles of breath. You may wish to increase the number of repetitions over time.

"Washing the Sternum" Breathing:

To begin, place your hand gently on the area in the center of your chest—the breastbone or sternum. On the inhalation, feel the sternum rising and imagine it lengthening. On the exhalation, feel the sternum relaxing downward. As you continue, imagine that each inhalation is "washing" the sternum with soothing energy; allow the soothing energy to move from the bottom of the sternum to the top. On the exhalation, imagine the "washing" action moving in the opposite direction. Continue for five or fewer cycles of breath. Over time, feel free to increase your repetitions—up to ten slow repetitions. As you practice this technique, you may choose to move your hand (or one finger) along your breastbone in sync with your breath, moving the hand or finger upward with each slow inhalation and downward with each slow exhalation.

"Feather Duster" Breathing:

This simple technique can be both fun and relaxing. If possible, lie down in a safe area where you feel relaxed (e.g., your couch, bed, or floor). Allow yourself to relax onto the supportive surface. When you are ready, breathe slowly and gently in and out. Repeat for two additional conscious cycles of breath. Then allow your breathing to remain slow and steady as you imagine a feather duster moving through your body. Let the feather duster move into the nooks and crannies where old memories, fears, anxiety, stress, holding, or tightness of any sort might be lingering. As you breathe gently, allow the feather duster to move through you, sweeping away any negativity. Repeat for up to ten relaxed cycles of breath.

"Letting Go" Breathing:

This breathing technique is particularly helpful when fear or anxiety just begins to arise or when you feel as if fear or another negative emotion is "stuck" inside your body. Begin in a relaxed environment where you feel safe and secure. It may be helpful to be in a seated position. Place your hand gently on the area or areas of your body that feel stressed, clogged, or anxious, such as your belly or your heart. When you are ready, breathe in slowly to the count of four as your chest expands. If possible, hold for a count of four. Then exhale slowly to the count of four as you draw your belly toward your spine. Focus on the area underneath your hands; simply notice, without judgment, how this area of your body feels. If anxious thoughts come to you, consciously let go of them as if they had wings. Return to another cycle of breath. After the next cycle of breath is completed, notice the energy in the areas under your hands. Notice the sensations, such as the experience of feeling throbbing, stuck, or cramped. Then visualize sending golden healing energy into that space. If a negative thought arises, detach from the thought—"give it wings." Then return to another slow, focused cycle of breath. Continue to repeat the breath cycles for five or fewer rounds. Over time, you may desire to increase the repetitions for several more cycles. The more you practice your "Letting Go" breathing, the more it will become part of your natural routine. In the same way, when you notice that a pocket of fear is stuck in your body (e.g., aching muscles and tension spots), breathe into these spaces and then practice mindfully releasing the fearful energy that is held in that space. When we expose a sore spot in the body or psyche, it is important to actually release that soreness. Otherwise, that soreness has merely been exposed without the benefit of being released to create freedom.

Stress-Reduction Strategies to Support Your Well-Being

The simple, powerful techniques described below won't eradicate life's stressors, but they will go a long way toward increasing your sense of inner calm. As you practice and utilize these strategies as part of your daily self-care toolkit, you will feel less anxious and stressed. Your mental clarity will increase. You will find yourself becoming less reactive and more responsive to the unique needs of every situation. You will find that you feel more powerful and capable to face what life brings your way.

Breathe and Breathe:

Pick your favorite exercises from the outline above. If you have another variation or favorite technique, write it down. Then put a "Remember to breathe!" sticky note on your mirror, on the refrigerator, or inside your desk drawer at work. Include just enough details of your favored breathing technique to remind you to use your breathing skills when stress or anxiety begin to arise.

Positive Messages:

Find a positive message or mantra that feels strong and calming for you. Keep a copy in your wallet, on your mirror, and on your desk. Repeat the mantra or phrase when you are calm and relaxed. Your brain will come to associate the gentle, supportive words with a positive, relaxed state. It can be helpful to repeat the words as you press a specific finger or place on your hand—"anchoring" the calming energy into yourself. At the slightest hint of anxiety or stress, repeat the mantra or phrase. If it feels better to touch the anchoring place on your hand or finger, add in this element for greater benefit.

Positive Self-Talk Tape:

Select a meaningful, positive phrase that will help you combat any negative, critical self-talk. The phrase can be simple, such as "I am a wonderful and valuable person with a good, caring heart." When a harsh, critical voice arises, simply stop and notice the voice without judgment. Then imagine "taking out" the old tape and inserting a fresh, positive one that offers supportive, uplifting thoughts. It is often helpful to post reminders (notes that detail your positive self-talk phrases) on the refrigerator, bathroom mirror, or doors. The more you use your positive self-talk tape, the more you will erase the negative, critical voice that wants to take center stage.

Positive Imagery:

Envision a real or imaginary place that feels serene. Perhaps the setting is a field of lavender, a quiet beach, or a tree-covered hilltop. Imagine yourself in this calm setting, perhaps inviting a favorite animal or trusted friend to join you. Whatever your positive image might be, practice envisioning it when you are relaxed. Etch the details of the beautiful, peaceful image into your mind—notice everything, from the colors and scents to the plants and sky. Allow this image to become a safe resting place. Then when a stressful situation begins to arise, take a break or time-out. As you imagine yourself in that beautiful, stress-free environment, your anxiety and stress will dissipate.

Journal Freely:

Great benefits can be had by writing down stresses, anxieties, and fears in a private journal. By keeping a journal specifically for this purpose, your psyche knows that it has a "safe place" to unload. Make a daily date with your journal—allow yourself to offload any negative energy. If possible, write in your journal at least a few hours before bedtime; this will allow any unwanted energy to dissipate as you move through the rest of your evening. When you write in your journal, try not to self-edit or worry about grammar and such. Simply let your emotions and thoughts flow freely. When you are finished, close the journal—resist the temptation to reread it, as this often brings up self-criticism and judgment. I encourage keeping the journal in an area outside of the bedroom to reduce the desire to read it at night. This strategy also keeps the offloaded, unwanted thoughts and energy in a different space as you sleep.

Write-Off Notepad:

Keep a notepad beside your bed for the purpose of "writing off" to-do list items or other thoughts that might interfere with sleep. All too often we worry that we'll forget to do something the next day, and the worrisome thoughts interfere with sleep. Once pesky thoughts are on the notepad, the psyche can unwind and rest.

Time to Worry:

If you are a constant worrier, make a daily time to worry—ideally a few hours before bedtime. At the set time, sit down with a pen and paper and allow yourself to worry for five or ten minutes. As counterintuitive as this may sound, it actually works. Instead of trying to force yourself not to worry, which can actually increase worrying, the busy mind often calms down once it knows it will be allowed to worry at a set time.

Catnaps:

Short naps can be incredibly stress-reducing. An afternoon nap of ten or twenty minutes can be restorative for both body and mind. Naps that are too long—generally over forty-five minutes—may cause grogginess and even interfere with nighttime sleep. To avoid the nagging worry that you might over-nap, set a gentle alarm to wake you.

Walk and Relax:

Unlike aggressive, high-adrenaline sports, walking has the wonderful benefit of allowing you to relax while you exercise. You benefit both your body and mind by using your walking time to consciously "let go" of life's stressors—to actually leave them behind you as move forward during your walk. Even a short ten-minute walk can elevate your mood significantly.

Stretch and Move:

Studies substantiate the soothing benefits of exercise such as gentle yoga, tai chi, and qigong. Such practices—which often combine gentle movement, stretching, breathing, and elements of meditation and mental imagery—can be helpful in reducing stress.

Shower Power:

A warm shower or bath can feel incredibly relieving after a stress-filled day. As you ease into a bath or shower, imagine your cares and stresses melting away. Indeed, a short shower before bed can do wonders to improve overall relaxation and sleep quality.

Calming Essential Oils:

Soothing essential oils such as lavender and chamomile can be go-to necessities for those who are stressed or anxious. Some essential oils are intended to be rubbed on the skin (e.g., behind the ears or on the wrists), whereas others are meant for diffusers. Make your selections in person at a store that allows you to smell and experiment. Whatever your choice, select quality essential oils that feel soothing and good to you. Not all essential oils affect everyone in the same way. As well, be sure to check for allergies.

Love Connection:

Stress and anxiety can ease away when a friend or loved one is close. Although in-person connection is often ideal, a chat via phone can decrease feelings of stress, anxiety, and isolation.

The Power of Touch:

Whether in the form of a hug or cuddle time, touch can be tremendously healing and stress-relieving. Additionally, hugging or petting a pet (whether your own or a friend's) can significantly reduce stress, decrease anxiety, and elevate your mood.

Laugh, Laugh, Laugh:

Laughter can be incredibly stress-relieving and mood elevating. Whether you call a friend to share comic memories or watch a rerun of your favorite laugh-inducing television show, remember that laughter is a very powerful medicine.

While you practice and enjoy your new tools for balance, mindfulness, and letting go, remember that you are well on your way to healthful transformation. As you continue to build your overall awareness, you will find that you enjoy life just a bit more each day. Be patient with yourself as you experiment with a new way of being. Allow constructive fear to guide you into behaviors and thoughts that reduce negativity and bring you greater joy. Listen to yourself. Listen to your needs. Move forward consciously and compassionately, taking one small step at a time. Remember that you are truly amazing.

CHAPTER 5

Welcoming Transformational Fear into Your Personal World

Getting Closer to You

It's wonderful to get to know yourself, to discover who you are and what makes you tick. When self-awareness begins to take shape, when you start tuning into yourself with loving attention, you get the joy of knowing how unique and precious you are. It is an incredibly beautiful process, one that many people never come to experience—often because they unconsciously fear discovering their interior world. Instead of getting through the muck to discover hidden internal treasures, they continue through life without the rich benefits of self-discovery. Yet here you are, already immersed in a journey that is taking you to places inside yourself that you may have never known. You have courage; you have undertaken a rare and extraordinary process that will change your entire life.

With increasing self-awareness, the heavy cloak of destructive fear will continue to fade away, leaving you to shine more brilliantly every day. You will come to know deep inside yourself that you are precious—with all of your strengths and frailties, successes and stumbles, courage and insecurities—and that you are divine. As you get closer to your true self, you will thirst for more of what feels right to you. On both physical and psychological levels, you will want to be kinder and more compassionate with yourself and with others. At the same time, you will naturally shy away from that which does not feel good; harmful or unhelpful ways of the past will become unappealing and will fade away. As you become more adept at listening to constructive fear and taking steps into transformation, destructive fear will have no choice but to relinquish its grip upon you.

Destructive Fear's Allies: Doubt, Criticism, and a Quick-Fix Mentality

You've already been introduced to a few of the forces that work in concert with destructive fear to hold you back in life. These powerful forces tend to be very sneaky, slipping into your mind and your being at every opportunity. As you are discovering, they are especially likely to take advantage of you when you're suffering due to issues such as chronic stress, lack of sleep, or overwork. This section will offer you a more in-depth look at how some of destructive fear's most common allies might be working against you behind the scenes. As you continue to move forward, a few of destructive fear's most effective henchmen—doubt, criticism, and a quick-fix mentality—may gnaw and growl at you regularly. In fact, these forces may become more intense than ever in their drive to push you back into your former unhealthy patterns.

So prepare yourself for the snarling jaws of doubt to come at you with added force. It might arise through self-doubt or a general sense of doubt. For example, as you take steps to make simple, concrete changes in your life, self-doubt might make you question yourself and your progress. It might tell you that you can't change. It might tell you that you're not making any headway at all or that you're doing it all wrong. It might leave you wondering if you're even worthy of change.

Doubt may arise to tell you that it would be easier to just accept life as it is. It might tell you that destructive fear doesn't really exist. It might tell you that it's not safe or necessary to change. Doubt will want you to *doubt*. It will pepper you with many words of negativity. It will want you to feel insecure, hoping that you'll stay bound in your old ways of uncertainty or immobilizing fear. By increasing your general sense of doubt, destructive fear hopes to keep you under its bullying control.

Don't worry, for you are now prepared. You are learning to listen for this voice and to know it for what it is. You are learning to take charge. When you hear this negative voice of doubt arise, you can now pause and say, "*Stop*. I'm not listening to this fearful voice of doubt. I am becoming more aware. I am making progress—I can feel it. I'm onto you, Destructive Fear." It's a powerful comeback, isn't it? You are learning to quell that nonstop voice of doubt and immobilizing fear. This is a most wonderful sign of transformation.

As you deepen your journey, be on the lookout, too, for the harsh voice of criticism. The critical voice is a strong enemy, whether turned in upon yourself or from others. It may sneak in quietly, criticizing you for not doing something "right." It might softly whisper that you are not smart enough, strong enough, or patient enough to transform your life. Just like destructive fear's other allies, it often comes in through the back door, worming its way into your mind. It also might bang loudly at the front door of your mind, openly telling you that you are "stupid," "hopeless," or just too "broken." This critical voice wants you to give up; it wants you to stay stuck in patterns that hurt you and hold you back. Destructive fear is often highly irrational, but it is savvy. It will try to convince you that *you* are irrational or unintelligent and that *it* is logical and wise. This is one of the many ways that it will try to fool you through critical words that press you into feeling unworthy or incapable. Yet the friendly, honest voice of constructive fear will walk in to help you know the truth. Constructive fear will help you transform the critical voice that fuels destructive fear.

Notice, too, that others might criticize you as your behaviors and attitudes shift. Those who are accustomed to the "old you" may feel uncomfortable as you transform, for humans crave homeostasis. Overt and quiet pressure from loved ones and friends to "keep doing what we *normally* do together" can be one of the strongest forces of all. Consciously and unconsciously, others may want you to revert to your former, familiar ways—even if those patterns were terribly unhealthy. Those close to you

may want you to stop changing; they may feel threatened by your transformation and may strike out with harsh criticisms. Your positive shifts
may make others unconsciously more aware of their own issues, yet it is
not your responsibility to fix another person's discomfort with your positive changes. However, it is your right to continue on your journey with
courage, dignity, and awareness. Know that others may poke at you in an
effort to get things back to the way they were. This is yet another one of the
strong, far-reaching tentacles of destructive fear.

Once again, there is no need to worry. You are gaining the awareness
and wisdom to do what is truly right for you. Whether criticism arises from
inside yourself or from others, you know what to do. Pause to notice the critical voice without judgment. Remember, judgment allows the critical voice
to sneak in again through the back door. Do not react to the criticism; just
notice it. Then you will be able to say to yourself, "This criticism is not wise
or true. It is trying to keep me stuck. Stop, critical voice. Stop plaguing me.
Leave me in peace, Destructive Fear." As you move away from the critical
voice—not reacting to it, just noticing it—you are increasing your ability to
listen to the kind voice of constructive fear. In this way, too, you are transforming your life—you are transforming your fear.

Notice that destructive fear can taunt you in a way that is linked to
both doubt and criticism—the quick-fix mentality. As our world is often
oriented toward quick fixes, destructive fear will use this mindset as a tool
to hold you back. It will use a sense of pressure to get you off track. For
example, it might tell you that you need or deserve instant change. It might
tell you that you should have relief *now*. It might tell you that it is unnecessary or ineffective to delve into your history to make sense of harmful
patterns; it might tell you that it simply takes too much time. The voice
will tell you that there are easier routes to take. It might tell you that it
would be better to numb yourself. It might tempt you to dull your anxiety,
worry, and pain with self-medication. It might prompt you to resort to
unhealthy habits of instant gratification. It might tell you to close this book
or even throw it away. Remember, destructive fear does not like change. It
wants to keep you immobilized in anxiety, depression, and stress. It wants
to fuel the doubt and criticism that will keep you stuck in old behaviors.
Destructive fear likes having you in its harmful grasp.

Take a deep breath, for you need not worry. Your awareness of the
quick-fix mentality is also growing. You have the ability to notice this forceful aspect of destructive fear. When it rises to tell you that you deserve a

quick fix, you will have a ready response. You might even say, "Destructive Fear, I hear your voice. Yet I am wise to the power of constructive fear. My hurts and pains didn't arise overnight, and it will take time and patience for me to understand them and tend to them. I am worthy of a life filled with peace and joy. I have the patience and determination to bring that to my life. Yes, my changes may be slow, with two steps forward and half a step back, but they are beautiful, hard-earned changes. I am worth it." As you press on with courage, you will continue to transform your life in the most profound and simple ways.

Noticing Thoughts of Doubt, Criticism, and Quick Fixes

You now have the opportunity to notice some of the ways that destructive fear creeps into your mind. As you prepare for this exercise, make sure that you are in a safe, relaxed setting and are psychologically ready to proceed. With your pen and notebook at your side, take a few cleansing breaths. Work without judgment; accept whatever thoughts arise. Notice if destructive fear tries to enter with a voice of judgment or criticism.

Begin by imagining the word "doubt." Close your eyes, allowing yourself to reflect on ways that doubt interferes with your progress. For example, you might think *I can't imagine ever not being anxious; I'll always feel this way.* Open your eyes when you are ready. Write down at least five thoughts that express your doubts, leaving at least two spaces between items. Breathe.

Follow the same steps with the word "criticism." Close your eyes. Reflect on ways that criticism (from yourself or others) hampers your life. For example, you might think, *My husband tells me I'm wasting my time on this self-help stuff. He says it makes me crazier than ever!* When you are ready, open your eyes. Write down at least five thoughts that describe the criticism you experience; leave space between each sentence. Breathe.

Then follow the same steps for "quick fixes." Close your eyes, pondering the ways that a quick-fix mentality affects you. For example, you may think, *I'm already forty-one years old. I've been on antidepressants for a year. I should have my issues fixed by now!* When you are ready, open your eyes. Write down at least five thoughts that express how a quick-fix mentality works against you. Leave space between each sentence. Breathe.

Now go back to each set of the sentences that you wrote. Starting with the section on doubt, read each negative sentence. Then let constructive fear guide you on reframing that doubt into a supportive, helpful comment. The first example above might be reframed to say, *There are moments when I can actually notice my anxiety lessening—the breathing exercises make me feel a little better every time I practice them. I know I can do this. I can move forward.* With the voice of constructive fear in your ear, reframe each of the sentences that are focused on doubt. Shift them, with conscious awareness, to a positive truth. Breathe.

Then move to the section on criticism using the same steps. For example, the thought above, *My husband tells me I'm wasting my time on this self-help stuff. He says it makes me crazier than ever!* might be adjusted to say, *I am getting stronger and more aware. I know this makes my husband uncomfortable and afraid, but I want to persevere. This feels good and right to me.* With the voice of constructive fear in your ear, reframe each of the critical-minded sentences. Shift each one to a positive message. Breathe.

When you are ready, move to the section on quick fixes. Notice that the thought, *I'm already forty-one years old. I've been on anti-depressants for a year. I should have my issues fixed by now!* could be adjusted with a dose of compassion. It could be reframed to say: *I've had quite a history that's really affected me. For the first time in my life, I am really understanding and appreciating what I've been through and how it has shaped me. I am gathering the awareness and tools I want and need to move forward.* Listening to constructive fear, positively reframe each sentence in the quick-fix category. Breathe. Congratulate yourself on a job well done. By practicing the concepts from this section, you will become increasingly aware of the many manifestations of destructive fear. The mindfulness you are creating is an invaluable aspect of your transformative journey.

Promoting Healthy Personal Patterns

The foundation you have been building will get even stronger as you practice the concepts you are learning. Some realms of life are less amenable to change than other areas, so be patient with your progress. Remember that this journey is a process; change will not happen overnight. Indeed, trust that your body and psyche require time to learn new concepts and even more time to effectively and consistently apply them. It might be helpful to remember that a seed planted in the earth needs plenty of time, water, and nutrients before it begins to germinate. Then, one day, it "magically" sprouts—but unseen, transformative work was taking place all along within the dark soil. It is the same with your own process. You might not see or notice the work taking place in your internal world, but the magic is happening nonetheless. Your unique process cannot be forced; it will have a time and rhythm all its own. Your psyche will know when it is ready for another step. With patience and perseverance, the seeds of your journey will germinate and grow. Trust your process with transformational fear. Trust yourself.

As you prepare to move into the heart of this chapter, remember that old behaviors can be highly resistant to change. Destructive fear will dig in its heels, doing everything it can to stop your progress. Allow yourself to slow down, breathe, and listen for the wisdom of constructive fear. Embrace the positive concepts and tools you have learned so far; carry them in your heart and mind. Know that the peaceful, joy-filled life you desire is not so very far away.

Your Unintentional Consumption of Destructive Fear

Destructive fear won't like you reading this section at all, for it directly targets destructive fear's most secret entry points and dwelling places in your internal world. Much of the self-doubt, anxiety, and depression you might experience is tied to destructive fear's furtive ways. In fact, destructive fear controls us most in the areas where we are deeply sensitive and fearful. We do all that we can to protect our secret hurts and wounds—our most vulnerable areas—and this gives destructive fear its greatest edge. When we are ashamed and embarrassed, destructive fear knows that it has us tightly in its grasp. After all, if we are too ashamed to talk—or even think—about our worst hurts and fears, how could we possibly effect change? In this way, destructive fear knows that it is safe. When we ignore or protect our aching, most wounded areas, we protect destructive fear.

There are times that we don't even know we are hurting inside. For some, the hurt is so deep and penetrating that they never feel as if they fit in anywhere in life—no matter what they say or do. For others, the sense of discomfort is so intense that they do not feel as if they are comfortable in their very skin. Destructive fear is at the root of this discomfort and lack of ease. It often sneaks in during childhood through parents' unkind, thoughtless, or outright destructive behaviors. In other cases, the hurts begin to form during school years through the slights of cliques, teachers, or friends.

As if critical words, hurtful behaviors, and destructive patterns aren't enough, destructive fear has moved into our psyches in the most pernicious, invisible ways. Day and night, it taunts us—often hiding in plain sight. Look around you for a moment. Chances are that you can find at least one item that is an ally of destructive fear. If your computer screen is on, notice if pop-up ads are on the side. Is a beauty magazine near you or a trendy catalog at your side? If your television is turned on, what images do you see? It's likely that something around you is unconsciously reminding you that you are somehow deficient. In essence, destructive fear uses the material world around you to make you unconsciously strive to live up to impossible standards—to look perfect, act perfect, and be perfect. It wants you to compare your life to your neighbor's. It wants you to compare your body to a magazine or television image. It wants you to buy cars, clothes, pills, food, jewelry, houses, and material items of all sorts in the hope that you'll feel just a little more like the pretty or handsome image selling the latest or biggest thing. It wants you to compare your smile, your body, and even your mood to the person next door. Destructive fear can infect your psyche with the unconscious drive to incessantly compare yourself to others, ultimately leaving you in despair.

The Disease of Comparison: A Case Study

It's time to introduce you to Isabel, who came to see me for anxiety and self-esteem issues. In her mid-thirties, Isabel was haunted by her perceived imperfections and lifelong sense of isolation. To the objective eye, Isabel was lovely, but she did not see herself this way. She could recount stories from childhood through current life where she felt like an outcast. As Isabel explained, "First off, my dad wanted a boy. I struck out there big time. My younger brother was the golden child; I was pretty much dirt. When I was a kid, I was always the scrawny one—always left out. Then, before I was eleven, I developed breasts and hips—way before the other girls. I got a lot of attention—often from older guys, but it wasn't what I wanted. I felt self-conscious and embarrassed, and that feeling never left me. I wanted to look like the other girls—thin and small. People sometimes tell me I'm pretty, but I've never felt pretty at all. I can hear the words, but they don't translate for me. I'm just too big and too curvy—I want to be a twig. I'd give anything to look like a swimsuit model, but it's impossible for me. I've dieted to death, but it doesn't work. I can't stand being in a bathing suit or even shorts. I *hate* being naked. I can't stand looking at myself in the mirror."

Isabel suffers from the disease of comparison—a very powerful disease crafted by destructive fear. Both men and women suffer from this serious affliction, for we live in a world where comparison has become a way of life. As you increase your awareness, you will have the power to immunize yourself against this debilitating disease. You will come to notice the ways that this element of destructive fear gives rise to many harmful issues that include self-doubt, insecurity, and feelings of anxiety and depression. Unfortunately, you can't eradicate this widespread disease, but you can learn to inoculate yourself against it.

If you were fortunate, the "look around" I asked you to do earlier proved fruitless. However, even if your current environment is free of ads, commercials, and other visual or auditory methods that propel you to compare yourself to others, it's likely that your days are not free of this aspect of destructive fear. Supermarket checkouts are lined with magazines that offer airbrushed perfection. Actors and actresses use a variety of tools from makeup, lighting, and body doubles to hide their imperfections. Paper advertisements and on-screen commercials often sell us on their models far more than their actual products. Through subliminal and overt advertising, we are promised that we will have better, happier lives if we buy the right pills, drive the latest cars, properly accessorize the perfect home, use the best-smelling deodorant, dress in the latest style, and smile our whitest smiles. It's exhausting. It's unachievable. It's ridiculous. It's no wonder that the disease of comparison creates such a high degree of self-doubt, self-loathing, and anxiety. It is no surprise that it leaves countless men and women mired in chronic insecurity and depression—ever striving for the illusion of perfection. This disease is one of the most debilitating and invasive claws of destructive fear. It is relentless in its quest to convince you that you are insufficient, unworthy, unlovable, or unacceptable as you are. Constructive fear wants to remind you that this is simply and utterly untrue.

Yet this aspect of destructive fear can create chronic, negative self-talk in your head. Just as it did with lovely Isabel, it can put a voice inside you that tells you that you are not enough. As Isabel confessed one day, "I can't even stand to watch television when my boyfriend is around. I could never tell him this, but I have this terrible fear that he looks at the women in the shows and commercials and compares me to them. I get this sick feeling in my stomach—like he's secretly attracted to the thin ones instead of me. It's gotten to the point where I can't even watch a football game with him. I'll never look like the women in the commercials—I constantly compare myself to them. It's not my boyfriend—he tells me I'm pretty and that he loves my curves, but that doesn't soak in. I have this voice in my head that says, 'You are not good enough. You are too fat. You're disgusting with your big boobs and curves.' Over the years, I've bought every diet and exercise book, diet pill, and body shaper I could find. I've joined gyms and weight-loss clinics. I've spent way too much money on diet plans and diet shakes. I've even bought fat-melting cream. Not a day goes by that I don't wish I looked like someone else." Isabel, like many of the men and women who tell me similar stories, was held in the grip of destructive fear.

In time, Isabel learned to routinely track her negative self-talk. She discovered that personalized positive self-talk tapes were a powerful force in decreasing her anxiety and increasing her self-esteem. Isabel chose positive phrases to combat her negative self-talk. She particularly enjoyed this positive tape: "I am beautiful just as I am. I am valuable and worthy of love." Isabel went through her closet and rid herself of clothes that she bought to "fit into someday." She bought a swimsuit—the first one she had owned since childhood—in the hope that she would wear it someday soon. She made a decision to no longer buy fashion magazines—one of her key triggers. Isabel took down and sold a vintage poster she had purchased that depicted the waif-like beauty she always wanted to be. She made a visit to her physician for a long overdue wellness check, allowing herself to soak in the truth that her weight was within a normal range for her body type and height. When she felt safe, Isabel discussed her fears with her boyfriend. She was overjoyed by her boyfriend's supportive, thoughtful response. Armed with his support and love, they worked together to create an environment that was less triggering to her as she worked on improving her self-esteem. They began exercising together and created healthy eating plans that supported a sustainable, healthy diet, replacing Isabel's yo-yo dieting lifestyle. As she pushed out destructive fear's negative self-talk, Isabel began to discover true and simple joy—she began to feel comfortable in her own skin. As she listened to the compassionate voice of constructive fear, Isabel's days and nights were no longer ruled by nonstop, comparative messages of destructive fear.

If this aspect of destructive fear is at work in your life, you can begin to immunize yourself to its toxic ways. As with most of destructive fear's patterns, one of your greatest tools is simple awareness. You will now be able to scrutinize your daily environment to notice the negative ways that devious comparison sneaks into your world. Again, you can't completely rid your world of advertisements and other comparison-inducing elements, but you can become aware of their impact on you. Through this simple act of noticing the impact, you will then make conscious choices to protect yourself from the constant onslaught of this comparative voice. You will also be able to notice and address any thoughts of comparison that arise inside of you.

Your Personal Immunization against Comparison

This exercise can have profound and lasting results. Once you notice where destructive fear's comparison-oriented force is at work, you will begin to feel more at ease with yourself.

Begin this exercise once you are in a safe, relaxed environment and feeling psychologically prepared for this next journey. Take care to work with a compassionate, nonjudgmental attitude. With your pen and notebook at your side, pause to breathe. Read the complete exercise. When you are ready, you may wish to proceed with your eyes closed.

Imagine the world that you walk through each day. Envision the ways that your mind might be filled with thoughts of comparison. Imagine the various ways that comparison comes to you—through your eyes and your ears. Let yourself envision the ways that destructive fear sneaks into your life and your psyche with incessant messages that make you feel unworthy, insufficient, or unlovable as you are. For example, you might have noticed thoughts of not being as attractive as your friends or as well-built as other gym members. You might have had thoughts of being too short, too fat, or too skinny. Perhaps you had thoughts of an airbrushed model who has perfect breasts and no wrinkles or blemishes. Maybe your thoughts turned to the guy next door who has a better car or bigger house. Whatever comes to your mind, just notice it without judgment. When you are ready, open your eyes and write down ten ways that comparison manifests in your world. For example, you might note, *I constantly compare my body to everyone else's at the gym.* Leave plenty of space between each item to allow for the next part of this exercise. Pause to breathe when you are finished.

When you are ready, close your eyes again. Imagine a world where you feel loved and accepted as you are. Imagine the shifts that might be possible to allow yourself to let go of the destructive voice of comparison. Listen for the wisdom of constructive fear. When you are ready, open your eyes. In the spaces below each item where you listed the negative effects of destructive fear, write down a positive message from constructive fear. For example, if you found yourself comparing your body to someone else's, you might write, *When I go to the gym, I am going to remind myself how blessed I am to have a wonderful, healthy body. If comparisons and negative self-talk comes up, I will repeat my self-talk that reminds me that my body type is curvy and good.* Let constructive fear come in to guide you each and every step of the way. Notice and feel the power of your positive inner voice. Notice how empowering it feels to address and silence the bitter voice of comparison. As you listen to and use the wise voice of constructive fear, the comparative voice of destructive fear will fade bit by bit. Take your time with the exercise, for it has the power to transform the way you view yourself and your world.

Home: Where Fear Hides in Plain Sight

When you open your eyes in the morning, what is the first thing you see? What is the first thing you hear? When you close your eyes at night, what is the last thing you see? What is the last thing you hear? You might be tempted to skim past these questions, but your honest response is highly significant. You are affected more than you know by the way you begin each day and the way you end each day.

Remember, destructive fear looks for opportunities to sneak into your life. Being the negative force that it is, it rather likes the idea of being present as you wake every morning. Destructive fear also feels powerful when it is present as you go to sleep every night. This gives it greater energy and more power to remain with you throughout the day. When this enemy side of transformational fear is able to wedge itself into your daily routine, it knows it has a strong foothold in your life. In fact, when you hear the word "routine," you might automatically think, *Routines and schedules are no fun. They're constricting and boring.* That's destructive fear talking to you, once again sneaking in the back door to thwart your progress. Constructive fear would tell you, "Routines simply give safety and stability to your life. They needn't be dull or tiresome. You have a great deal of freedom to create and utilize practices that feel right for you. Personalize your routines as much as you like!"

Step back in time for a moment. What were your morning and evening routines as a child? When you woke, did you have a morning routine that felt safe, allowing you to greet the day? Did you start your morning with a hug from your parents and a good breakfast? Did you brush your teeth? Did you put on fresh clothes that made you feel ready for school? Was your homework done and your lunch packed, giving you the comfort of being prepared for the day? Then recall your evening routine. Did you have a set time for homework? Did you have an opportunity for play? Was dinner shared at a table where discussions were inviting and supportive? Was the television turned off? Were you lulled to sleep by the sound of your mother's voice? Did your father stop by your bed to kiss you goodnight? Was a bedtime story part of your evening routine? Did you prepare for bedtime by brushing your teeth and taking a warm bath? Was there a familiar, comforting routine to your bedtime schedule and a set time for sleep?

The above might sound like a fairy tale or unrealistic television show, yet many home environments offer at least some predictable version of these familiar, healthy routines. What is most vital is the realization that even if you didn't grow up within a healthy environment, you have the power to create one now. Small, steady changes will help you create gentle, beneficial daily routines that will give you incredible relief. With an outside world that is terribly chaotic and unpredictable, such ordinary, familiar practices are all the more precious and necessary. When home life is steady and predictable, the external world can be far less stressful. When home life is chaotic and charged with frenzied energy, the body and psyche have no place to rest and relax. The routines that we live with day in and day out create hard-wired patterns and *felt* memories. No home environment or daily routine is ever perfect; indeed, the illusion of perfection hampers the true goal. The objective is simple: With gentle awareness, begin to shift your home life into one that makes you and your loved ones feel internally safe and free from the external world's stressors. As you allow yourself to notice how fear has infiltrated your life without you even knowing it, you will naturally become more aware of what does and does not feel healthy.

To deepen your awareness, return to thinking *nonjudgmentally* about how you begin most of your days. Do you wake to the alarm clock screaming at you? Do your first thoughts take you to work and to-do lists? Do you reflexively turn on the television to hear the news? Does news of the latest natural disaster or shooting spree rush into your mind? Can you hear sirens from your window or neighbors screaming at their children? Do you reach for your phone to read text messages or emails? Do you race through your shower and mindlessly dress for work? Do your children seem like just another stressor in life? Do you ignore breakfast and rush out the door with a coffee buzz? On the other hand, perhaps your mornings are not stress-inducing. Maybe you feel deeply rested as you open your eyes. Perhaps you wake to a kiss from your partner, the sound of your children's voices, or the furry warmth of your pet. Maybe the sweet sound of silence or gentle music fills the air. Perhaps you pause to meditate or offer a morning prayer. Maybe you brush your teeth, enjoy a warm shower, and then carefully dress. Perhaps you sit down to enjoy a healthy breakfast, noticing the taste and texture of your food. Perhaps you help your partner with the children, sending them safely on their way. Maybe, when it's time to head to work, you hug your sweetheart or pet goodbye, pick up your bag, and move out into the world with a smile. Whatever your routine may be, pause to look at the flow of your morning. Then, as you tune in to the wisdom of constructive fear, ask yourself, *Is this how I want to start my day?*

Give your evening routine the same objective review. Do you race home from work and take off your shoes? Do you head for the refrigerator, reaching for beer or a glass of wine? Do you check your phone throughout the evening? Do you mindlessly turn on your television or computer and sit down for the night? Do you throw a frozen dinner in the microwave or unpack the takeout food you brought home? Or did you eat your dinner in the car, the bus, or on the subway? Do your children frustrate and irritate you with their noise or homework needs? Do you fall asleep on the couch with the television on in the background? Do you bother to floss and brush? Do thoughts of work or home difficulties plague you as you lie in bed? Do you have trouble falling asleep or staying asleep? Do nightmares or bad dreams torment you? Do you take a sleeping pill or two, hoping to find some rest? On the other hand, perhaps your evening routine is gentle and relaxed. Maybe you come home to a hug from your partner, the laughter of your children, or the wag of your dog's tail. Perhaps you sit down in quiet to relax with a cup of herbal tea at your side. Maybe you reach for a book or help your child with homework. Perhaps you unpack groceries and prepare dinner with your partner. Maybe you sit at the kitchen table, enjoying the back-and-forth of gentle conversation. Maybe you help put your children to bed, reading them a story or two. Perhaps you sit quietly with your partner and talk about the highlights of the day. Maybe you slowly prepare for bedtime, enjoying the familiar routines of flossing, teeth-brushing, and washing. Perhaps you enjoy sexually intimate time with your partner with sweet kisses sending you off to sleep. Maybe you read a few pages of your favorite book before nodding off. Perhaps you give your sweetheart a few words of gratitude before closing your eyes. Maybe you doze off to sweet sleep alone or with a pet cuddled nearby. Whatever it may be, pause to look at your evening routine. Listen for the helpful guidance of constructive fear and ask yourself, *Is this how I want to end my day?*

Let me explain a bit more fully why all of this is so important. Home is where we start from, and home is where we end our days. As noted earlier, it's not about creating a "perfect" home environment that is absolutely free of distractions and ripples—such an environment is unlikely to exist. It's about creating a home environment that does not breed internal and external fear. It makes sense that you would want your home, where you spend so much of your sleeping and waking time, to feel peaceful and safe. Indeed, if you work outside your home, you likely are at work for about one-third of each weekday; the balance of your time may be largely spent at home. In many ways, you have the power to transform your home life. Maybe you can't change what goes on outside the walls of your home, but you can certainly affect what takes place inside. Remember, when the home environment is chaotic and disruptive, destructive fear moves in noiselessly.

Of course, there are situations where a living environment doesn't readily support—or is highly resistant to—positive change. For example, beneficial shifts may be particularly challenging if a controlling, inflexible spouse takes the attitude, "It must be my way or the highway!" Some households may suffer chronic upheaval due to toxic anger, substance abuse, or other difficult issues. Other homes may be disrupted by the caregiving needs of elderly parents or demands of significant health issues. Some households find that adolescent or grown children are a constant source of complaints and unrest. Many feel terribly stuck with unharmonious or disrespectful roommates. If you are in one of these more intractable situations, don't let destructive fear keep you immobilized. Trust that you are amassing the insight and power to make positive changes. Let constructive fear guide you to listen, reach out for support, and create small, achievable goals. As you move forward one small step at a time, you will ultimately transform your environment. The progress may be slow, but every positive change you make—no matter how tiny—leads you closer to your goal of a serene, positive home environment.

Childhood Routines

As you move into your next exercise, prepare a safe and comfortable environment for yourself. Check in with yourself, making sure that you are ready to proceed. Then, with your journal and pen at your side, read the complete exercise. Breathe. When you are ready, you may wish to proceed with your eyes closed.

Once again, reflect on your early childhood routines in detail. Notice what felt good and what did not feel good. Do not worry that you might misremember something from your childhood. Your memories are your own, and your perceptions are your own. Scan your morning routines, both for weekdays and weekends. First, look at the morning flow itself. Was a routine present, or was chaos the rule? Then notice the pace of the mornings. Was the pace slow and leisurely, fast and hectic, or somewhere in between? What was the energy? Did the mornings move fluidly and with a sense of gentle purpose, or was the energy frenetic and nerve-wracking? Did music play in the background or was the television blaring? Then look at how breakfast was handled. Was the first meal of the day ignored altogether? Was it cold cereal or a hearty, home-cooked meal? Was breakfast eaten at a table, while standing, or on the run? Finally, notice how prepared you felt for each day. Did you have your school assignments completed and in your backpack? Was your lunchtime food or lunch money ready? Did you set off for the day ahead feeling well-prepared? Most of all, notice if you generally left home in a calm or a stressed state. Make notes about all of these important details, for they are part of the vital environment in which you were raised.

Now review all of your notes carefully. First, notice which patterns, both healthy and unhealthy, you might be unconsciously repeating in your adult life; place an asterisk next to these. Second, place a large "F" by those patterns that are fear-based—these are the ones that create anxiety and stress. Finally, make a list of the positive patterns you would like to retain; add any new patterns that sound helpful. Make a second list of the fear-based patterns you would like to shift. Take several deep breaths.

Notice that you have used your awareness of destructive fear to create a list of those patterns that create stress and anxiety in your life. Notice that you have used constructive fear to create a very positive list that will support you in life. Focus on the positive list you have made. You have the power to bring these helpful changes into your life. As you extinguish the effects of destructive fear, your home environment will become an increasingly safe and supportive space. Congratulate yourself on a job well done!

You may have noticed from your work on the above exercise that destructive fear can sneak stealthily into your life. This surreptitious nature of destructive fear gives it great power. After all, who would think that a mere news broadcast buzzing in the background could rattle the nerves? Who would think that a crazy day at work could follow you home? Who would have known that the grimace on your face as you closed your eyes would be there to haunt you when you woke? We have become so used to our fast-paced, chaotic lives that we simply don't realize how much chaos may be present. It is in this constant chaos that destructive fear thrives. As noted by the brilliant psychologist and author James Hillman, "We awaken daily in fear of the things we live with, eat, drink, and breathe."[1] When we are at home, we often do not *feel* "at home." All too often, we are immersed in living environments that reverberate with fear.

Now it is time to visualize the rooms in your home. Scan each space slowly, noting the electrical appliances that are present. Are televisions, desktop computers, laptops, and gaming systems present? Notice all of your electrical devices, including security cameras, alarm systems, coffee makers, microwaves, lights, and anything else that might be plugged in. Pay special attention to any devices that emit blue light, the wavelength of which is disruptive to sleep at night due to its suppressing effect on melatonin production. Then objectively ponder which of the devices you personally equate with a peaceful environment and those that you would associate with increased adrenaline, stress, or anxiety. Notice that it might be difficult to be objective, because you might, consciously or unconsciously, know that the use of certain devices actually increases your level of stress or anxiety. Look at what you want to retain in your life; differentiate between the devices that bring you peace and joy and those that increase stress or disconnection from others. This is a perfect opportunity for you to notice how destructive fear might have snuck into your world in yet another way. Remember that noticing destructive fear is the first step to transforming it into constructive fear.

Changing Stuck Patterns with Specificity

Clearly, your home environment is a very important place. We've touched on some of the ways that destructive fear might be affecting the atmosphere in your home. In this next exercise, which is built on the exercise above, you will have a great opportunity to make changes in your home life. If you find yourself thinking, *Well, I did that in the last exercise! What more do I need to do?* you've found another spot where destructive fear has you in its grasp. The first exercise helped you outline the changes you want to make, but it didn't give you the opportunity to create the specific steps to help you *achieve* your goals. The previous exercise was constructed in that way to draw this critical point to your attention: so many plans for change don't come to fruition due to a lack of structure and specificity. Many people think that their hoped-for changes fall flat because they are doomed, lazy, or incompetent. In most cases, it's simply that tricky, destructive fear has taken control. It might tell you, *I don't like structure or routine* or *Oh, this is too much work!* or *I'll get around to it someday.* Remember, destructive fear likes you to be stuck in your old patterns; it doesn't like change. Destructive fear wants you to be blind to the freedom that arises from safety and routine. These are just a few of destructive fear's mind tricks. But now, you have cultivated the awareness that allows constructive fear to step in as your guide and friend; it can help you outline specific, achievable steps that will let you create a more stress-free home. Throughout your journey, keep in mind that destructive fear is terrified of structure and specificity, whereas constructive fear thrives on them!

As you move into this next exercise, make sure that you are physically and psychologically in a peaceful, relaxed space. Then, with your notebook open and pen at your side, look at the two lists you made for your last exercise. The first list outlines the negative patterns that create stress and anxiety in your life. The second list outlines the constructive patterns that you are choosing to create, retain, or enhance in your life.

Now, on fresh pages in your notebook, make a list of each negative pattern, leaving space below each pattern for additional notes.

After each negative pattern, write out several simple, realistic steps you can take to achieve your desired results. Next to each step, give yourself an achievable timeframe for completion. (Notice that destructive fear might want to interfere; it knows that a specific goal and specific time increases the likelihood that change will be made.) For example, if you find that your family watches too much television, you might write:

Reduce television use:

> Step 1—Donate the television in the playroom. Do this within seven days.
> Step 2—Reduce television watching to one hour per night on weekdays. Do this starting tonight.
> Step 3—Play a board game with my family every Saturday night. Start this weekend.

Then continue this process with your constructive list. After each positive pattern, write out several simple, achievable steps you can take to achieve your goal. Next to each step, give yourself an achievable timeframe for completion. For example, if spending time with your partner makes you happy, you might note:

Increase time spent with my partner:

> Step 1—Leave work on time. Start this today.
> Step 2—Take a walk together three days a week after work. Start this tonight.
> Step 3—Make a dinner date with my partner two times per month. Start this weekend.

After you have completed both lists, take a deep breath. Notice that you have used constructive fear to create steps that will allow you to make concrete, positive changes in your life. Congratulate yourself on the time and energy you are investing in creating a happier, less-stressed life. Well done!

The big and little shifts you are creating in your inner and outer worlds will have incredible payoffs. Remember, your old habits might be very resistant to change. This is completely natural, for they are hardwired into your very being. Destructive fear may try to interfere with your progress with words of doubt and negativity. When you hear this negative voice, simply remind yourself that you have what it takes to press forward to manifest the changes you desire. This positive energy—the flow that you create—will actually have a significant effect on your personal and work relationships.

As one of my favorite sayings wisely notes, "All things change when we do." Trust that you have incredible power inside of you—far more than you may know. As you become less controlled by destructive fear, you will feel more relaxed and at ease. As you listen to the wisdom of constructive fear, you will be less stressed and more at peace—and you will truly become a model for others. With the power of transformational fear in your pocket, you will change your world.

Constructive Fear: The Allure of the Slow and Silent Type

"Beware the barrenness of a busy life," warns a quote attributed to Socrates. Those seven simple words ring harsh and true, for a busy life can be all too empty of what matters most, such as inner peace, love, and tranquility. If the above exercises left you noticing that you are far too busy, maybe it is time to wonder *why*. The previous section gave you the opportunity to take a look around your world. This next segment will help you attend to pieces that may be falling through the cracks. Perhaps it is time for you to listen to your inner self, to notice what you really want and need out of life.

For example, how do you respond when you are asked "How are you?" Is your common response "Oh, I can't believe how busy I am!" or "I'm fine—just waiting for the weekend!" Or when you haven't checked in with a loved one, do you offer an explanation that says, "I've been so crazy busy!" or "You know how it is—there aren't enough hours in the day!" This is destructive fear at work, dragging you mindlessly through your days. What if, one day, you were to say, "Today, I will slow down. I will not rush. Today, I am not busy. I am not too busy to call my elderly mom. I am not too busy to brush my dog. I am not too busy to sit with my son while he does his homework. I am not too busy to spend ten minutes on the phone with my dear friend who left me a message a week ago. Today, I will make the time to breathe and to enjoy every single moment." When you let constructive fear lead you into a different way of being, your world opens up and transforms. So when someone asks, "How are you doing?" your response might be entirely different. You might smile, look them kindly in the eyes and say, "Thank you for asking. I'm doing really well. I am slowing down and choosing to do the most wonderful things with my day!"

Given our busy schedules and busy world, it can be difficult to change pace and slow down. Whether we bring it on ourselves or not, our schedules are often far too busy. Notice, too, that destructive fear might propel you to believe that you must constantly *stay* busy. Through subtle pressure from self-messages or society at large, it can feel "wrong" not to be busy. Destructive fear projects the mantra that says, "If you are not busy or actively creating your next to-do list, you're somehow not a 'whole' person." In fact, destructive fear might want you to believe that you are worthless if you are not busy. Constructive fear would counter such notions with honest awareness. Constructive fear would say, "Busyness does not make you a better, more whole person—busyness can actually keep you from coming to know and love yourself."

It's also important to differentiate between self-created, avoidable busyness and busyness that is necessary to meet basic needs. For example, an individual who is working two jobs simply to make ends meet may not be able to cut back on work hours at all. As such, helpful and realistic self-care tips for such a person might include carved-out personal time that could allow for short meditations, breathing exercises, and uplifting social interactions.

As you are coming to find, destructive fear desperately wants you to stay busy. It wants you to race around, chasing after money, material "stuff," and power. It wants you not to notice how empty that way of life can be. Destructive fear wants to brainwash you into believing that life is about amassing material wealth, fame, and fortune. But it's not. Research continues to show that after a certain point, money does not increase happiness or life satisfaction.[2] In general, the level of happiness plateaus once basic needs are covered. For those who are driven to busyness hoping to increase happiness, it's possible that their efforts are counterproductive. Destructive fear wants you to press ever forward; it wants you to avoid even basic self-care and self-awareness. It wants you to go off to work so that you can purchase and consume—and then go back to work so that you can purchase and consume even more. Destructive fear doesn't want you to stop and think about any of this, but constructive fear does. It wants to ask you if you *need* to stay so busy. It wants to ask what would happen if you slowed down. Would you make less of the money that you actually need? Would you have less to spend on necessities? Or would you have less to spend on things you don't need—things that aren't making you happy once the box is opened or the new item is put away? Before you go any further, constructive fear wants to ask you another question: Are you *afraid* to slow down?

The above questions are important to ask yourself, for your inner life depends upon your honest responses. Indeed, there are times in life that we must work very hard just to make ends meet—to have a home, clothing, and food. Yet sometimes destructive fear takes us down a path that leads to a life of nonstop work and ego-driven busyness that is focused solely on accumulating more and more. When that journey begins, there is often no end in sight until death finally comes to take us from all the material wealth we've desperately accumulated—leaving behind nothing but dust and disconnected souls. Without judgment, let yourself notice if you are on the right or wrong path for yourself and what truly brings you peace and joy. For a moment, let constructive fear be your guide to noticing what type of life would allow you to truly thrive.

In today's chaotic world, a busy life and a noisy life often go hand-in-hand. Notice, for a moment, how noisy your own world has become. Are you distracted by constant noise in your environment? Are your ears and your mind assaulted by auditory stimulation at every turn? If so, your environment is inviting and helpful to destructive fear. Constructive fear thrives in quiet and calm, but the opposite is true for its counterpart. Destructive fear wants your head filled with noisy chatter; it doesn't want you to think too much, especially about concepts such as change and transformation.

As you reflect on the day-to-day level of noise in your environment, imagine dialing it down a little bit. Notice if you are simply accustomed to noise or if you actually like noise. Let constructive fear guide you to home in on whether or not some spaces of quiet would be good for you. In fact, constructive fear wants you to consider what it might be like to eat in silence, walk in silence, work in silence, or even drive in silence. It wants you to notice if you have become so accustomed to the chatter of news, loud music, or talk shows that the idea of silence actually worries you. Constructive fear wants to ask you two more questions: Are you afraid of what you might think or feel if the external chatter stopped? Are you afraid to come face-to-face with the thoughts that are spiraling in your head? Notice, without judgment, if your daily world would improve with a bit of quiet. Notice, too, if you take the gift of silence for granted. As a dear friend who developed chronic tinnitus told me, "To contemplate never being able to experience utter silence again is very troubling . . . how precious true peace and quiet is!"

Fast, Loud, Empty, and Lonely: A Case Study

This is a perfect opportunity to introduce you to Richard, a bright and super-charged man in his late thirties. When I first met Richard, he asked me for help on two issues. Foremost, he wanted to understand why he kept repeating negative cycles in relationships. Second, he wanted to get relief from his chronic anxiety. During one of our early sessions, I asked Richard to describe his daily routine—even the smallest details. As I listened, I could feel his energy and anxiety rise.

Richard noted, "I like things busy, easy, and hassle-free. So from the moment I wake up, I'm on the go. I get a cup of coffee, then I get a fast shower, drink a protein shake, and jump in my car. I usually have the TV or music playing—I like it loud. I get in my car and head to the gym. While I drive, I listen to the radio or have my music on—I like old-school rock. It's the same when I work out every day—I have my earbuds in. After my workout, I get another quick shower before going to work. I'm there all day. I don't take a lunch; I usually eat an energy bar or two and drink a lot of coffee. The coffee keeps me going. I get more done when I work non-stop; it's a fast-paced office. I'm usually one of the last to leave the office. At the end of the day, I head to a restaurant or sometimes grab fast food. I usually have a beer or two—rarely more than that. Once I get home, the computer is on and television is on. Loud. I like the noise. Sometimes I smoke to chill out—truth is, I smoke every day. Then I usually fall asleep watching TV—sometimes I read with it on in the background. Half the time I wake up and the TV is still on. I don't sleep well most nights and often take a sleeping pill. No matter what, I always wake up between 2:45 and 3:00 in the morning. I hate that part—it's quiet. I don't like things quiet. It's too empty and strange without some sort of noise."

During his quick overview, Richard didn't just tell me a lot about his daily routine—he told me a great deal about his internal life. Over the course of several months, I came to understand a lot more about Richard. He grew up in a tumultuous, highly charged family where the pursuit of money and success was paramount. An only child, he was raised in a chaotic home environment where noise was constant and personal connection was not. Richard noted, "My father was always on the go. If I sat still for a second—even to do homework—he called me lazy. My mom was always busy, too. She worked nonstop just like my father. Whenever we were together, whether it was dinner or whatever, the television was always on—always loud. My dad liked it in the background. Now that I see things more objectively, I can see that they were just trying to avoid talking about anything other than work and money."

In his adult life, Richard unconsciously amplified the noise he had grown accustomed to throughout the first half of his life. Richard unintentionally copied the disconnected, unaffectionate ways of his parents in his personal relationships. The constant noise and buzz in his environment numbed him and drowned out any internal voices that hoped to be heard. Although he thought the noise and busy clatter eased his nervousness, they actually only covered up his anxious thoughts and feelings. Whether he listened to loud music, drank, smoked, or watched television, the anxiety was always waiting just below the surface. As he learned more about his inner workings, Richard once said, "You know, I thought I had my life pretty dialed in. Now I can see that I was actually empty and depressed. I was running and running to avoid how empty I felt. I was trying to outrun my anxiety. The nonstop noise and insane schedule—those were just my ways of going numb. I was repeating what my parents did. It seems crazy to me, but I get it. Now that things are changing, I can look back and see how I was running in circles to avoid myself. It's pretty sad."

Actually, Richard came to see that his story is far from sad, for he had the courage to explore his history and learn from it. Richard had the bravery to dive in, notice what was not working for him, and begin to transform his life. Driven and highly self-disciplined, the external changes he wanted were fairly easy for him to make. From stocking his refrigerator with fresh fruit and vegetables to making his bedroom a television-free zone, Richard steadfastly made thoughtful shifts that brought him a sense of pleasure and accomplishment. He told me, "My mornings are a little slower now. I've actually bought eggs and started frying them up each morning. It's a small thing, but it feels really good just to use my dishes and pans—to make something for myself. I still can't handle too much quiet, but I'm working at it. The music is lower, and the television is off unless I'm sitting down to watch something."

Richard's internal journey took quite a bit more effort and time. Richard came to discover that he was actually afraid of himself—of his internal world. He had never stopped to wonder who he was or what he really wanted out of life. He simply continued moving forward in life doing the next "right thing"—whether it was right for him or not. In our work together, Richard discovered that he had many desires and interests he had never thought to explore. Once he turned down the volume of his world, he found that he actually liked many aspects of the man he was. He also found that there were aspects of his being that he didn't like much at all. As he explored himself, he came to understand the fears that unconsciously drove him to work and push nonstop. He came to see why he had lived for so long in a world fueled by fear and the anxiety it created. In the most beautiful way, Richard came to understand and appreciate himself. As he learned the art of self-compassion, he naturally became more at ease with himself. In a much later session, Richard noted, "When I started seeing you, I thought it would take a few appointments—that you'd give me some information and send me on my way. I had no idea that I would actually learn about myself. I didn't know I even had an internal world to explore. If someone had told me my life was run by fear, I'd have told them they were insane—and I would have believed it. Here's the coolest part: I actually like myself now. I like who I am and who I am becoming. I don't even know the guy I was before. The guy I am now—well, I don't have to run from him anymore."

Indeed, during the course of his journey, Richard had learned that he had run from others as well as himself. He discovered that he had trouble letting anyone get close to him; he realized that he was terrified of emotional intimacy. Yet Richard didn't give up. Determined to be successful in all areas of his life, Richard worked doggedly to understand himself. Over time, Richard's courage allowed him to form a close relationship with a new partner. Although the going was tough for quite a while, Richard persevered. He discovered that fast hookups and shallow relationships were doing him far more harm than good. Once he slowed down and became more comfortable with himself, he became more aware and discriminating. He learned that he didn't need to push his new partner—a truly loving person—away. Now engaged to be married, Richard is working less, loving more, and quietly moving forward with the voice of constructive fear consistently in his ears. Richard discovered that his noisy, busy life was nothing but a powerful cloak for the wide-reaching arms of destructive fear. Life is slower and richer for Richard now, for he continues to create a life he desires with the power of transformational fear.

Now it's your turn. You have the opportunity to notice where *you* want to shift. This next segment gives you the opportunity to address the issues in your personal life that are keeping you stuck in the world of destructive fear. Perhaps you are weary of keeping a breakneck pace that is killing you. Maybe you are tired of working and working just so you can buy the latest thing. Perhaps you want less external or internal noise in your life. Maybe there is too much clutter in your head and your environment. It's possible that you are ready to listen to yourself just a little more. Maybe you are prepared to stop running from whatever ways destructive fear has you by the tail. If so, the next section is just for you. Whether you want to take a step as big as cutting an hour or two off of your workday or you want to simply turn off your cell phone at night, this is your opportunity to create specific changes in your personal world. Let constructive fear take you by the hand and help you make a few shifts that might make all the difference in your world.

Slow Down and Turn Down

This exercise will allow you to notice the spaces and places where destructive fear has gotten its hold on you through busyness and noisy chatter. As always, begin your exercise in a safe and comfortable environment and in a state of psychological readiness. With your notebook and pen at your side, read this exercise before proceeding. When you are ready, you may wish to proceed with your eyes closed.

Take a few breaths to notice the environment around you. Is it noisy or quiet? Is there a hum of electronics or busy activity in the background? Notice, too, if your mind is busy or quiet. Notice whatever you notice, keeping your mind free of judgment. Take a few deep, cleansing breaths. Notice when you are ready to proceed.

Then, with your eyes closed, reflect on the areas in your life that feel too busy or pressured to you. Notice how destructive fear might be pressing you to do too much or keep you working to exhaustion. When you are ready, open your eyes. Make a list of seven of the areas that could benefit from a slower pace, leaving a few spaces between each item. For example, you might note, *I commit to so many activities on the weekends that I am worn out by Sunday night.* Or you might write, *My work consumes me; I take it home every night.* Breathe.

Then let constructive fear guide you to consider seven ways that you might slow your pace. Write each positive change underneath the behavior you want to shift. Also note the date you will begin this shift.

Add any other details that will support your change. For example, as a response to the first issue noted above, you might write, *I will accept up to two invitations every weekend. I'll choose one or two activities that feel good to me and respectfully decline the others. This will leave me time to rest and relax. I'll make this change as of this weekend.* With the second example, you might note, *I will sit in my car for a few minutes before I get home to prepare myself for the evening. I will place a reminder on the dashboard of my car where I can see it. I will leave my work thoughts in the car; they will be there in the morning. I will start this new practice on Monday.* Pause to breathe.

Then, with your eyes closed, ponder the areas in your life that feel too loud or chaotic. Open your eyes when you are ready. Make a list of seven ways that your life feels too noisy, leaving space between each item. Remember that destructive fear can sneak in when the mind is busy and filled with chatter. For example, you might write *The television is always on when I am at home. Whether I am watching it or not, it creates background noise.* You also might note *My thoughts are loud and nonstop—they are way too noisy for me.* When you are finished with your seven items, pause to breathe.

As your next step, let the wise voice of constructive fear help you to consider seven ways that you might reduce the noise in your world. Write each helpful idea underneath the behavior you would like to shift, making note of planned starting dates and any other specifics you need to support this change. For example, as a response to the first example, you might write, *When I get home at night, I will take the time to put on relaxing music while I make dinner. I won't turn on the television unless I want to watch a show. I will start doing this tonight.* As to the second example, you might note, *When my thoughts are noisy, I will pause to breathe until my head is clear. I will make a commitment to do this each time my head gets busy, even if it feels inconvenient.* I will start doing this immediately, and I will put up a few sticky notes as reminders. Once you have finished your seven items, pause to breathe.

Congratulate yourself on your progress. You are doing excellent work. With every step you take forward with constructive fear, you are leaving old, destructive habits behind you. You are taking charge and creating the life that you desire—you are embracing and owning the power of transformational fear.

CHAPTER 6

Fear and Families

Traditional Family Life: Going, Going, Gone?

In the course of your journey thus far, you've had the opportunity to notice many ways that destructive fear has affected your life and the world you inhabit. In this segment, we'll be taking a closer look at how this negative face of fear is affecting children, teens, and families. Indeed, as the media is quick to report, the increasing pressures of today's world are having a deep and significant impact on our youth and families in general. Parents are overwhelmed by work pressures, busy schedules, interpersonal difficulties, and financial concerns. The rise of single-parent households has resulted in higher stress levels for parents.[1] Often by sheer necessity, families are forced to choose income-producing time over wellness and family time. Parents suffer, children suffer, and connective family bonds suffer.

It is time to investigate how we can use constructive fear to provide the guidance and assistance that is needed. The purpose of this section is to focus on how families, whatever their makeup might be, can be supported in creating healthier dynamics and habits. Regardless of race, sex, marital status, socioeconomic level, or number of children, we are all affected by the far-reaching impact of destructive fear.

On psychosocial levels and beyond, the changes in our culture and society at large are affecting our children—and adults—in many significant ways. Throughout this section, you might notice the critical, judgmental voice of destructive fear. When this arises, simply notice its power to shift you away from a positive, helpful mindset. Remind yourself that this section is not geared toward demonizing any person, group, or entity; the intention is to create awareness and, through this awareness, transformative change.

Our Children: It's a Scary, Scary World

Even if you are childless, this section is relevant for you. Today's children truly are the future of our world. The youngsters we see each day will become tomorrow's high school students, college graduates, employees, business owners, parents, community leaders, and caregivers. Yet today's children don't have it easy. Whether they are age three, ten, or seventeen, their young lives are chronically riddled with invisible, destructive fear.

Every day, our children wake up knowing that they are surrounded by very real threats. Their minds are doused in reports of disastrous climate changes, dangerous air quality, unsafe food, and unclean or insufficient water supplies. Today's youth are constantly reminded that they live on a polluted planet that often seems on the verge of global war. Given this atmosphere, it is no surprise that they feel generally unsafe and terrified. It's exhausting to be immersed in an environment that perpetuates extensive psychological pressure. It's no wonder our children are angst-ridden; they live, nearly 24/7, in a world filled with destructive fear. No matter where they turn—whether they are at home, at school, or with friends— they are reminded that a disaster of some sort is waiting. Although they might not speak the words, they live in constant agitation knowing that the air they breathe, the water they drink, and the food they eat might be toxic in some way. They know that their school could be the next target of a mass shooting. They know that even an ordinary concert could become a deadly disaster. They know that they—or someone they love—could be the victim of cyberbullying, suicide, or a drug-related death. This is the scary world that our children live in every day.

Some believe that today's children need to "toughen up." Parents and grandparents—many of whom suffered through wars, economic downturns, and other stressful circumstances—may complain that youngsters are spoiled and "just don't know how hard life can be." Yet today's youth, whether pampered or not, were born into a fear-filled world that is constantly changing and abuzz. They are raised in homes where the incessant pulse of technology is commonplace. Youth are taught that obsolescence occurs in shorter and shorter timeframes and "falling behind" is a fate worse than death. They look at parents who are weary, overstressed, and often distracted. They look up to skies that are often grayed by pollution. They look into waters that are contaminated by factory waste and debris. Their eyes see fear wherever they go. Their ears cannot escape the busy hum. Their brains have been hardwired to see and feel the world in ways that the generations before them never knew. Rates of drug use, suicide, depression, anxiety, and self-harm among our youth continue to rise.[2] Clearly, today's youth are extremely stressed and very fragile. They need—and deserve—our help in creating positive change.

Given the environment that has been created under our watch, it is our responsibility to be proactive on behalf of our youth. Although youths often dress and act in ways that make them appear to be "miniature adults," they are children and therefore are simply ill-equipped to cope with life's adult-level challenges. With parents and friends who often have their own personal difficulties, our youth often have nowhere to turn for appropriate support. As adolescents also pride themselves on increasing their sense of autonomy, many don't reach out for fear that they are being too dependent or weak. In their natural drive for personal independence, they often don't understand that even the most self-sufficient individuals need support and guidance. Through wise awareness, understanding, and constructive solutions, we have the power to create transformation. We each have the ability to make a positive impact, whether our efforts are directed to our own children, the cast-aside child down the street, or a struggling parent or two. Whether small or large, every action that supports the growth of constructive fear will reduce the negative impact of destructive fear. We have the power to utilize transformational fear to effect great change in the lives of today's children. In doing this, we help our world—and we also help ourselves.

The Adult Burden of Destructive Fear: A Case Study

Let me tell you about one of my clients whom we'll call James. The first time I met James, his wiry body was tight with anxiety. He sat in my office, barely making eye contact, with his arms folded stiffly in front of his torso. I listened carefully as he explained his situation in a methodical, cautious voice. "I'm here," he said, "because my doctor thought it was a good idea for me to get help. I was hoping he could just give me a pill to help me stay focused and feel less pressured. I realize that I should eat more—the doctor thinks I'm too thin—but I just don't have much of an appetite. I don't sleep well, and maybe it's because I'm under a lot of stress. I do my best to handle everything, but I just don't have enough time. As it is, I don't get to bed until almost midnight. There aren't enough hours in the day—my schedule is very, very full."

James is not an adult; he is a mere twelve years old. As I listened, James's story unfolded in greater detail. He unloaded his school concerns, from his rigorous homework assignments to his constant worry about not measuring up to his peers. With fearful eyes, he confided that his parents were on the verge of divorce. They didn't realize that their ongoing "behind-the-scenes" battles affected him deeply. He often heard them arguing about bills and financial issues behind their closed bedroom door. This made him feel worse, for he knew that his school expenses made matters more difficult. As James told me, "My mom wants me in a private school because the academics are better. She thinks the sports programs are better too. My dad has a good career, but he went to public school, so he thinks my private school is a waste of money. I don't care, but no matter where I go, they'd press me to be at the top of my class. They even fight about my sports—I play sports just to make them happy. Honestly, I don't even like soccer or baseball anymore. I just want them to stop fighting about me, about school, about everything. If they get a divorce, I know it will be because of me." Like many children, James believed that he was the cause of his parents' struggles. He carried this constant worry and guilt on top of his intense academic course load, sports schedules, church commitments, and peer-related concerns. At the end of his session, James noted in his careful, adult tone, "What I told you isn't even half of it. There's so much more. I wish I could just be a kid sometimes."

Yet, sadly, James was in a situation where he was not allowed to be a child. His well-meaning, highly educated parents wanted what was best for him in life. With successful professional careers of their own, James's parents simply wanted him to be in a position to achieve the success they had created for themselves. His parents did not intentionally want to stress James or make him into a "mini adult," yet they had unconsciously put heavy adult burdens on James's shoulders. It was fortunate that James's primary care physician suggested to James—and his parents—that he receive psychotherapy. It was very helpful that James's parents supported his coming to see me. Yet, as important as that step was, the family unit— headed by the parents—needed some significant, positive changes. To begin with, James needed to be seen as a child and supported in discovering and growing his sense of self. James's parents also had their work cut out for them. From seeking out a marriage therapist to resolve their interpersonal issues to addressing the various life stressors they had intentionally and unintentionally placed on their son's shoulders, James's parents had their own transformational journey ahead.

Unfortunately, James's story is more common than not. From difficult home lives to bullying issues, many of our youth are struggling to stay afloat in our hectic, disconnected society. When we pause to notice the uncertain, externally oriented, competitive world in which our children are raised, it is no wonder they are anxious and living in fear. It is no wonder that up to one out of every five children in the United States experiences a mental disorder in any given year[3] or that 80 percent of chronic mental disorders begin in childhood.[4] What is going wrong? In what ways has destructive fear taken hold of our children? What can be done to effect change—harnessing the power of constructive fear to lead to transformation?

Eight Stepping Stones for Destructive Fear

Children are affected by their environment from conception onward; this is a simple, well-researched fact.[5] For example, from a mother's stress level during pregnancy to early exposure to electronics such as televisions, studies show that children's levels of stress hormones are affected by their environments.[6] Although there are certain areas in life where we can't effect major change, we can focus on those arenas that we can control nearly every day. Utilizing many of the tools and concepts that were addressed in prior chapters, we can now turn our attention to eight key areas where destructive fear enters the lives of our children and erodes their overall wellness and self-esteem: media, technology, sleep, diet, exercise, school and achievement, social issues, and family connection. To support the growth of constructive fear, simple and effective tools will be introduced at the end of each section. You will be more successful in your steps toward transformation when you move forward with firm, consistent changes.

Mainstream Media

Children are highly impressionable by nature. Their young brains soak up information—positive and negative—like sponges. It is natural for children to look to external figures as they form their self-perceptions. Their young eyes turn to parents, teachers, media images, and friends for guidance on "who to be" and "how to be." From an early age, many have unhealthy standards set for them—if not by parents then by the media at large. Young children often look to storybook princesses, superheroes, and playful animated characters as some of their first role models. Given the wide-reaching presence of the media, children often leave these generally positive role models behind and look to Hollywood figures, fashion models, and sports figures as their role models. Unconsciously, they compare themselves against the images proffered by the media. They aspire to look like the unrealistic, often airbrushed images of models, singers, and television idols. They model their behavior after big-screen actors, hall-of-famers, and larger-than-life performers. No one, not even the idealized, unrealistic figures themselves, can live up to the images created by the media. Yet children—whose brains are not even fully developed—do not understand that all of this is illusory. They are left ever-striving after fantasy images—and often feeling secretly inferior.

We have created a culture that so highly prizes external appearances that psychological well-being suffers. Our youth are constantly assaulted with visual images that leave them feeling inferior and imperfect. The media capitalizes on children's impressionable brains and anxious fears, using its pervasive power to sell the fictional idea that happiness and self-esteem can be purchased. Given the biological changes that occur during puberty, teens are particularly vulnerable. Plastic surgery rates among those thirteen to nineteen years of age continue to rise as our youth endeavor to "look right" and fit in.[7] Feeling strong pressure to buy the right things, look the right way, and do the right things, many children are terrified of not fitting in with their peers. All of these factors and many more create an environment that fosters the critical, comparative mind of destructive fear.

Social media use continues to rise, with the vast majority of adolescents tuning in to various social media sites every day. Although social media certainly has its benefits, including additional social awareness, exposure to novel ideas, and increased opportunity for social connection and support, substantial risks are also present. For example, social media often exposes our children to highly inappropriate material or inaccurate information that is not questioned and is accepted as fact. Connections made through social media can also lead to unsafe and unhealthy interactions that include cyberbullying and age-inappropriate contact. Communication through social media also lacks the in-person elements such as facial expression and body language to contextualize comments and discussions, giving rise to interpersonal misunderstandings and conflict.

Social media use assuredly can have a negative impact on self-esteem. Wanting to appear perfect, many adolescents photoshop the selfies they proudly display. Indeed, on an unconscious level, many adolescents believe that they must look airbrushed and live near-perfect lives to be accepted. Those who are struggling with self-esteem issues are all the more at risk. Especially when anxious or depressed, an adolescent is likely to view positive images posted by peers in a highly comparative manner, automatically assuming that others are enjoying more fun-filled, happier lives. Many, however, hide their personal difficulties and imperfect moments and share only their most positive images and stories. As a result, it is easy to assume that others have near-perfect lives when, in fact, what is being viewed is a lopsided or fictionalized version of reality. And although viewing such images and information results in feelings of unhappiness, self-doubt, and negativity, addictive urges keep them coming back for more and more. Many youths simply can't differentiate between their real and online worlds.

A child's brain absorbs the environment in which it is immersed. If a child's psyche is bathed in soothing elements, the child's attitude and behavior will reflect those positive influences. If a child is exposed to chronic violence or other stressful influences, the child's attitude and behavior will reflect those destructive influences in some way. Research continues to show that exposure to violent media (e.g., video games) increases aggressive thoughts, angry feelings, and aggressive behaviors, yet media groups present strong opposition to protective regulations.[8] This leaves proper control and supervision squarely in the laps of busy parents, many of whom are unaware of the negative impact. Parents who do attempt to curb video game usage often encounter strong resistance from their children; eventually wearying of the battle, they often give up.

Due to the pervasive influence of technology and the media, children of all ages are increasingly exposed to physical, psychological, and sexual violence in video games, movies, television shows, and other media outlets. The media knows that sensationalized hype, horror, and sexuality sell far better than wholesome or upbeat stories. As a result, children's minds are filled daily with reports of mass shootings, growing crime, bullying, racism, sexism, poverty, job market concerns, alarming health statistics, increasing environmental toxins, and rising drug abuse rates. The threat of terrorism, global war, and economic uncertainty is a bleak, everyday milieu. Even on home soil, our youth are unable to escape the chronic infighting, scandals, and corruption within the government—the very entity that is charged with keeping their country safe. Although it is important for parents to discuss critical, age-appropriate issues with their children, it is unhealthy for our youth to grow up in environments filled with violence and sensationalized media accounts.

Because of the comparative lack of technology and a different world environment as a whole, previous generations simply were not raised in excessively stimulating, fear-riddled environments that overload the senses. Sadly, it is visions of unattainable perfection, war games, and nightmarish news reports—not lullabies and bedtime stories—that rock today's children into troubled sleep. If the children in your care are being subjected to a chronically agitating and activating environment, there is good news: *you* can create change.

Listen for the voice of destructive fear as you enter this next section. Its negative voice will step in to maintain and foster unhealthy habits. Destructive fear may say that change is impossible or that shifts are unnecessary. It might even tell you that your kids won't like you if you don't do what they want. Listen without judgment to whatever negative messages arise, and see them for what they are—the destructive side of fear. Then let the constructive voice of fear guide you toward wise changes. Let constructive fear become your ally. Let it remind you that *you* are the adult and that healthy guidelines are a necessity, not an option. Let constructive fear remind you of your privilege and responsibility to be aware and to raise children who are physically and psychologically well-balanced. Let constructive fear guide you toward being your child's wise parent—not their best buddy. When parents set and maintain simple, common-sense rules, their children feel safer—even when they feel annoyed. When parents refrain from making arbitrary rules, children will respect their parents and will also feel respected. When parents are consistent and avoid setting rules that exist one day and evaporate the next, they teach children constancy and self-control.

Without blame or judgment, open your eyes and your heart to create awareness. Listen as constructive fear offers healthy shifts that generate harmony, communication, and joy. As you attend to the positive voice of constructive fear, the wonders of transformational fear will take greater space in your life. You have the ability to create simple, small changes that will have a powerful and long-lasting positive impact on the children—and the adults—in your world.

Shifting the Effects of Mainstream Media with Constructive Fear

Whether you are a role model for children through parenthood or some other capacity, trust that you can make a difference in lessening the negative impact of media. For example, my office waiting room is devoid of fashion and news magazines. Instead, notepads, coloring pencils, and inspirational books await my clients. Instead of the noise of a television, a gentle tone flows quietly in the background. Many clients come early for their sessions to enjoy the meditative peace of my waiting area. This is a simple example of the effective, simple changes you can make in your own environments. Remember, destructive fear has less opportunity to take hold when your environment does not feed it. The tips outlined below will offer you simple suggestions that promote constructive fear while they decrease the hold of destructive fear.

Ten Constructive Media Use Tips

1. Allow children reasonable access to social media, yet monitor the use closely. Create a schedule and guidelines that are simple, clear, and consistent.

2. Do not assume from a child's external appearance that all is well. The negative impact of social media can be extremely hidden, silent, and pervasive. Children may hide difficulties or unrest.

3. Have children take frequent breaks from media use to exercise and engage in other tasks.

4. Put all forms of media "to rest" well before bedtime to promote healthy sleep.

5. Make yourself readily available to openly and nonjudgmentally discuss issues that arise.

6. Take care not to dismiss or minimize a child's experience, even if it appears minor or inconsequential to you. Children tend to feel as if they are center stage. Their experiences—even if they appear overly dramatic—are very real and important to them.

7. Encourage critical thinking. Foster age-appropriate, objective discussions to encourage open-mindedness and flexibility. Encourage looking at issues from various perspectives (e.g., "Can you put yourself in the other person's shoes?").

8. Model positive, restrained use of all forms of media, from television shows to social media.

9. Discuss why you use certain forms of media and the benefits. Have frequent conversations about the benefits and downsides of media, including advertisements and violence.

10. Make it a habit to discuss illusory perfection and its impact on self-esteem. Promote children's self-esteem by noticing and supporting their unique abilities. Focus on building their capacities in various realms, from creative expression through writing, music, and art to participation in sports. When the importance of external appearances is minimized and other arenas and capacities are highlighted, genuine self-esteem naturally grows.

Each of the above tips relies on your connection to the wise power of constructive fear. You can make a difference by ensuring that the children in your environment are not under the constant influence of the media by limiting television exposure, computer time, and smartphone use. Forget the old "Do what I say and not as I do" attitude; remember that your behavior has an impact on those around you. Tune into yourself and the children in your life and become an advocate of critical thinking, intelligent media consumption, and healthy habits. Of course, it's important to be attentive yet not overbearing. Children of all ages respond to clear, consistent guidelines that respect their individuality while also ensuring their safety. Older children often respond well to fair agreements that are co-created with adults. Although children may initially meet changes with strong resistance, your firm and consistent guidance is absolutely critical. Remember, destructive fear thrives on uncertainty and inconsistency. Destructive fear won't want you to make shifts that increase intelligent, conscious use of media—it knows that your wise changes will not let it thrive.

Changes for Healthier Media Use and Awareness

With your notebook and pen at your side, review the above list of suggestions for media use. Pause to breathe. Envision the changes that you can make in your attitudes and behaviors with media. After reflecting, you might also imagine unique changes of your own. Notice if destructive fear wants you to stop this exercise or devalue it in any way. If this urge arises, simply notice it without judgment. Then, when you are ready, make a list of at least five simple changes that you would like to see in your relationship with media use. Remember to keep your list simple and specific to support the changes. Let constructive fear be your guide in creating reasonable shifts that will make your home environment less stressful and more connected. For example, you might note, *Starting Saturday, our family media cutoff time will be 8 p.m. This will give me sufficient time to talk with my spouse about the changes and have a cooperative family meeting.* Remember that you are a model for those in your world, whether at home or at work. As you model positive changes with your own behaviors, your shifts will be an encouraging example for others.

Tireless Technology

It is only in the last few decades that most individuals—young and old alike—have a cell phone, computer, and television at the ready twenty-four hours a day. Our ubiquitous use of these products has affected today's use on many levels. Children's often unrestricted or under-restricted use of technology carries with it many of the same concerns that arise with media use in general. However, it is important to address a few additional noteworthy points.

In 2013, The American Academy of Pediatrics discouraged screen time for children under age two and recommended limiting screen time to one to two hours per day for all children over two. This report also recommended keeping children's bedrooms free of televisions and internet-connected electronic devices.[9] Although the recommendations were adjusted in 2016—limiting screen time for children ages two to five years to one hour per day and adding individualized restrictions for children ages six and older—the guidelines speak to the widespread, negative impact of largely unrestricted technology use.[10] Given portable handheld devices and the ready availability of technology in automobiles, homes, and other arenas, children of all ages are increasingly flooded with unhealthy amounts of screen time. Despite parental concern and substantial proof that overexposure to technology is harmful, research indicates that children aged eight to twelve use digital media six hours per day and those aged thirteen to eighteen have an average use time of nine hours per day.[11] With the majority of parents reporting that they do not supervise their child's use of technological devices, we must ask ourselves a few important questions: Are the guidelines having any positive impact? What can we do to effect much-needed change? And—most importantly—are we willing to do what is necessary to protect today's children?

Technology, while not inherently "bad" or "good," is increasingly taking over our lives and the lives of our children. Young brains simply are not physiologically mature enough to properly process much of the information they receive. Whether technology exposes our children to excessive violence, pornography, or hypersexual behaviors, their brains often don't distinguish between what is appropriate and what is not; through widespread technology use, the mass media are having an enormous impact on our children's behaviors, values, and beliefs. As the lines between reality and on-screen worlds blur, many children imitate the standards and behaviors presented by technology. This impact is less significant, however, when parents and other role models help children understand and avoid the possible problems and dangers. Additionally, when the use of technology is not moderated, vital face-to-face time with others is reduced, time for exercise is more limited, and sleep is often disrupted.

For a moment, step into the intense, often addictive world of video games and online gaming. As most adults have discovered, it's often difficult to stop or limit a child's (or one's own) engagement with technology. Violent video games—while often allowing the opportunity to interact with friends and even players from around the world—have an even more serious downside. If you've ever witnessed a youth playing an even moderately violent video game, all you need to do is notice their posture, facial expressions, and verbiage to know that they are engaged in a serious, combative experience. Research indicates a link between playing violent video games and increased cortisol levels and cardiovascular arousal; this suggests that such games may activate a fight-or-flight type of response.[12] As well, children who are overexposed to violent behavior often become desensitized to violence. Research continues to show that children may become less sensitive to the pain and suffering of others as a result of viewing violent, aggressive behavior, whether it is in the home environment or modeled on television, computers, and other electronic devices. The short- and long-term impact can be harmful, particularly when the violent and aggressive behavior being modeled depicts human or human-like characters. Additionally, given technology's hypnotic, addictive qualities, it can be difficult for children and adults to turn away from chronic use. Research continues to show that children who are exposed to violent media may behave more aggressively or engage in harmful acts toward others.[13] Destructive fear absolutely thrives in technology's addictive, violent forums; it wants you to turn your back and let your child steep in this type of environment. It wants you to pretend that you don't see or hear the perpetuation of violence. Destructive fear wants to tell you that "It's no big deal—it's just a video game." Destructive fear wants you to turn a blind eye to these issues; it does not want you to believe that electronic media violence may be a factor in violent, aggressive behavior. Constructive fear asks you to be aware and proactive. Constructive fear knows that simple, positive shifts are possible. It knows that you can be part of the healthy changes that are sorely needed.

Violence is also increasing among children in the form of cyberbullying. Bullying in any form is highly destructive; impressionable youth are particularly vulnerable to its toxic effects. Cyberbullying—which takes advantage of the vast, instantaneous reach of the digital world—can be especially harmful for a number of reasons. Traditionally, a bully had a name and face on the schoolyard or in high school hallways. However, the perpetrators of cyberbullying are often shielded by anonymity. Their virulent attacks can be nonstop, arising at any time of the day or night. With the capacity to spread destructive attacks quickly through texts, social media, and emails, cyberbullies can do a great deal of harm in no time at all. Additionally, information spread by cyberbullies can become public and permanent in the digital world, affecting their targets in many realms. Studies show that cyberbullying is related to a host of issues, including reduced academic performance, suicidal thoughts, low self-esteem, feelings of isolation, and intense humiliation.[14] Destructive fear knows that bullying has incredible power to increase anxiety, depression, and a sense of terror. Constructive fear wants you to know that bullies of any type are weak; they lose their power when safely confronted and deflated.

Sex and technology make great bedfellows; this often highly toxic combination has an especially negative impact on our children. When sexuality is consumed and disseminated as if it were nothing, it becomes nothing; this attitude ultimately leaves a dark, empty hole in the soul. Yet, from sexting to chat room sites that provide a perfectly veiled forum for sexual offenders, technology provides greater opportunities for inappropriate and unsafe sexual connections. With our youth increasingly feeling at ease sharing highly sexualized images for all the world to see, the line between what is appropriate and what is not continues to fade. Modeling the behaviors of their peers, older friends, and family members, many youths have been desensitized to highly sexualized images. Often in the hopes of gaining attention by sharing provocative photographs, it is all too easy for youth to ignore the implications of such images—as well as the long-term impact on reputation and self-esteem. As if these issues aren't worrisome enough, a variety of dating apps allow for quick sexual hookups that leave many feeling used and lonely after the excitement of the sexual encounter fades. Destructive fear thrives on the dark power it finds in debasing sexuality. Constructive fear wants you to remember that sexuality is a precious form of intimacy that—when honored—can be powerfully connective. Constructive fear wants to encourage sexuality that is based in emotional maturity and mutual trust. Destructive fear and judgment are left behind when sexual behaviors are in line with an individual's mature, intentional personal ideology. With an emphasis on wise personal choice, constructive fear can lead the way into a world of sexuality that is loving and free of shame.

Eight Powerful Technology Use Tips

1. Set simple, clear limits for non-academic screen time. Ensure that babysitters and caregivers are aware of the guidelines. If a child presses for more screen time, avoid destructive fear's push to "give in." Instead, be ready with suggestions and materials for other ways to have fun, including puzzles, crafts, board games, books, and outdoor exercise.

2. Whether screen time is for academic or extracurricular purposes, monitor the content of the material being viewed.

3. Utilize a child's interest in technology to create an opportunity for rewarding good behavior with limited extracurricular screen time. Require proper exercise and home contributions as a condition for the agreed-upon screen time. Avoid the temptation to give additional screen time as a primary reward. Instead, create other healthy rewards, such as a walk with your child, making a treat together, or other connective behavior.

4. Model positive behavior, remembering to keep bedrooms free of televisions, computers, and other devices that allow internet access.

5. Openly discuss family values. Create an understanding of what is appropriate and expected regarding technology, violence, sexuality, and the respectful treatment of others.

6. Openly discuss cyberbullying and traditional bullying. Include a discussion about expected, safe reporting of bullying. Caution children to report bullies immediately to responsible adults (e.g., parents and school authorities) and to *never* confront bullies directly. Parents should retain evidence of any bullying incidents. In cases of anonymous cyberbullying, block the cyberbully and alert both the social media site and internet service provider. Contact law enforcement when criminal activities are involved. If a child has been the victim of bullying, take proactive steps to provide proper psychological support through private counseling or other means.

7. Notice the ratings on children's video games. If it's not labeled "E" (Everyone), consider the ramifications. No matter the game, look at the actual content. Let constructive fear ask you one

question: "Do you want to perpetuate the behavior modeled in the video game?" If not, do not buy or permit use of the game.

8. Supervise and interact with your child. Avoid destructive fear's tempting idea to let technology in any form "babysit" your child.

Changes for Wiser Technology Use

With your notebook and pen available, review the above list of suggestions for technology use with children. Pause to breathe. Envision the changes that you can make in your technology-related attitudes and behaviors. After reflecting on the suggestions, you might also consider unique, positive changes of your own. Notice if destructive fear wants you to skip this exercise or devalue it in any way. If this occurs, simply notice these thoughts without judgment. Then, when you are ready, create a list of at least five simple changes that you would like to make in your relationship with media use. To support change, keep your list simple and specific. Let constructive fear be your guide in creating shifts that will make your overall environment less stressful and more connected. For example, you might note, *Tonight, I will talk to my spouse about healthy screen time guidelines. We will craft a solid outline for our family—an outline that will generate more connective time and no more than two hours of screen time per day. Then, this Sunday afternoon, we will have a family meeting to discuss the positive changes that we will begin instituting right away.* Remember that—for better or worse—you are a model for those in your world, whether at home or at work. As you model the changes with your own positive behaviors, those in your world will notice.

Destructive Fear's Role in Children's Sleep, Exercise, and Diet

It's no secret that children require a great deal of sleep, yet their schedules and habits often rob them of the precious hours they need for healthy physical and psychological development. School-age children are developing habits that keep them up late even though they need to wake up early for school. The American Academy of Pediatrics recommends that children age six to twelve years regularly obtain nine to twelve hours of sleep and that children age thirteen to eighteen sleep eight to ten hours per night.[15] Many children in these age groups are awake until midnight or later, yet they often need to wake by 6 a.m. to prepare for school. The National Sleep Foundation indicates that a mere 9 percent of adolescents in grades nine through twelve obtain optimal sleep each night.[16]

Children of all ages feel pressured from many angles; without proper sleep, they are ill-equipped to meet their many developmental and psychosocial challenges. Poor sleep habits negatively affect many aspects of a child's daily quality of life, including mood, emotional regulation, ability to concentrate, memory, and attention span. It is no surprise that insufficient sleep is associated with poor academic performance, increased injuries, obesity, diabetes, low self-esteem, negative body image, anxiety, and depression. Additionally, those who have faced the rigors of daily life with a sleep-deprived child know that situations can be far more difficult and tempestuous than when that same child is well-rested—the difference can be like night and day.

Yet even with increased awareness regarding the negative effects of insufficient sleep, many parents do not limit children's access to screen time during the day or in the evening hours. A compelling study from the *British Journal of Medicine* notes that 97 percent of American adolescents reported having at least one electronic media device in their bedroom. This same study found that four or more hours of total daily screen time was associated with an increased likelihood of less than five hours of sleep per night.[17] Given that adolescents require nearly twice this amount of sleep for healthy development, it is clear that appropriate limits on screen time and healthy sleep routines are absolutely necessary to protect the well-being of our youth. Remember that destructive fear will utilize sleep-deprived states as an opportunity to create angst, turmoil, and unrest.

In the not-too-distant past, exercise and childhood went hand-in-hand. Aside from school time, children played outdoors, enjoying vast stretches of time running, playing games, bicycling, and engaging in face-to-face contact. Before television and other electronic devices lured children into living rooms and bedrooms, outdoor activities were the norm. The ever-present reach of technology now creates an environment that often nudges us onto couches, chairs, and beds. Habits that lead to chronic inactivity are worrisome enough for adults, but the results can be particularly harmful for children's growing bodies. Indeed, the sedentary routines learned in childhood often pave the way into a lifetime of inactivity.

The CDC reports that almost one in five children age six to nineteen in the United States is obese—a rate that has more than tripled since the 1970s.[18] A wide variety of studies show a correlation between obesity and heavy use of televisions, computers, video games, and other electronic devices. This is not surprising, for the time that children might otherwise have spent exercising is now often devoted to sedentary activities. Children often spend seven hours a day sitting in classrooms only to return home and sit in front of computers or television screens. According to the US Department of Health & Human Services (HHS), the average child spends more than seven and a half hours per day in front of a screen of some sort. The HHS also reports that on an average school day, nearly one-third of high school students play computer or video games for three or more hours.[19]

Once again, it's not that technology itself is the problem; it is the misuse of technology that creates a lack of balance. Destructive fear wants your children captive; it wants them in front of television and computer screens where it holds their rapt attention. Constructive fear wants something far different; it wants you to encourage healthy exercise and provide firm limits for sedentary, electronics-based activities.

Now, let's digest some disconcerting statistics on the all-important area of food and health. As the importance of healthy eating was discussed in an earlier chapter, this section will focus on foods with poor nutritional value and empty calories. Empty calorie foods are those which are composed solely or primarily of sugar, fats, or oils and have little or no nutritional value. According to the HHS, "Empty calories from added sugars and solid fats contributed to 40 percent of total daily calories for two- to eighteen-year-olds."[20] Half of these empty calories consumed by our youth come from items such as soda, fruit drinks, pizza, desserts, and whole milk.

Many families are fortunate to live in areas where fresh, healthy food is widely available. Yet we often resort to giving our children prepacked food, unhealthy snacks, and sugary drinks. Our busy schedules lead us to the interior aisles of supermarkets where frozen foods, sugary cereals, cookies, and chips line the shelves. The perimeter aisles, however, are where the fresh, affordable alternatives are stocked. Healthful grocery shopping habits promote healthy eating.

A few years ago, I worked with juveniles on probation. During many of our group sessions, I would weave healthy living concepts into our meetings. One particularly engaging and helpful exercise was the "virtual grocery store" shopping game I developed to help them learn healthy food purchasing habits. First, I would "give" each child one hundred dollars to spend in the store. I would then let each child fill up an imaginary personal grocery cart, logging the estimated cost of each item put inside the cart. Once the shopping money was exhausted, we would discuss the cost and health value of each item. Often, their imaginary carts were chock-full of sodas, energy drinks, candy, prepacked foods, desserts, and salty snacks—many noted that they were simply mirroring their caregivers' shopping habits. As a follow-up, I would take each child on a virtual shopping excursion with me by their side. With the same one hundred dollars, we would fill up the cart with healthy alternatives. For example, the children found that their money went further when they selected large bags of potatoes, bunches of bananas, and unsweetened cereals such as oatmeal. They learned to consider low-cost, healthy alternatives to prepackaged snack foods such as fresh watermelon and carrots. The groups were consistently amazed to discover that one jar of nutritious peanut butter and a loaf of whole-grain bread—which could create a week's worth of lunches—cost less than one fast food meal. Through such exercises, I not only discovered a great deal about each child's personality and habits, but the youths also learned healthy options and behaviors they may have never known.

When it comes to healthy food habits, destructive fear wants you to stay stuck in old, unhealthy habits. Destructive fear knows that people simply do not feel or behave at their best when operating on a poor diet. Destructive fear knows that a child's haphazard, unhealthful eating can lead to many issues including obesity, diabetes, mood swings, poor body image, and lower self-esteem. Constructive fear wants you to take yourself on virtual grocery shopping excursions that will ultimately translate to grocery purchases that are truly healthy. Constructive fear wants you to shake things up for the better. When you purchase foods that are healthful and model a healthy diet, you are supporting your own well-being and the well-being of the children in your life.

Ten Achievable Tips for Sleep, Exercise, and Diet

1. Regardless of a child's age, set clear bedtime routines and sleep
   times that support the recommended sleep hours for the individual's age. Ensure that babysitters and caregivers are aware of the
   guidelines. If a child exerts pressure to change the bedtime, avoid
   destructive fear's desire that you "give in." Keep expectations
   simple and clear!
2. Keep all bedrooms free of all electronic media devices (phones,
   computers, and televisions).
3. To support better sleep, make certain that children discontinue
   use of electronic media devices at least one hour before bedtime.
4. Encourage daily exercise. When screen time is limited, a child
   will naturally have more interest in other activities. Encourage
   extracurricular sports, outdoor play, or chores that involve exercise (e.g., washing the car, mowing the lawn, or vacuuming).
5. Connect with your children through exercise. Whether walking,
   hiking, or playing an outdoor game, model positive exercise
   habits by creating and joining in playful activities.
6. Shopping is key to creating healthy food habits. Prepare a
   healthy list in advance, sticking to the list to avoid impulse buying. Avoid shopping when you are hungry or tired. Do your best
   to shop in the healthy perimeter sections of the store where fresh
   produce and other fresh groceries are found. Avoid prepackaged
   goods, fried foods, processed snack foods, sugary drinks, and
   other unhealthful products.
7. Many grocery store chains now offer online shopping for
   delivery or pickup. Consider online shopping to help you avoid
   impulse buys. If you're not physically wandering through the
   grocery store, you're less likely to pick up items that "just look
   good" in the moment.
8. When possible, send children to school with healthy lunches
   prepared at home. Connective time can be created when parents
   and children prepare and pack lunch food together. Morning
   busyness can be lessened by preparing lunches the night before.
9. Take the time to research healthy food with your children. For
   example, by seeing and digesting information that shows the
   long-term health implications of unhealthy foods, children are

more likely to realize that attention to a healthy diet is not a penalty but an act of love.

10. Create and offer healthy snacks and desserts. This will help avoid the dynamic of creating cravings for "forbidden" foods. Let fresh fruits, low-sugar yogurts, and other healthy options become a natural, rewarding delight.

Changes for Sleep, Diet, and Exercise

Prepare for this exercise with your notebook and pen available. When you are ready to proceed, review the above list of suggestions for sleep, diet, and exercise. Pause to breathe. Envision the changes that you can make in these important areas. Feel free to imagine additional changes of your own. Notice if the voice of destructive fear wants you to discontinue this exercise or diminish it in any way. If negative messages arise, simply notice them without judgment. When you are ready to proceed, create a list of at least five simple changes that you would like to create for the children in your life. Remember to keep your list simple and actionable. Let constructive fear be your guide in creating shifts that will make your daily habits and routines healthier. For example, you might write, *As of tonight, I will take a daily thirty-minute walk with my children to the park.* You might also note, *This Saturday, I will work with my teenagers to create solid guidelines that will provide them with at least eight hours of sleep every night. The new, healthy routines will start Saturday night.* As to diet, you might write, *I will begin buying fresh fruit every time I shop. I will no longer buy sodas or energy drinks.* Although these changes may seem difficult or even radical at first, you will be surprised at how quickly the shifts will become your new normal. As you discuss, create, and model healthy changes in your own environment, your children will be more likely to make healthy choices even when you are not present. In addition, other children—and even other parents—may notice and adopt positive behaviors as a result of the changes you create in your own environment.

School and Achievement Pressures

From competitive school environments to a fear of never finding employment in an increasingly competitive market, today's youth live in an aggressive, high-pressure world. These are important issues to discuss with children when they are at an appropriate age. There is a fine line between supporting a child's success with firm guidance and pressuring a child to a point that is highly stress-inducing. Destructive fear can step in quickly to convince a parent that unrelenting pressure on a child is for his or her own good. All too often, it is a parent's ego—a form of destructive fear—that pressures a child beyond a personal capacity. Constructive fear would moderate demoralizing pressure with this idea: "To avoid damaging a child's self-esteem, guide a child to perform at his or her personal best—regardless of the score or grade achieved."

It is vital that parents and caregivers become attuned to each child's individual needs. When it comes to academic environments, some children are hardwired to garner straight As with almost minimal effort, whereas others find themselves struggling to earn a B or a C. Parents can support their child's success by promoting the truth that a child's best efforts are what ultimately matters. Whether in academic or sports achievements, it's vital that parents allow their children to fail now and again. Even if sincere effort results in falling short of a certain goal, the effort is what matters most. Yet many parents' fear of failure or imperfection leads them to behaviors and attitudes that don't allow children to fail successfully. Parents can support successful failure in two ways. First, support natural consequences for poor or substandard effort—avoid the urge to rescue your child. Second, provide positive reinforcement for "best efforts," even if they fall short of certain hopes or expectations.

Indeed, it is vital that parents model a healthy response to failures in their own lives. When parents share both their successes and their failures, children are far more likely to accept their own natural failures. Many parents want to appear to be superheroes to their children, yet such an attitude models an inhuman, unachievable ideal. Parents serve their children far better by modeling behaviors that reflect honest, humble pride in embracing a strong work ethic—whether it leads to the expected result or not. When parents model comfortable, conscious awareness regarding both successes and failures, their children feel far more in tune with their own efforts and the ultimate outcomes. Indeed, children see their own lapses and disappointments far differently when parents help them believe that failures are an opportunity to pause, reflect, and learn. Destructive fear wants to perpetuate the illusion of perfection and continuous success. Constructive fear wants to remind you—and the children in your world—that life's disappointments often offer the best learning opportunities.

Notice, too, if destructive fear secretly urges you to live vicariously through your children. Many parents consciously and unconsciously propel their children to achieve in ways they could not—or in ways that duplicate or reflect on a parent's own path. This prevalent force can be highly destructive to a child's nascent desires and inherent capacities. Although a parent may have the best of intentions, pressing a child toward a certain area—be it a sport, academic achievement, creative interest, or career—may not help the child find the ideal personal fit. Constructive fear would ask that you be aware of any tendencies that would interfere with your child's unique abilities and desires. By remaining conscious of your child's unique natural desires and interests, you will be able to positively support your child in creating a joyful, fulfilling life.

As you move forward, notice when destructive fear wants to sneak in with its critical, negative voice. Remember that destructive fear can find power through self-criticism and criticism of others. If you find that you are critical of yourself or the children in your life, pay attention to the negative voice. Notice, too, if destructive fear wants to exert its negative power through sarcasm, ridicule, or other harmful commentary. Let constructive fear nudge you toward a gentle, helpful voice that is truly empowering. Pause to notice the ways that destructive fear might have crept into your communication patterns with your child. For example, destructive fear might prod you to think *Davis should be performing better; he won't amount to much because he is so obstinate and lazy.* Constructive fear would shift this to say *I want to pay more attention to Davis to help him discover the learning style and subjects that really interest him. He is very bright and capable—he just needs some guidance and support from me. I will take time tonight to review his homework with him and offer gentle encouragement.* Such small shifts are extremely beneficial in the long term. As you make positive changes and maintain consistent standards, you and the children in your life will notice the transformative effects.

Seven Supportive Tips for School and Achievement Pressures

1. Set your child up for success by making sure that your child has clear, achievable goals that are in line with his or her abilities. Support your child in reaching the goals with helpful, positive attention.
2. Avoid the temptation to do your child's homework or other tasks. Guide your child toward success, but let the child's effort and abilities be the focus. Remind yourself and your child that it is not perfect results that matter but the child's diligent efforts, focus, and self-responsibility.
3. Set aside clear times for homework in distraction-free zones where an adult is available for support and guidance.
4. Explore the world of possibilities with your child. Let your child's unique interests—not your private, personal agenda—be the guide in extracurricular activities and vocational direction. Expose your child to different arenas to maximize discovery, engagement, and success.
5. Keep it positive! Consistently pay attention to your child's positive behaviors and regularly reinforce those behaviors with affirmations.
6. Watch out for criticism and blame. A critical, blame-oriented attitude can absolutely erode a child's self-esteem and sense of personal capacity. When a child makes an error, gently focus on the constructive lesson that can be learned from the error.
7. Be a bird, not a stealth bomber or helicopter. By discussing and modeling a healthy relationship with achievement—neither bombing your child's success nor hovering over it—you will raise a child who will become a successful, free-flying adult.

Changes to Support School and Achievement

With your notebook and pen available, consider the above tips. Pause to breathe. Envision the changes that you would like to make in the realm of school and achievement, whether using the above tips or unique ideas of your own. If the voice of destructive fear arises, simply notice it without judgment. When you are ready to proceed, create a list of at least five simple changes that you would like to create regarding school and achievement. By keeping your list specific and clear, changes will be easier. Let constructive fear be your guide in creating shifts that will promote the success of the children in your life. For example, you might write, *Starting today, I am going to focus on supporting my daughter in more positive ways. I am going to put a sticky note on my bathroom mirror to remind me to listen, notice what she does right, and give her positive feedback.* You might also note, *As of this evening, I will have my daughter do her homework at the kitchen table while I am making dinner. This will give me the opportunity to support her if she needs help.* The positive changes you create will foster your child's inherent capacities and promote a lifetime of high self-esteem, personal achievement, and true success.

Social Issues: Friendships, Peer Pressure, and Bullying

The ability to form close friendships during childhood is important for a child's psychosocial development. Healthy friendships help children of all ages grow and thrive. Unfortunately, given the nature of childhood, early friendships are often easily fractured. Undeveloped interpersonal skills give rise to many difficulties that leave children feeling excluded and distressed. By nature, humans are tribal and often highly exclusionary. On a very primitive level, a child understands that less safety and support are available when outside the inner circle of acceptance. By observing the behavior of parents, elder siblings, and television shows, children learn from an early age that there is safety in being part of an "in" crowd. In this way, destructive fear steps in to foster the concept that being popular and part of a clique provides safety. This idea leads to the reality that those who are pushed outside the inner circle of acceptance are often left feeling rejected and unsafe. Taking this one step further, those who are cast out—or never accepted at all—are often subjected to insults, bullying, and other destructive behaviors.

When popularity and clannish behavior become all-important, destructive fear thrives. Those who are less popular can feel cast aside and disconnected and are often subjected to general negativity and ridicule. Once it gains exclusionary traction, destructive fear often propels a divisive groupthink mentality that leads to judgmental and emotionally unsafe environments. On the other hand, constructive fear understands the importance of individuality, acceptance, and connection. Unlike destructive fear, which would have others shunned to provide greater exclusivity, constructive fear would ask for nonjudgment and mindfulness. This attitude acknowledges our inherent human affinity for certain types of people (those with whom we feel a more natural connection) while it purposefully avoids sidelining those who may not be as like-minded or familiar. When differences are honored and seen as a way to build greater awareness, destructive fear loses its grip. By inviting individuality with an open, nonjudgmental attitude, a wider variety of friendships and connections blossom. In these ways, constructive fear builds intrapersonal and interpersonal awareness and tolerance. An individual with high intrapersonal intelligence is more likely to be in tune with his or her own strengths, weaknesses, and internal capacities. When this is coupled with healthy interpersonal skills—the ability to relate to and communicate with others—relationships are enhanced tremendously. When the focus is on being generally accepting and inclusive, the tribe becomes more cohesive and the environment becomes safer for all, whether at school, online, or in social settings.

It's important to re-emphasize that online and school bullying are added stressors in children's lives. Today's youth are well aware that a single photo, social media post, or text message can do them irreparable harm. Whether online or in the school environment, bullies often sneak in and wreak silent havoc on their victims' self-esteem. Sadly, children who are considered "different" are often bullied by their peers. Destructive behavior can arise through physical and non-physical aggression. Whether in the form of insults, spreading harmful rumors, pushing, or other threatening behaviors, bullying behavior is unacceptable. Yet many incidents of bullying go undetected by even the most aware, well-meaning parents. As children struggle with issues from weight to gender identity, it is crucial that parents remain vigilant and also maintain open lines of communication with their children. Remember, destructive fear thrives in environments that are filled with pressure, judgment, and secrecy. Constructive fear invites transformation through clarity, transparency, and attentiveness.

Given the influence of technology and social media, the very concept of friendship has become blurred. Without understanding that different types of friendships exist—from best friends to minor social acquaintances—youth can feel pressured to compete for friendship numbers. Indeed, it is vital to have open, honest discussions about various friendships types—from one's small, trusted circle of intimate friends to a larger group of peripheral acquaintances. By discussing the various types of friendships and the important role that each type plays, children are more likely to understand that having hundreds of "friends" on a social media site is far different from actually having an intimate, bonded friendship. Although individuals often benefit from having smaller groups of close friends rather than larger social circles, children of all ages often feel pressured to have a greater number of friends. Research shows that there may be cognitive constraints on friendship network size.[21] Children are less likely to feel pressured to accumulate social connections when they understand the vast difference between supportive, intimate friendships and social connections. These distinctions are important to acknowledge and discuss, as children are usually unaware of the differences.

Simple, clear guidelines and non-invasive conversations are an excellent tool for supporting children through the often-murky areas of friendships, peer pressure, and bullying. Parents can support their youth by inviting open conversation as they model positive, inclusive social behaviors. Discussions on family values—behaviors that are acceptable and those that are not—are vital. For example, a child raised in a highly accepting, open-minded environment may confuse the acceptance of others with the need to accept inappropriate behavior. What might seem basic or routine to a parent is not necessarily clear to a child. Finding the perfect balance of being available and communicative without being invasive can be tricky, but it can be done. When in doubt, keep it simple. Ask open-ended questions rather than "yes" or "no" questions. Allow for connective times of quiet when a child might naturally reveal a concern or question. Remember that destructive fear will have its own negative agenda. Constructive fear is your greatest ally; a generally open, transparent, and nonjudgmental attitude will provide the keys to transformation.

Seven Practical Tips for Social Issues

1. Stay connected and available to your child; be aware of sudden
    or worrisome shifts in behavior or attitude. Openly discuss any
    concerns with your child, and seek appropriate support when
    necessary.
2. Keep lines of communication open. Ask open-ended questions;
    refrain from judging your child's responses. Allow your child
    plenty of opportunity to safely discuss even the most difficult
    subjects with you.
3. Openly discuss friendship issues, focusing on an inclusive atti-
    tude, healthy boundaries, and respect for self and others.
4. Model healthy, positive interpersonal behaviors and friendships
    in your own life. Avoid behaviors and relationships that are gos-
    sipy, judgmental, or bullying in nature, as children will uncon-
    sciously imitate what they see and hear.
5. Make your home a "safe space" for your child and your child's
    friends. Offer a supportive, structured environment that will
    allow your child's friends to feel at home—while giving you the
    opportunity to make certain that your own child is safe.
6. Get to know the parents of your child's friends. If your child is
    at a friend's home, be certain that an adult is home and that the
    other family's values are generally aligned with yours (e.g., sub-
    stance use, parental supervision, etc.).
7. Openly and continually discuss family values and current social
    issues, including the immediate and safe reporting of bullying,
    abuse, or other harmful behaviors.

Changes for Healthier Social Behaviors

With your notebook and pen at your side, review the above list of
suggestions. Pause to breathe. Using the tips above, imagine the
changes you would like to create in the realm of social behaviors.
You may also envision unique changes of your own. If the negative
voice of destructive fear arises, simply notice it without judgment.
When you are ready to proceed, create a list of at least five simple
changes that you would make to create healthier social behaviors.

A specific, clear list will support positive change. Constructive fear will guide you toward creating shifts that will support more positive social behaviors. For example, you might write, *I want to meet the parents of my daughter's friends. It's important for me to know the environment my child will be in if she visits their home. I will make the necessary introductory calls this weekend.* Although some of the changes you outline might feel weighty or unfamiliar, let constructive fear be your guide in making positive steps that will protect and support your child in loving ways.

Family Connections

Although technology and social media can provide healthy ways of connecting and obtaining social support, overuse can be problematic. For adults, it's tempting to de-stress by tuning into television or computers after a long day. For workaholics, hyperconnected types, and social media fans, it's also tempting to spend evenings and weekends checking emails, texts, and social media sites. After school, children often want to retreat to a bedroom where cell phones, computers, or televisions provide easy distractions. When parents and children follow this trend, disconnection results. Vital face-to-face time with loved ones is replaced by screen time of one sort or another. As a result, children and parents often feel disconnected from each other even when at home. This type of environment is ripe for the grip of destructive fear. When family members feel disconnected from each other, unhealthy attitudes and behaviors can take hold.

The negative effects of our overexposure to technology and social media are becoming more apparent. Family members report an increasing level of disconnection as a result of technology use.[22] Whether youngsters are imitating parents or parents are imitating youngsters, the trend toward detachment is alarming. Many people are hyperconnected to their phones, computers, and televisions—and often not very connected to the people in their own home environment. Although it might be tempting to unplug completely, technology and media have their advantages. Many individuals and families have not yet found the path to a healthy, balanced relationship with technology and social media.

Two stress-related surveys by the American Psychological Association revealed many worrisome trends that include the following:

- Those who constantly check emails, texts, or social media accounts (43 percent of Americans) have higher stress levels.
- 58 percent of parents report worrying about the influence of social media on their child's mental and physical health.
- 45 percent of parents and Millennials report that due to technology, they feel disconnected from family even when together.
- 48 percent of parents report that regulating their child's screen time is a constant battle.
- Only 28 percent of parents report not allowing cell phones at the dinner table.[23]

You can make a difference in your own life and the lives of today's youth. When you take the time to envision and create positive changes, you have more control in your own world. Destructive fear wants you to remain unaware; it wants you to bury your head in the sand. Constructive fear wants your eyes and mind wide open to both the positive and negative effects of technology and the media at large. Constructive fear wants you to make healthy choices that will bring you—and those around you—joy and serenity over time.

Remember that children's brains are not fully developed until they are twenty-five. Today's youth may look and act older than their years, yet they are physiologically and psychologically undeveloped in many ways. Destructive fear knows that young minds are highly impressionable and that their emotional reactions are often impulsive and unpredictable. A child's needs and troubles feel extremely urgent and often highly overwhelming. It is vital that parents and caregivers understand these basic issues. When parents listen and do not minimize a child's concerns, the child feels honored and supported. When parents do not take the easy way out by giving in to a child's incessant requests, the child ultimately feels safe and valued. When parents shift their focus from their computers and phones to their children—whether during meals or on a weekend day— they are modeling behavior that says *I value you. I value our connection. I value our relationship more than I value the distracting devices in my life.*

Although the changes might seem difficult at first, trust that every step you take toward interconnectedness will benefit you, those around you, and your larger world. Life ultimately becomes easier when routines are established and steady. Although children might display an initial spike of resistance, they will become accustomed to the new routine once they understand that their parents will remain unswerving. The entire household benefits when firm consistency and stability are present. Remember that destructive fear will want to hold you back from making changes. It will want you to remain tethered to technology and media at the ultimate expense of bonded relationships. Destructive fear will want you to take the path of least resistance. It will shout, "Don't make changes! It's not worth the effort—it's too tiring. Things are fine as they are." Constructive fear has a wise, gentle voice that says, "Your changes will make a tremendous impact on your children and their future. You can create a peaceful, loving home environment built on true connection." Constructive fear will want you to make simple, steady changes. It will guide you to bring greater consistency, structure, and balance to your family life.

Ten Connective Tips to Improve Family Life

1. Model positive behavior for the youths in your life. Whatever you ask of them, do your utmost to demonstrate those actions in your own life.

2. Take the time and energy to institute changes that will benefit you and the children in your life in the long term. When possible, co-create balanced technology and social media guidelines with the children in your life. When a child's opinion is heard and slight compromises are made, guidelines are more likely to be embraced than fought.

3. Once the guidelines are determined, strive to enforce them routinely. Children thrive on stability and structure. Although they may initially press you to revert to old habits, hold firm. You will need patience and determination as the old, unhealthy habits are extinguished and new, positive patterns take their place.

4. Create a "no-tech" time for unplugging and detoxing. At first, you might set aside one weekend day to disconnect and detox. The benefits might be so delightful that you add additional days over time.

5. Replace the no-tech time with positive, connective activities, such as board games, card games, or exercise. Avoid the temptation to replace no-tech time with chores alone—this will increase resistance to the changes.

6. Create plentiful quiet time. Whether in the car, at home, or exercising, allow for quiet spaces. Children often speak their minds when they don't feel pressured or distracted by television, computers, or other devices. It is during quiet, distraction-free times that parents and caregivers can give thoughtful attention to children—often noticing behaviors that might otherwise be missed.

7. Utilize media to fuel discussions. This connective, highly valuable element is often underutilized or ignored. Make time after watching movies or television shows to discuss themes, characters, and values.

8. Some families discuss sports, television shows, books, and politics on a superficial or agenda-ridden level. Do your best to create a connective and nonjudgmental environment that allows for non-combative, in-depth discussions that honor the feelings and opinions of others. When in safe, supportive environments, children often reveal a great deal.

9. When media reports or other issues stimulate fear and anxious feelings, have honest, age-appropriate discussions regarding the issues. Acknowledge your child's fear and anxious feelings without avoiding the issue at hand or becoming dramatic. Be sure to acknowledge and process your own fears and anxiety as well so that you can sensibly support your children.

10. Offer your ongoing, nonjudgmental emotional support without being invasive. For example, have conversations that destigmatize mental health care. Children often fear that their issues will be undervalued or seen as a sign of weakness or being unlovable. Additionally, children can be fearful of being a hardship or burden on the family unit. Make yourself available for discussions with an open, compassionate, and transparent attitude. The more genuine you are with the children in your life, the more genuine they will be with you.

Changes for a Supportive, Connected Family Environment

With your pen and notebook at your side, review the previous list of suggestions for an improved family environment. Pause to breathe. Consider the shifts you would like to make in this vital area of your life. Imagine unique changes that will benefit your family. If destructive fear wants to offer negative messages, simply notice them without judgment. When you are ready to proceed, create a list of at least five simple changes that you would like to make to improve your family environment. Remember to keep your list simple and actionable to support your success. Let constructive fear be your guide in creating shifts that will improve the supportive, connected energy in your family. For example, you might note, *This evening, I am going to ask my son about the movie he saw with his friends last weekend. I am going to listen to his thoughts without judgment to create greater safety in our communication. I will use this experience as a template for future discussions about other shows he watches, whether with me or with others. I will model positive behavior as I listen to him and acknowledge his personal opinions.* Every positive change that you make in your family environment—particularly those that create a connected and supportive environment—will have lasting and wide-reaching benefits. Your commitment to transformation will improve your life and your children's well-being.

A Fragile, Worthy Generation

Allow yourself to take a step back in time. Based on the knowledge you now have, nonjudgmentally imagine the changes you might have made several years ago. For example, you might imagine playing board games with your children or spouse. Maybe you envision a quiet weekend playing in the park or playing dominoes on a rainy day. Perhaps your imagination finds you removing televisions and computers from bedrooms. Envision any changes that would bring more joy and less stress to your life. As if you're watching a movie, imagine how different your world might be—if the changes would have improved your world or not. Close your eyes, honestly imagining if you and those in your world might be more peaceful, more connected, and less stressed. Then open your eyes. Wipe that movie image clean, for you can't change the past. However, you can envision a different future. You can use the wealth of knowledge you are accruing to create vast changes from this moment forward. You can and *will* make positive changes. How do I know this? Because I trust your wisdom. I trust that once we become aware that something is not healthy for us and our children, we will make changes to do better. Why? Because it is our responsibility and because we can.

Destructive fear might already be telling you that everything's fine and that change isn't necessary. But you might now know that everything isn't fine and that change *is* necessary—that every choice you make matters. Every time you purchase or consent to a violent game or movie, you have made a choice. Every time you text when your child wants your attention, you have made a choice. Every time you check your cell phone when your spouse wants to enjoy your company, you have made a choice. Every time you choose healthy food for your family instead of fast food, you have made a choice. Every time you turn off that television or computer to honor that your mind, body, and family connections truly want something else, you have made a choice. Every time you pause to discuss and honor family values, you have made a choice. When in doubt, choose connection, choose health, and choose transformation. Why? Because you are inherently wise—and because you can. By listening to the wise voice of constructive fear, you will transform your life and the lives of generations to come. With every positive step you take, you are bringing transformational fear alive for yourself and all the world to see. Well done.

CHAPTER 7

Creating Personal Freedom: Touchstones for Balance

The Truth of Personal Power

Women and men have incredible personal power yet often don't realize their own multifaceted power or know how to use it appropriately. The understanding of power is often limited to behaviors that involve being controlling, aggressive, or having influence over others. Personal power has nothing to do with these traits; personal power evolves through knowing, honoring, and optimizing the whole of one's being. True personal power arises through self-awareness—becoming conscious of one's positive and negative capacities. Personal power grows when we work to understand who we are and how to become more of who we want to be. As constructive fear grows, personal power thrives. As the grip of destructive fear fades, its controlling tendencies also fade and are replaced by self-awareness, acceptance, and love. In this chapter, you will embrace and balance certain personality traits to optimize your personal power. As you see beyond the limits of traditional gender roles, you will see yourself in new ways. You will also gain insights that will help you understand, appreciate, and support others in your life.

When it comes to gender, it can be tremendously helpful to understand how destructive fear works to create unnecessary division in our own psyches, our relationships, and our view of others. As we move forward, you will notice that constructive fear wants to promote awareness and connection. Indeed we become healthier and more synergistic when we understand and utilize our differences to become collaborative and complementary rather than divisive antagonistic.

Society often impregnates us with images of how a "real" woman or man should look or act. From romanticized images of Cinderella to television and movie versions of Superwoman, the ideal homemaker, or the perfect girlfriend, it's easy for women to forget that *real* human beings—real women—are unique in demeanor, shape, size, appearance, and capacities. Messages about womanhood are often confusing and contradictory. A woman is often taught that she must be pleasing, caring, maternal—and tough. She must need her man and be submissive, yet she must also be self-reliant and independent. She must be sexy and passionate but not in charge of her sexuality. She must be compassionate and caring but not too emotional. She must be intelligent but never smarter than the man next to her. The ideal woman must be petite, tall, thin, curvaceous, brunette, blonde, athletic, domestic, career-oriented, nurturing, and more. This setup is created by destructive fear. It wants women and men to perpetuate impossible expectations. Constructive fear wants you to know that there is great power and freedom in setting yourself free from the expectations of others.

Men struggle with their own list of impossible expectations. With media images that perpetuate the idea of the perfect man as tall, dark, and handsome, men have visions of the ideal man plastered in front of them. This towering, muscular man has broad shoulders, strong abs, and tremendous physical strength. He must guard his woman, children, and home, yet he must not be overpowering or forceful. Whether the image is Superman, James Bond, or a Navy SEAL, men often feel the need to be some idealized version of manhood—smart, savvy, sexy, and wise. He must never show his emotions out of fear of being weak. This ideal man must also be compassionate, attentive, thoughtful, and loving. He must be aggressive—but not too aggressive—and independent—but not too free. This ideal man must be fun-loving, strict, easygoing, sensitive, tough, formidable, gentle, wild, tame, protective, and tender.

Destructive fear wants women and men to go in circles—always chasing impossible ideals. Constructive fear wants you to notice that these impossible standards are the source of much intrapersonal and interpersonal conflict for both men and women.

What Makes a "Real" Woman?

So what is a "real" woman? We each have the right to consciously create our unique definition of womanhood. Guided by the basic principles of constructive fear such as self-optimization, love, and respect for self and others, authentic descriptors of womanhood may come to mind. For example, I see a "real" woman as one who constantly strives to know who she is and what she wants in life. This woman truly acknowledges that her early environment and past have affected her in many ways; she works through the negative aspects so as to not harm others or carry negativity forward. She claims the positive aspects and enlivens them to offer these capacities to herself and the world. My version of a real woman proceeds in life with courage, dignity, and grace. She knows her power, her strengths, and her weaknesses. She laughs at the idea of perfection, knowing that life's lessons and imperfections are teachers. A diligent person who knows the value of work and effort, she strives continuously to hone and expand her abilities. Aware of the need for self-care, she treats her body, mind, and spirit with loving kindness. She honors her sexuality, respecting the precious nature of sexual intimacy. She honors her partner and children, treating them with loving respect in behavior and thought. Such a woman knows the value of her emotions and sensitivities; she does not hide them or devalue them but honors them as messengers. She prizes her integrity, values, and morals—acting and speaking her truth with respect for herself and others. She seeks harmony and balance in her internal and external worlds. Ever guided by growing awareness and compassion, such a woman strives to help and support others. This woman does not look to others to save or complete her; she knows that she is her own savior and friend. She loves her independence but is also highly capable of being interdependent and intimately bonded. My version of a "real" woman is one who evolves throughout her life into greater balance, wholeness, and wisdom. You may note that my outline of a "real" woman could also be applied to a "real" man. This neutrality is a reflection of balance and wholeness.

The above is my version; it has changed as I have changed. It will continue to evolve as I do. Destructive fear may want to keep you from considering your own version or to contaminate you with judgmental thoughts. Yet constructive fear wants you to know that awareness and acceptance are key. Constructive fear wants to guide every one of us to form a working image of what it means to be a balanced, powerful being.

Your Version of a "Real" Woman

Create a safe and relaxed environment. With your notebook and pen at your side, pause to breathe. Close your eyes. Without judgment, envision your own version of a "real" woman, letting the voice of constructive fear act as your guide. Open your eyes when you are ready. Breathe.

Next, make notes about the qualities and characteristics that you believe make a whole, "real" woman. Be as detailed and creative as you like. Pause to breathe. Well done. You can now embrace your version of a "real" woman. You are allowing the voice of constructive fear to create more wholeness in your own being. You may even be freeing yourself of another judgmental layer of destructive fear.

What Makes a "Real" Man?

What is a "real" man? Here, again, each person has the right and ability to consciously create a version of what it means to be a man. Once again, enlightening descriptors will flow from an attitude focused on self-realization, love, and respect. My version of a real man is broad and focused very much on the internal capacities—not the external appearance—of the person. This man knows that his childhood and history have affected him deeply. He acknowledges this truth and takes steps to work through the negative effects of the past; he takes care not to perpetuate cycles of violence, negativity, abuse, and harm. The real man does not need to be in absolute control of everyone and everything; he knows that his own judicious self-control is the most essential aspect of his power. This man strives toward balance of strength, gentleness, and kindness. He knows that he and others make mistakes, and he honors those mistakes as teachers in life. He is not critical or blaming of himself or those around him—he knows the power of positive reinforcement and love. Such a man works to communicate openly and honestly—striving for connection, not conflict. This man is able to bond with loving intimacy, not using sexuality as a tool for mere self-gratification or power. He is a provider, a supporter, and a coworker. He does his utmost to give of himself to help others. This man honors family and relationships, taking care to respect his partner and children in word and deed. He uses his natural abilities to create stability, consistency, and safety for those in his world. Such a man is filled with integrity; he is a man of his word. This man continues to evolve and change throughout his life, ever striving to be the best version of himself. You may note that my outline of a "real" man could also be applied to a "real" woman. This is balance and wholeness at work.

This is my version of manhood; it will continue to evolve as I evolve. Notice if destructive fear wants to step in with judgment of any sort. Let constructive fear guide you toward creating your own version with accepting, conscious awareness. Constructive fear wants to guide every person toward their own version of what it means to be a balanced, powerful being.

Your Version of a "Real" Man

Create a safe and relaxed environment. Pause to breathe. With your notebook and pen at your side, close your eyes. Allow yourself to envision your own version of a "real" man in a genuine, nonjudgmental way. Let the voice of constructive fear act as your guide. When you are ready, open your eyes. Pause to breathe.

Next, make notes about the qualities and characteristics that you feel make a whole, "real" man. Be as specific and creative as you wish. Pause to breathe. You now can honor your own version of a "real" man. Well done.

Seeking a Balance: Nurture Energy and Power Energy

The next section has its roots in the work of Carl Jung and his concepts of the anima (the unconscious feminine aspect of a man's personality) and animus (the unconscious masculine aspect of a woman's personality). In the individual's journey into maturation and wholeness, Jung emphasized the importance of psychic integration, a part of which is awareness and balance of the unconscious masculine and feminine aspects of the personality. As a Jungian-oriented psychologist, I believe terms such as "masculine" and "feminine" were not meant to be divisive or binary but instead were intended as archetypal descriptors. In today's world, the terms "masculine" and "feminine" can seem stereotypical or even harmful. Therefore, I have coined the terms "nurture energy" and "power energy" as descriptors of these archetypal traits. Although the terminology is different, the Jungian roots are much the same.

In looking at nurture energy, your understanding of this force will grow as we focus on some of its vital capacities. Well-developed, balanced nurture energy is absolutely glorious to behold, for it provides a shining warmth and radiance that is beyond physical appearance. At its finest, nurture energy has the quality of light illuminating a person's being from the inside out. Indeed, well-developed nurture energy is divinely loving, receptive, compassionate, and patient. These nurturing qualities support the natural desire for open, positive communication and bonding. Our nurturing qualities allow us to be astute leaders, attentive caregivers, and tender nurturers. Nurture energy is not combative or war-mongering; it is oriented toward safety, peace, justice, fairness, and harmony. The intuitive abilities of nurture energy can bring forth profound insights that lead to understanding, growth, and change. The wise nurturing side also has a remarkable ability to appreciate positive morals and values that support connection. Our nurturing side also knows the importance of balance, play, sharing, and a gentle touch. The warm, nurturing aspect has a sense of flow and mysterious sensuality. The radiant nurturing side is also the home of joy and a wealth of feelings. With its sensitive, emotion-oriented capacities, nurture energy is vital for healthy relationships. The well-developed nurturing side deeply treasures family and connective activities, supporting and sustaining a healthy family structure. The nurturing aesthetic sense allows for the creation and maintenance of beautiful environments—at home and in the world. Indeed, nurture energy has vast creative potential—from creating life to beautiful artistry.

Each woman or man has all of these capacities—and so many more—waiting to be cultivated and honed. Much to the delight of destructive fear, many of these capacities lie hidden and even fossilized within the psyche. It is possible that you have been unconsciously indoctrinated to shy away from your nurturing side or to let it become withered and dormant. Perhaps you have confused nurture energy with behaviors that are weak and passive, ultimately becoming a doormat for others. Maybe you have overcompensated, becoming aggressive and overly domineering. Perhaps your nurturing side has become distorted or even unrecognizable in some ways. Constructive fear wants you to unearth what it means to you to be nurturing. It wants you to create your version of a powerful, optimized woman or man with balanced nurture energy.

If this concept seems unfamiliar to you, take heart. Some men and women have no idea what it means to be a balanced, powerful, optimized human being. Others have fragile, undeveloped conceptions that need attention and strengthening. Still others have distorted ideas that they don't even realize are distorted. Indeed, you might find yourself wondering how you can define or articulate what it means to be your best self when you feel incapable of figuring out the basic pieces. This is destructive fear talking to you; it is trying to hold you back. Every journey has a starting place. Whether you are near the beginning of your journey or further along the way, simply work from where you are today. Your ideas will grow and evolve as you evolve. Trust that all you need is a starting place. Honoring your own heart and personality, hold these three thoughts in mind: What feels right to my own heart? What qualities make me feel good and at ease? What capacities and characteristics give me a sense of balance? Let constructive fear remind you that you already have everything you need inside your own being. All you need do is continue on the slow and steady path of self-discovery, taking care to keep self-judgment and criticism at bay. Trust that any thoughtful step forward is a most precious and beautiful step toward becoming your optimal self—whatever that may be. Your version will be unlike any other person's. Your version will be perfect for you—a reflection of the qualities and capacities you find most precious. In this journey, you will have the opportunity to understand, develop, and balance your nurture energy side.

The power-energy side has tremendous, exemplary wealth of its own. Balanced power energy is incredibly attractive and compelling in a way that has nothing to do with a person's exterior and everything to do with the interior life. Power energy gives us strength, fortitude, and courage. The powerful aspect is splendidly brave, dignified, and adventurous. With its focus on achievement, the powerful side is often highly motivated. This energy fosters follow-through, allowing for the completion of tasks. Power energy is goal-oriented, ever pressing forward to gain ground. This side also offers a protective, firm energy that is vital in creating physical safety. Power energy bestows the gift of providing—bringing shelter and sustenance to the family. The powerful side brings with it the essential qualities of structure and order. As a necessary complement to the free-flowing energy of the nurturing side, the well-developed powerful aspect contributes consistency, discipline, and clear direction. True power energy offers a fiery passion that is balanced by commitment and dedication. The powerful side enjoys freedom and independence, yet it also knows the importance of stability—the rooted quality of the tree. With its logical capacity, the powerful side has the ability to focus, plan, and calculate. The well-developed powerful side does not bully; it has excellent leadership capacities that are grounded in wise awareness. Balanced power energy has a wise, hunter-like quality; it wants to search and obtain—but never to attain more than it needs. At its finest, power energy rises from strong self-esteem built upon a foundation of genuine integrity. In many ways, well-developed power energy has the quality of a peaceful, righteous warrior.

Whether you are a man or a woman, these tremendous powerful qualities—and so many more—are waiting inside of you. There may be aspects of your power energy that you have let languish. Perhaps there are powerful qualities that you always wished for, not knowing that they were waiting to be developed. Maybe some of these aspects are over-dominant—controlling you rather than working for you. The secret is in learning to acknowledge these traits within your own being and then doing the work necessary to bring them to life in a balanced, harmonious way.

You might naturally wonder if this process will make you "too much like a man" or "too much like a woman." If so, notice that destructive fear is already striving to fill you with doubt. Let constructive fear step in to tell you, "Trust that this part of your journey will be tremendously fulfilling. You won't become any more or less of a specific gender as you transform;

you will simply become more aware and balanced—a more whole, splendid version of who you already are."

You may now be ready to entertain these questions: How do I see and hold nurture energy? How is nurture energy at work in my life?

Your Version of Nurture Energy

Whether you are a woman or man, these next exercises are a vital part of your journey. As you embark on this next exercise, create a safe and peaceful environment for your work. With your pen and notebook by your side, relax and breathe. Notice if destructive fear wants to stop you with a voice of judgment. Notice if it steps in with thoughts of bias or negativity. Take note if it presses you to stereotype yourself, your roles, or your own way of being. When you are ready, pause to breathe.

Begin by making your own creative and thorough list of nurture-energy qualities—your outline may contain different qualities from those described previously. For example, your list might contain qualities such as these: gentle, kind, compassionate, flexible, agreeable, thoughtful, nurturing, sexy, mothering. Without judgment, take a look at your list.

Next, write a plus sign next to each quality that you would like to foster—those areas of your nurturing side that you would like to expand. Place an equal sign next to the qualities that you feel are balanced within you. Next, write a minus sign next to the qualities that you would like to diminish—those that might control you in certain ways. Pause to breathe.

When you are ready, close your eyes. With a nonjudgmental attitude, envision the person you are right now. Imagine the qualities that you currently embrace with balance. Next, imagine the nurturing qualities that you want to increase—those that you would like to foster and amplify. Next, imagine those that you would like to decrease to create better balance. Pause to breathe. Open your eyes when you are ready.

Take another look at your list, giving careful attention to each notation. Make additional notes as you like. When you are finished, close your eyes once again. Imagine nurture energy coming to life in your world. Consider how the various shifts might affect your relationship with yourself. Envision how the changes might benefit your relationships with others—your partner, your family, your friends, and those at work. Imagine how embracing nurture energy—bringing it into greater balance—might positively affect many areas of your life. When you are ready, open your eyes. Feel free to make notes about your thoughts or feelings. Breathe. Congratulate yourself on a job well done.

Nurture Energy in Action: Creating Greater Balance and Wholeness

You might wish to take a break before this next exercise. When you are psychologically ready to proceed, ensure that your environment is safe and relaxed. With your notebook and pen at your side, pause to breathe. Check in with yourself to notice how you are feeling. Perhaps this process creates feelings of being energized, anxious, or weary. Simply notice whatever feelings arise. Then, using the previous exercise as a foundation, create a list of the nurture-energy qualities that you want to increase in your life. Next to each item, write three actionable ways that you can foster this quality. For example, you might note, *Compassionate: (1) I will be more compassionate with myself—I will notice and pause my negative self-talk; (2) I will show my husband more compassion by listening to him attentively when he talks about his work stress; (3) I will nurture my compassion by volunteering at the animal shelter once a month.* Follow this example for every item on your list of qualities you would like to increase. Pause to breathe.

Next, create a list of the nurture-energy qualities you would like to diminish—to put into greater balance. For example, you might note: *Agreeable: (1) I will stop saying "yes" to every request and will consider requests carefully, prioritize them, and select those that give my life greater ease and balance; (2) I will give clear, firm, and unapologetic responses to create clear boundaries; (3) I will be honest with myself and others, saying "no" when necessary rather than saying "yes" in the moment just to please others.* Breathe.

Next, look at the items where you feel you have balanced energy. Notice and appreciate the areas where you feel in sync. Applaud yourself for having embraced and nourished these qualities within your own being. Pause to breathe. If thoughts or feelings arise, feel free to make notes. When you are finished, pause to breathe. Give yourself solid appreciation for engaging in this vital aspect of your journey. Well done.

Your Version of Power Energy

As you embark on this next exercise, ensure that your environment is safe and relaxed. Ensure that you are psychologically ready to proceed. With your pen and notebook by your side, pause to breathe. Take note if destructive fear wants to stop you with a voice of judgment or criticism. If it steps in, just notice if it pushes you to stereotype or otherwise judge who you are, your roles, or your own way of being. Pause to breathe.

When you are ready, make your own thorough list of power-energy qualities—your outline may contain different qualities from those described previously. For example, your list might contain qualities such as these: logical, rational, unemotional, forceful, dominant, aggressive, virile. Without judgment, take a look at your list. Next, place a plus sign next to each quality that you would like to foster—those areas of your power-energy side that you would like to foster and expand. Put an equal sign next to the qualities that you feel are well-balanced. Next, place a minus sign next to the qualities that you would like to diminish or shift in some way—those that control you or certain aspects of your life. Breathe.

When you are ready, close your eyes for a moment. With a non-judgmental attitude, envision the person you are right now. Imagine the power-energy qualities that you currently embrace in a balanced way. Next, imagine the power-energy qualities that you would like to expand and amplify. Then imagine the qualities that you would like to decrease or shift to create better balance. Pause to breathe. When you are ready, open your eyes. Look at your list again, giving attention to each notation. Make additional notes if you wish. Close your eyes for a moment to imagine balanced power energy coming to life in your personal world. Consider how the changes might affect your relationship with yourself. Then begin to imagine how the shifts might benefit your relationships with others—your partner, family, friends, and coworkers. Envision how a more balanced power energy could positively affect many areas of your life. When you are ready, open your eyes. Add notes about whatever thoughts or feelings come to you. Breathe. You are doing great work.

Power Energy in Action—Creating Greater Balance and Wholeness

When you are ready, proceed with this exercise in a space that feels safe and relaxed. With your notebook and pen close by, pause to breathe. Notice your feelings—perhaps you are feeling eager, interested, or tired. Just notice how you feel. Next, create a list of the power-energy qualities you would like to increase in your life. Next to each item, write three actionable ways that you can foster this quality. For example, you might note: *Accomplishment: (1) I will begin setting achievable, daily micro-goals for myself; (2) I will take action, following through with the goals I set; (3) I will monitor my progress, taking note of what is and is not effective for me.* Follow this example for every item on your list of qualities you would like to increase. Pause to breathe.

Next, create a list of the powerful qualities you would like to diminish—to put into greater balance. For example, you might note: *Aggressive: (1) I will foster a win-win approach that considers the needs of others as well as my own; (2) I will refrain from interrupting others and assuming that my words or opinions are more important than another's; (3) I will ask my partner to gently remind me when I am becoming aggressive, and I will take a time-out to reflect.* Pause to breathe.

Next, look at the items where you feel you have balanced power energy. Notice and appreciate the areas where you have created a healthy and balanced power energy. Applaud yourself for having fostered these tremendous qualities in yourself. Pause to breathe. If thoughts or feelings arise, feel free to make notes. When you are finished, pause to breathe. Give yourself solid appreciation for engaging in this vital aspect of your journey. You are making excellent progress. With every step you take, you are transforming your life.

Who Are You?

Maybe you truly know who you are—or maybe you don't. Maybe you love the qualities you have accepted and embraced—or maybe not. Whatever your story is and however you got to be where you are today, you have so much ahead of you. Whether you are a self-growth enthusiast like me or someone who simply wants a more joyful life, perhaps you are craving a better understanding of how to optimize your extraordinary self.

As with other aspects of our personhood, women learn "how to be women" early on in life. By watching mothers, elder sisters, grandmothers, aunts, teachers, and media images, we learn from—and ultimately mimic—whatever role models we were exposed to from early childhood forward. Men learned "how to be men" by watching their fathers, older brothers, grandfathers, uncles, coaches, and media images. Whether born male or female, we simply tend to model what we observe; we can't help it. Coupled with our unique DNA, the environment around us often makes us who we are—and the formative impact occurs before we have the cognitive capacity to understand what is taking place. As a result of these natural influences, we are unconsciously molded into a being that we did not fully choose to be. Now, as a more aware adult, you can choose to change what does not work for you and create more of what makes you feel like who you *want* to be. As you are finding, constructive fear wants you to have a choice to move beyond the dictates of your childhood and history; it wants you to embrace transformational fear. Yet destructive fear wants your past patterns and influences to hold you back; it doesn't want you to question who you are or how you came to be.

In essence, all children learn by paying attention to certain behaviors in their environment. They form ideas about what they have seen and ultimately mimic the behaviors. Children then tend to strengthen the behaviors that result in approval or other forms of attention. Children also learn by observing the consequences of others' behavior; they are more likely to mimic behaviors that are rewarded in some way. Interestingly, many parents and caregivers unwittingly reinforce negative behaviors by giving children far more attention for what they do *wrong* than what they do right. Children, particularly those who don't receive enough positive attention, may choose "acting out" behaviors that will get them some sort of attention—even if it is negative in nature. Some become combative, often imitating an aggressive parent's behavior. Some children may observe the negative behaviors and outcomes and elect to run in fear, freeze, or become invisible in some way. Others become peacekeepers and people-pleasers, striving to keep family unrest at a minimum. In general, children unconsciously adopt a medley of functional and dysfunctional patterns that help them navigate their world. In many ways, a child's script of "how to be" is an amalgamation of whatever behaviors were observed, encoded, and reinforced in some way. Fortunate children grow up in healthy environments that consistently provide opportunities to observe loving, respectful interactions between parents and other family members. Unfortunately, many children are reared in homes that model unkind, disrespectful treatment of spouses, children, and even family pets. Many are raised in environments where women and nurture-energy qualities are disrespected, devalued, and even hated. In this way, destructive fear begins its work when a child is very young. It gets inside the body, mind, and spirit. It tells the child how to be—how to act—even when that behavior is destructive to the self and others. It is by listening to the wise voice of constructive fear that change is possible. By taking this positive energy and using it for active change, transformational fear comes to life to create the necessary shifts.

The Fairy Tale of Sweet Marie: A Case Study

Let me tell you the story of Marie, a lovely British friend who wanted to share her transformational journey with you. Self-described as "warm, soft, and personable," Marie is a genuinely kind and gentle soul. Single, hardworking, and energetic, Marie has found herself contemplating her roles in life. Now in her thirties, Marie is investigating who she is and who she would like to become. As Marie offered, "I never paused to consider the type of future I wanted. Like many little girls, I'd dream about meeting a kind man, having a family, and living a nice life. That's as far as it went for me. Whatever dreams I might have had were quickly dampened by my father who told me from a young age how I must get a good job and save for the future as 'no one else was going to do it for me.' As it happens, I took that literally and started two part-time jobs at age fourteen, saving and worrying about the future at a young age. I had very mixed messages growing up, for my mother wanted nothing more than to be a stay-at-home mom. When she had to work three jobs after Dad lost his job, she wasn't happy. On one end, I had my father pressing me to be self-sufficient, yet my mother modeled the idea that a woman is happiest when dependent and domestic. My parents wanted what was best for me, but I now see that their conflicting agendas weren't helpful. I believe that I craved opportunity—something far beyond the roles they had accepted in life—but the family message was to 'get by.'"

When she was just seventeen, Marie fell for a charismatic man, Jon, who was ten years her senior. Jon had two young children and a flourishing mechanic's business. Jon wasn't her—or her parents'—idea of a suitable boyfriend. As Marie said, "He was a foul-mouthed smoker, covered in offensive tattoos, and generally disrespectful to anyone or anything. At the time, I prided myself on being open-minded and not judging a book by its cover. I used justifications and clichés to mask the reality of the situation; I didn't want to face what I knew deep inside, that it wasn't a healthy fit. But I saw vulnerability in him. I saw a little boy looking for praise and appreciation. I thought I could be the one to rescue him." At the time Marie met Jon, her parents' own marriage was tenuous. Their home life was volatile and difficult, yet Marie's mother could not accept the truth that her relationship had deteriorated significantly. Unwilling to see her own part in the destruction, Marie's mother placed the blame on her husband. As Marie stated, "She had failed to see that her marriage was in trouble. She conveniently forgot about her drunken kisses at Christmas parties or the dinner dates with other men. She didn't want to see that all of these behaviors—and so many more—had built up over time to create nearly constant battles." Seeking stability and relief from the constant turmoil, Marie moved in with Jon—unaware that she was jumping from the frying pan directly into the fire.

During this time, Marie became aware that her father was having an affair with a woman he had met at work; she knew of her father's adultery before her mother did. Marie, then nineteen, felt it was her duty to support her father as an accepting and caring peer. Pushing aside her natural anger and disappointment, Marie did her best to face the situation without emotion. As her parents' marriage deteriorated even further, her father left. For the next two years, Marie supported her mother through the difficult separation and ultimate divorce. Marie noted, "I watched my mother play the role of victim incredibly well. She had a complete emotional breakdown. I had to talk her out of bed every morning, encouraging her to start a new life as an independent woman."

In the background, cracks were also beginning to appear in Marie's relationship with Jon. The "charming" man she had dated slowly faded away. An emotionally abusive, manipulative man took the place of the sweet, attentive Jon she had fallen for originally. Marie was confused and frightened, uncertain how to cope with the "real" Jon. Although she wanted to pretend that the changes weren't occurring, she could see that Jon was increasingly controlling and critical—he wanted things his way. Marie began to eat comfort food and drink more alcohol to drown her anxiety and internal pain. She gained weight, and her self-confidence suffered even more. In time, Jon also began to dictate what Marie wore and, at times, what she ate and drank. He interfered with her relationships, making it difficult for her to socialize and connect with her supportive friends. Marie also knew something else was awry in their relationship—she sensed Jon was being unfaithful. Her instinct triggered her to investigate further, and she found multiple messages to various women on his phone. The messages made it obvious that he'd been having sexual relationships with several women while he claimed fidelity to her. Her exploration also revealed another issue—Jon had a hidden drug habit that had been secretly draining their joint finances. This information also helped Marie understand Jon's previously inexplicable mood swings. As Marie shared, "I felt my world falling apart. Jon had been the only 'stable' thing in my life for several years." Marie unconsciously began restricting her diet to have some sense of control in her otherwise out-of-control life. Not realizing that she had developed an eating disorder, Marie became thinner and thinner.

Marie knew that the relationship was destroying her, but she didn't have an easy way out. She was fearful of confronting Jon about his behavior, yet she also felt that she couldn't leave. Jon shared custody of his daughters, and they were regularly in the home. Jon was somewhat detached from his daughters, but Marie felt very close to them. She couldn't imagine being separated from the two young girls she had come to love and care for deeply. Additionally, Marie and Jon had two dogs that Marie loved. Jon could be violent and abusive to both of them. Marie was their protector, and they were hers; she could not envision leaving them with Jon.

So Marie plodded forward, doing the best she could. She noted, "I spent the next two years on autopilot. I cared for his children, his dogs, and his house. Jon retired from work, and this aggravated my situation. He was heavily into drugs, and his mood swings worsened. He would spend days in bed, and the financial burden began to affect me. It took a terrible, physically abusive argument to finally persuade me to leave; I walked away with just a suitcase and the dogs. For three years after that, I was in and out of depression—something I didn't even have the capacity to recognize at the time. I was suffering terribly; the years of mental torture had finally taken their toll. I realized that the dogs were also now controlling my life. I was constantly worried about them and unable to commit to anything too time consuming. I found myself in a spiral of drunken nights out. I justified my behavior as 'making up for lost time.'" Yet Marie did a good job of making it look like she had things under control. She continued to function very well at work, continuing the job she had held for many years. Her friends, who were busy with their own lives, didn't notice her depression and stress.

During this time, Marie's mother had begun rebuilding her own life. Fortunately, her mother's new partner recognized that Marie was struggling—he noticed that she was eating poorly and drinking excessively. He told Marie that he feared she was becoming a danger to herself. His concerns prompted Marie to seek outside support. As she actively engaged in workshops and individual therapy, Marie realized that she could change her life for the better. In Marie's words, "I realized that the only limits I had were the limits I placed upon myself."

This period of time offered Marie challenges as well as opportunities for growth and healing. She was incredibly close to both her paternal and maternal grandparents, all of whom lived nearby. When her father's parents fell ill, Marie helped care for them. Her beloved paternal grandparents ultimately passed away within six months of each other. Marie became a source of practical and emotional support for her father as he coped with the death of his parents and the loss of his marriage. During this period, Marie made the difficult decision to find a new home for her dogs. As Marie offered, "Although I knew it was for the best, it was—and continues to be—the worst experience of my life. We'd been through so much and shared an extremely difficult journey. I'd seen them as my protectors during my time with Jon, and I was also their protector. I learned a great deal through all of this. It was a difficult time filled with stress, loss, and grief. I was determined to make positive changes for the following year and going forward. I knew that I could put what I'd learned and experienced to good use."

Marie used her new awareness and skills to move forward. She had become wise to the ways of controlling, destructive fear. Yet she knew that she had to keep consciously shifting her behaviors to continue her transformative journey. Marie decided to take a few calculated risks that would strengthen her internal awareness—as well as her courage and bravery. Uncharacteristically, Marie decided to discover life outside her limited world. Never having ventured solo beyond her hometown, she contacted relatives in Vancouver and arranged a short visit. Her two-week trip expanded to a three-month tour of America and Canada; this adventure had wide-reaching, positive effects.

Marie shared the ups and downs of her beautiful, challenging journey with honest, insightful details. "This experience changed my life. I'd been brought up to believe that you don't take risks. I was taught that you stay loyal to an employer, you save, and you build a future. Yet there I was, giving up my job of eight years and jetting off to explore the other side of the world! My trip was filled with emotions; it tested my anxiety, fear, self-confidence, self-safety, and self-doubt. I was terrified of having a blinding migraine attack, not ideal when traveling alone. I was always a very nervous person, having been mugged, molested, and attacked before the age of twenty-one. I never thought I would overcome all of my challenges. Yet every host I stayed with helped me to grow, learn, and adjust my way of thinking in some way. I was completely overwhelmed at people's generosity and kindness; I often felt that I was not worthy. I realized that I needed to make changes. I wanted to really move on from the past, but I felt strangely guilty for wanting to. Yet, new courage slowly grew inside of me."

Marie began to delve more deeply into her history to ensure that she did not repeat it. She took the opportunities presented in her physical travels to deepen her psychological journey. Marie shared her exploration thoughtfully and noted, "I spent time reflecting on my past decisions and trying to understand why I chose to be in a relationship with Jon. I wondered if it was because I'd grown up watching my dominant father dictate the household while my submissive mother happily let him. I wondered if it was because my loud, aggressive, and manipulative older sister ruled the house—and my parents. I began to acknowledge that, despite being a product of my upbringing and environment, I—like every person—could choose to create change. On my return home from traveling, I felt slightly removed from my family; it seemed a necessary distance. I had a newfound hunger to think differently. I was more at ease. I had no regrets—only lessons learned. I could regret meeting Jon, regret not confronting him sooner, and regret not finding another way to help the dogs. I could regret not taking my trip before my grandparents died so that I could share my journey. But I realized that such regrets have no value. Instead, I began to focus on the valuable lessons I'd learned. Now, eight years on, I've accomplished so much more than I ever imagined. I now accept that the *thought* of facing something challenging—such as change and the unknown—is often worse than actually doing it. I once feared change but now I embrace it, for change brings opportunity."

Marie invested incredible time, thought, and effort in her journey. She pulled in resources from every arena—psychotherapy, traditional medicine, natural remedies, and alternative modalities such as hypnotherapy and acupuncture to alleviate her migraines and improve her overall well-being. She looked at her relationship with alcohol. She came to acknowledge that she used alcohol as "a way to mask reality." No longer willing to suffer depressing hangovers and other negative effects, Marie began to carefully manage her alcohol consumption. Rather than letting alcohol control her, Marie placed her health and overall wellness at the forefront of her life. In much the same way, Marie has consciously worked to develop a healthy and balanced relationship with food and exercise.

In one of my most recent exchanges with Marie, she told me, "I continue to think about how destructive fear can control my life if I'm not careful. I continue to realize how my upbringing and environment tend to dictate many of my unhealthy automatic responses in life. As I started my new job, I could feel myself getting highly anxious. Then I reminded myself that change can lead to growth and opportunity. This positive mindset actually provided me with great confidence in my first week of the new job. The job is a complete unknown, so there is massive uncertainty. But rather than wondering or assuming what can go wrong, I'm completely excited about what will go *right*! I continue to challenge other automatic thoughts that appear to me, questioning their validity and whether they are worthy of further thought. I listen to my positive, constructive voice. It stops my anxiety from getting the best of me. This pattern makes me think, feel, and act in more positive ways!"

Marie continues to evolve, learning more about herself and the path she wants to take. Even now, she is re-envisioning her roles in life. She noted, "I feel a daily pull between my career path and desire to have a family. I question why I'm so restless and confused. I now link it back to my younger days and lack of direction. It seems that I did what my father instructed—I focused on getting ahead in life at the expense of being happy. For too long, I've made sacrifices for work progression and success. I felt like the poster girl for my last employer. I always needed to perform perfectly—to say and do exactly the right things. This put intense pressure on me, and I sometimes felt as if I couldn't breathe. My new position is enjoyable and less stressful than my former job, yet I still feel drawn to do something different. In truth, I stand at a crossroads, unsure of what profession I truly wish to follow. I'm surrounded by friends who all have determined their paths. I wonder if it's too late to retrain and focus on something new. Yet I am aware that this is destructive fear talking; I now see that it wants to immobilize me and hold me back. As I become more aware of the voice of constructive fear, I am realizing that I do want to do something different—and I will. I have left behind the roles of victim and people-pleaser. I am sloughing off the role of 'woman without a cause.' I envision a career that will allow me to balance home life with work life, one that does not make me sacrifice one for the other. I've become so much more aware of my passionate nature—and a balanced, passionate blend of home and work is what calls to me. I envision my role in life as a woman who helps others and loves well but who first helps and loves herself."

As Marie continues to envision and create the future she craves, she also knows that she has more work to do in her relationship realm. With frank awareness, she shared, "Even though I have a lovely new man in my life, I know that some of my old patterns are still alive. Although the dynamics in this relationship are quite healthy, I know that work provides a safe haven for me. It is always there in the foreground, giving me stability when relationships fail. In some ways, my focus on work has perpetuated my inability to commit. If I think back to my upbringing, my parents didn't show love between each other. Both displayed unhealthy behaviors; the impact is obvious now. Given their behaviors, I understand why it's been exceedingly difficult for me to trust. My father, mother, sister, and I have failed to succeed in healthy relationships. Yet I am determined to succeed. I am determined to continually notice and shift my old, destructive patterns. I am honoring constructive fear in my current relationship. In the past, I'd have clung to the relationship or run from it. Now, I am allowing it to unfold. This relationship is being built on behaviors that are loving and honest. It's coming to life through open discussions, play, and thoughtful effort. I don't know where it will lead, but that's fine. I am focused on creating joy in the here and now."

This tale is a real-life story with a happy new beginning that will continue to unfold. Marie's tale isn't unfolding beautifully by chance but as a result of her conscious dedication to her personal transformation. Marie discovered the courage to face her past and her future with awareness. She lives with the willingness and bravery to ever confront the destructive fears that want to hold her back. Marie has embraced the wisdom of constructive fear; she has made it her friend and ally. Indeed, Marie is dedicated to continuing her life journey with transformational fear at her side.

Marie's tale is a reminder that life is not easy and that the past can truly haunt us in the most destructive ways—unless we choose to work through the negative, fear-based issues. When women and men tell me their stories, their childhood experiences are often highly visible in the background. Whether their experiences were positive, negative, or somewhere between the two poles, they had lasting effects. Each person learns the treatment of self and others early on in life. If the impact was negative, the journey of self-work can create relieving understanding and change. In situations where childhood influences were largely positive, self-work can provide greater awareness and energy to support others. In truth, becoming a positive, self-aware person can be the work of a lifetime. Yet many individuals operate under the misconception that they should know who they are and "how to be." Some believe that the problems they experience are the result of their being unlovable or "defective" in some way. Many do not realize that their issues are a result of childhood environments that simply didn't provide appropriate, positive modeling for womanhood or manhood. Indeed, many parents and other role models are confused and struggling in their own lives. Often trying their best to "get by," many don't realize the negative impact they are having on their children. As a result, unhealthy behaviors and attitudes are perpetuated generation after generation. This negative cycle can be changed by facing destructive fear's impact and learning new ways through the ongoing guidance of constructive fear. Transformational fear will work its magic when you embrace this process with interest, commitment, and effort.

Learning who you are deep inside is not an easy task. Given the significant changes in traditional roles and societal expectations, it is easy to become confused about one's unique personhood. Many people move through life striving to be who they think they should be and acting as they think they should act. Others take automatic, oppositional attitudes that are controlling in their own way, driving the adoption of contrary roles or

behaviors that may be unsuitable. Some seem rather ambivalent, unconsciously thinking and behaving in ways modeled by parents and dictated
by society. Now that you are aware of your relationship with both destructive and constructive fear, you may see that you have a choice. You may
realize that you no longer need to accept the thoughts and behaviors that
work against your highest self.

Any trait, be it power energy or nurture energy, can become overly
amplified or left to wither away, and this lack of balance can cause significant difficulties. Marie's story provides an example of how a person
can unconsciously imitate negative behaviors as certain positive capacities fade away. Marie learned destructive, passive behaviors that led her
unwittingly into an abusive relationship. Additionally, her necessary,
positive sense of personal power wasn't nourished during her early childhood. Growing up in the shadow of a domineering father and abusive
elder sister, she shrank back. Following her mother into a role of passive
acceptance, she did not develop many of her positive capacities. Marie's
naturally caring and helpful qualities were not balanced by wise, internal
power. As a result, her self-esteem did not flourish, and she reflexively
followed the self-destructive path modeled by her mother. Marie's loving mother, of course, intended no harm to herself or her daughters; she
likely adopted the behaviors her own mother had modeled for her. In the
same way, Marie's overbearing father was likely perpetuating behaviors
he had learned from his own role models in life. The beauty of tales such
as Marie's is their ability to guide us forward into consciously learning
more about the self and those in our world. Fueled by the life experiences
of others, the true work lies in finding the balance that creates a sense of
being one with the self in a way, allowing you to transform your life in the
most beautiful way.

Destructive fear wants women to remain in chains—whether the chains
are crafted by other women, men, or society. It wants to foment reactive
behavior and unproductive anger for the misogyny women have suffered.
Constructive fear has a different attitude. It wants righteous anger to be
channeled into lasting changes that will create respect, equality, and balance. It wants women and men to better understand each other. It wants
to replace prejudice with understanding and conflict with discussion.
Constructive fear sees the benefit in the valuable synergy that is possible
between women and men. Constructive fear wants women and men to
honor each other in words and in actions. By moving in this direction, our

lives and the world we live in will be transformed—we will free ourselves from the negative forces of destructive fear.

Marie's story may resonate with you, propelling you to consider the roles you have adopted in life. Many individuals come to feel as if life forced them to become someone they do not understand or even like. Far too many unconsciously follow set patterns and expectations as they proceed through childhood and into adulthood. Indeed, for those who struggle to simply get through each day, the unfamiliar concept of self-work is often low or nonexistent on the list of priorities. Some continue mechanically on their way, reacting to one challenge after another, ever struggling and barely staying afloat. Others—as was the case for Marie—pause to take notice of their internal being only when life begins to spiral. Yet no matter how or when the desire for transformation arises, it can be done. With Marie's story as a reminder, trust that it truly is possible to notice destructive fear's negative patterns and begin the life-changing journey forward with constructive fear.

Of course, men also have their challenges. In our patriarchal world, power energy is too heavily emphasized; without the balance of nurture energy, the psyche—and the world—suffers. For example, given certain fear-induced imbalances in power energy, many men compartmentalize their emotions. By shutting off such vital aspects of the self, amazing capacities wither and fade. Indeed, more men than women seem to be out of touch with their interior world—some, in truth, hold fast to the singular power of the "logical" mind. Many do not know who they are apart from roles they have taken in life such as provider, businessperson, employee, or athlete. Some truly have no idea that they are far more than their external successes or failures. Sadly, such individuals are completely out of touch with the vast array of other self-capacities that lie dormant and await discovery.

Destructive fear has its hand in all of this. Destructive fear has divided men from many of their vital nurturing-energy capacities. It has taught men to fear vulnerability in an undiscriminating, controlling way. It has fooled men into believing that emotions are irrational and that their sensitivity is a threat. It has duped men into believing that nurture energy is weak, insipid, and even unnecessary. In doing so, destructive fear has robbed men of half of their inherent wisdom—half of their capacities. It has sent many men on a mindless, reactive quest for power and control. Destructive fear has confused men into thinking that a "real" man is tough, angry, and combative. Destructive fear has led some into reflexively aggressive behaviors that feed negativity and anger. Others have assumed passive stances that leave them feeling emasculated, sometimes leading to hidden angst that fuels passive-aggressive behavior. Whether it is highly charged aggression or powerless emasculation, polarized behavior gives too much weight to certain aspects, leaving the underweighted qualities to fade or even perish. It is balance—the thoughtful balance created by the wise voice of constructive fear—that is the key to freedom.

The Tale of Frightened, Tyrannical Thomas: A Case Study

When I first met Thomas, an aggressive man in his late forties, he noted that he simply needed assistance with stress that had "apparently become noticeable to others." Thomas sought psychotherapy at the suggestion of his trusted accountant who had noticed that Thomas appeared increasingly stressed and forgetful. Over the course of several lunch meetings, his accountant nudged him to make an appointment with a psychologist. From the onset, Thomas made it clear to me that he was not a believer in psychotherapy, that he "didn't expect it to work," and that I had one appointment to change his mind.

Much of our initial session was spent on Thomas's basic history. When I asked about his childhood, Thomas said, "My childhood was absolutely fine. I had two hardworking parents and two older siblings—a brother and a sister. That about covers it. I don't want to waste my time addressing it further." Intrigued by Thomas's terse response, I moved to focusing on other areas, including his current life stressors. When I asked Thomas what he thought might be at the root of his stress, he matter-of-factly noted, "It is possible that the death of my parents might have affected me, yet they were old—I was prepared for it. My mother had cancer and didn't respond well to treatment. Several months after her death, my father passed away. Also, two of my closer friends recently died from heart attacks—almost back to back. I imagine it's logical that all of this affected me in some way. What I find problematic is the fact that *others* perceive that I'm stressed. I'm used to operating effectively and at a very fast pace. I can't have this affecting my business or my life. I don't have time for it."

As we discussed more of his personal history, Thomas gave a short, humorless laugh. "I was married once—very young. I married because I was expected to, not because I was in love. Of course, it's no surprise that the marriage didn't take. After that, there's been a stream of women, but never anyone meaningful to me. I just didn't care; my focus has always been on my business and my personal pursuits. Success is vital to me, particularly in the business realm. Relationships with women are not a good bet—look at the divorce rate. Besides, women are a pain—illogical, disruptive, and needy. I'm self-sufficient, intelligent, and hardworking. I've never met a woman who is half as hardworking or intelligent as I am—nor one who is self-sufficient. Thus I've never found a woman I can respect. In fact, I doubt such a woman exists. Besides, I've watched too many marriages end. But enough about relationships. None of that is actually important. I am here to get my stress under control; I don't want stress—or anything else—interfering with my life."

Before the end of our first session, it was clear to me that Thomas had an exceedingly tough armor. Yet he was motivated to address his stress—if only to be able to continue in his role as a self-contained, highly effective businessman. I wasn't intimidated by Thomas's abrasive attitude; my office had been home to other men who were similar in many ways. Some had become highly involved in their internal journeys, and some had decided not to make the effort. I wondered which avenue Thomas would take. As he left, he asked for another appointment, saying that I "might be worth" his time. I smiled. Thomas would not be an easy client.

In our second session, Thomas talked about his chronically busy schedule and how he had no time to think about unnecessary matters such as grief and loss. He noted, "I can't prevent death; I've no control over it. When it comes, you accept it and move on. I don't waste my time on touchy-feely issues." Extremely adept at compartmentalizing his feelings, Thomas had not processed the deaths of his parents. When his mother passed, he worked matter-of-factly with his siblings to handle funeral and burial arrangements—and then moved on with his life. When his father died, he did the same, handling the necessary details with businesslike detachment. As he discussed the unexpected deaths of his two friends, he showed a hint of emotion. Their sudden deaths affected him more than he was prepared to acknowledge. These friends—both within a few years of Thomas's age—left him staring at his own mortality. With not much more in his life than a successful business, material wealth, and a few friends, Thomas was unaware that he was frightened to the core. He had operated on the premise that everything he had accumulated in life was all that he needed and wanted, but the recent deaths of his two friends had pricked his inner world. Thomas was staring at the emptiness of his future—and his past. A lifetime of unprocessed anger and sadness seemed to be welling up inside of him. Yet, even in our second and third sessions, Thomas didn't want to delve into his childhood or his past. Thomas professed that he didn't want to be in my office, routinely noting that psychotherapy was "a waste of time," but something kept him coming back.

As we moved into our fourth session, I asked Thomas to tell me about his favorite hobbies as a child. His eyes lit up as he said, "I loved to play with army men. I liked riding my bicycle. I spent a lot of time alone. When I wasn't doing chores, you'd find me building models or reading. Everyone else in my family was busy—there was always organized chaos. I found it better to be alone." When I asked him to tell me more, Thomas shifted to talking about his business, one of his customary means of deflecting my queries. I used the opportunity to ask Thomas why he chose his profession—if his family supported him in finding the career of his dreams. Thomas looked at me quizzically. "No, my family wasn't in the dream-supporting business. No one asked me if I'd like to sail, fence, play tennis, or do something enjoyable for a living. My family was in the do-what-is-expected business. More accurately, my father was in the do-what-is-expected-and-do-it-right business. Dreams weren't discussed. Doing what was expected—being successful and making money—was a given."

Pressing forward, I asked, "When you were little, what did you want to be when you grew up?" Thomas looked at me blankly. I continued, "Young boys often have visions of becoming policemen, firefighters, or doctors. Some want to be sports stars. What did you want to be?'

Thomas tersely responded, "I never gave it a thought." I looked into Thomas's eyes, and he shifted the conversation toward politics. Indeed, Thomas was most comfortable talking about three issues: business, politics, and sports.

In our next session, I casually asked Thomas to tell me about his favorite childhood superhero. "Superman, of course. I was just a kid. Like any boy, I wanted to believe that Superman existed. Someone out there had to be good—to protect people." When I asked Thomas who needed to be protected, he was silent. For a split second, he seemed frightened. I asked him if there were any "bad guys" in his childhood—people or situations that had scared him. Thomas paused and said, "I understand the way your mind works now. You want me to say something like my father and brother were the bad guys, but I decline to do that. You'll have to up your game. Besides, I don't really have any memories of my childhood. There's nothing there for you to explore. So sorry to disappoint you."

I later asked Thomas to tell me about his favorite childhood book. He smiled, knowing that my questions always had an underlying purpose. "I liked *Ivanhoe*—it was about knights and such. I imagine that the fantasy of knights and doing good was compelling to me as a kid. I also liked tales of Robin Hood—he was quite cunning and strategic. *Robinson Crusoe* was a favorite, too." As we talked more about the book characters and their qualities, I saw fragments of the young, idealistic Thomas. It seemed that young Thomas had wanted to be an adventurer and a knight in shining armor—he just didn't know how.

As is often the case, Thomas originally didn't want to believe that his childhood had any impact on who he was as an adult man. In his intractable way, he declared, "Who I was as a kid doesn't matter. I'm not going to blame anything on my childhood; that's an absurd concept. I had good parents. People liked my father. He was a hard worker—a good provider. There was always food on the table and a roof over our heads. I'm not going to blame anything on my mother, either. She was a great woman—always very busy." I reminded Thomas that we weren't exploring his past to cast blame but to understand how his childhood and his overall past affected his thoughts, behaviors, and the various roles he played in life. Thomas wasn't ready to consider this concept. With a hard look in his eyes, he stared at me and said, "My role is to be successful and to make money—lots of it. Your role is to take the money I give you to fix whatever is wrong." Thomas was used to intimidating both men and women with his combative, aggressive attitude. I looked into Thomas's eyes and caught a glimpse of unfiltered rage—the destructive fear—inside.

In time, Thomas's substantial armor of defenses slowly began to give way—though it often appeared to revert to its former strength between sessions. Yet more and more, I saw the terrified little boy underneath as he slowly began sharing excerpts of the distressing early-life experiences he began to recall. Thomas shared how fearful he was to make mistakes, for his father's critical eye focused on the perceived errors of every family member. His father's alcoholic, highly inconsistent behavior made Thomas feel as if he were "constantly walking in a field of landmines." Thomas shared bits of his father's sarcastic commentary which, although intensely hostile and destructive, was disguised as "joking" banter. Thomas also recounted memories of his father mercilessly teasing his mother about minor mistakes. "My mother wasn't always the best with numbers—he never let her forget any error. He made constant, sarcastic jokes at her expense. He wouldn't let *anything* go. My mother took it. She never said anything."

It took a few months for Thomas to share a deeply poignant, unforgettable memory with me. As a small child—likely in first grade—Thomas decided that he wanted another child's lunch more than his own. He took his schoolmate's lunch and happily devoured it. The incident came to the teacher's attention, and she asked Thomas why he'd taken the other child's lunch. Thomas manufactured a story, sheepishly telling the teacher that he didn't have food at home. When the teacher contacted Thomas's parents, trouble unfolded. Little Thomas—barely six years old—was met at the door by his father. Without displaying emotion, Thomas recounted the incident: "My father grabbed me by the neck and crammed my head into every cupboard in the kitchen. He stuffed my head into every drawer and cabinet, saying over and over again, 'See, this is food! This is what food looks like. There is plenty of food in this house. Don't you dare ever tell anyone we don't have food. Do you hear me?'"

"That must have been terrifying," I said.

Thomas ignored my comment. "Knowing you, I imagine that you see some fault with my father's behavior, but it was effective. I got the message. I never took another kid's lunch." After sharing this troubling memory, Thomas seamlessly segued to tales of how wonderful his father was at putting gifts in Christmas stockings. Without pause, he then dove into stories of horrific dinnertime battles between his drunken father and elder brother—some that turned the tyrannical behavior in his direction. Thomas noted casually, "But my dad was great at telling stories. Sometimes he'd tell adventure stories at the dinner table—he could surely weave a tale." Yet clearly Thomas could never predict which version of his father would appear. Little Thomas grew up in a tremendously unpredictable environment that was ruled with an abusive hand.

Bit by bit, Thomas reconstructed his childhood. Some of Thomas's later stories told of a home life that did not permit entry of "outsiders"—normal childhood activities such as having friends over for dinner and sleepovers were prohibited. With his parents focused on work, he was often placed in the naïve care of his too-young older siblings. Thomas described a home life that was a highly inconsistent blend of chaos, rules, criticism, humor, and inflexibility. In matter-of-fact tones, Thomas described a history where emotional intimacy—in fact, the existence of an interior world—simply did not exist. Piece by piece, Thomas's childhood unfolded in my office over several months. As his childhood history came to life, so did my understanding of Thomas.

At first, Thomas refused to believe that his father's chronic belligerence and volatility could have affected him. Thomas couldn't comprehend that his father's angry, unpredictable eruptions—often focused on others, but sometimes directed at Thomas—could have done him any harm. He couldn't imagine that his father's constant criticism had any relationship to his own constant inner critic. Additionally, he didn't want to believe that his mother's pointed, critical voice also still reverberated inside of him. Thomas also couldn't accept that he had suffered as a result of his mother's fear-based unwillingness to stand up to his father. He didn't want to see that her accepting, passive behavior had a serious downside. Thomas did not want to see or believe that his childhood or parents—his physical role models in life—had contributed in any way to the empty, unfulfilling personal relationships that had plagued him his entire life. Indeed, as Thomas was successful in the material world, he was truly mystified that his destructive childhood could have affected some areas of his life but not others.

Yet Thomas persevered. A sharp, highly educated man, he was now invested in understanding why certain areas of his life were highly successful and others were not. Although he enjoyed many aspects of life, from competitive sailing and fencing to his high-caliber tennis abilities, he often found himself retreating from contact with others. This tendency became more understandable as Thomas shared other memories about his father's often unfeeling, heartless behavior. As Thomas once noted, "My father cut off contact with his own brother after a disagreement; he wouldn't say what it was about, but he never spoke to him again. He did the same thing with me and my siblings at different times. I said something he didn't like—it was something very minor about his business—and he didn't talk to me for nine years. For nine solid years, he pretended I didn't exist. He did the same thing with my brother and sister. I don't fault him for this; if someone doesn't do what you believe they should do, it's your right to cut them off cold." In the same session, Thomas quipped, "I wouldn't say this to anyone but you, but I'm a loner at heart. As a child, I preferred my army men and my bicycle. They were reliable; they didn't let me down. I feel the same way about solo sailing. I prefer not having to rely on anyone. In fact, I don't particularly like that I've come rely on you somewhat." I smiled at his progress. It was difficult for Thomas to trust anyone. Although Thomas felt safe with his tough armor, he was very lonely and very alone. He had unknowingly followed in his father's footsteps, cutting off access to his own heart and soul.

Thomas was a highly complex man who, on many levels, was not who he appeared to be. His persona was far different from the terrified man underneath the mask of cold aggression. I came to learn that Thomas was once a heavy drinker and that two DUIs propelled him into forced sobriety. Yet, like his father before him, the patterns that led him to drink heavily were never addressed. In Thomas's view, the cause of the drinking didn't matter—what was paramount was that he stopped "cold turkey." Despite his penchant for smoking, his excessive spending, and a long line of difficult relationships, Thomas didn't yet see that the addictive behaviors modeled by his father were alive inside of him. His friends knew him as the sarcastic, competitive, funny guy—a "good guy" like his father. And, like his father, Thomas was highly aggressive. In his domineering way, he operated his thriving manufacturing company with a firm hand and a tight fist—just as his father had done in his own business. Thomas noted that his father prided himself on his calculated business dealings, noting, "My father's favorite thing in life was 'the art of the deal'—he loved working situations to get what he wanted." Yet Thomas could not see the connection to the tale of his self-admitted pattern of "saying and doing whatever is necessary to get what I want." In the same way, Thomas could not see that his father's disrespectful attitude toward his own wife had infected Thomas's ability to respect women. Although Thomas once noted, "My relationships with women were largely built on sarcasm, condescension, aggression, and indifference," he couldn't yet see the connection to his father's behavior. Thomas wasn't ready to see that he had inherited his father's behaviors and attitudes—destructive fear didn't want to release Thomas from its grasp.

Given his longstanding patterns, it was difficult for Thomas to move out of his myopic, black-and-white world. He wanted to believe that the roles his father and mother had played were "all good." He struggled to see that this "all good" attitude left him attributing any "bad" to himself or others. The middle spectrum—the gray area of balance—was unfamiliar to Thomas. As we explored his childhood together, our work sometimes focused on envisioning new attitudes and alternative behaviors. If he were able to open up to new possibilities, Thomas could create his own future rather than following in his father's footsteps. Yet he balked at allowing constructive fear to come in to guide him, to show him that he was poised for greater awareness and growth.

One day, Thomas ranted longer than usual about my "wholly ineffective penchant for examining personal history to uncover patterns."

I looked at Thomas with curiosity and said, "So, if I hear you right, you're telling me that you weren't affected at all by your parents. Your father's ability to retract his 'love'—to cut off family entirely—has had no effect on your ability to form safe, intimate relationships. Your father's antagonistic, emotionally abusive treatment of your mother—sarcasm, ridicule, and disparagement—didn't affect how you see women or learned to treat them. You're telling me that your father's violent and verbally abusive behavior of your elder siblings, your brother in particular, didn't affect you. It also seems that you weren't affected when your father impulsively upended your beds, threw your toys outside, or drove drunk with you in the car. And, if I've listened well, you believe that your father's constant criticism, teasing, and belittling ways—often directed at you—had no impact on the man you are today."

Thomas stared at me. "Say more," he invited flatly.

"Okay," I replied, watching him carefully. "We've talked before about a way you might have been parented differently—a way that would have not been so hurtful to you. So I am curious to know if you can envision some adjustments that would have been helpful."

"Go on," Thomas directed.

"You might imagine that parents could work as a team to love each other and their children with respect and kindness. For example, I wonder if you would have possibly preferred a father who sat down to gently talk with you when something went wrong and also to commend you when things went right. It might have felt wonderful to be the positive focus of both your parents' attention as they read you bedtime stories, gently helped you with homework, and attended sporting and school events. I imagine you would have liked it if friends were permitted to stay the night—you may have yearned for a playful and inviting home environment."

Thomas cleared his throat, and I paused. "Continue," he stated.

"Okay. So it is possible that you might have felt more secure if your father treated your mother with tenderness and respect. It might have made you feel warm inside if your father had been physically and emotionally affectionate with your mother. You might have felt safer if your father wasn't chronically abusive to your brother. It's possible you would have preferred a home life where you weren't alternately ignored and terrorized. You might have felt safer if you were not the constant target of frightening behavior and criticism. Perhaps you wanted kindness and acceptance. I wonder if you might have liked knowing that you and your family—not work and other pursuits—were your father's priority."

"I might consider that," Thomas said with hint of sorrow in his voice. "Go on."

"Well, maybe it would have felt good to have a childhood that felt safe. One where your mother protected you and nurtured you. One where your father was kind, stable, and loving. I imagine it might have felt good to know that you mattered—your emotions, your thoughts, and your hopes for the future. Perhaps, Thomas, it would have felt good to know that you were a priority, not a burden."

Thomas looked at me, and his jaw tightened for a moment. "I have to go now," he said. "It's almost the end of my appointment, in any event." He turned back to me as he left and said, "I'll give consideration to what you've said."

That particular session proved to be a significant turning point in Thomas's psychotherapy journey. As Thomas later commented, "It was the first time I could actually hear the constructive fear you talked about. In that session, I was struggling to release something that was very negative, very powerful—I imagine you would term it 'destructive fear.' I could actually hear constructive fear—or, perhaps, I could hear your voice giving me constructive messages. Regardless, it felt as if a battle were waging inside of me. Something was trying to get me to close off—to shut down as I would have in the past—yet something else was stronger than that. That aspect allowed me to listen, even when the other voice wanted me to become angry and sarcastic with you."

Thomas realized that, like his father, he had carried on in life as a hardened, aggressive businessman who "did whatever it took, often at the expense of integrity." Thomas slowly discovered that he had lost his sense of respect for himself—and for others in the process. In one particularly profound session, Thomas offered, "You know, my father was a sensitive man inside. He really was. Yet all of the challenges he had experienced in life—whether growing up with an alcoholic mother, friends taking advantage of him, or business difficulties—had turned him into a hard, calloused, self-absorbed man. He was absolutely unforgiving. He could hold a grudge like no one I've ever seen." All of these realizations were bitter pills for Thomas to swallow. He struggled, angry that he had unconsciously become a version of his father. His evolution into self-awareness was slow and arduous, and he often reverted to his former patterns. Yet he continued to pry back his armor sheeting, even if sometimes begrudgingly. In one session, Thomas barked, "Do you enjoy evaluating me? Has my 'success as an evolved man' become your *raison d'être*?"

I paused, smiled, and responded, "No, Thomas. It seems to me that your internal journey is becoming *your* reason for being." Thomas stared at me with steely eyes, and then he actually smiled.

As our sessions progressed and Thomas evolved, he came to a point where he could imagine in a nonjudgmental way how his parents might have done things differently without feeling as if he was betraying them or his upbringing. He came to see that his parents had tremendous positive capacities and also certain weaknesses—many of which had affected him deeply. Thomas noted, "I can see that my father had a very troubled and volatile side. Among other things, he was bigoted, cruel, angry, and extremely critical. Yet he was also creative, hardworking, fabulously mechanical, and humorous. I now see that his sensitivity was not well-used; instead, he hid behind a tall, thick wall of sarcasm and cruel behaviors. As to my mother, she was wonderful and amazing in many ways—too many to list. Yet, she was hyperfocused on work and very task-oriented. She could also be highly critical—I came to fear that side of her. And I can see now that it would have been terrific to have her hug me—to get something in the way of physical affection. It's clear to me now that I have become in many ways the sum of both their negative and positive capacities. It is my goal to continue to amplify the positive traits and to do my utmost to extinguish the negative."

Thomas began envisioning a few new roles in life. He began to consider donating money and time to various causes. Before long, he found himself volunteering for a local nonprofit. He then discovered that his tennis abilities could be utilized to offer tennis instruction to underprivileged children. With a grin, Thomas noted, "I never imagined volunteering could be fun. The kids are so great that I'm considering teaching a fencing class. I also learned about a group that teaches sailing to veterans to help them heal from trauma. That would be a terrific experience." Thomas was becoming kinder and more compassionate before my eyes—not by chance but as a result of his commitment to being a more complete man.

In the course of volunteering, Thomas met a lovely attorney who had lost her husband to cancer; she soon became the apple of his eye. He described her as good-hearted, patient, and tolerant but absolutely unwilling to accept his abusive, volatile tendencies. Thomas began learning what it was like to be in love—to actually care for and focus on another human being. He admitted that it was exceedingly difficult for him to remember to put another's needs above his own—or at least on the same level—but he continued to create greater awareness within himself and to *act* on his awareness. Now motivated on another level, his life began to change even more. Thomas reflected, "I see myself as more than an aggressive businessman now. I might, someday, even find myself married. Although I can't imagine having children at this stage in my life, I have come to realize that I truly do want a healthy relationship. This is quite hard for me to admit, but clearly I used people I didn't care about to temporarily fill voids in my life—in myself. I was in difficult, immature relationships because I was a difficult, immature man. It is rough in some ways for me to look back and see how I let my self-absorbed, destructive side control me for so long. Yet I keep focusing on the future. My journey so far has made me far more mature emotionally, but there is clearly hard work ahead. I am a high achiever, so it will happen. I'll stay the course so that I can be as good a partner to someone as I expect someone to be to me. It didn't compute for me that helping others could make me feel better about myself, but I am seeing that it's true. As I learn to focus more on others and less on my own selfish needs, I feel more positive and alive. I want to enjoy the rest of my life knowing that I am the best I can be in all realms—not just the material world; I've already conquered that. I am continuing to learn that the business side of life is easy when compared to self-work. Business is business, but being a truly good person and this self-discovery work—*that* takes vast effort. It's all about turning all of your capacities on—not running from them or turning them off. I see how easy it has been for me to hide in fear behind work and sports where I knew I would excel. I used the roles of businessman and sportsman to shield myself from the imperfect and difficult—yet very real and very human—journey of life."

By accepting that his parents were human and therefore not "all bad" or "all good," Thomas became more accepting of the imperfect nature of all aspects of his humanity. As he appreciated his parents' significant strengths and forgave them for their human weaknesses, his own sense of truth and forgiveness grew. By envisioning behaviors and attitudes that would have felt better to him—those that would have enlivened him rather than terrorized him—he was able to free himself of criticism and blame. By acknowledging that his younger self would have naturally wanted more love, acceptance, consistency, and support—and less criticism, passive-aggressive behavior, and anxiety-inducing volatility—his sense of compassion developed. Slowly, Thomas came to see his history and his life for what it had been. With constructive fear in his mind and his heart, he saw his capacities; he saw what he wanted to become. Thomas chose to embrace the journey of transformational fear in the most powerful of ways.

The stories of Marie and Thomas may give you insight into your own roles in life. You may now be pondering your own roles as a man, woman, and human being. You might be considering how your roles came to be—if you consciously chose your life roles, unconsciously adopted them, or if they evolved through a blend of internal and external forces. You might be noticing the ways that destructive fear held you back or pigeonholed you. You might be hearing the voice of constructive fear guiding you to make changes. This next exercise will allow you to more fully explore this vital aspect of your life.

The Evolution of Your Life Roles and Personal Characteristics

To prepare for this series of exercises, create a safe and relaxed environment. This multi-level segment may take you some time to complete. Be patient with yourself, as the various layers address important elements of your work with transformational fear. Indeed, many aspects of this section are the culmination of work you have done so far. Take special notice that you will be continuing your work with both power-energy and nurture-energy qualities; remember that these traits are often out of balance.

As always, make certain that you are psychologically ready to proceed. With your pen and journal at your side, take a few cleansing breaths. Proceed with an attitude of nonjudgment, letting thoughts and images arise as they will. Destructive fear may step in with thoughts of blame, guilt, or judgment; allow yourself to set these thoughts free. When you are ready, close your eyes.

Imagine your parents, caregivers, and any other chief role models in life. Allow yourself to envision the roles that these individuals embodied. When you are ready, open your eyes. For each role model, whether a parent, grandparent, dominant sibling, or influential teacher or coach, write their names in your notebook. Use a separate page for each person. You may want to work with one role model at a time.

Next to each person's name, list the various roles that you believe this person embodied. Using Thomas's father as an example, the roles might be *provider, bully, father, businessman,* and *tyrant.* Avoid destructive fear's push to tell you that there is an "all good" or "all bad" role model. Notice if destructive fear uses judgment to tell you that you are "right" or "wrong" by viewing your role models in a certain way— your unique, personal impressions and perspectives are what matter. Remember, your purpose is to notice how the roles affected you in both positive and negative ways. After listing the roles for each person, pause to breathe. Next, consider each role you listed. Without judgment, put a plus sign next to those that had a positive impact on you. Then put a minus sign next to those that affected you negatively. Breathe.

Next, look at the name of each role model; again, you may wish to work with one role model at a time. Close your eyes, imagining the various traits—both positive and negative—that were most pronounced in each person. Take care to remain accepting and nonjudgmental. When you are ready, open your eyes. Breathe. Below each person's name, make two columns, one marked "positive" and the other marked "negative." List the person's positive traits in one column and the negative traits in another. Using Marie's mother as an example, the positive list might read: *kind, nurturing, hardworking, patient,* and *compassionate.* The negative list might read: *passive, passive-aggressive, unfocused,* and *unmotivated.* With Thomas's father as an example, the positive list might read: *humorous, hardworking, creative, diligent,* and *focused.* The negative list might read: *domineering, disrespectful, cruel,* and *insensitive.* With an attitude of nonjudgment, create lists for each role model. When you are finished with this section, pause to breathe.

This next portion gives you the opportunity to notice that certain traits have a positive core but can become negative when the positive core is either overly amplified or underdeveloped. This is an important, if sometimes difficult, concept to understand. Look at the negative list of traits for each person. Imagine the root positive trait at the core of each item. Using Thomas's father as an example, the core of "domineering" might be the positive trait of personal power that became destructive due to an overamplification of power and control. As another example, "disrespectful" would be the underdevelopment or demise of respect for self and others. Work with the negative traits of each person, investigating which are the result of an overly amplified trait and which are the result of underdevelopment. Make notes of your discoveries, taking care to remain nonjudgmental. When you are finished, pause to breathe.

In these next segments, you will have the opportunity to look at your own roles and traits without judgment. Pause to breathe. When you are ready, close your eyes. Imagine your own roles in life as they currently exist. Next, open your eyes and make notes about your various roles in life. For example, you might note: *workaholic, provider, doer, pleaser,* or *victim.* Pause to breathe. Then close your eyes again. Imagine the roles in life that you would like to open up or claim as your own. When you are ready, make notes about your desires. Be as specific as possible. For example, you might note: *lover, volunteer, active parent, tender husband, balanced provider, healthy being,* etc.; leave plenty of space between each role. Pause to breathe. Then, next to each role, write out three very specific actions you can take to enliven your existing roles and create new ones with passion. Let constructive fear be your imaginative, supportive guide. For example, next to *lover,* you might write: *(1) I will make a date night with my partner once a week; (2) I want to become more playful in the bedroom—I will invest in sexy lingerie and massage oil; (3) I will make more time to play attentively with my partner so that our relationship has more playful intimacy.* Pause to breathe.

In this section, constructive fear will guide you into further transformation. It will help you notice the positive traits you would like to maintain or nourish. It will also help you notice traits that need downsizing or greater development. Without judgment, imagine your positive and negative traits. Feel free to close your eyes. Refrain from judging yourself—simply allow yourself to notice those traits that are helpful for you (those that improve your life) and those that work against you (those that create hardships in your life). Pause to breathe. Next, make two lists—one for the positive traits that work for you and one for the negative traits that work against you.

Pause to breathe. Then put a plus sign next to those positive traits that you would like to increase or balance. For example, you might note in your positive column that you are considerate. If you are satisfied with your level of consideration, you would make no mark. If you would like to increase your level of consideration, you will make a plus mark. Next, put a minus sign next to those negative traits that you are truly willing to invest in decreasing or balancing. For example, you might have noted that you are sarcastic. If you want to invest in decreasing this trait, you would place a minus sign next to it. Although you might feel pressure from destructive fear, let the tender, supportive voice of constructive fear act as your guide. Pause to breathe.

Finally, allow yourself to envision ways that you can create shifts in your own life. Remember, destructive fear will not want you to be concrete or detailed; it knows that you are less likely to create change without specificity and consistency. Notice all the traits—positive and negative—that are asking for your attention. Let constructive fear guide you into making a list of three specific, actionable ways that you can create balance and beneficial energy in these areas. For example, if you are sarcastic with your partner or others in your life, you might create change through steps such as these: *(1) I will ask my partner to gently let me know when I am being sarcastic; (2) When my partner tells me I am being sarcastic, I will not become combative or defensive—I will listen; (3) I will take responsibility and rephrase my comment so that my message is direct and kind.* Complete this for each trait on your list. Pause to breathe. Well done.

It can be very difficult to put your goals into action. Change is challenging, even under the best of circumstances. As such, you may naturally stumble now and again. Trust that what you write in your exercises will always be available for ready reference. Your hard work in each exercise will never be lost—you can turn to your exercises at any time for guidance, reinforcement, and support.

Although change is, by nature, often very difficult and demanding, the journey is ultimately rewarding beyond belief; this is the very essence of transformational fear. You can absolutely achieve your goals with patience, dedication, and effort. As a friend once told me, "Even the strongest ballet dancer stumbles and falls. The secret is to get up again and dance." So trust that you have what it takes to live the life you want to live—and dance the way you want to dance.

Believe in yourself and your journey. Trust that the series of exercises you have completed will help you enliven your journey with transformational fear. As you embrace the roles that you choose in life, you will notice that you become more joyful and passionate. As you foster the characteristics that make you feel good about yourself and your actions, your self-esteem will flourish. As you diminish or let go of the traits that hold you back, stifle you, or make you less than proud, you will find that you truly like—and even really love—the person in the mirror. By embracing constructive fear more fully as a man or woman, you become the role model you wish you had—and you become the type of role model the world truly needs. Remember that destructive fear will want to hold you back. It wants to make you less than the tremendously self-aware, joyful individual you are meant to be. Constructive fear wants to free you. It wants you to know that you matter—that your life matters. It wants you to recognize that regardless of how negative or destructive your past might have been, you are creating the awareness and tools to set yourself free. You—amazing you—are transforming your life.

CHAPTER 8

Shifting Relationships Bound by Fear

True Relationships

R elationships have the extraordinary ability to push us to be our best selves. The most priceless relationships have the capacity to press us to evolve in ways that we cannot experience alone. At the heart of such relationships is the divine energy of constructive fear. Far different from the superficial, self-oriented, immobilizing, or manipulative relationships borne of destructive fear, the most inspiring relationships are held and nourished with the wise, loving ways of constructive fear. Not being bound by destructive fear in relationship with the self or others may be one of the greatest goals and rewards in life. With constructive fear as the guide, relationships have the power to lead us into the arms of transformational fear—and, thus, into freedom.

After digesting this chapter, it is possible that you will never see your relationships in the same light again. Those that are healthy may become more deeply valued and cherished. Some that have languished may draw your attention. There may be some that you thoughtfully choose to let fade away. Wherever these pages lead you, trust that the supportive energy of constructive fear is at your side. Destructive fear will want to impede your understanding and acceptance—it will not want you to change. Yet constructive fear will help guide you forward into the open, loving ways of transformational fear.

Relationships come in many forms throughout life, from temporary childhood playmates and lifelong friendships to social acquaintances and necessary business relationships. All of these relationships have a prized place in life, yet there is one type of relationship—what I term a *true relationship*—that is the oxygen of intrapersonal and interpersonal life. Those who have a true relationship with the self often make the most excellent partners in relationship, yet a true relationship with the self can be nurtured and enlivened in the embrace of a true relationship with another. You may find that true relationships thrive when essential qualities, shared values, and shared moral codes are present. And so you might find yourself asking, "What do you mean? What is a true relationship?"

After asking many individuals for their personal thoughts on the qualities that are essential for forming a true relationship,[1] this list outlines the most common responses: honesty, kindness, respect, loyalty, trust, generosity, connection, emotional availability, interdependence, equality, nonjudgment, patience, dependability, emotional intimacy, sexual intimacy, love, independence, partnership, tenderness, compassion, transparency, shared values, common and separate interests, empathy, authenticity, balance, laughter, selflessness, and good communication. Although we might tend to think of these qualities as applying only to romantic relationships, each one of these words (with the exception of sexual intimacy) could also describe the best of friendships, family relationships, and work relationships. Indeed, a genuine friendship built on trust, loving kindness, and mutual respect is at the core of every true relationship.

In looking at the final results of my informal survey regarding necessary qualities for a true relationship, it was not surprising that honesty was the most common response. As one participant noted, "The most important thing in a good relationship is honesty. This means honesty about *all* aspects of your life, including all of your past history—the good and the not-so-good. Being honest creates trust and understanding about who you really are." The quality that took second place was respect. One contributor noted, "Respect is the foundation upon which everything else in a relationship is built. Mutual respect gives you faith that even when you disagree or have problems, your partner will have your best interests at heart and you, theirs." Kindness was the third most common element. As one person shared, "I absolutely believe in being as kind as possible to your partner. Have you ever witnessed someone snap at their partner and then say something nice to a stranger? It's important to be kindest to the one you love the most." The quality of trust was a close fourth. One contributor succinctly offered, "Trust grows when a partner is reliable and true. Trust is so important because it's what makes a relationship feel safe." Interestingly, the word "love" was the least common response, perhaps reflecting the very real truth that qualities such as honesty, respect, kindness, and trust reflect the necessary qualities that allow love to grow.

Each individual has the right to ascertain the qualities and values they find essential for a true relationship. Values—what one finds most significant in life—can refer to essential principles and behaviors as well as more externally oriented needs and desires. For simplicity's sake, we will refer to an individual's vital, core list of the qualities and values as "essential qualities." The essential qualities that are prized by some may not be prized by others. By acknowledging this truth, an objective and honest attitude can be maintained; different people will simply value different things. Destructive fear might want you to have a black-and-white mindset geared toward believing that there is one "right" list of essential qualities. It might also tempt you into believing that it's not important to know or understand one's essential qualities. Constructive fear would say, "A few key values such as integrity, honesty, respect, and kindness are essential for any true relationship. Beyond such basics, let your wise self be your guide. A vital element of self-awareness is the nonjudgmental knowing and cherishing of what is important to you. In this way, you can understand and honor what you find essential. Without self-awareness, you are constricted and bound by the beliefs you unconsciously adopted throughout life—going whatever way you might be led. Through self-reflection, you gain awareness of your own personal values and needs." Armed with the wisdom of self-awareness, you can then take actions that lead you closer to your values. In this way, you evolve consciously, moving ever forward with the power of transformational fear.

The first step, then, is to generate awareness of one's unique conception of essential qualities. As an individual becomes more self-aware, a personal "list" of essential qualities can be used both to form and to guide relationships. A firm understanding of one's essential qualities allows for the open and honest communication of these essential needs to others. The more important the relationship is, the more critical it is to have a meeting of the minds and spirits on the necessary qualities for that relationship; when a relationship is more peripheral or less significant, there is often greater leeway. When it comes to core, true relationships, these precious connections tend to thrive when both individuals value and offer the same essential qualities. When one person lacks a quality that the other person finds absolutely essential, the relationship often suffers. When many key qualities are missing, disaster often results. For example, if a certain woman prizes honesty, integrity, kindness, thoughtfulness, and communication above all other qualities, she will do best with a partner who values and offers these qualities. However, if this woman's partner is dishonest, disrespectful, unkind, self-oriented, or uncommunicative, she will suffer deeply in the relationship. Her partner will also suffer—even if only unconsciously—by not honoring and offering the better parts of the self. Of course, if both partners in a relationship lack certain fundamental essential qualities, such a relationship would also fail to thrive. As we will explore, many qualities are beneficial for creating and sustaining true relationships; these qualities are often dependent on the unique needs and desires of each partner. Yet there are certain non-negotiable qualities that no true relationship can do without: integrity, honesty, respect, and kindness. Although a relationship without these qualities may appear functional and may, indeed, be convenient for one or both parties, there is no capacity for a true relationship if the fundamental qualities are absent.

The word *relationship* carries many connotations—it means different things to different people. Therefore, it is often helpful to look at the roots of a word to regain a true and deeper sense of the original meaning. The "ship" portion of the word *relationship* indicates a state or condition, whereas "relate" stems from the Latin *re*, which means "back or again," coupled with *lātus*, which means "borne, carried, or endured."[2] As such, it may be that a relationship is a state where those involved return to each other to bear, carry, and endure. This interpretation resonates with me deeply, for society uses the word "relationship" so loosely that it can become almost meaningless. Like the word "friend," the word "relationship" has come to include those to whom we feel little or no trusting connection. Yet people are somehow surprised and left wondering what is "wrong" when a sense of trust or bonded intimacy is missing. They find themselves confused, hurt, and angry when disrespected and even betrayed.

What is missing—what has gone awry—is that many "relationships" do not involve bearing, carrying, and enduring the journey of life. Far too many relationships do well in good times and when immediate needs for companionship, sex, fun, or money are being met, but when it comes to weathering life's truths, challenges, and deepening intimacy, the relationship has little or no strength. These generally superficial associations, which are often mere infatuations or connections of convenience, lack the essential elements that allow for bonded, lasting love. Many such connections are consciously or unconsciously built on the theme of "I'll use you just as much as you use me." Sadly, such situations are the breeding grounds of destructive fear—they perpetuate negative behaviors and throw mud on the concept of loving connection and growth. Indeed, a "relationship" formed or continued on a lack of integrity—disrespect, dishonesty, manipulation, and the like—is not a true relationship. "Convenienceships" is the term I have coined for such connections.

To bear, carry, and endure the journey of life, those involved must always bring integrity to the table; integrity is nonnegotiable in a true relationship. Additionally, such a relationship offers transparency and open communication. It supports the acknowledgment and honoring of each other's strengths and weakness. True relationship does not expect perfection; it offers compassionate support. It does expect—it absolutely requires—integrity, respect, kindness, and honesty. True relationship also asks for the fostering of genuineness, independence, interdependence, sharing, and equality.

Perhaps these qualities sound too foreboding or impossible to find in others or even achieve in oneself, yet they are absolutely necessary for your evolution in relationship with yourself and with others. When these factors are not present, the "relationship" lacks the necessary foundation on which to build an intimate, trusting connection that can weather both life's storms and sunshiny days—it lacks what is required to earn the appellation of true relationship. Again, true relationship does not demand perfection; it asks that the essential qualities—those that the partners in the relationship find key—be honored, nurtured, and refined with awareness. When the necessary qualities of a true relationship are present and ever evolving, loving intimacy is able to blossom and grow.

As a society, we are increasingly programmed to focus on the super-ficial qualities of people and life. It is easy to be drawn in by good looks, pretty things, and monetary wealth. However, these external qualities say nothing about the person underneath. A handsome or pretty face means nothing if the person underneath is dishonest, selfish, disrespectful, or unkind. This section asks that you turn your attention largely to *internal* essential qualities—the lasting characteristics that make a person truly attractive. If you desire a true relationship, take this element to heart. Take care not to get distracted by mere words, external appearances, and mate-rial things. When in doubt, observe an individual's actions over time; look at what a person does. Ask yourself this question: *Is this person's overall behavior attractive to me—or is it not?*

Your Journey into Essential Qualities and True Relationship

These next exercises may be challenging, for they require substan-tial introspection, self-honesty, and nonjudgment. Allow yourself to proceed with a patient, gentle attitude. Remember that it is normal to feel uncomfortable at times in the course of self-reflection, yet as with any self-exploration, objective honesty is essential. When you are open to gentle reflection on your old patterns and ways of being, the strong arm of destructive fear has no choice but to slowly release its grip. Indeed, our most amazing improvements come as a result of noticing and attending to the areas where destructive fear has silently grown and festered. Now is your opportunity to shine conscious awareness and healing light into this area of your life. Listen for the friendly, nonjudgmental voice of constructive fear; let this voice be your guide and ally as you move into another realm of transformation.

As with every exercise, make certain that you are in a safe and relaxed environment and that you feel psychologically ready to proceed. With your notebook and pen by your side, take a deep breath. If you feel destructive fear stepping in at any time, simply notice that it is present. When you are ready to proceed without judgment, allow yourself to envision the idea of a true relationship.

Close your eyes if it is helpful. Imagine every quality that is important to you in a true relationship. When you are finished, open your
eyes. Make a list of the qualities you noticed; your list can be as
exhaustive as you desire. When you have finished your list, pause
to breathe.

In this next segment, place an E (to signify "essential") next to
every item that is essential to you; these are the traits that you find
absolutely nonnegotiable in your true relationships. For example,
a short list might read: *integrous, honest, loyal, generous, playful,
loving, tolerant, fun-loving, creative, respectful, kind,* and *tender.*
You may find yourself marking every quality on the list with an
E. You may, however, find that you are led to mark relatively few
items with an E. Allow the process to unfold without judgment.
When you have finished, pause to breathe. The items marked with
an E constitute your list of essential qualities. Make notes of any
thoughts that come to mind. Breathe.

In this next phase, take a fresh look at your complete list of
qualities—your personal outline of the qualities you find important
for a true relationship. Pause to breathe. Then place an O (signify-
ing personal ownership) next to every quality that is something you
embrace and honor in your own life. Remember, you don't have to
be perfect in embodying these qualities—what is vital is that you
honor your essential qualities and strive to hone them in your life.
Destructive fear might step in with criticism or judgment; simply
notice if it does. Allow constructive fear to guide you into honestly
evaluating the characteristics that you actively strive to treasure
and embody. When you have finished, pause to breathe.

Next, take objective notice of the items that have both an E and
an O. Take note of those items that only have an O and no E or
vice versa. For example, for an individual who values and embod-
ies honesty as an essential trait, an E and an O would both appear.
Yet even an exceedingly honest person may not demand honesty
in relationships; in such a case, only an O would appear next to the
word *honest*. On the other hand, an individual may demand honesty from others yet may not be honest in relationships with others
and with the self. In this instance, only an E would appear next to

the word *honest*. Once you have reviewed your E and O markings, pause to breathe. Make notes of any thoughts that come to mind. Breathe again.

In this next step, simply make a separate list of your essential qualities. Every item marked with an E will become part of this list. In the course of completing the above exercises, you may notice that you want to add or delete items from this list. Feel free to make any changes you find important. Ultimately, you will have a list—short or long—of your essential qualities. This list has the potential to be a most vital guide and ally in your life.

Finally, prepare to ask yourself five important questions with clarity and honesty. If destructive fear steps in with judgment or criticism, simply notice its presence. If discomfort, irritation, or other feelings arise, allow yourself to notice the feelings. Allow yourself to feel the kind, gentle wisdom of constructive fear. Allow yourself to remember that constructive fear wants to help you obtain wellness, fulfillment, peace, and joy. Pause to breathe. Now, ask yourself these five questions:

1. Am I searching for qualities in another person that I do not have within myself?
2. If so, am I willing to do the work necessary to engender these qualities in myself?
3. Am I accepting a relationship with someone who does not have the qualities I find essential?
4. If so, am I willing to talk to this person about my needs with honesty and dignity?
5. If the other person is unwilling or unable to honor my essential needs, am I willing to walk away?

Write out your responses to each question. You need to do nothing but allow yourself to process your responses at your own pace. Pause to breathe. You are doing excellent work. Well done.

As you continue your journey into relationships, destructive fear may consistently feed you with negative, judgmental thoughts. Destructive fear may press you to become impatient, anxious, angry, or irritated. It wants you to accept unfulfilling, paralyzing, or harmful relationships simply because it thrives on stagnation. Constructive fear, on the other hand, knows the transformative power of relationships. It wants you to know that conscious self-reflection will let your relationships become the greatest teachers in your life. Constructive fear wants to tell you, "Though relationships often bring significant challenges, they also offer the fuel for the greatest personal growth." It is within relationships that we can be pressed ever forward to become our better selves, but it is within true relationships that *both* parties support each other in a conscious, purposeful development of the self and the relationship. Destructive fear knows this, fears this, and wants to put up as many roadblocks as possible. Destructive fear wants you to accept relationships that are not beneficial for you. It does not want you to optimize yourself. For this reason, destructive fear will press you to avoid introspection. It might chime in with thoughts of doubt, criticism, embarrassment, or shame. You might feel destructive fear's critical voice welling up to create anxiety. You might feel irritated or confused, worried that you have too few true relationships in your life. You might even worry that you do not have any true relationships in your life. Notice, too, if destructive fear wants to force you into believing that any *close* relationship is a *true* relationship. If such thoughts arise, simply notice them without judgment. Let constructive fear come in to tell you, "True relationships are rare and take time, focus, and conscious awareness to create and nurture. This is your opportunity to come to terms with the actual nature of the relationships in your life. Destructive fear will want to deceive you. It may have you believing that people who lack or refuse to embody the qualities you find essential—such as respect, honesty, and loving kindness—are true friends and that you share true relationships with them. It may have you ignoring a person's disrespectful or dishonest actions to keep you stuck in an unhealthy relationship. Do not worry. Your understanding and awareness will increase, allowing you to create true relationships in your life."

The True and Untrue Relationships in Your Life

Proceed with this exercise when you feel emotionally ready. Make certain that you are in a safe and relaxed environment with your notebook and pen by your side. Pause to take a deep breath. If you feel destructive fear stepping in at any time, simply notice without judgment that it is present. First, allow yourself to envision your conceptualization of a true relationship. Close your eyes, imagining the qualities and capacities that are most vital to you. Then, imagine those relationships in your life that feel like true relationships to you. When you are finished, open your eyes. Make a list of those in your life with whom you have a true relationship. Notice if destructive fear wants to chide you if your list is short or even empty. Instead, listen as constructive fear says, "It is better to have a short or empty list rather than one filled with names of people who do not possess the qualities you find absolutely necessary, such as loving kindness, honesty, and respect." When you have finished, pause to breathe.

Next, pause again to consider and honor the qualities and capacities that each person on your list possesses. Breathe. Then, next to each person's name, write out the qualities you value in that individual—those that allow you to have a bonded, true relationship. Pause to breathe. If your list was empty or shorter than you might find desirable, trust that you are gaining the awareness and skills to create true relationships in your life. In completing these exercises with honest self-awareness, you have shown tremendous courage and strength. Trust that you are moving ever closer to creating a balanced, joy-filled life. You are making excellent progress.

Clarity and Awareness with Self and Others

Much of this next section will focus on romantic relationships such as marriage and dating, yet you may find that many aspects are applicable to other relationships in your life. As noted above, the tenets of a true relationship are intertwined with the essential elements of a true and bonded friendship. With your idea of a true relationship now in your head and heart, you may begin to ask more of yourself and others in regard to relationships. You may become increasingly aware of your essential needs in your relationships with yourself and others. You may be gaining clarity on the importance of knowing what is vital to you and then being able to honestly and kindly articulate those needs. Indeed, you may begin to notice that you have a lower threshold for disrespectful behaviors in general. You may notice that you have a higher benchmark for qualities such as honesty, transparency, and kindness. This is constructive fear at work; this is the light of constructive fear guiding you into the positive, freeing embrace of transformational fear.

The Cycle of Unaware Ava: A Case Study

When Ava made her first appointment with me, she noted that her top concern was "repeating the same unhealthy patterns in relationships." Her second priority was "to learn to like" herself. Her third concern was "to learn to be vulnerable." Ava, an attractive woman in her early forties, is educated, hardworking, and honest—and terrified of a romantic, intimate relationship. Yet, as Ava told me during a later appointment, "I love being in love. I absolutely adore being in relationships. I crave the companionship, sex, and general fun. But my relationships never last. I get drawn in by something or other—usually good looks, money, or great sex. But sooner or later, the 'nice guy' disappears and the real jerk comes out. Yet I get hooked. I stay in the relationship too long, even though I know I shouldn't. Sometimes I get back with the guy over and over again, especially if there's no one better on the horizon. I forget all of the negative issues and remember only the fun times—until I'm back in the relationship again and remember why it went bad. I just don't get why I do what I do; it's so frustrating and unfulfilling. I end up being so mad at myself and disappointed. If you knew me in the real world, you'd see that I'm self-sufficient. I actually don't really 'need' a man. I have a great career and have my own home. I have a good family, a dog, and my girlfriends. But I always end up wanting a man in my life. Now that I'm over forty, I feel like I've wasted so much time and energy on guys and relationships that were not good for me. In hindsight, I can see that I put up with a lot of crap—dishonesty, disrespect, and loads of manipulative behavior—just to have male companionship. It's my pattern; I'm a magnet for the wrong kind of guy. It's almost as if I date the same man in a different body over and over again. I feel terrible saying this, but most of the men I've dated had looks and money but weren't good people. I don't know what these choices say about me—I'm afraid to find out. I don't know why I chose to be with men like that. I want to figure out what's been going on with me, because I don't want to repeat this cycle for the rest of my life."

Ava's words echo the stories I have heard from hundreds of men and women of all ages. In the very normal quest for companionship and attention, many people enter into convenienceships seeking to have their needs met. Whether a person's needs are monetary, sexual, companionship-oriented, or simply to "have fun," the voicing of clear and honest expectations is essential. When those in a convenienceship have conflicting or differing expectations, significant disappointment, hurt, and anger can result. Misunderstandings can be avoided by openly and honestly sharing, acknowledging, and discussing each other's desires, needs, and goals in a relationship. Sadly, many people avoid this critical step out of ignorance, fear, selfishness, or indifference.

Although it takes time and awareness to "slow down" to ascertain and evaluate one's needs, this is a critical first step—one that is necessary to face before seeking a relationship. An individual must first know their own needs and expectations to be able to communicate them effectively to others. The second critical element is the voicing of one's needs with honesty and respect. Although this step can be uncomfortable, it is absolutely necessary. Many people skip this step in the hope that things will magically "turn out well." Others avoid this step because they are not invested in the relationship or out of fear of being rejected. For some, a combination of these factors is at play. Many people simply don't bother to sit down with the other person from the onset of the relationship—and at various points throughout—to check in with each other on their goals and desires for the relationship. As a result of omitting necessary communication, the relationship continues to limp along until someone or something gives in or gives up.

In Ava's case, she simply didn't have the awareness to slow down and give attention to her relationships. As she came to discover, she didn't know how to engage in a healthy relationship; she dove in, hoping that things would work out. Ava came to see that her habit of diving thoughtlessly into dating—into convenienceships—created cumulative harm. Ava had selected her companions based on physical and material characteristics, not at all considering the most important qualities—those of the person's values and moral code. Ava didn't consider whether or not the man before her was well-matched to the qualities that she found most important in life. In fact, Ava had never assessed her "essential needs." Although Ava was exceedingly adept at evaluating people, situations, goals, and needs in the business realm, she never paused to apply these same skills in her personal life. Instead, she took the men that life brought her without scrutinizing their inner qualities and capacities. Ava once noted, "I'm not even sure how I ended up with some of the men I was with—it just happened. I didn't actually choose them, it just evolved. Before I knew it, someone was either in my bed or I was in theirs. I didn't bother slowing down to get to know someone—to tell them my life story or to hear theirs. It just didn't matter to me then. But I can tell you that it is going to matter to me from here on out."

As is very common, Ava hadn't paused to evaluate what she wanted and needed during the various phases of her life. In her younger years, she may have wanted to date various men, have a variety of experiences, and not settle down. Later, she might have decided that she wanted a life partner and then paused to use her experiences to understand her essential wants, needs, and goals. Although Ava would have readily taken these steps for a business deal, she didn't know that these steps were even *more* vital for the success of her personal life. By not slowing down to clearly evaluate what she wanted without judgment, she moved thoughtlessly and unconsciously from one convenienceship to the next.

If Ava's clear goal was to have superficial, short-term connections, she may have felt more in tune with herself and others by acknowledging this goal and honestly sharing it with others to ensure that they wanted the same. Without judgment of herself or others, Ava may have felt empowered by stating her needs openly and directly. Self-honesty on Ava's part would allow her to be open and clear with others about her true intentions. Such an attitude would allow Ava and her potential partners the ability to ascertain if their goals were similar. As a result of such honesty and clarity, a conscious choice could be made about whether or not to proceed with a superficial, temporary connection. Here, again, honesty is absolutely key.

In the same way, if Ava discovered that a long-term relationship was her true goal, she would share this goal with others openly and honestly. She could then choose to move toward those who shared similar values and goals and away from those who did not. Ava would then use her conscious awareness to further evaluate potential mates. Through this careful process, she would deepen relationships with those who exhibited the qualities she found essential for a true relationship. Although Ava could not be guaranteed that the "right" partner was the one at her side, her heightened level of self-awareness would help her ascertain if the connection might evolve into a romantic, *true* relationship. Additionally, by being respectful to herself and others, Ava would be increasing her chances of forming lasting friendships—even if a long-term romantic partnership was not meant to be.

Although Ava might eliminate certain connections by following such a thoughtful, direct procedure, she would be left with potential partners who were like-minded and more suitable. Ava's pool of potential partners might be smaller than someone who "took whatever came," but her pool would likely be of higher quality—a quality that was better aligned with her needs and goals. In the most profound way, such a process actually increases self-esteem. By knowing one's value and refusing to "go out with just anyone," one's sense of self-respect increases. In being willing to be alone—enjoying one's own company rather than "any" company—the individual learns to value the self even more. When individuals become self-aware and selective about their relationships, they inherently tell themselves and the others, *I value and prefer the company of myself rather than the company of those who do not improve me—or I them. When honest, kind, respectful company is unavailable, I prefer being by myself.* Destructive fear may tell you that this is judgmental. Constructive fear would tell you, "There is no judgment in knowing what feels best to you. Your time on Earth is limited. When you choose your company, choose wisely and well. When possible, choose to spend time with those who give you the support, fuel, and space to be your better self. Whenever possible, give this same gift to those you choose to have by your side. This is the essence of true relationship."

Although direct, honest communication with the self and others is often unfamiliar and anxiety-inducing, it does become easier and more familiar with practice. Additionally, your sense of self-respect will increase once you become used to being straightforward and clear. You will learn to take pride in knowing your personal values, preferences, and goals. With practice, you will learn to voice your needs and intentions with clarity, kindness, and honesty. You might discover that others don't share your values and goals, yet you will feel heartened in knowing the disparity sooner rather than later. Although you cannot control another person's level of honesty and respect, you can control your own honesty and clarity from the onset. If the other individual is honest and respectful, your personal honesty and clarity will be valued. In such cases, both individuals have the ability to make informed decisions as to what does and does not suit them. This is a critical element of any fledgling healthy relationship.

In Ava's case, her state of unknowing led to her chronic sense of feeling unfulfilled. Without internal, wise direction, Ava unconsciously sought out the next guy who might be "the one"; this caused harm to Ava and others in the process. Ava once commented, "I now see that not one of the relationships made me a better person. I never even thought about that before—the idea that a relationship could make me or my partner better. I didn't think that way; I was only looking to have my needs met. Whether I was using the guy or he was using me, I can see that I actually devalued myself in some way in the course of each relationship." Indeed, a few of Ava's former partners cheated on her and, as she admitted, she cheated on some of them. She had great adventures with several yet found the fun times overshadowed by emotionally abusive behavior. One man who appeared to have it all borrowed some money on a vacation and never repaid the sum. And, as Ava relayed, "The worst one—the only one I might have actually liked—proved to be married in the end. I actually found his wife's business card as the marker in a book he was reading. We were on a trip in Mexico—it didn't end well." Ava simply hadn't pause to screen her potential companions for the vital qualities of integrity, kindness, respect, and honesty. Ava knew what her companion's general resume contained, but she had no idea what sort of person was waiting inside. As Ava noted, "In the end, I have to admit that I simply didn't like being alone; I didn't know how to be alone. When there was a void in my life—when I wanted to take a vacation or have someone to share empty nights with—that was when I wanted a man in my life. I guess that attitude left me with whoever was available at the time. On some level, I had the attitude that 'something was better than nothing'—yet look where that got me. Now I see that I would have been better off investing that time and energy in myself, because here I am, still needing to learn how to be with myself—how to actually enjoy who I am without distractions." With her attention on her career, goals, and personal desires, Ava simply had not yet discovered the importance of conscious awareness—the fundamental need to look inside both herself and any potential partner. By focusing on a man's superficial qualities, Ava had unconsciously let destructive fear control her world of relationships. Although an intelligent woman, Ava had been ignorant regarding how each relationship choice affected her self-esteem, her life, and the very treasure of her soul. Ava had become accustomed to the quietly destructive attitudes and behaviors that had controlled and limited her internal and external life.

Destructive fear thrives in relationships that lack clear intention and conscious awareness. Many kind, well-intentioned individuals suffer after blindly entering a relationship that ultimately feels superficial, stuck, or unfulfilling. Some believe that "being smart" offers a protective factor, but it doesn't. Regardless of an individual's overall level of intelligence or good-heartedness, any person can become the target of deceivers, manipulators, bullies, and the like. On the other hand, when both individuals are manipulative and self-absorbed, the relationship can become a chess game of maneuvering—each person often unaware that the other is doing exactly the same.

Regardless of the underlying issues, many unhealthy relationships continue long after their expiration date. Many factors contribute to this pattern, including ignorance, sheer indifference, embarrassment, a "love of the game," or a simple willingness to settle for *any* companion rather than being alone. Some of these associations evolve into long-term relationships or even result in marriage. Yet no matter the form such relationships take, the underlying theme is often the same: the partners in the relationship did not explore or confirm the existence of essential qualities, shared values, and shared moral codes. As a result, when the initial motivating factors no longer exist or are insufficient "glue," the relationship often falters.

As Ava and many like her eventually learn, physical attraction and sexual desire can be heady relationship starters, but they are not sufficient to build a true relationship. In the same way, financial needs motivate many to enter convenienceships. Whether it is a desire to have a home, save on rent, enjoy wonderful dinners, go on lush vacations, or obtain health care, many people have sought convenienceships to obtain material benefits. For some, the financial benefits reaped are enough to hold the convenienceship together. Without essential qualities such as kindness, compassion, honesty, communication, loyalty, and devotion, such relationships are often a matter of sheer expedience. The desire for companionship draws many

lonely souls together, yet without the connective power of true relationship, such people often find themselves very lonely within the relationship.
Although a person may not be physically alone, the lack of vital elements
such as emotional connection can leave a person feeling extremely lonely
due to the inability to connect with the partner. Many relationships simply do not have the foundation necessary to support true connection and
intimacy.

Ava never realized that true relationships require intense focus and
introspection. Like many men and women, Ava unconsciously subscribed
to the false notion that "a relationship will just work out if it is meant to
be." True relationships are one of the most extraordinarily wondrous—
yet often the most challenging—adventures in life. Ava noted, "I guess I
thought that good relationships 'just happened.' I didn't see my parents
work on their relationship. I didn't know that a good relationship took
work." I gave Ava two small bits of homework. The first was to make a
list of her business successes that "just happened." The second was to
have an open discussion with her parents to determine how much energy
and effort was required for their marriage. Ava smiled in response to the
homework. "Fine," she noted, "I'll bring you a blank piece of paper for the
first assignment. Every really successful business deal I've been involved
with has taken focus, planning, and work. I get your point. I need to apply
this same focus—and more—to the idea of a true relationship. I wanted it
to be easy, but I can see that the gain will be in line with my investment,
just as it is with business." As to the second element of her homework, Ava
was excited to talk with her parents. "I'd never thought of asking them, but
I will. They are both so forthcoming; it will be a terrific discussion."

In a later session, Ava shared the highlights of her discussions with her
parents; her initial inquiry was so helpful to her that she enjoyed many
additional discussions about relationships and marriage with her parents.
Ava laughed, "They were truly excited to share their history with me. I am
surprised it never came up before. As an only child, I guess I was always
focused on myself. Yet my parents have so many stories to share. I always
thought their lives were easy—they made it look easy. I didn't realize that
they had their share of struggles on many issues, from finances to my
mother not being able to conceive a second child. They shared with me
how they nearly divorced a few times early on in their marriage, and that
if it weren't for my mother's Catholic upbringing and their joint commitment to making the marriage work come what may, they might not have

stayed together. It's a frightening thought, actually. But if you were to see them together, you'd know why I thought that relationships didn't take work. Apparently, they used the rough challenges they faced early on to become closer—to become better people and a better team. I am so glad that I discovered this; it makes me feel hopeful."

It was wonderful to witness the evolution of Ava's personal journey. As she worked diligently to determine her essential qualities, needs, and goals, she became more self-assured. Indeed, as Ava came to honor and value her own wants and needs with courage and awareness, her increased sense of personal value translated into a tangible, gracious luminosity. Ava began to notice that her inner strength gave her the ability to speak honestly and assertively. Where she previously resorted to being either coolly passive or fiercely aggressive, she found the power of speaking her truth with gentle firmness.

Over time, Ava and I discussed the progress she was making on her three original concerns—the repetition of unhealthy relationship patterns, her goal of learning to like herself, and the desire to be more vulnerable. Reflecting on her former attitudes and dating habits, Ava once noted, "I shake my head when I think about my old patterns. I used to secretly believe that I was more valuable or worthy when I had men chasing me— as if my value was dependent on how many men found me desirable. I never realized that not being choosey made me feel worse about myself and the men I was with. In fact, I can see that I often didn't say 'no' to a man because I was afraid that someone else wouldn't be in line. I also see that I said 'yes' to many situations lacking respect and kindness because I didn't value myself enough to have standards. On some level, I had a mantra going that said, 'You're not good enough to have high expectations. You should just settle for money, good-enough looks, and sex—that's better than nothing.' I guess I didn't believe I could have what I really wanted. In fact, I didn't know *what* I wanted, so I took what came my way. My old patterns aren't in sync with what I want for my life. Things are changing—I'm learning to look at what really matters to me."

Ava also came to acknowledge that low self-esteem was at the heart of many of her patterns. During her journey, Ava crafted a personal moral code that felt right to her; this code became a constant guide. She offered, "I thought I had great self-esteem because I had accomplished so much in life. I didn't make the connection that I could appear confident yet not have a true sense of self-worth. I feel so much better now that I have clear standards—now that I know what is important to me." Ava came to know, for possibly the first time in her life, the power of true internal confidence and self-esteem. As she began respecting and valuing herself, she turned away from relationships that didn't have the potential to offer what she desired and deserved.

Making progress in the arena of vulnerability wasn't easy for Ava. As she noted, "I know that I want a life companion, but the road to get there is scary for me. I guess I'd much rather be alone than settle for anyone who is less than what I really want. Trust and vulnerability aren't easy for me." Indeed, Ava had a long journey in front of her, for the idea of a true relationship was both compelling and frightening. Yet she persevered, crafting a meaningful list of essential qualities to guide her. As Ava worked on these vital qualities in her own life, she increased her capacity to recognize them in others. She came to find that the more she trusted herself, the more she felt safe slowly opening up to trustworthy people. Ava also discovered that by holding true to her essential qualities, she felt more capable of creating relationships with like-minded individuals—those who would respect and cherish her vulnerability and all that she had to offer. Over time, Ava learned that it was safe to be vulnerable with trustworthy people—the type of souls who valued true relationship.

Ava found that the grip of destructive fear had held her back in the realm of personal relationships; it had kept her enmeshed in patterns that made her feel stuck, alone, and often unvalued. In the course of her journey, Ava learned to listen for the gentle, wise voice of constructive fear. She took the time to home in on her essential qualities, strengthening and honing those vital aspects of her own being. Ava learned to turn this same careful awareness to the relationships in her life, valuing herself enough to connect with those who were willing to work at knowing themselves better. Ava didn't stop at tuning into the voice of constructive fear—she put her newfound wisdom into action, embracing the full power of transformational fear.

How Wishes and Worms Hinder True Relationship

A wish can be a beautiful thing. When a wish drives us to achieve a goal, whether for personal growth, success in life, or necessary material items, wonders can result. However, when a wish creates cloudy vision and

interferes with wise objectivity, the relationship with the self—and therefore with others—can suffer tremendously. As an optimist and believer in
the power of rose-colored glasses, I have also learned to value the objective,
firm counterpoint of wise, constructive fear. Indeed, those who are naïvely
unaware can become easy victims of manipulators or bullies. Of course, at
the other end of the spectrum, those who are jaded and suspicious allow
the worm of cynicism to obstruct any chance of intimacy. Destructive
fear is at work at both poles; neither the unmindful wisher nor the worm-
riddled cynic allows for the freedom of objectivity and resulting growth.
When in an unhealthy relationship, it is easy to get stuck in a wishful
place, ever praying and hoping that the relationship and the other person
will somehow change. In this way, what we wish to see—what we hope
to see—halts the voice of constructive fear. This false hope is an aspect
of destructive fear, preventing self-honesty and conscious awareness. Yet
constructive fear wants to be your ally in learning to see and form true
relationships. Although constructive fear does not pretend that it is easy
to create true relationships, it does say, "If you learn to observe what is
actually present in yourself and others, you will see that actions—not mere
words—speak the truth. When you objectively observe a person's actions,
you will see if they are congruent with what the individual claims to value.
You can see if the relationship is what you deserve, desire, and want to
accept. In this way, you will learn to see things as they are, not as you might
wish them to be."

By looking at all of the relationships in your life in this way, you will see
the truth of the relationship. Without judging any relationship as "good"
or "bad," you will simply ask yourself this question: Does this relationship
truly honor and support the qualities that I value most in life? Your honest
answer will help you know if you are stuck in a world of wishes or worms.
Once you know the honest truth in your heart, you can embrace the active
power of transformational fear to create the changes that will bring you
closer to relationships that value and put into action qualities such as honesty, respect, and kindness. In this way, you will create the changes that
will transform you and your life.

Destructive fear likes to hamper true relationship, and it employs a
wide variety of harmful ruses to reach this goal. Whereas constructive fear
thrives on honesty, respect, and transparency, destructive fear loves the
power of deception. Indeed, many relationships are harmed by deception
and manipulation. Although a genuine lack of awareness may sometimes

be at play, a truly dishonest, manipulative person will continue the unhealthy patterns even when fully aware of the destructive behavior. This type of person, who is often disguised with a mask of charisma, is normally concerned with one thing: how to have his or her needs met. The needs or desires of the other person simply don't matter. Such a person often continues through life in a self-absorbed way, taking no responsibility for the hurt and damage created. Due to the superficial qualities that can disguise the manipulative core, this type of person can leave the innocent party questioning what has gone awry. Indeed, as one client noted, "He was so good at his games that he had me believing that I was the crazy one. He'd tell me I was too sensitive, too needy, or irrational—all to cover his tracks. He'd make promises he wouldn't keep. He was emotionally abusive, calling me names and saying horrible things I can't bear to repeat. He had this way of turning things around so that I felt bad about myself—as if I was somehow wrong to want kindness and respect."

Indeed, dishonesty can arise in many forms in a relationship, whether through misleading statements, empty promises, false impressions, overt lies, omission of key details, or other forms of manipulation and deceitfulness. This is destructive fear at work, for it thrives in the realm of lies, manipulation, and confusion. Once in the throes of a relationship, it can be difficult to objectively see the many ways dishonesty and manipulation manifest. A practiced manipulator can leave an individual questioning his or her own reality. Yet constructive fear is a wise, objective ally. It will help you determine whether a negative behavior is due to a lack of awareness or a serious character defect that will likely not change. Constructive fear would offer this simple tip: "An honest, respectful individual who is capable of introspection will take responsibility for an error and then take concerted action to avoid repeating the hurtful or negative behavior. A dishonest, manipulative person will avoid personal responsibility, using all manner of excuses and deflections to avoid accountability. Such a person will not make an effort to change but will instead put effort into rationalizing and continuing the old behaviors. Beware this type of deceptive, manipulative person, for destructive fear has this individual in a strong, devilish hold."

Compassion is necessary during this process, for developing a solid relationship with truth and honesty can be a journey of its own. Many individuals are raised to fear being honest with themselves and with others. Some even find it easier to live within a web of half-truths, white lies, and secrets. Others make a habit of overt deception, with dishonesty as their normal code of conduct. To one degree or another, all of these patterns reflect the dark power of destructive fear at work. Yet even the unhealthiest patterns may be shifted with patience and concerted perseverance. A new, healthy normal can come to life through self-awareness. By listening to the wise voice of constructive fear, the truth becomes familiar and grounding. Although truth and honesty may, at first, feel odd and even scary, they can ultimately come to feel so very right. Indeed, by putting truth and honesty into action, transformational fear steps in with substantial power. Truth and honesty with yourself and others can truly change your life.

Brandon's Ignored Instinct: A Case Study

Brandon first came to see me after his fairly new marriage began to falter. It took several sessions for his story to come out, for he was terribly confused and embarrassed about his situation. Although he thought he had done his due diligence in selecting his wife—indeed, she appeared to have the qualities he desired—he discovered, too late, that she was not the woman she had pretended to be. This was not due to carelessness on Brandon's part. As he noted, "I'm a strong businessman. I actually had a checklist, and Kit fit the bill. We share common interests, have similar family and educational backgrounds, and hold strong religious beliefs. Our life goals are the same—we wanted one child and substantial material success. I thought I had it covered, because we even have the same work ethic. Up until a month ago, we worked at the same firm in similar roles. I didn't know anything was off—it seemed like a perfect match on paper. The only area that could have been better was the passion and sex department, but I figured that would improve with time. Now, I realize that I ignored a critical piece—she was not interested in me romantically. I guess I just didn't want to see what was right in front of me. We weren't married for more than a few months before she moved to a separate bedroom. She's now taken a leave from work to regroup. I don't know what her next step will be. Two weeks ago, she informed me she's a lesbian and has a long-term girlfriend. She wants to stay married—she said it works for her—but she's not in love with me. I can't believe it. We had such incredible potential."

Understandably, Brandon was disappointed, confused, angry, and hurt. His pain was palpable. Brandon stared at the wall and continued, "I never thought someone could make a fool out of me. I am smart—I have an MBA, for God's sake. I should have seen this. Now, looking back, I can put the pieces together. There were times she'd tuck her cell phone away when I came in. There were other times that she'd be on the computer, and when I came into the room, she'd close the screen. When I asked her about it, she'd tell me that it was a confidential work product and that I was being suspicious. I guess I bought her story, even though I knew in my gut that something was wrong. I particularly remember one instance that I came home early from a business trip. It looked like someone had been over— the bed was different, she smelled different, and there was something off. I asked her about it, and she told me I was being paranoid. Again, I overrode my instinct and just figured I had to accept that it was my issue—even though I'm not a distrusting kind of guy. She's a smart businesswoman, and I didn't see that she was manipulating me. Because we generally got on really well as a team—we work well together in so many ways—I just believed whatever she said and continued on. I could kick myself for not putting the pieces together. You know, it was on our wedding night that I really should have known. We had a fabulous destination wedding in Mexico—it was perfect. On our wedding night, Kit said she felt really ill and needed to go for a walk. We had just gotten into bed. I got up with her and began to dress. She told me she preferred to go alone. I was fine with that and decided to sit up and wait for her. An hour or so passed, and she didn't come back. I put on my clothes and went out for a walk—maybe I knew something was up. By chance, I caught her coming out of one of the bungalows, the one where her maid of honor was staying. I called out to her, and she met me on the path. When I asked her what she was doing with Jen—her maid of honor—she said she was getting stomach medicine. Once we were back to our room, she said she still didn't feel well and wanted to go to sleep. Needless to say, we didn't have wedding night sex. That was the beginning of the end of our sex life. Now that I put the pieces together, I think—but I don't have proof—that Jen is her girlfriend. I think she played me all along. I wouldn't have cared if she was a lesbian—I don't have any judgment about that. We might have been good friends, but I surely wouldn't have married her." Brandon paused and asked one key question. "Or, since the truth was really right in front of me, do you think

I would have married her anyway? Was I just too set on how perfectly we matched up on paper?"

I smiled and said, "It is difficult to see things objectively when we want something very much. When we become focused on the end result—our personal wishes—we often see things as we want them to be rather than as they are; this is human nature. You experienced how difficult it is to remain completely objective in your personal realm. Although you are able to be objective and detached in business, this skill doesn't translate perfectly into personal relationships. Actually, it wouldn't be great if it did, for then your personal relationships would feel businesslike—emotionless, detached, and disconnected. There is a 'sweet spot' between the two poles, one where emotion, wisdom, intellect, and instinct work together to allow us to see truth as it really exists."

Brandon was extremely disillusioned—this very disillusionment contained both the source and the healing of his suffering. When an illusion shatters the wish and hope of what we want a person or situation to be, incredible pain can result. Yet from this painful place, the voice of constructive fear can move in to offer healing wisdom. Constructive fear would say, "It can be painful to see what really exists behind the illusion. But it was only an illusion after all. From this space of seeing things as they are, you now have the choice to go forward in a way that is beneficial for you. Evaluate the situation as it truly is and use it as fuel for learning. Do not let destructive fear grip you with what you should have noticed or done. That is the past, where destructive fear would like you to stay. You have today. You have a future before you. Move forward in a conscious, loving, and honest way."

Brandon thought he had done his due diligence in selecting his wife-to-be. Yet Brandon didn't realize that his then-fiancée was not honest about very key issues. Given Kit's many attributes, he had not paused to give attention to *all* of her qualities—the good and the not-so-good. Brandon simply was not able to see the full woman before him with objectivity. As is so human and common, Brandon saw only what he wanted to see. Now faced with reality, Brandon's work was to discover how he wanted to move forward with courage, respect, and honesty. Brandon also had to consider the healing work ahead—he was deeply embarrassed, hurt, and angry. Throughout his days, Brandon found himself immersed in negative feelings and thoughts of his wife's betrayal. Brandon once noted, "I see that I have to forgive not only my wife—my soon-to-be-ex-wife—but I have to forgive myself. I want to stop beating up on myself for having had such bad judgment. I tend to make great decisions in life. I still can't wrap my mind around how I made such a blind mistake. I am embarrassed about my failure; this stands out like a red flag for me and everyone to see."

Various levels of deception and manipulation such as what Brandon experienced are sadly common in relationships. Although Brandon's situation might seem dramatic, aspects of it are similar to what many women and men face in life. Because it is so easy to get swept off our feet in romantic relationships, Brandon's situation highlights the general importance of building a true relationship. Brandon was on the right path; he knew the characteristics, goals, and general values that were important to him. Yet, as he came to discover, he stopped when he had checked off the items of religion, children, money, shared interests, work, and financial goals. Brandon later came to see the lack of intimate connection—not just sexually but in their overall interactions as well. He put the lack of tenderness, kissing, and bonding intimacy down to their busy schedules. But as he later noted, "I knew something was off. I had been in previous relationships that had a strong romantic and emotional connection. I knew it wasn't present with Kit. Yet all the other line items were present. I knew deep down that she wasn't into me. And, in truth, I can now see that I knew that she was hiding something from me. I represented the ideal lifestyle that would let her move up the ladder in a traditional, male-dominated industry. Being married to me was a shield that allowed her relationship to go on behind the scenes; she didn't have to confront the truth of being a lesbian with her family, siblings, or church. Kit wanted the nice appearance—the sham—of it all. I was just her means of getting it. Maybe I knew all of this on some level and just didn't want to burst my own bubble. Thank God we didn't have kids. I'm glad everything is out in the open. I'm starting to feel free—really relieved. I can move on with my life. As you say, a big piece of my work will be to not wall myself off. I am terrified of women now and so afraid that I'll get used again. But I am wiser now; I know that."

Many people find themselves in relationships that share common threads with Brandon's situation. In Brandon's case, he had the courage to move out of the relationship with respect and dignity. Brandon accepted the reality in front of him rather than continuing to wish for something that would never be. Although Brandon once believed that the relationship had incredible potential, he was strong enough to see that this was an illusory belief. Indeed, it can be tremendously difficult to come to such a place of honest awareness and acceptance, for destructive fear thrives in a world of dishonesty and illusion. With the voice of constructive fear in his ear, Brandon found the courage to put his wisdom into action. Brandon faced the sad, problematic truth of his situation. In the most respectful, loving way possible, he made necessary changes. As a result, his personal life—his overall world—transformed. His life wasn't as he envisioned it, but the new life he had was built on truth. Had Brandon chosen to preserve the façade, he wouldn't have found the freedom he discovered in the arms of transformational fear.

Your Relationship Goals

This exercise will help you ascertain and evaluate your personal relationship goals. As you proceed, strive for an attitude of non-judgment, for there are no "right" or "wrong" responses. Some may find this exercise easy and basic, whereas others who have never paused to consider relationship goals may find it challenging. Use these exercises as an opportunity for honest self-reflection, knowing that you can adjust or update your responses at any time. As you change and evolve in life, your relationship goals may surely change; this exercise may provide you with a reference point as you move forward. Notice that your work in this exercise may be enlivened by your previous efforts on the "essential qualities" exercise.

As always, ensure that you are feeling physically and psychologically ready to proceed. When you are in a safe, relaxed space with your pen and notebook by your side, pause to breathe. First, write out a general list of your relationship goals. For example, if you are already in a relationship, you might note: *(1) I want to learn to communicate in a loving way with my partner; (2) I would like my relationship to be healthy and loving; (3) I would like to have two children with my mate.* If you are single and would like a committed, long-term relationship, you might note: *(1) I would like to find a like-minded partner to share my life with; (2) As I continue my self-work, I want to date one person at a time to thoroughly explore each relationship; (3) As I date, I want to practice my values of being genuine, honest, respectful, and aware.* However, if you are single and have no desire for a committed relationship, your notes might look very different. You might note, *(1) I want to be unattached and date a variety of people for at least a few years; (2) I would like to discover myself and others within a variety of uncommitted relationships; (3) As I continue my self-work, I want to practice and utilize my tools, communicating my goals and needs to others with honesty, clarity, kindness, and respect.* Whether your list is short or long, use this portion of the exercise to gain clarity about your needs and desires. When your list is complete, pause to breathe.

Next, look at your general list of goals. For each goal on the list, write out three specific, actionable micro-goals for each item. Remember that destructive fear will want you to avoid clarity and specificity. Let constructive fear be your guide in creating actionable micro-goals that will generate greater health in your world of relationships. Using the first example above, an individual in a committed relationship might have the following three micro-goals for the first goal: *(1) I will talk to my partner tonight about taking a communication course for couples and will enroll us by the end of the week; (2) I will practice complimenting my partner every day; (3) I will make respectful eye contact with my partner when we talk.* An individual desiring a long-term relationship might have the following three micro-goals for the first goal: *(1) In the next week, I will refine my list of essential qualities to better my chances of finding a like-minded partner; (2) By the end of the month, I will have a greater understanding of my personal goals, for this will help me better notice those who share my important goals; (3) By the end of the month, I will complete an online dating profile, and I will make certain that the profile clearly represents my essential qualities.* For the individual who prefers uncommitted dating, the three micro-goals for the third goal might be: *(1) I have not been honest with some people who are in my life about my true goals, and I will do soul-searching on this tonight; (2) I will honor my natural desire to avoid this uncomfortable process by journaling and talking to my best friend; (3) By this weekend, I will have honest, considerate discussions with those I have misled.*

When you have completed your specific micro-goals for each section, pause to breathe. Congratulate yourself on a job well done.

Getting to Your Truth

For a variety of personal reasons, many women and men remain stuck in unhealthy or stagnant relationships, consciously or unconsciously choosing to stay when there is no hope of true relationship. As noted above, many relationships are bonded by convenience or need with the partners lacking a desire for true relationship; this is a choice that the two partners can make and accept honestly. In unhealthy situations, however, one or both partners may suffer tremendously in the relationship, often exhibiting psychological and physical manifestations of their distress. It is in these situations that one or both partners may cry out for change. Often suffering in painful confusion, some know nothing more than that they feel stuck and hopeless. Others seethe in anger and resentment, seeking temporary solace in infidelity, cycles of violent abuse, or the numbing effects of alcohol and other substances. With destructive fear creating conflict and confusion, these individuals cannot hear the wise voice of constructive fear.

It is not always easy to detect if a relationship has no hope for a positive future. It can be extremely difficult to accept that a relationship is not—or possibly never was—truly healthy, appropriate, or beneficial. Indeed, as a firm believer in the human ability to effect change, I also recognize that it can be difficult to conclude that a relationship simply is not viable. Particularly when a great deal of time, effort, energy, and hope have been invested, it can feel devastating to accept a relationship's demise. Some people make the error of giving up too soon—fearful and unwilling to face the journey of personal and relationship growth. Others stay far too long, investing in a relationship that has no potential. Some erroneously believe that "unconditional love" requires the acceptance of dishonesty or abuse. Even when faced with glaring patterns of deceit and disrespect, many individuals say, "The relationship has such potential. I really hope it will change." This is a common misuse of the power of hope, for the dream of potential can be an illusion. What's more, even true potential is a mere wish if not actuated. How, then, can a person determine when a relationship has no hope or if true potential is being abandoned?

In essence, the true potential of a relationship can be discovered with one particular key: deep honesty with the self and with the partner. Although this may sound easy enough, it can be difficult for one critical reason: self-honesty relies on self-awareness, something that may be lacking in one or both parties involved in a dysfunctional relationship. It can be difficult to be honest with the self for a variety of reasons. For example, objective clarity and self-honesty can be elusive if a person is generally lacking self-awareness, under emotional duress, or in dire physical circumstances. Indeed, many individuals simply have not developed enough psychological maturity to understand the importance of honesty in a relationship. Yet remember that it is never too late to develop a solid relationship with honesty. With patience, practice, and the wise voice of constructive fear in your ear, you will learn to cherish honesty in yourself and your relationships. You will become so familiar with truth and honesty that any other way of being will simply not feel right to you. In this way, a solid relationship with honesty will set you free.

Five Steps toward Diving In or Letting Go

This next exercise will help you evaluate your important relationships including, of course, your relationship with yourself. As you will be working with sensitive material, ensure that you are in a safe, secure environment and that you are psychologically ready to proceed. This process may not be easy, but it has the potential to be very illuminating. Indeed, the work you undertake during this section has the power to transform your life in significant ways. In looking at yourself and your relationships with absolute honesty, you will be able to evaluate what your highest self requires. As a result of this work, you may decide that certain relationships—those that you value or want to value as true relationships—deserve greater commitment and energy. You may come to realize that a key relationship has no potential for healthy evolution. You may find that your partner's essential qualities are incompatible with your own. Additionally, you may come to realize that a person is unwilling or unable to work on the relationship with you. Trust that your levels of emotional and overall psychological maturity have grown substantially during this journey. Know, too, that the work you are about to embark on may trigger an earthquake of sorts in your life. Wherever this next journey might lead you, move slowly and with loving care. As you entertain possible shifts in your life, seek outside guidance and support when needed.

When you are ready, ensure that you are relaxed and that your notebook and pen are at your side. Pause to breathe. Reflect on only one personal relationship at a time. You may choose to focus only on your relationship with your spouse or partner. You may also choose to evaluate all of the key relationships in your life. Choose what is best for you. (You will note that the word *partner* is used throughout this exercise. Feel free to adjust this term to reflect your focus and needs.) Now, armed with the wise power of self-honesty and nonjudgment, consider these vital questions:

1. Am I actively working on my personal journey, taking necessary steps to be my optimal self?
2. Does my partner have the essential qualities I require for a true relationship?
3. Is my partner willing to invest the time and energy necessary to make this relationship evolve and flourish?
4. Is my partner taking the necessary active, concerted steps for personal growth and the evolution of the relationship?
5. Do I have the desire to invest my time and energy to make this relationship evolve and flourish?

Pause to breathe.

Before proceeding further, read the paragraphs below. Feel free to take a break to reflect after reading. This next section will allow you to investigate and examine your possible responses to the five questions outlined above. As always, take care to be aware of your needs; work at a pace and level that feel right for you.

Question One: Am I actively working on my personal journey, taking necessary steps to be my optimal self? This first question can be answered only with fearless honesty; you must be willing to do your personal work consistently, remaining ever responsible and aware. If you are actively working on your personal journey through this book, with a psychotherapist, or via other means, you can rest assured that you are taking the foundational step in creating a true relationship with yourself and being capable of being in a true relationship with others. Remember, this journey is a process that is seemingly endless. It's not about "being a perfectly evolved person"; it's about knowing that the evolution of personhood is an imperfect process that asks for consistent, dedicated effort.

Question Two: Does my partner have the essential qualities I require for a true relationship? This second question can be answered by an honest review of your list of essential qualities. Indeed, you might find it important to review this—and other—sections of your work with your partner to ensure that you are moving forward with awareness. As you review your list of essential qualities, you might find that your partner possesses these qualities or is actively working on them. But, after honest reflection, you may realize that your partner is uninterested or incapable of embracing the qualities that are essential to you. This step requires an honest, holistic evaluation of your partner's capacities, qualities, values, and traits. Destructive fear may step in to cloud your vision, distracting you with what you want to see—what will allow you to continue on with illusory hope. Yet your wise mind and instinct know the truth. Listen for the wise voice of constructive fear as it gently pushes illusions aside. If your partner does not have the essential qualities you need or hasn't the interest and ability to actively embrace them, the potential for a true relationship does not exist. With this awareness, you can choose to exit the relationship with honesty and grace.

Question Three: Is my partner willing to invest the time and energy necessary to make this relationship evolve and flourish? This third question is key. As you gain clarity on your desires, needs, and goals in your relationships, honest discussions with your partner are essential. By kindly and clearly articulating your needs, your partner will gain awareness of your expectations and needs. You may have never taken these steps in your relationship, but it is never too late. You both may feel uncomfortable, but clear communication is vital for this step. Whether your relationship is new or years-old, your partner needs to know and understand what you expect. It is only from this place that you and your partner can ascertain if there is a willingness to invest the necessary time and energy to create a successful relationship. If your partner is not willing or able to invest in the relationship, you can then choose to move away from the relationship in a clear and honest way.

Question Four: Is my partner taking the necessary active, concerted steps for personal growth and the evolution of the relationship? Your honest response to this fourth question is an essential component in getting unstuck. Many relationships remain stuck at this junction. A partner may promise to change yet the critical component of action is missing. Sometimes the promise of change is made with sincerity yet the individual lacks the drive or other capacity to follow through. In other cases, insincere promises are made to temporarily ease the situation. The latter case adds the element of manipulation—this may make a decision to exit the relationship all the easier. Yet, in either case, observation of the partner's change-oriented actions is critical. If the individual is unwilling to actively work on improving unhealthy or dysfunctional patterns or ways of being, there is no hope of true relationship. However, if the partner is making a concerted effort, the relationship has potential. Indeed, change may be slow in coming, for old patterns can be very hard to break. Although lapses may occur, the critical element is the sincere, consistent effort toward personal growth and evolution in the relationship. When missteps occur, personal accountability is a key component in moving forward. The relationship has potential when partners work without blame to actively improve themselves and the relationship. If promises are not being translated into action, you may elect to exit the relationship with courage and dignity.

Question Five: Do I have the desire and willingness to invest my time and energy to make this relationship evolve and flourish? Your objective evaluation of your mind, heart, and personal qualities is critical in answering this fifth question. You may know deep down that you have exhausted your best efforts and that change is impossible. You may have been deceived by your partner with false claims and other dishonesties. You may realize that you made a poor decision by entering a relationship with someone who is not healthy—whether due to a lack of personal awareness, selfish goals, or other issues. However, if you feel tired of working on yourself or the relationship, pause to notice if destructive fear is at work. If you are in a committed relationship with a partner who is honest, true, and invested in the relationship, pause to notice if you are making excuses. Indeed, if you have a tendency to tire of "working on relationships," this may indicate that you are not doing your own personal work. In such a case, it is important to revisit your own essential qualities to assess issues such as commitment and integrity. Yet in the end, there is no possibility of a true relationship if you are unwilling to do what it takes to make the relationship work. However, if you are able and willing to put sincere effort into the relationship—doing everything you can without compromising your dignity and self-respect—then the relationship has the potential to transform into a true relationship. If your answer to the fifth question is "no," then it is your responsibility to do what is necessary to tend to the relationship with dignity, kindness, generosity, honesty, and respect.

Next, write out each of the five questions in your notebook. Again, due to the intensity of this exercise, it is best to work only on one relationship at a time. Allow plenty of space between each question. When you are ready, write out your responses to each question with as much objectivity as possible. You may not particularly like your authentic, honest responses to these questions. You may hope that reality is more in line with your wishes. However, if you wish to change unhealthy patterns, your genuine responses are a necessary first step. As you move through the series of five questions, you will become aware of how your genuine, self-reflective responses will lead to an objective, appropriate conclusion. This step-by-step process can be utilized in nearly all important relationships in your life. Pause to breathe often during this process. This exercise takes tremendous honesty, clarity, and perseverance.

If your response to each of the five questions is "yes," you and your partner have the ability to craft a most beautiful and rare true relationship. If not, you can wisely decide what is best for you, your future, and those in your world. Whatever choices you make, remember to listen to the wise voice of constructive fear. Remember that destructive fear will push you to make excuses. Its clamoring voice may offer rationalizations and try to distract you. Yet you know in your deepest heart what is best for you and those you love. It is natural to fear change; this is destructive fear at work. Trust the voice of constructive fear, for it will remind you that healthy changes are an essential element of a balanced, fulfilling, and joyful life. Although you may initially feel worried, guilty, or heartbroken as you contemplate and prepare for necessary changes, trust that your wise courage will create inner freedom. Indeed, your wisdom and courage may be just what your partner or others in your life need to begin their own changes. When your heart and soul are good and true—when you put your essential qualities into action in your own life—you will be in a true relationship with yourself. From this place, you will have the capacity to be in true relationships with others. Pause to breathe. Make any notes that you find important and helpful. Congratulate yourself on a job very well done.

In being honest with yourself, you have opened up your world of relationships to the wise guidance of constructive fear. By noticing where destructive fear has held you in stuck patterns and unhealthy relationships, you will be able to free yourself. Through noticing where your essential qualities demand to be inserted in your own life and your own relationships, you will be able to enliven these qualities and enhance your capacity for true relationship. By noticing where you have not been honest with yourself—and, therefore, incapable of being honest with others—you may now see a new pathway opening before you. As you move forward in an honest, courageous way, you will be living with the power of transformational fear.

The Changeable Web of Intimacy, Partnership, and Communication: A Case Study

Felicia and Arturo, a young couple in their early thirties, sought my assistance in resolving their marital difficulties. The couple had dated and lived together for several years before marriage and both felt secure in their shared values, goals, and loving commitment to each other. Yet although they cared for each other deeply, the relationship began to falter during their first year of marriage. The situation worsened after the much-anticipated birth of their child. Hardworking and dedicated, Arturo felt cast aside as his wife focused all of her energy on her job, household duties, and their young son. Arturo craved the passion and loving attention that he had become accustomed to before the birth of their son. With angry frustration, Arturo stated, "If I knew having our son would create constant conflict, I would have thought twice. What we had before was great—we had our ups and downs like any couple, but our commitment was always strong. Life was fun; it was just the two of us. In some ways, I wish things could go back to the way they were. There are times that I am so resentful that I want to give up. I won't, of course, because I love my wife and son. To be honest, I really hate feeling this way. I know I must sound selfish, but I just don't know what to do to make it better. We have tried to talk through our issues, but we end up going in circles. I've gotten so angry at Felicia lately that she said we had to get help. I agree. Instead of resolving issues, things keep getting worse."

Felicia, clearly exhausted and frustrated, noted, "I agree with everything Arturo said. His angry outbursts are what prompted us to make an appointment. They actually scare me, because he's not usually an angry person. Something in him switches lately—like an anger switch gets flipped. I am doing the best I can—I am just worn out. On some levels, I also miss the closeness we had—but sometimes I am just too tired to do anything more. I want Arturo to be happy. I want to be a good wife and a good mother. I just don't know how to make everything work. Honestly, I feel resentful too. I've told Arturo this. Neither of us had perfect parents with perfect marriages. We've both seen resentments and conflict destroy some of our friend's relationships. We prided ourselves on being different—we used to make the greatest team. So, even though I'm exhausted, I want us to get back to that place." This young couple's marriage was not suffering from a lack of love or commitment; it was suffering as a result of life changes and the lack of tools to face them.

During our first session, it was clear that both Felicia and Arturo were committed to making the marriage work. They were both willing and engaged, desperate to put an end to the conflict that had become the "new normal" in their lives. This obvious commitment to each other and the marriage was critical for the success of their marriage. When they discovered that they didn't have the tools to understand and face their challenges, they proactively reached out for support. Felicia and Arturo gave their relationship a far greater chance of success by not avoiding the issues or waiting until one or both collapsed under the strain. As Arturo wisely said, "We both grew up in families where many issues weren't talked about. Seeing a psychologist or any therapist would have been seen as a weakness—it just wouldn't have been an option. But Felicia and I have a different attitude. We see it like going to the mechanic for a car issue. Yes, there are certain things that Felicia and I can do ourselves—like changing the oil or adding coolant—but there are things that are beyond our skill set right now. That's how we see this situation. It feels like we are out of alignment. We want you to help us diagnose what's wrong, understand how to repair things, and give us the tools we need to get back on the road and stay there!" Arturo's metaphor encapsulated the couple's willing, can-do attitude.

Unlike Felicia and Arturo, many couples simply go through the motions of trying to make their marriage work. Whether married or not, it is common to have one partner "drag" the other into therapy after a prolonged period of difficulty. The non-invested partner often has already emotionally and mentally abandoned the relationship. These situations—far different from one like Felicia and Arturo's—are not promising. Yet even those that look rather hopeless can change course if both partners ultimately choose to truly invest in the relationship.

When issues are resolved within the relationship, both partners can benefit tremendously. Indeed, if their work together is successful, they both move forward stronger, more aware, and with greater confidence in their commitment to themselves and the relationship. This alone can be incredibly powerful—knowing that one has what it takes to make it through challenging times can be one of the most powerful self-esteem builders in life. On the other hand, if an individual walks away from commitment due to indifference or unwillingness, self-esteem ultimately suffers, for there can be a sense of inner failure in knowing that one has not done all that was needed or required to honor a commitment. This goes back to the original definition of true relationship—the willingness to share in and carry the burdens (not just the delights) of the relationship over and over again. It is important to remember that there are times when it is appropriate to walk away from a commitment. For example, if a partner is abusive or dishonest and lacking in the desire or willingness to actively change, the only healthy solution is to exit the relationship.

Fortunately, Felicia and Arturo sought help for their relationship before it devolved into a chronic cycle of negativity and resentment. In our subsequent sessions, we teased apart the issues. First, the couple fine-tuned their communication skills; reflective listening (mirroring) became their favorite tool. The couple discovered the importance of gentle eye contact, "slowing down" to attend to each other, and making agreements about how and when to talk about their concerns. Arturo attended a confidential anger management group, and both he and Felicia were delighted by his quick progress. The couple discovered that these skills allowed them to face their new roles—and the changes that came with them—with greater confidence in their ability to truly listen and attend to each other.

In a later session, Felicia noted, "I feel so much better now. I didn't realize how many resentments I was carrying. I thought I'd done a good job of talking about what was bothering me, but I realize that unresolved issues were stacking up inside me. Now that we are getting to the bottom of things, I see that I was covering up a lot of anger and hurt."

Arturo nodded in agreement, saying, "We now make time every evening—once the baby is asleep—to talk about our days. We share the good things and the not-so-good things. Even if we are tired, we give each other positive affirmations. We make sure to talk about issues as they come up. The reflective listening really works. I say how I feel without being blaming, angry, or sarcastic. I keep it simple and clear. Then Felicia repeats what I said to make sure she understands. We work on it a little bit to fine-tune things. If Felicia has something going on, I give her the same respectful attention. It's amazing—absolutely amazing—how this little tool makes such a huge difference. Instead of fighting, we now have discussions about things as they come up. I feel closer than ever to Felicia—closer than before our marriage for sure. The process we are going through is making things real. I get the idea of a true relationship now—the idea of how getting through the tough stuff with kindness is actually the heart of it. Before we were married, it was different because we were free and easy. Now, we are actually going through real life together—now we are really a team."

No matter the duration of the relationship, the ability to adapt and change is absolutely critical. Indeed, change is a certainty and necessity in life. Relationships and the people in them cannot grow and evolve without change. Constructive fear knows that intrapersonal and interpersonal relationships require constant positive adjustments and change. Destructive fear perpetuates the belief that relationships "should be easy." Romanticized movies and fairytales can lead the unwary into believing that they will "meet the right person and live happily ever after." This belief leaves out a few critical elements: Meeting the "right person" is a necessary element, and so is actively *being* the "right person." What's more, "happily ever after" doesn't come by chance. It results from the magic of facing life's challenges and changes with patience, dedicated effort, honest commitment, and heavy doses of loving kindness.

Although Felicia and Arturo understood that changes and challenges might come with marriage and a child, they weren't quite prepared for reality. The couple didn't have the tools to adapt. Arturo once reflected, "I thought it would be easy once we were married. We were pretty much in tune with each other when we lived together. Now I see that the stress of change brought out our weaknesses. I see that I was unconsciously getting into patterns of anger that I probably learned from my dad. I thought it would be easy to segue from being a boyfriend to being a husband and then a dad. I was on board for all of that conceptually, but I was absolutely unprepared for the actual changes that came. Just being a husband—that's a huge responsibility on its own. That's a lifetime commitment. Then the idea of being a dad—caring for a little baby that is totally dependent on us for everything—it's a twenty-four-hour job that will last for another eighteen-plus years. No one can prepare you for the full reality of that."

Felicia and Arturo discovered that their partnership needed recalibration. When single, they had operated as a team yet were also highly independent in certain ways. Not only did marriage bring a commingling of funds and other material changes, but they had also unconsciously stepped into roles modeled by their parents. Arturo, who had been helpful in the kitchen and household duties, had unconsciously retreated from these areas. Felicia, accustomed to her own mother's domesticity, assumed the full weight of the duties without a word. Additionally, in the hope of owning their own home, the couple had created a stringent savings plan. They now accounted for every penny, different from the carefree days they knew before marriage. Arturo also took on a second job when Felicia returned to work. Caught up in their busy schedules, they didn't realize that their many changes had taken a heavy toll.

The couple came to realize that they would benefit from a few shifts in their partnership and their priorities. As a team, Felicia and Arturo sat down to revise their goals. They developed one-year, five-year, and ten-year plans. Knowing that their relationship was suffering from their intense demands, the couple decided to give themselves a few additional years to achieve their homeownership goal. This allowed Arturo to give up his second job, and it also allowed Felicia to reduce her work schedule by several hours per week. Their level of physical exhaustion decreased, and their time together increased. As Felicia noted, "We've made some tradeoffs, but we are much happier. We can still save quite a lot, and our childcare costs have also decreased. But the big difference is our home environment. We are so much happier. Arturo is home more, and we are playing like we used to do. Arturo is also picking up more of the chores—he cooks at least half the meals. The changes are a win-win for us. Even the baby seems happier. We know we are a family—that we are there for each other. We put each other first. I put Arturo before anyone and any-thing—my parents, my sister, my best friend, and even our son. I had to get re-centered and reconfigure my priorities. We have each other's backs even more than we did before we were married. I think we really under-stand our relationship—and each other—in a more real-life way. We are emotionally intimate—we can talk about anything and everything way more than we did before. We have no secrets from each other. We are absolutely honest and transparent. This is amazing, because it allows this deep, real sense of trust to exist. It's the best feeling in the world. I feel safe. I feel loved. I know it won't always be easy, but I know we have the tools we need to move forward through anything."

True relationship is a most priceless, beautiful entity. It transforms each partner, allowing for the unselfish evolution of all aspects of the self and the other. In this way, there is nothing to ever fear in a true relationship, for no such partner would ever consciously do something to harm the other. Although misunderstandings surely occur in even the truest relationships, they are viewed as natural, minor stumbles in the journey. Constructive fear would say, "Survival in relationships is a human condition, but suc-cess in relationships is a conscious choice. Manipulative relationships are based on getting your partner to do something so that you 'win.' True rela-tionships are based on doing all that you can so that your partner and your relationship can benefit. In this way, you cannot help but win in the long run, for your partner in a true relationship will be turning this same loving energy toward you." This awareness will allow you to step forward into actions that embrace the power of transformational fear. In doing so, you will transform yourself, your relationships—and your most precious life.

CHAPTER 9

Fear and the Greater Good

Creating Your Reality

Throughout the pages of this book, you have had the courage to engage in a fearless survey of many aspects of your soul, your life, and your world. In this last chapter, you will have the opportunity to further expand your journey. After you read the last page, I pray that you move ever forward using the insights and tools you have garnered. I see the journey of life as a constant evolution—one that we can take part in consciously and actively or leave fairly much to chance. Although it seems that the winds of fate are always at least a bit in play, we do have the choice to create and affect our own reality at every turn.

The reality of life is not always pleasant or what we might have hoped for, yet we cannot escape it. We have three basic choices when we don't like the truth of reality. The first option is to face reality and actively work to change what we do not like. The second option is to try to escape, whether by running, hiding, or pretending reality does not exist. The third is to passively or irritably accept the status quo. Only the first option actually has the potential to create conscious, lasting change. Only the first option embraces the wise voice of constructive fear. The other two options are fueled by destructive fear, for they allow other forces to take charge of your life, your future, and your world. The choice is yours. You can become active in changing your world for the better, or you can live in relative resignation. The first option doesn't ask you to become a martyr, leader, or sign-bearing activist. It only asks that you lead your life in a way that allows you to model the healthy wisdom of transformational fear.

Our world is busy and often frightening. The daily pressures, noise, and fast rate of change can be stressful and terrifying. As a result, many people either fear or do not like their reality. Possibly unaware of or uninterested in other options, they elect the route of escapist behaviors. Whether a person escapes by turning to drugs, alcohol, food, overspending, or to the virtual worlds of television, video games, or social media, the outcome is the same. The distraction is only temporary. Reality waits, unchanged— or sometimes worse—for the escapee's return. Destructive fear is quite pleased with escapism.

The third option—acceptance—is always a possibility. In fact, as each person has a finite amount of time and energy to invest in change, we often accept situations unknowingly or by default. There are times when acceptance is the best choice—when efforts have been exhausted and change is impossible. Many individuals, however, seem to accept the status quo with angry words, bitter outbursts, or complacent resignation. Some may grumble and gripe about their lives, society, or the world. But in the end, an attitude of "it is what it is" takes hold. Acceptance of this sort does not lead to change. Destructive fear smiles at blind or willing resignation.

So what's a person to do? Destructive fear would urge you to ignore or avoid problematic issues in your life, environment, and the greater world. It might even try to convince you to outlive or outfox problems rather than tending to them. Constructive fear knows that there is another way. Constructive fear knows that you can change your reality so that you don't want to escape it. Constructive fear wants you to address problems now so that you can transform your world and the world that will be met by future generations. Constructive fear wants you to take all that you have learned thus far and use it to create a better reality—one of self-awareness, peaceful interconnection, respect for self and others, and lasting joy. The truth is that no one person can change the world, yet each individual can strive to stay aware and active in trying to change certain aspects—whatever areas are most important to that person. As a result of cumulative effort, great changes occur over time.

You may now notice how fear is at work in your personal being, your home life, and the outside world. You may be aware of how destructive fear works to create chronic anxiety, depression, and disconnection. You might see how destructive fear has connected you and your family into a web of hysterical fear by drawing the world's chaos into your home. You may now be wise to the vast, controlling role of destructive fear—a role that you may have never understood or noticed in the past.

As a result of your courageous journey, it is possible that you are less afraid of change—and you may even welcome it. You may now realize that destructive fear wants you to be afraid of change, whereas constructive fear wants you to welcome the changes that set you free. Indeed, it is possible that you have already begun making steady, wise steps to creating change where you can. Perhaps you have made constructive fear your ally, making positive changes that increase your sense of self-efficacy and personal power. Every step you take with constructive fear leads you one step closer to the life you desire—a life that increasingly exemplifies the wisdom, balance, and joy of transformational fear.

Your Core Life Fears: Your Most Vulnerable Space

You may now be ready for this next vital aspect of your journey, for you have explored and learned a great deal about your personhood and your own world. Knowing that the entity of fear is a natural part of life, you may now be ready to make peace with your innermost fears. What I have come to call "core life fears"—each person's deepest, often secret personal fears—can be an incredibly powerful force of immobilization and struggle. Yet, once acknowledged, these same core life fears can become a source of wise awareness and self-compassion. Core fears are not normally associated with rational, realistic fears such as the inability to pay one's bills when a bank account is low or being attacked by a mountain lion when walking through a forest that is a home to wildcats. Rather, core fears tend to be rooted in an internal place of worry and doubt, a place where faith is shaky. These fears are often deep and silently lurking and are often off-limits to investigation and discussion. Being afraid of core life fears is absolutely understandable, for these fears seem to hold the secret key to our vulnerabilities. It can be scary to be vulnerable, particularly if one has suffered many wounds in life. As such, it makes perfect sense that awareness and discussion of these core life fears is "no one's business." Yet this is destructive fear talking, for individuals often know their core life fears even if they refuse to acknowledge them. In the same way, people who are close to each other are often acutely aware of each other's core life fears—and some may even use this knowledge to cause harm. In any case, it can be rare to acknowledge and speak about core life fears, yet the core life fears are present nonetheless. Why not then be true to the self by knowing them, befriending them, and freeing the self from the stranglehold of ignorance or avoidance? Why pretend that invulnerability arises by not being vulnerable? In truth, the vulnerability exists either way.

When I began investigating fear over a decade ago, I realized quickly that fear is a slippery entity. I noticed that people responded in very interesting ways to my research. I noted that men often became defensive and wary—even declining to participate. Although men were generally amenable to talking about fears such as motorcycle accidents and work issues, more personal fears were often off-limits. Given that men are generally raised to avoid emotions and a sense of vulnerability, the male resistance to discussing fear-based issues made sense. I noticed that women tended to be much less defensive and, once a sense of safety was established, were often willing to share intimate details, hurts, and worries. However, when my research was confined to anonymous quantitative and qualitative surveys rather than in-person discussions or non-anonymous surveys, men were nearly equally as likely to respond as women. This held true through over seven hundred qualitative and quantitative anonymous surveys. My research also revealed that most people have an average of three core life fears.[1] Of course, some had fewer core fears and some had more.

Core life fears take many forms and can be articulated in countless ways. Yet three general themes surfaced, only one of which pointed toward a fear of a specific situation or item (e.g., a fear of spiders). The other two themes reflected very basic human vulnerabilities: fear of failure and fear of abandonment or loss. No matter the words that were used to express these two core fear themes, the message was often the same: *I am afraid of failing—of making a mistake. I am afraid of being abandoned or losing someone I love.* In essence, it seems that most—if not all—humans are afraid of not being worthy, losing the essence or object of love, and being alone. Perhaps this can be distilled to a single fear that unites us all—a fear that we might ultimately be unloved and alone. Constructive fear steps in to say, "Ah, rest easy. With faith in divine connection—whatever that connection and power means to you—you are never alone."

In two recent, more unstructured qualitative fear surveys,[2] participants shared many poignant thoughts. Some responses focused on specific fears such as financial instability, relationship concerns, or aging issues. Others shared more general core fears. Interestingly, the key themes of fear of failure and abandonment or loss arose again. The most common response was a fear of being unsuccessful—a fear of failure. Second in line was a fear of rejection—of not being worthy or lovable. The third most common response was a fear of "not being good enough." As one candid individual noted, "Fear of hearing 'no' was always my thing. I suppose another way of describing the fear would be a fear of rejection. From asking out a gal to applying for a great job, the fear of 'no' and the associated sense of rejection—of not being good enough—has slowed me down."

Destructive fear has many tentacles: insecurity, unworthiness, abandonment, betrayal, failure, shame, loss, and countless more. Regardless of the words used to convey the underlying fears, the nature of core fears remains constant. Indeed, the themes noted in the two unstructured fear surveys further emphasized the basic nature of core fears. In short, situational or specific fears (e.g., monetary concerns) make up one of three common categories. The two remaining categories tie back to two powerful, central themes: a fear of failure and a fear of abandonment or loss. And, again, these two fears can be further distilled to a simple fear: the very human fear of being unloved and alone.

As you begin to acknowledge and investigate your own core fears, a good dose of self-compassion is in order. It can be difficult to acknowledge one's deepest life fears, yet these fears exist whether we acknowledge them or not. Why not move toward them? Why not allow constructive fear to lead you forward into awareness? Why not let the action of transformational fear attend to—if not heal—this part of your life? Of course, you need not share your core fears with anyone at all. If you do not have others who will honor and tend to your fears, then—at this time—your core fears are yours alone. Yet if you have someone who will respect and honor your core fears and not use them to disparage you or do you other harm, then you may wish to share your core fears. For example, if you determine that your core fears are failure or betrayal, you may want to share these fears with a good and loving soul. You might wisely share a fear of failure with a supportive, loving person who would embrace you unconditionally through failure and success alike. You might also wisely share a fear of betrayal with an integrous friend who would never give you cause to suffer the serious wounds of betrayal and thus allow you to build true trust. Whatever the core fears might be, sharing them with honorable, conscious souls can increase self-awareness, faith, and binding love. As inner vulnerabilities are shared and honored, the psyche says, "I feel safe. I feel seen. I feel honored. I feel loved." In this way, the sharing of core fears can be a powerfully connective and healing experience for all those who embrace the process with loving kindness and respect.

Your Core Life Fears

This exercise will allow you to discover and investigate your own core life fears. As you are delving into sensitive territory, make certain that you are psychologically ready for this work. Ensure that you are in a safe and relaxed environment with your pen and journal at your side. When you are prepared to proceed, pause to breathe.

Envision your core life fears. You may wish to close your eyes. Imagine what forces hold you back, make you feel immobilized, or fill you with doubt and worry. Many thoughts or images may come to mind. Whatever they are, allow them to arise without judgment. Pause to breathe. When you are ready, write out your thoughts in your journal. Allow your words to flow on the page without censure or judgment. Pause to breathe.

When you are done, notice what you wrote. Again, refrain from judgment. You may notice that certain themes have arisen. For example, you may notice a theme regarding a fear of death, loss, abandonment, unworthiness, imperfection, betrayal, failure, or being unlovable. If you notice fear-based themes, feel free to make note of them as they arrive. Notice those that have the strongest emotional impact on you and underline these themes. If certain themes don't seem to be present, simply underline those fear-based thoughts that tend to have the greatest hold on you. Pause to breathe.

Look at whatever words or sentences you have underlined. It is likely that these are your core fears. Make any notes or adjustments that feel appropriate to you. Now, using whatever language feels right, make a list of your core fears. Breathe. You may wish to read the next five sentences many times over, for they are very powerful.

Your core fears are sacred. You can choose to give them power over you, or you can strive to release their control over you and your actions. These core fears are not the monsters they seem to be. They represent tender wounds that need your compassionate love. These core fears represent wounds that have the power to chain you or set you free.

Pause to breathe. Congratulations on a job very well done. You have taken yet another courageous step with constructive fear. Your life will continue to transform.

Purpose and Meaning: What Is Your Life Banner?

Along with safe and loving relationships, supportive social connections, and basic financial resources, having a sense of purpose in life is critical for overall well-being. It is human nature to crave meaning and purpose in life. It is fulfilling to know that one's efforts make a difference in the world. It does not necessarily matter if the impact is small or large; it is the felt nature of the impact that counts. A life powered by passionate energy tends to inspire others to follow their own dreams. Destructive fear would have you stay small. It would have you stay on the couch, focus on instant gratification, and leave the future to come as it will. In this way, destructive fear wants to suffocate your potential, your passion, and your drive. Constructive fear wants you to thrive; it wants you to find fulfillment. Constructive fear wants you to utilize the nascent power of your hopes and dreams to actively create a life of purpose and meaning.

We often don't pause in life to really ponder who we are or who we want to be. We may take more time to create a shopping list or plan a trip than to evaluate our unique purpose or meaning in life. Your work in other chapters may have increased your awareness of your patterns, your ways of being, and your roles in life. You may better understand yourself, your relationships, and the various life positions you have adopted. Now you have the opportunity to expand on all of this, to take a step back and envision who you are and who you truly, deeply want to be in the world.

When I was younger, I was both intrigued and confused by the likes of beauty pageants. I recall looking at the pretty women and wondering who they were behind the makeup and toothy smiles. I watched most attentively when the talent and interview portions arose. Even at a young age, I wondered why the participants seemed artificial and unnatural. I wanted to see real women I could understand and look up to, yet the banners the women wore told me nothing about the person inside. The budding psychologist in me wanted to know what was truth and what was illusion. I wanted to see what mattered most to me—the person's heart and soul.

It wasn't long before I learned that what mattered to me often didn't matter to others. Ever naïve, I was disappointed time and again when the actions of others were not what I hoped reality would be. Yet I ultimately realized that what mattered most was my own attitude—my focus on being a good and kind soul. So I eventually created my first "Miss Carla" banner—what I came to call a "life banner"—to gain my balance. It was a wise decision, for that invisible banner—a pledge to my higher self—helped me set my course in the right direction. In consciously creating my own banner, I became truer to my real self. Indeed, I was proud to wear and live my first banner. It wasn't perfect, but it suited me, for I am not perfect either. Of course, there were times when my banner got a bit muddied or frayed, yet one of the beauties of such a banner is that it is meant to be recreated again and again. My personal banner now reads: *I will strive every day to live my truth with courage, dignity, and respect for myself and others. I will ever be a dedicated and true wife, mother, friend, and helper. I will not be complacent and will give of myself and my resources to improve the world. I will be forgiving yet wise. I will do my utmost to put my essential qualities into action every day—embracing and living their essence both in private and in the greater world. In times of doubt and challenge, I will strive to let loving kindness be my guide.* I smile, knowing that my banner has always been—and always will be—a humble work in progress.

Your Life Banner

When you are in a safe, relaxed environment with your pen and journal by your side, pause to breathe. When you are ready to proceed, imagine your own life banner. Envision it as your own mission statement of sorts, one that you can hone and change as you change. If it is helpful, close your eyes and visualize the banner as if you wore it for all the world to see. Imagine a banner that you will be proud to wear day after day. Let the wise voice of constructive fear be your guide. Pause to breathe.

When you are ready, make notes in your journal that describe your personal banner. Breathe. Then study the words you have written. Imagine being able to actually bring these words into action during the course of your days. Remember, the idea is not to create a banner that you must embody every moment of every day; let your banner reflect the ideals you strive to embrace. Make changes to your personal life banner as you like. Breathe.

Now, on a separate page, write out—in as large a print as you like—your personal life banner. Whatever your banner contains, it holds your essence. Your work in this exercise has allowed constructive fear to guide you closer to your highest self. This is most beautiful. Well done.

Your life banner is your own work in progress. It may reflect your life goals, your values, and your moral code. Whatever your life banner contains, strive to make it come alive, to let it become more than words. As you strive to put your life banner into action every day, you will have true pride—humble, real pride—in your own being. Your self-esteem will grow through knowing you are proud of whatever you choose to make your own. You may find yourself being kind to coworkers and strangers alike. You may begin donating time or financial resources. You may use your personal power to create positive change where you can. You may become a more dedicated employee, boss, or coworker. You may be more respectful to your spouse, children, coworkers, and customers. You may be increasingly genuine and transparent—proud of your actions in public and private. You may become kinder and gentler—with yourself and with others. As you become one with your life banner, your actions in the outside world will mirror those at home and vice versa. As you live in this seamless, honest way, your life will continue to transform. Indeed, as you put the wisdom of constructive fear into action—making your life banner come alive—you will be walking with the power of transformational fear at your side.

Your life banner is more powerful than you might know; it holds the vital power of passion, power, integrity, and so much more. Indeed, your life banner may reflect your highest self. Whatever positive goals and qualities it represents for you, allow the power of your life banner to grow by keeping it front and center in your life. If complacency sets in, simply return to your life banner; let it fuel you into loving and attending to your highest self. Indeed, if it feels right to you, make a copy of your life banner to place in your wallet, your bedroom, or above your front door. Perhaps you will want to place a copy by your desk at work or on your laptop. Whatever you do, allow your life banner to become an active force in your life.

A Life Banner in Action: The True Story of Cramer

In preparing for this chapter, I considered using case studies, friends' stories, and even interviews with Navy SEALS and firefighters to highlight the importance of putting constructive fear—and one's life banner—into action. In the course of my research and outreach, the most perfect, true story came my way. It is shared with the full permission of the courageous, humble man who offered it to me. In the most fearless way, he shares his tale—including painfully intimate details—to light the way for others. Indeed, this fifty-six-year-old gentleman, Chief of Police Stephen Cramer, puts his life banner into action in the bravest of ways.

Cramer, as he likes to be called, has worked in law enforcement for nineteen years. A dedicated husband, Cramer has been married for twenty-three years to a wife he adores and cherishes. His blended family includes his wife's four children (whom he adopted), his two children, and one child of their own. A dedicated and loving father, Cramer is also the proud grandfather of eight. Actively involved with his children and his community, Cramer coached Pop Warner football, Little League, and Babe Ruth baseball for ten years. But Cramer didn't stop there. A believer in the power of education, Cramer has earned a bachelor of arts in public administration, a master of arts in leadership, a master of science in organizational development, and a juris doctorate. These accomplishments alone make Cramer an extraordinary man. Yet there is more to Cramer than all of this. Cramer is a six-time cancer survivor. Shunning both sympathy and accolades, Cramer shares his story, below, as a guiding light.

"I have battled throat cancer—squamous cell carcinoma—on and off for over seven years. From the moment I was diagnosed, I wanted to face my journey with humor and courage. I decided to treat this disease as 'vanilla cancer'—not letting it take my spirit away. As I have never smoked tobacco and am free of HPV, my oncologist determined that my cancer was environmental in nature. Several years ago, I underwent three months of chemotherapy and thirty-six rounds of radiation. The cancer returned two years later, resulting in a radical right-side tonsillectomy. Three years later, I underwent an eighteen-hour neck dissection; the doctors removed the right side of my throat and twenty percent of the back of my tongue. Surgeons sewed a thigh muscle into my throat to protect the area and allow me to continue swallowing and eating normally. The cancer spread, and my thyroid was removed that summer. The cancer returned thirty months later. This led to the removal of my lymph nodes and left tonsil. I underwent a second eighteen-hour neck dissection that August; the left side of my throat and my vocal cords were removed. The surgeons sewed a second thigh muscle into my throat and created a new esophagus for me to continue swallowing and eating normally. I now breathe out of a stoma. An extended nine-month medical leave from work was required due to three additional throat cancer surgeries and three rounds of chemotherapy. During this time, I became acclimated to using a tracheoesophageal voice prosthesis (TEP) implant. I made it through each hurdle by focusing on healing and returning to my regular life and my work. With the support of city managers and the city council, I am thrilled to finally have returned to the career I love—the work that allows me to contribute to my agency and community. I believe I am the first police chief in the nation to work with a TEP and am grateful to be accepted back in my profession with my new communication abilities. There is much on the horizon, including the once-in-a-lifetime opportunity of taking the lead on planning and designing our new police facility. Those who know me are aware that my personality, work ethic, and work product remain the same; only my voice has changed.

"In truth, I would not have survived my journey without the love and support of my beautiful wife, Tami, and my seven children. Tami, the centerpiece of my life, has been my sole caregiver over seven years and six surgeries. She has been with me through every medical appointment, ER visit, chemotherapy infusion, surgery, and hospital stay. Tami transitioned from wife to caregiver, sacrificing her own career goals until I recovered. She pushed me to be a better man, and we are stronger as a couple as a result of our journey. Tami is the cornerstone of a marriage well-cultivated and a family sculpted with hard work, dedication, and love.

"I know how fortunate I am. My profession expects me to look behind the blinds and exposes me to the horrors of humanity. All that I see makes me more aware of my blessings in life. Other paths could have brought roadblocks to hinder my personal goals and life ambitions, yet I was lucky to have a path that bestowed so much goodness on me and my family. Yes, I have battled cancer. I am fortunate, though, to have been given abundant acceptance and support. I truly believe that I survived my cancer journey because I still have much to offer my family, my agency, and my community.

"Today, I consider myself the luckiest man on the face of the Earth. I cuffed cancer, and I'm back to work. I have the support of my wife, my family, my coworkers, and my community. I have so much more to accomplish, both professionally and personally. I look forward with anticipation to my children's achievements, three more weddings, and countless more grandchildren. I look forward to the next chapters in my life, from breaking ground on our new police facility to earning a second doctorate degree. I am a survivor, a living example of what people can endure when backed by courage, perseverance, and love. In his book, *Man's Search for Meaning*,[3] Holocaust survivor Viktor Frankl wrote, 'Everything can be taken from a man but one thing: the last of human freedoms—to choose one's attitude in any given set of circumstances, to choose one's own way.'"[4]

Cramer's story reveals the power of a positive attitude brimming with faith, gratitude, and love. His tale is also a testament to a courageous life journey filled with passion and purpose. Cramer has found great meaning in life through marriage, family, vocation, community, and giving back through volunteering. He has crafted a beautiful life filled with love and courage in action. In asking Cramer to share the contents of his life banner, he noted that he'd never actually given thought to this concept; he simply lived in accord with his beliefs and life goals. As a result, Cramer's

Life Banner formally came into being: *I am a focused and dedicated man. I believe in the value of family, community, education, and hard work. Every day, I strive to give my best self to my wife, children, coworkers, and community. I honor the power of humor, loyalty, truth, courage, and perseverance. I believe in striving every day to be a better man and a better human being.*

Cramer moved a step beyond sharing a story that reveals both significant challenges and successes. Unexpectedly, Cramer also chose to share his three greatest fears. To share such fears—to be so very vulnerable—is an act of courage and humility. Prepare your heart and mind for Cramer's honesty as he reveals his three greatest fears:

"1. Fear of intimacy/performance: I hope this does not make you uncomfortable; it is certainly meant with no disrespect. During the course of my seven-year battle with cancer, my body has undergone significant trauma—from multiple surgeries to rounds of chemotherapy and radiation. The result has been a slow 'disintegration' of my virility, libido, and sex drive. For sixteen years, my wife and I had a consistently phenomenal sex life. Now I am limited in my 'abilities,' physical positioning, and stamina. My wife has been remarkably accepting of this change in our sex life, but it weighs on me. My fear is that I am no longer able to 'satisfy' my partner as I did seamlessly prior to cancer.

"2. Fear of professional acceptance: Since August of last year, I have been unable to speak normally due to cancer-related surgeries and have transitioned through different modes of communication, from a handheld electrolarynx device and a keyboard speaker system to a surgically implanted TEP. Much was required of me to assure city administrators that I could still perform my duties as police chief. I am monitored and evaluated to ascertain if I can consistently communicate with coworkers, community members, and city leaders. I know I can fulfill my myriad responsibilities successfully and do not see my condition as a disability, but not everyone shares this view. I have worked hard to return to my profession after my medical leave, yet the fear of losing my career has been at the forefront of my mind.

"3. Fear of another cancer recurrence: Being a six-time cancer survivor is an incredible achievement on its face, yet the reality has been exhausting and irritating. Each time I beat cancer, I was in remission for approximately two years. I am determined to fight this disease with every cell in my body, but it takes a toll each time it returns. There was a two-week period last autumn when I thought I would succumb to the disease. I wasn't able to take my liquid nutrition, slept nearly day and night, and was weak. Before that time, I had never had thoughts that I wouldn't survive. That period scared the hell out of me. I had to face the fact that I might not have more time with my family—more time to enjoy life. My fear revolves around another cancer recurrence in my throat area where I have nothing left to remove. The surgeries, the infusions, the MRIs, the feeding tube—it can be terrifying to stare at the mountain knowing I may have to traverse the rugged terrain again."[5]

You have Cramer's honest fears before you. They are human fears that most every person can understand. His first fear cuts to the heart of intimate sexual connection. It also reveals the very human fear of not being good enough—not being worthy or capable in a loved one's eyes. Cramer's second fear, the fear of not being accepted back into his chosen vocation, again goes directly to a core human need of acceptance. This also speaks to the basic fear of not being found worthy or capable. Finally, Cramer's third fear tells of his battle with death. Although he refuses to give in, he is afraid of losing his life. Death and loss are undeniable facts of life, but this does not make them any less feared or any easier to accept. From the day a person is born, these fears are alive. Indeed, these fears are so very human. Spoken or unspoken, they live within each of us.

Cramer's story offers a glimpse into the life of a courageous, dedicated man. His tale reveals his humanness and the profound beauty of a life banner not consciously conceived yet put into daily action. Cramer's honesty also allows a soulful, poignant look into the heart of fear. Constructive fear gave Cramer the courage to acknowledge, explore, and reveal his fears; destructive fear would have had him pretend they did not exist. By acknowledging and sharing his deepest fears, Cramer offered both his truth and his vulnerability. Through this journey, Cramer freed himself from self-isolation. Cramer's courage in facing destructive fear allows others to share in his pilgrimage. It allows loved ones near and far to offer their support. Cramer's offering also provides a deeply connective element—the truth that every human does, in some way, share his fears.

In the end, the journey with core fears is essentially the same for each one of us. Core fears are an element of the human condition. If core fears are ignored, they still exist—festering in the dark, silent grip of destructive fear. Yet if such fears are made conscious, revealed, and brought into the light through constructive fear, awareness and love can soothe and even heal them. This makes the journey—wherever it may lead—not quite so dark and solitary. Through all of this, transformational fear waits as your ally, giving you the strength to forge ahead.

Spirituality, Faith, and Interconnection

Throughout this book, we have explored many vital elements of well-being, from biological and psychological components to social issues. During your reading, you may have noticed an undercurrent of spirituality. This would make sense in that I am a deeply spiritual person. You may also be quite spiritual in some way or another. Indeed, spirituality can manifest in countless ways, such as involvement with a specific religion, meditation, prayer, family connection, the cathedral of nature, or creative pursuits. The essence of spirituality is the sense that one is not alone—that one is connected to someone, something, or some power beyond the self. In this way, deep spirituality can offer reassurance. It can soothe the worried soul. Constructive fear might say, "Even with all your real and manufactured fears, you will ultimately be okay. Life will bring you suffering, loss, and pain. It will also bring you joy and love. Through all of this, you are never alone. You are connected and intertwined with love and life itself." Spirituality can give us great faith that allows us to move through our fears with awareness. Spirituality and the faith it brings can give humanity the power to face fear and use it to learn, grow, and ultimately transform.

One important aspect of spirituality is its ability to provide support and connection. Although not all spiritual practices are social in nature, some—such as religious services, group meditation, and certain yoga classes—have the potential to offer a sense of community and caring support. Given that humans are tribal in nature, the need to interact with others is ingrained in our very genetic makeup. A lack of social connection can lead to a very primitive, aching sense of vulnerability. When desired social connection is absent, feelings of being unwanted and unloved commonly arise. Research shows that feelings of isolation can be damaging to psychological and physical health. Indeed, one study revealed that a lack of social connection can be as damaging to one's health as smoking fifteen cigarettes every day.[6]

It is important to note that it's not the number of friends that matters; the key seems to be an individual's personal sense of having others to turn to for true support and connection. For some who are more solitary by nature, one or two close connections and occasional contact may be sufficient. Others may prefer a larger number of friends and more connective time. The quality of contact and a sense of being valued are critical. An individual will suffer physically and psychologically when feelings of loneliness and isolation are ignored, for we are communal creatures.

Having a sense of community and interconnection is a fundamental requirement for overall well-being. Despite growing awareness of this significant issue, reported rates of loneliness continue to rise.[7] This issue does not affect only the elderly or disenfranchised; many individuals across all demographics suffer in silent isolation. The issue of loneliness is a global one with wide-reaching effects, but connecting people with each other is both vital and doable. Where one lonely person waits in hurt and fearful silence, there is another corresponding soul to provide time and companionship. Destructive fear would have you turn a cold, blind eye to such issues. Constructive fear would ask you to pause with compassion, and then transformational fear would ask you to move forward—to take action to transform your life as you transform the lives of others. Indeed, by tending to the loneliness of others, you will tend to your own soul.

This truth provides incredible opportunity on a win-win basis. When an individual turns spare resources to help others, that person's own well-being benefits on several levels. By reaching out to support and help others, new social connections are automatically formed. Time spent giving to others also increases one's sense of purpose and meaning in life. It can be incredibly fulfilling to know that one's actions make a difference. Being a volunteer—as a participant or leader—can increase one's sense of self-worth. Great joy and connection can be found through giving of the self.

Your experience of spiritual connection—your sense of being part of the true essence of life—may increase as you engage in connective actions. Indeed, a lasting sense of spirituality can be vital for one's well-being. Given the abundant nature of life, there are many different paths to establishing and expressing one's personal spiritual identity. For some, organized religion of one form or another may be optimal. For others, a blend of practices may enliven the connection to self, others, and a divine power. Increasing one's spiritual life can result simply from slowing down and becoming more attentive to one's moral code, life duties, and responsibilities. Indeed, spiritual connection can be increased through volunteer efforts and charitable contributions. Whether through formal meditation or by bringing a meditative quality to daily rituals, a sense of non-distracted presence can promote spiritual connection. Spending time in nature—whether walking, hiking, gardening, or sitting—can offer a truly spiritual experience. Indeed, solitary and contemplative periods are necessary for both restoration and spiritual connection. Spirituality can be accessed by noticing beauty and magic in the world in a way that appreciates the simplest treasures—a child's smile, a flower, a beloved's kiss, and the humanity within a tear. Spirituality turns inward for discovery, not seeking meaning through ownership of material things. Daily life itself can become a deeply spiritual experience. In truth, an individual who ever strives to be the best version of the self may—in that striving alone—be living a deeply spiritual life. Spirituality can certainly increase one's sense of having purpose, connection, and meaning. In taking one's unique spirituality seriously, one can learn more about the self and existence as a whole. This next exercise will offer you the opportunity to explore your own relationship with spirituality. It's yours to create, experience, and live.

A Spirituality of Your Own

As you move into this exercise, ensure that you feel safe and relaxed, both physically and psychologically. With your pen and journal by your side, pause to breathe. Consider what spirituality means to you. If you wish, close your eyes to envision your personal image of spirituality. When you are ready, write out your unique definition of spirituality—using whatever thoughts and images come into your mind. For example, you might find yourself sketching an image of your higher power. You may be drawn to write a few paragraphs or a few simple words. When you are finished, pause to breathe.

Next, imagine ways to cultivate or deepen your spiritual life. For example, you may already have a spiritual practice such as going to church, yet you may wish to deepen your practice through reading or by attending church groups. As your spiritual practice may not involve organized religion, you might imagine many other ways to enliven your spiritual life. When you are ready, write out nine actionable ways that you can enrich your spiritual journey. As examples, your actionable goals might note:

- I will meditate every evening for ten minutes.
- I will visit a space in nature for quiet contemplation one Saturday a month.

- I will garden without distractions, using the time for self-reflection.
- I will wake five minutes early every morning to sit in quiet with a cup of tea.
- I will brush my dog every Sunday, taking the time to be mindful and loving.
- I will be more present when I attend religious services.
- I will volunteer at the local soup kitchen one evening a week.
- I will take out my elderly neighbor's trash.
- I will read in quiet for one hour every Thursday evening.

Destructive fear might try to impede your progress, for it wants you to be wary of spirituality. Listen for the wise, assuring voice of constructive fear; it wants you to know that your spirituality is unique and boundless. Feel free to be imaginative, for spirituality thrives in the realm of creativity. When you are finished, pause to breathe. Well done. Transformational fear will give you the power to bring your goals into action. By increasing your spiritual connection, you will increase your connection to yourself and the world around you.

Goals, Choices, and Commitment

As your journey with me concludes, imagine the many ways you can turn your energy toward actively creating a joyful life of wellness. By applying the concept of wellness to your endeavors, you will continue to create a more optimal lifestyle that recognizes your potential and encourages you to fulfill it. As you reach toward the greater world, allow yourself to offer others this same gift—the ability to help others see and build upon their strengths. Do not let destructive fear deceive you into believing that your singular life does not matter. Let constructive fear tell you the truth. Every action you take has one of three outcomes: (1) goodness; (2) harm; (3) nothingness. This is where your life can make a radical difference. By consistently doing your best to choose option one—to strive for goodness—you have the power to truly transform your world.

As you move forward, you may choose to apply the skills you have learned to increase your global sense of well-being. Indeed, there are areas of wellness that the specifics of our work have left untouched. You can utilize what you have learned to view your life through the lens of transformational fear. Embrace this power. Use the awareness of destructive fear to guide you into hearing the wisdom of constructive fear. As you become active in steadily addressing the imbalanced or unhealthy areas of your life, your world cannot help but transform.

For example, you may turn your efforts toward bringing your financial world into greater balance—doing your utmost not to spend more than you have or accumulate more than you need. Indeed, overconsumption not only harms our environment but also leads to having more material items to care for, which can bring additional stress. Strive for balance in your financial world both literally and figuratively, ensuring that the pursuit of money does not negatively affect your attitude, life, or soul. When possible, give to others—using the resources of time or finances to model a healthy, balanced approach.

You may turn your efforts toward environmental wellness, striving to live in a way that is respectful of the natural world and your daily surroundings. You may decide to take action to protect your environment, whether through taking shorter showers, cleaning up a beach, or being diligent with recycling. Resist destructive fear's persistent voice as it tells you that your running faucet or other wastefulness make no difference. Constructive fear would remind you that small changes can have incredible, cumulative positive impact. When you translate your conscious awareness into action, transformation of the environment will result.

Of course, continued growth can also be found in the realms of intellectual and occupational pursuits. Strive to keep these areas of your life alive and in balance. Allow your mind to be continually challenged with new ideas and experiences, whether through continued education or social and cultural activities. Engage in a variety of stimulating mental activities, whether taking up a foreign language, art class, or other new adventures. Encourage an attitude of openness with the ever-curious nature of a child. Bring this energy into your workplace, infusing your work with new ideas, passion, and creativity. Strive to enrich your workplace and endeavor to be part of a work world that also enriches you. Destructive fear would have you settle for less than you can be. Let constructive fear remind you that you are amazing, with capacities that you may not yet know you have. You will only discover and fulfill these capacities by spreading your wings—by becoming active with the force of transformational fear driving you forward.

You may choose to enliven your sense of activism, working to improve your community and the world at large. Your sphere of influence may be small or large, but it is an important sphere regardless of its size. It often feels most fulfilling to put effort into areas where you can see and even feel the impact. For example, a woman I know, Mina, has taken a firm stand against gun violence. Mina did not stop at writing letters, signing petitions, and marching in rallies. Facing resistance from both her husband and three sons, she took her activism one step further—and one step closer—by ensuring that violent video games and violent movies were unavailable in her home. In this way, she not only took a stand against gun violence within her community, she also took a stand against violent behavior in her own home world. Shored up by her actions, several other parents made similar changes in their own homes. By bringing her activism into her home life, Mina changed the world for her children and other families, too. Like Mina, your sphere of influence may be larger than you think. Whatever you find worth putting your efforts behind, do it—and live it.

Your Life Goals—Increasing Meaning and Purpose

This exercise will help you ascertain and evaluate your personal life goals, to breathe greater life and purpose into certain areas of your life. As you proceed, strive for an attitude of nonjudgment, for there are no "right" or "wrong" responses. Remember that destructive fear may step in to circumvent your progress. Allow constructive fear to guide you forward with gentle wisdom. Use these exercises as an opportunity for honest self-reflection, knowing that you can adjust or update your responses at any time. As you change and evolve in life, your goals may change. In some ways, your values and moral code may also change over time. As such, use this phase of your work as a starting place. Allow it to be a simple reference tool during your continued journey.

As always, ensure that you feel physically and psychologically ready to proceed. When you are in a safe, relaxed space with your pen and journal by your side, pause to breathe. In these exercises, you will be taking a general look at your life goals, gently bringing your desires into greater focus.

First, write out a list of your major life goals. Your list can be as short or long as you choose. Below each item, leave a few spaces for notes. For example, you might note:

1. I would like to change careers and become a nurse.
2. I would like to own a home someday.
3. I want to find a good partner and get married.

Pause to breathe. Below each major goal, write out at least three specific micro-goals with actionable clarity (e.g., dates). For example, the first goal noted above might be followed by notes such as this:

- I will begin looking at various nursing programs as of this weekend.
- I will immediately work on revamping my budget to save money toward school.
- By the end of this month, I will begin a search for nursing scholarships.

Follow this same process for each one of your major life goals. Pause to breathe. Well done.

Next, list your ten-year goals, leaving space under each item for your micro-goals. Be as creative as you like, listing as many goals as you find meaningful. For example, you might note: *I want to own my own e-commerce business. I want to visit Australia. I want to build a cabin. I want to adopt a child.* Following each ten-year goal, list at least three specific micro-goals with actionable clarity (e.g., dates). Pause to breathe.

Follow this same procedure for your five-year goals; leave space under each item for your additional micro-goals. Be creative, allowing yourself to home in on creating greater purpose in your life. You might note: *I want to return to school to obtain my master's degree. I would like to skydive. I want to own my own car. I would like to have a dog.* Following each five-year goal, list at least three specific micro-goals with actionable clarity (e.g., dates). Pause to breathe.

Next, list your one-year goals following the same procedure. Leave space under each goal for your micro-goals. For example, you might note: *I want to go on a dating website. I want to plant a garden. I want to learn to play the guitar. I want to volunteer at an elderly care facility. I want to donate money every month to my favorite charity. I want to buy fewer unnecessary products. I want to take a three-week vacation.* Following each one-year goal, outline at least three specific, actionable micro-goals. Be as clear and detailed as possible. Pause to breathe.

Finally, follow this same procedure for your six-month goals, leaving space under each item for your additional micro-goals. Be creative, allowing yourself to consider goals that are achievable in the shorter term. Ponder goals that would give your life a greater sense of ease, joy, and meaning. The goals need not be grand—they can be simple and pure. For example, you might note: *I want to walk my dog every evening after work. I want to visit my parents within the month. I want to do better at drinking water during the day. I want to volunteer at the animal shelter one day a week. I want to read my son bedtime stories every night.* Following each six-month goal, list at least three specific micro-goals with actionable clarity (e.g., dates). Pause to breathe.

Well done. In completing this exercise, you have taken another step toward creating the life that you desire. As you take steady, active steps to fulfilling your goals, your life will become more beautiful. Remember, you might not see progress as quickly as you might like, but trust that your steady efforts will pay off. Before you know it, you will have achieved your six-month goals. Soon after that, the completion of your one-year goals will be a source of personal pride. Achievement of your other goals will follow in time. In this way, you will continue to create a life that is filled with joy, love, meaning, and purpose. This will be no accident; it will be due to your diligent, loving efforts. You will do all of this—and so much more—with the wise power of transformational fear.

Sweet Choice: We Are as We Choose to Be

Y ou may now realize that a life well-lived serves the self yet also the greater good. You need not be a version of Cramer nor Mother Teresa. All that is required is that you live each day striving toward becoming your higher self. I knew a soul like this, a woman so passionate and filled with love that she wanted to rescue life itself. Reading braille and with a cane at her side, she excelled in college. With courage, she made it through her too-short life suffering from a multitude of issues, including blindness. Her goal was to become an activist for women, to protect those who could not fend for themselves. And though her heart gave out while she was in law school, the effects of her passion and love live on within me. Her brief life is a testament to the extraordinary power of a life geared toward becoming one's highest self.

You have this same extraordinary power within you. You now know yourself better. You now know love and life just a little bit more. You know the power of destructive fear, you know the light of constructive fear, and you know the strong, positive force of transformational fear. You can never not know what you now know. What has been inscribed in your heart, soul, body, and mind is with you forever. The choice is yours. You can let destructive fear hold you back, or you can choose another path. You can take the awareness you gain from constructive fear, put it into action, and change your world with the power of transformational fear.

Thank you for allowing me to be with you during your journey. Thank you for the opportunity to be a small lantern—a light of faith and love. It is truly my honor and privilege to have been at your side through this process. May you ever continue your wise and courageous journey with transformational fear. May you be blessed with faith, love, and peace. May you create Joy from Fear.

Your friend,
CARLA MARIE MANLY

NOTES

Introduction

1. Descartes, R., & Williams, B. (1996). Meditation VI. *Descartes: Meditations on first philosophy: with selections from the objections and replies* (Cambridge Texts in the History of Philosophy) (J. Cottingham, Ed.). Cambridge, UK: Cambridge University Press.

2. Thoreau, H. D. (September 7, 1851). Journal entry.

Chapter 1

1. Anxiety and Depression Association of America. (n.d.). About ADAA: Facts and statistics. Retrieved January 30, 2018, from https://adaa.org/about-adaa/press-room/facts-statistics#.

2. National Institute of Mental Health. (2017). Statistics: Any anxiety disorder. Retrieved February 17, 2018, from https://www.nimh.nih.gov/health/statistics/any-anxiety-disorder.shtml.

3. Novotney, Amy. (July/August 2015). Are preschoolers being overmedicated? *Monitor on Psychology, 46*(7), 64–7. http://www.apa.org/monitor/2015/07-08/preschoolers.aspx.

4. Smith, B. L. (June 2012). Inappropriate prescribing. *Monitor on Psychology, 43*(6), 36–40. http://www.apa.org/monitor/2012/06/prescribing.aspx.

5. National Institute of Health. (Last updated August 21, 2018). What is pharmacogenomics? National Library of Medicine. Retrieved June 25, 2017, from https://ghr.nlm.nih.gov/primer/genomicresearch/pharmacogenomics.

   Scott, S. (December 2011). Personalizing medicine with clinical pharmacogenetics. *Genetics in Medicine 13*(12): 987–95. https://www.ncbi.nlm.nih.gov/pmc/articles/PMC3290900/.

6. Clay, R. A. (September 2011). Advocating for psychotherapy. *Monitor on Psychology, 42*(8), 48. http://www.apa.org/monitor/2011/09/psychotherapy.aspx.

7. Goodheart, C. D. (2011). Psychology practice: Design for tomorrow. *American Psychologist, 66*(5), 339–47.

8. Smith, Inappropriate prescribing.

9. Greenberg, P. E., Sisitsky, T., Kessler, R. C., Finkelstein, S. N., Berndt, E. R., Davidson, J. R. T., Ballenger, J. C., & Fyer, A. J. (July 1999). The economic burden of anxiety disorders in the 1990s. *Journal of Clinical Psychiatry, 60*(7), 427–35. http://www.psychiatrist.com/jcp/article/pages/1999/v60n07/v60n0702.aspx.

10. Smith, Inappropriate prescribing.

11. Pratt, L. A., Brody, D. J., & Gu, Q. (August 2017). Antidepressant use among persons aged 12 and over: United States, 2011–2014. NCHS Data Brief No. 283. Centers for Disease Control. https://www.cdc.gov/nchs/products/databriefs/db283.htm.

12. Smith, Inappropriate prescribing.

13. Ibid.

14. Psyche, (n.). (n.d.). Online Etymology Dictionary. https://www.etymonline.com/word/psyche.

15. Moore, Thomas. (August 7, 2001). *The original self: Living with paradox and originality.* New York: HarperCollins Publishers.

Chapter 2

1. American Psychological Association. (n.d.). Stress effects on the body: Musculoskeletal system. http://www.apa.org/helpcenter/stress-body.aspx.

Chapter 3

1. American Psychiatric Association. (2013). *Diagnostic and statistical manual of mental disorders* (5th ed.). Arlington, VA: American Psychiatric Publishing.

   National Center for PTSD. (Last updated February 22, 2018). PTSD and *DSM-5.* US Department of Veterans Affairs. https://www.ptsd.va.gov/professional/ptsd-overview/dsm5_criteria_ptsd.asp.

2. American Psychiatric Association, *Diagnostic and statistical manual of mental disorders* (5th ed.).

National Center for PTSD, PTSD and *DSM-5.*

3. The National Institute of Mental Health. (Last updated November 2017). Statistics: Post-traumatic stress disorder (PTSD). Retrieved February 4, 2018, from https://www.nimh.nih.gov/health/statistics/post-traumatic-stress-disorder-ptsd.shtml.

4. The Nebraska Department of Veterans' Affairs. (n.d.). Post traumatic stress disorder. Retrieved February 4, 2018, from http://www.ptsd.ne.gov/what-is-ptsd.html.

5. Ibid.

6. Child Mind Institute. (2016). Children's mental health report. Retrieved January 31, 2018, from https://childmind.org/2015-childrens-mental-health-report/.

   (If needed, the download page for the full report is https://childmind.org/download-document/?document=cmhr_2015.)

7. Van der Kolk, B. A. (1994). The body keeps the score: Memory and the evolving psychobiology of post traumatic stress. *Harvard Review of Psychiatry, 1*(5), 253–65.

Online version retrieved February 28, 2009, from http://www.trauma-pages.com/a/vanderk4.php.

Van der Kolk, B. A., & Fisler, R. (1995). Dissociation and the fragmentary nature of traumatic memories: Overview and exploratory study. *Journal of Traumatic Stress, 8*(4), 505–25. Abstract retrieved June 23, 2009, from http://www.trauma-pages.com/a/vanderk2.php.

Van der Kolk, B., Pelcovitz, D., Roth, S., Mandel, F. S., McFarlane, A., & Herman, J. L. (1996). Dissociation, affect dysregulation & somatization: The complex nature of adaptation to trauma. *American Journal of Psychiatry, 153*(7), Festschrift Supplement, 83–93. Abstract retrieved June 23, 2009, from http://www.trauma-pages.com/a/vanderk5.php.

Schore, A. N. (2001). The effects of a secure attachment relationship on right brain development, affect regulation, and infant mental health. *Infant Journal of Mental Health, 22*, 7–66. Abstract retrieved June 23, 2009, from http://www.trauma-pages.com/a/schore-2001a.php.

Schore, A. N. (2001). The effects of early relational trauma on right brain development, affect regulation, and infant mental health. *Infant Journal of Mental Health, 22*, 201–69. Abstract retrieved June 23, 2009, from http://www.trauma-pages.com/a/schore-2001b.php.

Schore, A. N. (2002). Dysregulation of the right brain: A fundamental mechanism of traumatic attachment and the psychopathogenesis of posttraumatic stress disorder. *Australian and New Zealand Journal of Psychiatry, 36*, 9–30. Abstract retrieved June 23, 2009, from http://www.trauma-pages.com/a/schore-2002.php.

8. Schore, The effects of a secure attachment relationship on right brain development, affect regulation, and infant mental health.

Schore, The effects of early relational trauma on right brain development, affect regulation, and infant mental health.

Schore, Dysregulation of the right brain.

9. Jack, R. E., Garrod, O. G. B., & Schyns, P. G. (January 20, 2014). Dynamic facial expressions of emotion transmit an evolving hierarchy of signals over time. *Current Biology, 24*(2), 187–92. Abstract retrieved from https://www.cell.com/current-biology/fulltext/S0960-9822(13)01519-4.

10. Cowen, A. S. & Keltner, D. (September 5, 2017). Self-report captures 27 distinct categories of emotion bridged by continuous gradients. *Proceedings of the National Academy of Sciences.* Abstract retrieved from http://www.pnas.org/content/early/2017/08/30/1702247114.

11. Plutchik, R. (January 1, 1980). *Emotion: A psychoevolutionary synthesis.* New York: Harper & Row.

12. Love is not included in the list of basic emotions because it arises from joy (or happiness). Love is experienced when the emotion of joy is connected to a person or object through experience. In essence, we learn to feel love or loving feelings when we connect the positive emotional state of joy to someone or something. For example, the experience of falling in love results from the wonderful, feel-good sensations that arise when joy occurs as a result of pleasurable sensations and experiences connected to a certain person.

13. Cozolino, L. (2002). *The neuroscience of psychotherapy: Healing the social brain*. New York: W. W. Norton & Company.

14. Ibid.

15. Ibid.

Chapter 4

1. Centers for Disease Control. (Last updated March 29, 2018). Alcohol and public health: Frequently asked questions. Retrieved January 15, 2018, from https://www.cdc.gov/alcohol/faqs.htm.

   Wood, A. M., Kaptoge, S., Butterworth, A. S., Willeit, P., Warnakula, S., Bolton, T., Paige, E., et al. (April 14, 2018). Risk thresholds for alcohol consumption: combined analysis of individual-participant data for 599,912 current drinkers in 83 prospective studies. *The Lancet, 391*(1012), 1513–23. https://www.thelancet.com/journals/lancet/article/PIIS0140-6736(18)30134-X/fulltext.

2. Esselstyn Jr., C. B. (January 31, 2008). Prevent and reverse heart disease: The revolutionary, scientifically proven, nutrition-based cure. New York: Penguin Group. First trade paperback edition 2008; original work published 2007.

3. American Heart Association. (November 13, 2017). Plant based diet associated with less heart failure risk. American Heart Association Meeting Report Poster Presentation M2081—Session LB.APS.10. Retrieved February 24, 2018, from https://newsroom.heart.org/news/plant-based-diet-associated-with-less-heart-failure-risk.

4. Research shows that 6 to 9 percent of households don't have access to healthy foods. While healthy food may seem like an impossibility to those in poverty or living in a food desert, this research also means that 91 to 94 percent of Americans *do* have access to healthy foods. In fact, a 2013 study found that healthy diets cost approximately $1.50 per day more than less-healthy diets.

   Bell, J., Mora, G., Hagan, E., Rubin, V., & Karpyn, A. (2013). Access to healthy foods and why it matters: a review of the research. PolicyLink: The Food Trust. Retrieved January 19, 2018, from http://thefoodtrust.org/uploads/media_items/access-to-healthy-food.original.pdf.

Rao, M., Afshin, A., Singh, G., & Mozaffarian, D. (Published online December 4, 2013). Do healthier foods and diet patterns costs more than less healthy options? A systematic review and meta-analysis. *BMJ Open*, *3*(12), e004277. Retrieved February 23, 2018, from https://www.ncbi.nlm.nih.gov/pmc/articles/PMC3855594/.

5. Centers for Disease Control. (Last updated February 16, 2016). 1 in 3 adults don't get enough sleep: A good night's sleep is critical for good health. Retrieved January 31, 2018, from https://www.cdc.gov/media/releases/2016/p0215-enough-sleep.html.

6. Harvard Health Publishing. (January 2006). Importance of sleep: Six reasons not to scrimp on sleep. Harvard Medical School. Retrieved February 5, 2018, from https://www.health.harvard.edu/press_releases/importance_of_sleep_and_health.

7. National Heart, Lung, and Blood Institute (NHLBI). (n.d.). Sleep deprivation and deficiency: Why is sleep important? Retrieved February 24, 2018, from https://www.nhlbi.nih.gov/node/4605.

    Centers for Disease Control, 1 in 3 adults don't get enough sleep.

8. Division of Sleep Medicine at Harvard Medical School. (Last reviewed December 18, 2007). Sleep, learning, and memory. Retrieved February 24, 2018, from http://healthysleep.med.harvard.edu/healthy/matters/benefits-of-sleep/learning-memory.

9. National Heart, Lung, and Blood Institute, Sleep deprivation and deficiency.

10. Nett, Stephen. (May 17, 2018). A prescription for better health: Go outside. *The Press Democrat*. Retrieved May 21, 2018, from http://www.pressdemocrat.com/lifestyle/8326921-181/a-prescription-for-better-health.

    Godman, H. (April 9, 2014). Regular exercise changes the brain to improve memory, thinking skills. *Harvard Health Blog*. Retrieved January 31, 2018, from https://www.health.harvard.edu/blog/regular-exercise-changes-brain-improve-memory-thinking-skills-201404097110.

    According to the US Department of Health & Human Services, a mere one-third of adults engage in the recommended amount of physical activity (e.g., 150 minutes per week of moderate exercise such as brisk walking). Less than 5 percent of adults engage in 30 minutes of exercise on a daily basis. Only one-third of children exercise every day, yet the average child spends more than 7.5 hours per day watching television, playing a video game, or sitting at the computer. As noted, this is more time than many children spend getting growth-supporting, restorative sleep.

    Centers for Disease Control, 1 in 3 adults don't get enough sleep.

    US Department of Health & Human Services. (Last reviewed January 26, 2017). Facts & statistics: Physical activity. President's Council on Fitness, Sports,

& Nutrition. Retrieved January 31, 2018, from https://www.hhs.gov/fitness/
resource-center/facts-and-statistics/index.html.

Rideout, V. (2015). The Common Sense Census: Media use by tweens and
teens. Common Sense Media. Retrieved February 3, 2018, from https://www.
commonsensemedia.org/sites/default/files/uploads/research/census_executive-
summary.pdf.

11. US Department of Health & Human Services, Facts & statistics: Physical activity.

12. Godman, Regular exercise changes the brain to improve memory, thinking skills.

13. Ibid.

14. Weir, K. (December 2011). The exercise effect. *Monitor on Psychology, 42*(11), 48.
Retrieved January 11, 2018, from http://www.apa.org/monitor/2011/12/exercise.
aspx.

15. Mish, F., et al. (Eds.). (1983). *Webster's ninth new collegiate dictionary.*
Springfield, MA: Merriam-Webster Inc.

Esteemed (adj.). (n.d.). Online Etymology Dictionary. https://www.etymon-
line.com/word/esteemed.

16. Gračanin, A., Bylsma, L. M., & Vingerhoets, A. J. J. M. (May 28, 2014). Is crying a
self-soothing behavior? *Frontiers in Psychology, 5*(502). Retrieved January 4, 2018,
from https://www.ncbi.nlm.nih.gov/pmc/articles/PMC4035568/.

17. Clay, R. A. (January 2011). Stressed in America. *Monitor on Psychology, 42*(1),
58–63. http://www.apa.org/monitor/2011/01/stressed-america.aspx.

18. Ibid.

19. Ibid.

American Psychological Association, Stress effects on the body:
Musculoskeletal system.

Cozolino, The neuroscience of psychotherapy.

Bernstein, R. (July 25, 2016). The mind and mental health: How stress affects
the brain. Retrieved January 31, 2018, from http://www.tuw.edu/content/health/
how-stress-affects-the-brain/.

Chapter 5

1. Hillman, J., & Ventura, M. (1993). We've had a hundred years of psychotherapy—
and the world's getting worse. San Francisco: HarperOne.

2. Jebb, A. T., Tay, L., Diener, E., & Oishi, S. (January 8, 2018). Happiness, income
satiation and turning points around the world. *Nature Human Behaviour,*
2, 33–8. Retrieved January 23, 2018, from https://www.nature.com/articles/
s41562-017-0277-0.

The exact dollar amount varies by country and city. For example, $75,000 per year is generally considered sufficient to afford well-being to those who live in North America. More information can be found here: https://www.realclear-science.com/articles/2018/02/15/how_much_money_does_it_take_to_be_happy_110551.html.

Chapter 6

1. American Academy of Pediatrics. (Last updated November 21, 2015). Stresses of single parenting. Healthy Children.org. Retrieved May 30, 2018, from https://www.healthychildren.org/English/family-life/family-dynamics/types-of-families/Pages/Stresses-of-Single-Parenting.aspx.

According to the 2016 US Census, two-parent families now comprise 69 percent of households with children under the age of eighteen; the period between 1960 and 2016 saw a drop from 88 to 69 percent in the number of dual-parent families. (United States Census Bureau Newsroom. [November 17, 2016]. The majority of children live with two parents, census reports. Retrieved February 11, 2018, at https://www.census.gov/newsroom/press-releases/2016/cb16-192.html.)

2. The National Institute of Mental Health, Statistics: Any anxiety disorder.

NIMH notes that "an estimated 31.9 percent of adolescents had any anxiety disorder." The statistics reflect that 38 percent of this group was female and 26.1 percent was male. (By contrast, the NIMH estimates that 31.1 percent of all adults in the United States "experience any anxiety disorder at some time in their lives.")

The National Institute of Mental Health. (Last updated November 2017). Statistics: Major depression. Retrieved February 17, 2018, from https://www.nimh.nih.gov/health/statistics/major-depression.shtml.

3.1 million adolescents in the United States suffered from at least one major depressive episode in 2016. "This number represented 12.8 percent of the US population aged 12 to 17." The rate reported for adolescent females was 19.4 percent, almost three times as high as the rate of 6.4 percent reported for males. (By contrast, the NIMH reports that 6.7 percent of the adult population in the United States suffered from at least one major depressive episode in 2016).

Kerr, P. L., Muehlenkamp, J. J., & Turner, J. M. (March–April 2010). Nonsuicidal self-injury: A review of current research for family medicine and primary care physicians. *Journal of the American Board of Family Medicine, 23*(2), 240–59. http://www.jabfm.org/content/23/2/240.full.pdf+html.

15 percent of adolescents admit to some form of self-injury. The rates of self-injury skyrocket in college populations, where the number is 17 to 35 percent. (By contrast, the rate in the United States adult population is between 1 and 4 percent.)

3. Centers for Disease Control. (Last updated July 27, 2016). Key findings: Children's mental health report, May 16, 2013. Retrieved February 28, 2018, from https://www.cdc.gov/childrensmentalhealth/features/kf-childrens-mental-health-report.html.

4. Child Mind Institute, Children's mental health report.

5. Schore, A. N. (2003). *Affect dysregulation and disorders of the self.* New York: W. W. Norton & Company.

6. Schore, The effects of a secure attachment relationship on right brain development, affect regulation, and infant mental health.

7. American Society of Plastic Surgeons. (2016). 2016 quick facts: Cosmetic plastic surgery demographic trends. *Plastic Surgery Statistics Report.* Retrieved January 31, 2018, from https://www.plasticsurgery.org/documents/News/Statistics/2016/plastic-surgery-statistics-full-report-2016.pdf.

8. Huesmann, L. R. (2007). The impact of electronic media violence: Scientific theory and research. *Journal of Adolescent Health, 41*(6), Supplement, S6–S13. Retrieved January 23, 2018, from https://www.jahonline.org/article/S1054-139X(07)00391-6/pdf.

9. American Academy of Pediatrics Council on Communications and Media. (November 2013). Policy statement: Children, adolescents, and the media. *Pediatrics, 132*(5), 958–61. Retrieved January 23, 2018, from http://pediatrics.aappublications.org/content/pediatrics/132/5/958.full.pdf.

10. American Academy of Pediatrics Council on Communications and Media. (October 2016). Policy statement: Media and young minds. *Pediatrics, 138*(5). Retrieved January 23, 2018, from http://pediatrics.aappublications.org/content/pediatrics/early/2016/10/19/peds.2016-2591.full.pdf.

11. Rideout, The Common Sense Census: Media use by teens and tweens.

12. Huesmann, The impact of electronic media violence.

13. Ibid.

14. National Institute of Health. (September 21, 2010). Depression high among youth victims of school cyber bullying, NIH researchers report. Eunice Kennedy Shriver National Institute of Child Health and Human Development. Retrieved February 18, 2018, from https://www.nichd.nih.gov/news/releases/092110-cyber-bullying.

   StopBullying.gov. (Last reviewed September 28, 2017). Facts about bullying: Statistics. Retrieved February 18, 2018, from https://www.stopbullying.gov/media/facts/index.html#stats.

15. Jenco, M. (June 13, 2016). AAP endorses new recommendations on sleep times. *AAP News.* Retrieved January 23, 2018, from http://www.aappublications.org/news/2016/06/13/Sleep061316.

16. National Sleep Foundation. (2006). 2006 Sleep in America poll: Summary of findings. Retrieved January 23, 2018, from https://sleepfoundation.org/sites/default/files/2006_summary_of_findings.pdf.

17. Hysing, M., Pallesen, S., Stormark, K., Jakobsen, R., Lundervold, A. J., & Sivertsen, B. (Accepted December 2, 2014; first published February 2, 2015). Sleep and use of electronic devices in adolescence: results from a large population-based study. *British Medical Journal, 5*(1), e006748. Abstract retrieved January 23, 2018, from http://bmjopen.bmj.com/content/5/1/e006748.

18. Centers for Disease Control. (Updated January 29, 2018). Healthy Schools: Childhood obesity facts. Retrieved February 12, 2018, from https://www.cdc.gov/healthyschools/obesity/facts.htm.

19. US Department of Health & Human Services, Facts & statistics: Physical activity.

20. Ibid.

21. Hill, R. A., & Dunbar, R. I. M. (March 2003). Social network size in humans. *Human Nature, 14*(1), 53–72. Abstract retrieved February 23, 2018, from https://link.springer.com/article/10.1007/s12110-003-1016-y.

   Dunbar, R. I. M., & Spoors, M. (September 1995). Social networks, support cliques, and kinship. *Human Nature, 6*(3), 273–90. Abstract retrieved February 23, 2018, from https://link.springer.com/article/10.1007/BF02734142.

22. American Psychological Association. (2017). Stress in America: Coping with change, part 2. *Stress in America 2017: Technology and Social Media.* Retrieved January 23, 2018, from https://www.apa.org/news/press/releases/stress/2017/technology-social-media.PDF.

23. American Psychological Association. (2017). Stress in America: Coping with change, part 1. *Stress in America 2017 Snapshot: Coping with Change.* Retrieved January 23, 2018, from https://www.apa.org/news/press/releases/stress/2016/coping-with-change.PDF.

   American Psychological Association, Stress in America: Coping with change, part 2.

Chapter 8

1. Two informal surveys I conducted, one in a women's group and one on social media, January–May 2018.

2. Mish, F., et al. (Eds.). (1983). *Webster's ninth new collegiate dictionary.* Springfield, MA: Merriam-Webster Inc.

   Relate (v.). (n.d.). Online Etymology Dictionary. Retrieved February 7, 2018, from https://www.etymonline.com/word/relate.

Chapter 9

1. Greco, C. M. (2010). Transformational fear as an instrument of self-awareness: A quantitative and qualitative analysis from an in-depth psychological and neurobiological perspective. ProQuest.

2. Two informal surveys I conducted, one in a women's group and one on social media, January–May 2018.

3. Frankl, V. (1946). *Man's Search for Meaning.* Originally published in 1946 in Vienna, Austria, by Verlag für Jugend und Volk; published in 1959 in Boston, Massachusetts, by Beacon Press.

4. Personal contact with Stephen Cramer, Cloverdale Police Department Chief of Police (Cloverdale, CA). Business network messaging and email, March 2–April 27, 2018.

5. Ibid.

6. Holt-Lunstad, J., Smith, T. B., Baker, M. Harris, T., & Stephenson, D. (2015). Loneliness and social isolation as risk factors for mortality: A meta-analytic review. *Perspectives on Psychological Science, 10*(2), 227–37. Retrieved February 18, 2018, from https://www.ahsw.org.uk/userfiles/Research/Perspectives%20 on%20Psychological%20Science-2015-Holt-Lunstad-227-37.pdf.

   Holt-Lunstad, J. (April 27, 2017). Testimony before the US Senate Aging Committee. Retrieved February 18, 2018, from https://www.aging.senate.gov/imo/media/doc/SCA_Holt_04_27_17.pdf.

7. American Psychological Association. (August 5, 2017). Press release: So lonely I could die. Retrieved February 18, 2018, from http://www.apa.org/news/press/releases/2017/08/lonely-die.aspx.

   Holt-Lunstad, Testimony before the US Senate Aging Committee.

ACKNOWLEDGMENTS

I am honored to acknowledge all those who have supported and enlightened my journey.

I am deeply grateful to my parents; they gave me more than I could appreciate in my youth.

Brian, I have come to understand true relationship more fully with you in my life; your love is your greatest gift to me.

Adam, I am blessed to have had your unswerving love and support through every joy and hardship.

Cody, your love and drive have been a strong, sweet light in my life.

Erika, I am ever grateful for your deep friendship and devoted guidance.

Genevieve and Rich, I am truly blessed by your loving friendship and support.

Cali, your friendship and compassionate support are true gifts to me.

Linnea, I am deeply grateful for your kindness and supportive insights.

Thomas Moore, you embody the wisdom and magic my soul has always craved. You are a treasured friend.

Orchid, I am blessed by your friendship and loving support. Thank you for sharing in my journeys.

Brooke Jorden, thank you for diligence in the final polishing of *Joy from Fear*. I am most grateful.

Katie Hale, you have been a diligent force in honing this book into its final form.

Kate Farrell, your thoughtful, enthusiastic marketing and public relations efforts will ensure that we reach as many souls as possible.

Familius publishing team, you have been simply invaluable.

I am deeply grateful for every friend who has loved me, every mentor who has guided me, each profound writing that has informed me, and every client who has reached out along the way.

And, of course, I wish to acknowledge every reader; without you, I would have no reason to share so passionately that which is within my own soul.

About the Author

DR. CARLA MARIE MANLY has become recognized as an authority on fear and fear-based disorders such as trauma, anxiety, and depression. Dr. Manly maintains her clinical psychology practice in Sonoma County, California. With her doctorate in clinical psychology and her master's degree in counseling, Dr. Manly merges her psychotherapy skills with her writing expertise to offer sound, digestible guidance. Dr. Manly is committed to working with individuals and groups to improve personal growth, enhance relationship connection, and increase life fulfillment. Through a highly personalized approach that focuses on utilizing transformational fear in the self-growth and healing process, Dr. Manly's psychotherapeutic model offers incomparable benefits. Blending her strong clinical knowledge with a holistic body-mind-spirit approach, Dr. Manly focuses on the multidimensional needs of the individual. Recognizing a need for greater somatic awareness in society, Dr. Manly has integrated yoga and meditation practices into her private psychotherapy work and public course offerings.

About Familius

Visit Our Website: www.familius.com

Join Our Family

There are lots of ways to connect with us! Subscribe to our newsletters at www.familius.com to receive uplifting daily inspiration, essays from our Pater Familius, a free ebook every month, and the first word on special discounts and Familius news.

Get Bulk Discounts

If you feel a few friends and family might benefit from what you've read, let us know and we'll be happy to provide you with quantity discounts. Simply email us at orders@familius.com.

Connect

- Facebook: www.facebook.com/paterfamilius
- Twitter: @familiustalk, @paterfamilius1
- Pinterest: www.pinterest.com/familius
- Instagram: @familiustalk

FAMILIUS

The most important work you ever do will be within the walls of your own home.

CPSIA information can be obtained
at www.ICGtesting.com
Printed in the USA
FSHW010240270219

9 781641 701211